EPIDEMIC NARRATIVES

THE CULTURAL CONSTRUCTION OF INFECTIOUS DISEASE OUTBREAKS IN INDIA

EPIDEMIC NARRATIVES

THE CULTURAL CONSTRUCTION OF INFECTIOUS DISEASE OUTBREAKS IN INDIA

Dilip K. Das

Orient BlackSwan

EPIDEMIC NARRATIVES: THE CULTURAL CONSTRUCTION OF INFECTIOUS DISEASE OUTBREAKS IN INDIA

ORIENT BLACKSWAN PRIVATE LIMITED

Registered Office
3-6-752 Himayatnagar, Hyderabad 500 029, Telangana, India
Email: centraloffice@orientblackswan.com

Other Offices
Bengaluru, Chennai, Guwahati, Hyderabad,
Kolkata, Mumbai, New Delhi, Noida, Patna

First published 2025

040841

ISBN 978 93 5442 778 7

Typeset in Minion Pro 11/13.5 *by*
K. Divya, Hyderabad 500 060

Printed at
Avantika Printers Private Limited, New Delhi 110 020

Published by
Orient Blackswan Private Limited
3-6-752 Himayatnagar, Hyderabad 500 029, Telangana, India
Email: info@orientblackswan.com

This book is about human suffering and compassion.

I dedicate this book to the memory of my nephew Bhabani, whose capacity for compassion was rare.

And for Manu, my son.

Contents

Acknowledgements

The inspiration for this book comes from a talk that I gave at the University of Hyderabad on the theme of plague in U.R. Ananthamurthy's novel *Samskara*, during the peak of the COVID pandemic. Professors Pramod K. Nayar and Anna Kurien had organised it as part of a series of podcasts on 'Literature and Disease'. That inspired me to design an MA course on epidemic narratives, which I taught for two semesters at the English and Foreign Languages University in 2020 and 2021. Many of the insights that figure in this book came from discussions with my students. During the last three years I have had the opportunity to speak on the cultural dimensions of epidemic outbreak, and the discussions that followed helped me formulate arguments that appear in this book. Professor Nandana Dutta of Gauhati University invited me to deliver the sixteenth Anita Baruah Sarmah Memorial Lecture on 'Pandemic Nationalism'. Professor Anand Mahanand of the English and Foreign Languages University, Hyderabad, invited me to speak at a Folklore Foundation event on 'Epidemic Goddess Traditions in India'. Mr Abhishek Varghese of Delhi Comparatists invited me to speak on cultural studies and COVID-19. I was also invited by Dr Upamanyu Sengupta of Maharashtra National Law University, Dr K.M. Johnson, then of Sacred Heart College, Kochi, and Dr Rose Sebastian of Bharat Mata College, Kochi, to speak on the theory and methods of interdisciplinary humanities, which frames my approach to epidemic narratives. As always, Professor P.C. Kar, Director of the Centre for Contemporary Theory and the Balwant Parekh Centre for General Semantics and Other Human Sciences, Vadodara, listened to my nebulous arguments and helped me fine-tune them.

The suggestions made by the anonymous reader of this book have helped me immensely in revising it for publication, and making it more readable. Mr Sreenath Sreedharan, Managing Editor, Humanities, at Orient Blackswan also provided many valuable inputs. Mr James Kanjamala helped ensure publication deadlines, and Ms Oli Chatterjee did an excellent job in meticulously copy-editing the manuscript.

Mr S. Mukundan, my former student, agreed to write an essay on *Plague Sindhu* by Anthony Muthu Pillai, which is a lesser-known Tamil narrative on the outbreak of plague in Madras Presidency. This book would not have been complete without the essay, which appears as its epilogue. Dr K.A.S. Mani, a hydrogeologist with an abiding interest in society and culture and a close personal friend, listened to many of my ideas during our daily morning walks, agreed to many and disagreed with many, and provided me with perspectives that were vital for the book.

I have received unstinting support from my family during the writing of this book. Sumitra listened patiently to my readings of the chapters, with their multiple revisions. To her goes the credit for the parts of the book that read well, to me the blame for the parts that don't. When the work of seemingly endless reading and writing proved too tedious, Manu provided me much-needed relaxation in the form of video games, re-re-reruns of movies we had watched and enjoyed, and evening drives in the family car.

To all of them, and many more, I am beholden.

Introduction

I have put away the packets of N95 masks and PPE kits I had bought two years back, for the time I'll need them again when COVID returns or some other microbe emerges to take its place, as microbes have done throughout history. The coronavirus may have declined in potency in India, but it still rages elsewhere as I write. The emergence of new microbes or resurgence of old ones will shape our way of life now, as we face another century of pandemic outbreak. It had been so throughout the nineteenth century with cholera, smallpox and plague, the last century opened with Spanish flu, and the present with SARS, swine flu, MERS, Ebola, Zika, Nipah, COVID-19, Mpox ...

Epidemic Narratives is about this way of life, recounted in stories by people who lived through precarious times brought on by disease. It focuses on some of the notable outbreaks in India in the last hundred-odd years, and the real and imagined accounts of them in scientific reports, newspaper stories, autobiographies, fiction and cinema. Having gone through a major life-threatening pandemic a couple of years ago, these stories find resonance in our own experience. It was at the peak of the first wave of COVID-19 that I decided to teach a course (online, of course, something I had never done before!) on epidemic stories from India. While putting together material for the course, I found very little in the nature of theorisation of epidemic narratives in general and on Indian narratives in particular. Hence, this book.

Epidemic Narratives puts together concepts and methods drawn from the humanities, medicine and the social sciences. It uses the method of interdisciplinary studies, which, as Lawrence

Grossberg writes of cultural studies, poses its questions not on disciplinary grounds but on the context of study. Epidemic being the context of the book, it explores epidemiological literature and media stories on particular outbreaks to get a sense of their scale, duration and effects. Biomedical reports provide objective information, which media reports build on, and add to it what is called the 'human interest' angle—that is, the subjective experience of people affected by the outbreak. This ranges from the emotional impact of the suffering it causes to socio-political conflicts that it brings to the fore as collective crisis. The understanding of an outbreak is framed by these objective facts, subjective perceptions and their social contexts, and it shapes public as well as personal response to the crisis. Literary and cinematic renderings of outbreak draw on this understanding, attributing meaning and value to its different aspects, which are then reconfigured into a coherent narrative with a well-defined plot. *Epidemic Narratives* poses two questions in analysing such narratives: what kinds of plot do they employ, and what significances do they attribute to outbreaks as complex human events? The book being a study in interdisciplinary medical humanities, its fundamental exercise is to uncover these significances through close textual analysis. My assumption here is that the interpretation of human phenomena requires insights from both the humanities and the human sciences: the latter dealing with patterns, laws and cause and effect mechanisms that give rise to these phenomena, and the former with the meanings attributed to these causes, effects, laws and patterns. Human beings are not just objects of what happens to them, but also subjects who try to comprehend and respond to these happenings. As such, therefore, understanding what an outbreak of epidemic disease means is a matter of taking account of the entire range of objective facts and subjective perceptions that construct its reality as a critical event.

In the first chapter I discuss the social understanding of epidemic using a theoretical framework drawing on Charles Rosenberg, Peter Berger and Thomas Luckmann, Stanley Tambiah, Roy Rappaport, Marcel Mauss, Mircea Eliade and others, to show how this understanding both derives from and adds to the biomedical view of disease. The chapter examines how, in pluralistic societies, epidemic reality is constructed through both biomedical and cosmological paradigms, leading to contrary ways of responding to it. Thus, in the outbreak of COVID in 2020 people both worshipped a goddess called Corona Devi and wore masks, observed social distance and isolated themselves if infected. In South Asian societies, such polar conceptualisations of outbreak coexist, though not without contention.

The second chapter is about the impact of pandemic on the nation as a community that imagines itself as healthy yet vulnerable to the threat posed by pathogens and pathogenic outsiders. For a national ideology based on ethnic community, the 'outsider' is any group perceived as different on racial, religious or cultural grounds, while for an ideology founded on civic community the outsider is the immigrant or foreigner within national territory. Ideologically, however, nations are a mix of both civic and ethnic models, so that the difference between people who are considered as 'other' within the national boundary and the territorial 'other' gets blurred. During the initial years of the COVID pandemic, when national hysteria was at its peak, the targeting and vilification of both kinds of 'other' was common. Since most cases of outbreak in recent times soon assume the proportion of pandemic due to increased global movement of people, international agencies like the World Health Organisation are tasked with controlling the spread of disease. But whether nations cooperate with WHO and other international public health agencies in this task remains the question. The COVID pandemic has made it clear that the future of public health in a rapidly globalising context depends on how nationalism and internationalism balance mutual interests. Such balance, however, proves impossible unless disease is de-nationalised.

Chapters three to ten deal with specific outbreaks. Chapter three discusses two narratives of the plague outbreak in

Pune in 1897 which culminated in the assassination of Plague Commissioner Walter Charles Rand. The first is the autobiography of Damodar Hari Chapekar, who was convicted and hanged for the assassination, and the second is *22 July 1897*, a film made on the incident by Nachiket and Jayoo Patwardhan. The chapter reads these two narratives intertextually with scientific reports on the outbreak, newspaper accounts and retrospective memorials of Chapekar, to show how the outbreak was constructed and framed as a political event, marking the emergence of militant nationalism and anticipating the freedom struggle. It shows how epidemic as a critical event provides the starting point for a much wider range of meanings and values in its narrative reconfiguration.

Chapter four reads U.R. Ananthamuthy's novel *Samskara* as an epidemic narrative inspired by an outbreak of plague that the author witnessed as a child. Most interpretations of the novel have been confined to the themes of caste and religious orthodoxy, the role of tradition in a modernising society, and the tension between allegory and realism, without taking into account the function of the plague story. In this chapter I argue that plague not only provides the inspiration for the novel and its point of departure, but also serves the function of a focaliser. It brings into sharper view the frameworks of meaning that critics have identified to be central. *Samskara* is about the question of social order, how a particular code of conduct becomes oppressive when it becomes rigid. In this regard the outbreak serves as a metaphor for larger social and ethical crises. Chapters three and four are, thus, about plague in India at the turn of the twentieth century, which took a heavy toll of life and caused enough human suffering for a goddess to be installed in its name. Variously called Plague Amma, Bombai Mai, Uramma and Plague Mariamma, she found worship in many parts of present-day Maharashtra, Karnataka and Tamil Nadu as well as parts of Uttar Pradesh.

Chapter five is about Spanish flu, which broke out (like plague) in Bombay in June 1918 and was rapidly carried to the rest of the country by soldiers returning from the First World War. The outbreak abated by early next year, but in these few months it claimed an estimated fifteen to twenty million lives in India. The chapter begins with two official reports on the flu by the assistant health officer of Bombay municipality and the sanitary commissioner of India. The scale of the tragedy was such that it moved both authors to express their emotional response in what were otherwise impersonal bureaucratic reports. I examine newspaper accounts of the outbreak and two literary narratives to show how the outbreak was variously framed as a lapse of colonial public health, a personal tragedy and a cosmological crisis. The final section of the chapter discusses the memory of the Spanish flu pandemic in the time of another pandemic that broke out a hundred years later, COVID-19. Focusing on a number of media reports and a novel, it shows how, long after Spanish flu had been forgotten, it was remembered and reconfigured in another crisis of similar, if much less, severity.

Chapter six deals with an outbreak of viral hepatitis, a disease that is largely endemic but has occurred intermittently in epidemic form in India in the last hundred years. The chapter analyses Satyajit Ray's film *Ganashatru* as an epidemic narrative, drawing on epidemiological literature on infectious hepatitis in India and Henrik Ibsen's *An Enemy of the People*, the nineteenth-century Norwegian play on which the film was based. Ibsen's play has been read as an allegory of the individual standing up against the majority, in asserting commitment to ethics as against manipulation of truth for personal gain. Though Ray follows the script of the original broadly, he makes a number of changes in the plot, characterisation and context. The spa town in Ibsen is replaced by a temple town, thus bringing into focus Ray's criticism of religious dogma especially when it contradicts rationality and places at risk the health of people. The film ends with the doctor's final victory, as public opinion veers round to his defence, and the triumph of reason over blind faith and vested interest. Ray changes the character of the doctor accordingly, from the Nietzschean hero in *Enemy* to a socially-committed individual whose primary concern is the welfare of the community as a whole, and not his personal fame.

Chapter seven analyses narratives of the HIV/AIDS epidemic, which broke out in India in 1986. It examines a range of media articles, literary and cinematic texts and an AIDS awareness video, to track changes in the social understanding of the disease and those affected by it. From the stigmatising accounts of risk groups and HIV-positive individuals that was characteristic of the early decades of the epidemic in India, the focus shifted at the turn of the century to empathy for them. While the narratives draw on popular conceptions of AIDS, they do not necessarily reproduce them but quite often call them into question. The chapter examines the dialectical relation between social understanding and narrative in bringing about this change.

In chapter eight, I discuss a Malayalam film on an outbreak of Nipah virus disease in Kerala in the summer of 2018. Aashique Abu's *Virus* is a fictional reconstruction of the event in terms of biomedical explanations as well as accounts of personal suffering. The chapter draws on scientific reports and media stories to bring these dimensions of the film into focus. Reading it in terms of Rosenberg's schema of social understanding and Priscilla Wald's schema for analysing outbreak narratives, the chapter shows how *Virus* constructs the event as the disintegration and renewal of community and as a sign of the vulnerability of human life. It also shows how the ending denies any assurance that the crisis is over and will not recur, thereby opening up the closure that both Rosenberg and Wald give to the structure of epidemic outbreak.

Chapter nine is on the recent outbreak of COVID-19 in India that resulted in a nationwide lockdown in 2020. It discusses stories of the pandemic and the lockdown in terms of the suffering they caused, the loneliness, disruption of everyday life, time-space disorientation, loss of life and livelihood, the lack of institutional support, and the precariousness that resulted from all of these. It focuses on two kinds of stories, those of personal suffering like the video *Infected 2030* and the *Times of India* blog

'My COVID Story', and those of collective suffering like Vinod Kapri's documentary *1232 KMS* and the book that followed from it, *1232 km: The Long Journey Home.* While all epidemics trigger a sense of insecurity and vulnerability, the experience of COVID-19 as it is constructed and framed in these stories emphasises a precarity that results not just from microbial attack but equally the inability of governments to deal effectively with so complex a crisis.

Chapter ten attempts to explain why narrative is the genre best suited to represent the experience of epidemic, and why epidemic in turn calls forth narrative as its most suitable mode of representation. Narratives are about events that unfold in time and space, which is also how epidemics are structured in the way they come to be understood socially. We make sense of an outbreak in two ways, as an objective event and as subjective human experience. Narratives bring out both these dimensions, by emphasising emotional responses to disease, death and suffering as well as making cognitive sense of it. As a corollary, epidemic outbreaks as happenings demand to be interpreted for what they signify as human phenomena, drawing on cultural memory of similar happenings in the past, and pre-narrative frames that find repose in culture. Narratives do not simply represent such happenings, they make them comprehensible as social reality.

The epilogue by S. Mukundan examines *Plague Sindhu* (1924), a narrative poem by Anthony Pillai on the outbreak of plague in his home district of Theni in Madras Presidency. When plague spread from Bombay to the south, it inspired a fairly large corpus of literary texts both oral and written. Mukundan discusses *Plague Sindhu* as a literary account of the causes of the outbreak, the steps taken by the colonial government to control its spread, and the suffering caused to the people both by plague and the antiplague measures. The poem is an apt example of how an outbreak of infectious disease comes to be socially constructed in terms of both modern scientific ideas of disease-causation and traditional ideas of disease as divine punishment for wrongdoing.

Though it does not seek to be representative of popular opinion in general, it provides a good index to what people thought and felt in this time of crisis. Mukundan also provides an English translation of a number of verses from this hitherto untranslated poem, which can be a source of inspiration for further research into the subaltern literature on epidemic outbreaks.

Epidemic Narratives takes as its main theme Charles Rosenberg's argument that the social reality of disease is constituted in the frames of explanation provided by biomedical, political, cultural and social ideas and practices. Narratives play a key role in this construction, in the way they both draw upon and critique these explanatory frames. As such, therefore, they are an important source of the way we know disease, both personally and collectively, and the impact it has on our lives. The reality of disease has been predominantly biomedical, understood as an objective condition that is knowable through visible signs and symptoms. *Epidemic Narratives* calls attention to the subjective experience that stories alone can express, which is as much a part of its reality as the interpretations of science.

1

What Is an Epidemic?

In April 2020, in the midst of the COVID pandemic and a country-wide lockdown in India, groups of women gathered near ponds to perform the worship of a new goddess they variously called Corona Devi, Corona Mata or Corona Mai. This seems to have been a spontaneous occurrence across widely scattered regions in Assam, Uttar Pradesh, Bihar and West Bengal, not orchestrated by any individual or group. These women dug a hole in the ground, sang songs to the goddess, and offered her flowers, incense, jaggery, flattened rice and sesame laddus. A woman devotee claimed that the goddess had appeared in the form of a cow and had said that she would protect them from the pandemic if they worshipped her (Das, 2021, pp. 11–13; 'Fear', 2020; 'Superstitions', 2020). The government, meanwhile, had invoked sections of the Disaster Management Act, 2005, empowering public authorities to cordon off containment zones, enforce the wearing of face masks and impose fines on those who violated COVID safety norms (Ministry of Home Affairs, 2020). While the women devotees of Corona Devi were performing her worship in large gatherings, ignoring the government's norms, a priest in Kerala set up a shrine to her at home, conducted worship online, and dedicated it to 'corona warriors, including health workers, scientists, and Fire and Rescue Services personnel' ('Just', 2020). In the same month, a fortnight after lockdown was imposed, the Prime Minister requested people to light lamps and candles at nine pm to illuminate 'the common purpose we are all fighting for' ('Light', 2020). These heterogeneous practices reveal how multiple perspectives come together in making sense of an epidemic outbreak, some drawing on religious ideas, some on scientific, and some ritualising the event in shows of solidarity. This chapter examines how an outbreak of infectious disease, consequently, comes to be constructed as a social crisis, shaping the way people respond to it.

1.1. The Social Understanding of Epidemic

Epidemics signify a crisis of society on multiple levels. They cause death, suffering and economic distress on an unprecedented scale. They strain the health resources of the community, which is caught unprepared for such a contingency. They lay open latent social divisions, intensifying stigma against people perceived as cultural outsiders—like the poor, religious minorities and immigrants. Finally, by the sheer randomness with which they strike, rendering everyone vulnerable, they unsettle belief in the stability of human existence, without which life becomes unbearable. In this, they are akin to what Clifford Geertz calls chaos: 'a tumult of events which lack not just interpretations but *interpretability*' which breaks in upon man at three points: 'at the limits of his analytic capacities, at the limits of his powers of endurance, and at the limits of his moral insight' (1973, p. 100, italics in original). Such events, therefore, demand to be interpreted. The divergent responses to COVID in 2020 show how people drew on widely different ideas to make sense of it, in order to reduce its randomness and mitigate its emotional and bodily effects.

In 'What Is an Epidemic? AIDS in History', Charles E. Rosenberg proposes a model for understanding how societies have historically dealt with the crisis of epidemic. Using a dramaturgical metaphor, he states that outbreaks unfold as a sequence of three 'acts' followed by an 'epilogue'. The metaphor seems appropriate because of the spectacularity of the outbreak, and the way it comes to be emplotted in social understanding: 'Epidemics start at a moment in time, proceed on a stage limited in space and duration, follow a plot line of increasing and revelatory tension, move to a crisis of individual and collective character, then drift toward closure'.[1] They are spectacles of community bonding in which people 'act out proprietory rituals that incorporate and reaffirm fundamental social values and modes of understanding'. Finally, as a real-life drama they reveal insights into the relationships between 'ideology, social structure, and the constitution of particular selves' (Rosenberg, 1989a, p. 2).

The first 'act' of this drama opens with people falling ill and dying in unusually high numbers, followed by growing apprehension of an outbreak, and ends with its grudging acknowledgement by public authorities. The delay in the declaration of the coronavirus disease as a pandemic is an apt instance. China reported the outbreak in Wuhan on 31 December 2019; but it was only on 11 March 2020, when it had spread to 114 countries causing more than 118,000 infections and 4,291 deaths, that WHO declared it as a pandemic (Global News, 2020, 07:10). Because an outbreak disrupts the political, economic and social order of life, authorities are 'usually unenthusiastic about publicly acknowledging the presence of so dangerous an intruder' (Rosenberg, 1989a, p. 4).

The second 'act' concerns attempts to comprehend the outbreak. People draw on already existing cultural frames from the collective memory of past epidemics—the two most important being the religious and the scientific: 'For most previous centuries that framework was moral and transcendent; the epidemic had to be understood primarily in terms of man's relationship to God; consolation was grounded in submission to the meaning implicit in that framework. … Since at least the sixteenth century, however, such spiritual assumptions have always coexisted with—and gradually yielded in emphasis to—

[1] Rosenberg, who wrote the essay in 1989, was obviously thinking of localised outbreaks 'limited in space and duration'. With the increase in global travel now, this no longer seems valid, as the SARS and COVID pandemics show. Even duration, as COVID shows, is much longer, especially as new variants emerge. Moreover, the almost annual recurrence of outbreaks makes epidemics seem like an interminable reality.

more secular and mechanistic styles of explanation' (Rosenberg, 1989a, p. 5).[2]

The third 'act' in Rosenberg's schema concerns collective attempts to control the crisis, drawn from the type of explanation that is most widely accepted: scientific measures to prevent disease transmission and religious rituals to address supernatural causes. Despite their differences, both take the form of ritual: 'the imposition of a quarantine, let us say, or the burning of tar to clear an infected atmosphere, the gathering of men and women in churches for days of fasting and prayer, all play a similar role—the visible acting out of community solidarity. At the same time, these collective rituals affirm belief—whether in religion, in rationalistic pathology, or in some combination of the two—while those beliefs promise a measure of control over an intractable reality' (Rosenberg, 1989a, p. 7). In the following sections I elaborate on the key arguments in Rosenberg's account.

1.2. Ritualising Epidemic Outbreak

Let me take the first argument, the ritualisation of response. If ritual refers to an organised sequence of coded acts designed for a specific effect[3], both scientific and religious practices are ritualistic

[2] Mark Harrison points to an important limitation in generalising Rosenberg's model, in particular acts two and three, across different epidemic events. The attempt to make collective sense of an outbreak and respond to it depends to a great extent on existing 'belief systems and modes of governance'. During the cholera epidemics of 1817–1821, for instance, the East India Company's rule had not yet been established, as a result of which there were different types of political authority ranging from that of the Company to that of local chieftains and customary rulers. Moreover, biomedical ideas of disease lacked wide acceptance and traditional belief systems prevailed. Consequently, public comprehension of what caused cholera and what steps needed to be taken was not as clear-cut as Rosenberg's model suggests. In the absence of a coherent public sphere, as it was in early-nineteenth-century India, the matter becomes even more complicated. Despite these limitations, however, Harrison admits the model's heuristic value in explaining the social dynamics of outbreak (2020, pp. 505–506).

[3] Roy Rappaport defines ritual as 'the performance of more or less invariant sequences of formal acts and utterances not encoded by the performers' (1979, p. 175). Ritual exists in culture as a reiterated practice that is

in the way they enact predefined codes of action. Participants presume that they will work, because they have done so in the past. Rituals, states Marcel Mauss in *A General Theory of Magic*, are '*traditional actions whose effectiveness is sui generis*' (1972, p. 25, italics in original). The role of acceptance or belief in ritual, however, is more complex than this would suggest. We perform a ritual when we believe it will be effective. As a corollary, in performing the ritual we believe in its efficacy, as Louis Althusser says of religious ideology: 'Kneel down, move your lips in prayer, and you will believe' (2001, p. 109).[4] Ritual has, in this sense, been compared to what J.L. Austin calls 'performative', in the way it produces what it refers to, the felicitous performance of ritual (Rappaport, 1979, pp. 176–179; Tambiah, 1980). In *How to do Things with Words*, Austin differentiates between performative utterances and those that state or refer to a verifiable fact, which he calls 'constatives'. A promise, for instance, does not state, refer to, or describe the act of promising, it performs that act: it is in saying 'I promise' that I make a promise. In contrast to this, the statement 'I promised' refers to something that I did in the past and is therefore a constative. The difference between the two kinds of statements is that one *points to* a referent while the other *produces* it. Other statements that belong to the category of performatives are orders, requests and wagers. According to Austin, there must be an already existing convention or code for a performative speech act to be 'felicitous' or effective: it is the code or convention that constitutes its performative force (1962, p. 14). There must be a tradition of promising, ordering, requesting or

presumed to be effective, whether or not actual experience confirms it. Most often, its failure to ensure the desired effect is attributed to factors external to the ritual, like an improper performance or the inexperience of those who officiate over it.

[4] Althusser is explaining how ideological beliefs have a material existence, and are not just ideas in the head. For the subject of ideology they are '*his material actions inserted into material practices governed by material rituals which are themselves defined by the material ideological apparatus from which derive the ideas of that subject*' (2001, p. 114, italics in original). Althusser's argument implies a link between ritual and ideology, which is the point I am trying to make: in enacting a religious or a scientific ideology, one also produces, reproduces and replenishes it.

laying a bet for one to do so in speech. Similarly, the imposition of quarantine or the worship of a goddess follows an ordered convention of acting in response to an outbreak, and each derives its force or authority from that convention. In a cultural context in which scientific knowledge is privileged over the religious, the ritualisation underlying scientific practices becomes obscured. In an essay on ritual in medicine, John Welch states: 'While we generally think of the hospital or medical clinic as a space for practicing objective, rigorous, scientific biomedicine that is very different from the shaman's blend of religion and medicine, it is not difficult to recognize ritual motifs at work in both the modern hospital's structure or in its practitioners' interactions with their patients' (2003, p. 22). As instances of the way in which clinical and shamanistic relationships are both structured by ritual, he draws analogies between the patient and the ritual supplicant, the shaman and the doctor, ritual regimen and therapeutic regimen, and the sequestration and isolation of the patient from the world of everyday life that are common to both hospitals and religious settings. The distinction commonly made between religion as ritualistic and medicine as non-ritualistic, Welch argues, has a history that is founded on the hegemonic status of science in modern societies.

A defining characteristic of performative utterances is that, unlike constatives, they are not subject to the criterion of truth/falsehood. As Austin puts it, 'they do not "describe" or "report" or constate anything at all, are not "true or false"' (1962, p. 5). To ask if X made a false promise is not to ask whether he did or did not make it for he must have uttered 'I promise' for it to be a promise in the first place, but whether X carried out what he had promised. 'His utterance is perhaps misleading, probably deceitful and doubtless wrong, but it is not a lie or misstatement' (p. 11). Austin calls such cases 'infelicities', when the person who utters them does not intend to carry them out, or is not the appropriate person, or the context is inappropriate (pp. 21–24). This has an important bearing on the question of belief in ritual efficacy. For those who participate in it, the failure of a ritual to produce its desired effect is not taken to prove that the ritual is false, but that it was not performed in the appropriate way. 'The ceremony *itself*', writes Stanley Tambiah of the Thai ritual of blessing a new house, 'cannot ever be said to have been proved to be false or untrue or ineffective; however, any particular enactment of it may be said to be void, unworthy or defective. A bigamist who on false pretenses has gone through a second marriage ceremony, does not on that account make the institution of marriage false, wrong or ineffective; what can be said is that he has undergone the ceremony in bad faith and that he has not properly 'married" a second time' (2017, pp. 468–469, italics in original). Thus, if an outbreak of COVID does not recede even after people worship Corona Devi or wear masks, the failure is attributed not to the practices themselves but to other factors: that the worship was not performed correctly, that the masks were not worn properly or were of poor quality and it is presumed that they would have succeeded if the right procedures had been followed. The performative approach helps to clarify that it is not rationality which makes a scientific ritual 'true' and a religious rite 'false', but the epistemic privilege accorded to science in modern societies.

1.3. Medical Pluralism

The second argument of Rosenberg's schema is the coexistence of multiple explanations. Rosenberg's account of the way epidemics are framed refers to his own cultural context (that is, Euro-American), but it also helps explain the frames present in non-Western cultures that have undergone colonisation. Multiple explanations of ill-health coexist in such societies, some based on ideas introduced by colonial modernity and others taken from indigenous literate and oral traditions. 'In such modernizing societies', writes Arthur Kleinman, 'one finds social realities that are a strange amalgam of modern and traditional beliefs, values and institutions, held together in varying patterns of assimilation, complementarity, conflict, and contradiction' (1980, p. 37). Health beliefs constitute an important domain of social reality, and contradictory belief systems can quite often exist side by side, serving different goals. This was prevalent in colonial South Asia, especially among the rural peasantry, and continues to be so, as the worship of Corona Devi shows. Ranajit Guha illustrates this by citing the petitions for ritual expiation submitted to the local brahmin priest by patients or their caregivers in colonial Bengal, even as others sought the help of medical practitioners. Malady of the body was, for the petitioners, a sign of spiritual pollution, which could only be removed by performing purificatory rites. Guha interprets this to mean that European medicine failed to achieve hegemonic status and that local health practices continued in utter disregard for it. 'What our petitioners sought therefore was prescriptions for moral absolution rather than medical ones for cure, and the authority they turned to was not doctors but priests' (Guha, 2009, p. 309). That is, European and indigenous health beliefs contended against each other in a struggle for hegemony, but people chose what they found to be more persuasive. This may very well have been the case, but it could equally well have been that people sought ritual expiation for only those illnesses that had been framed in moral terms, and turned to European medicine for those that had not. For instance, Andrew Strathern and Pamela Stewart note that in Hagen, Papua New Guinea, people seek the services of local healers only for ailments that they presume to be beyond Western medicine's purview, such as those caused by sorcery. 'When a Hagener becomes ill, western biomedical treatments, Christian notions of healing, and indigenous religious concepts may all be applied' (Strathern & Stewart, 2010, p. 107). Why people choose one system instead of another, which they would prefer on a different occasion, is a matter more complex than any single perspective can illuminate. Mark Harrison mentions the case of a British resident in eighteenth-century Calcutta who donated large sums of money for building temples to the cholera goddess, Ola Bibi, when his Indian wife survived a serious bout of cholera (2020, p. 509). Mr Duncan, the resident, may not have sought the goddess when his wife fell ill, but the fact that he felt grateful enough to build temples to her is proof of how prevalent alternative explanations of cholera were in the way the disease came to be imagined. It would perhaps, then, be more accurate to view modern biomedicine and traditional sacred rites not as rival systems but as serving different ends for those who seek them.

To understand the difference between the two systems, we can take the help of a distinction made in medical anthropology—curing versus healing. Curing 'refers to an act of treating successfully a specific condition, for example a wound or a case of diarrhea or infestation by worms. Healing, by contrast, refers to the whole person or the whole body seen as an integrated system with both physical and spiritual components' (Strathern & Stewart, 2010, p. 7). Linked to this is another distinction in medical anthropology, disease versus illness. Disease, writes Arthur Kleinman, 'refers to a malfunctioning of biological and/or psychological processes, while the term *illness* refers to the psychosocial experience and meaning of perceived disease' (1980, p. 72, italics in original). Similarly, Cecil Helman defines disease as 'the named pathological entities that make up the medical model of ill-health' and illness as 'the subjective experience of the patient to being unwell', including 'not only his experience of ill-health but the meaning he gives to that experience' (1981, p. 548). Biomedical therapy focuses on organ-systems affected by disease and is directed towards cure; traditional health ritual focuses on the whole person, body, mind and soul, and is directed towards healing. The distinction is, of course, only schematic: physicians also try to heal if they want their cures to be effective, as in the case of cancer, and most systems of healing also include curative components. The experience of being unwell is at once cognitive, affective and moral, involving reflection on the body's condition and its evaluation in spiritual terms, which are both equally lodged within one's personality and reflected in interpersonal relations. As John Welch explains, disease 'threatens not only our physical well-being, but also our ability to maintain our current relationships with the people and the world around us' (2003, p. 25). The success of any health practice depends on how well it integrates both dimensions—healing and curing. Hence, the simultaneous prevalence of scientific and religious frames and the practices they generate, as Rosenberg explains in outlining the second and third acts of his schema.

1.4. The Construction of Epidemic as Social Crisis

The third argument in Rosenberg's essay is that epidemics intensify existing social divisions and provide an occasion for reaffirming dominant hierarchies. Explanations of how an outbreak originated provide 'a framework within which moral and social assumptions could at once be expressed and legitimated' (Rosenberg, 1989a, p. 5). On this view, public health measures are performances that serve to contain not just the outbreak but threats to the social order as well, by isolating those of its marginal members suspected of spreading disease—foreigners, immigrants, the poor, religious (and sexual, in the case of AIDS) minorities. The outbreak of pneumonic plague in Los Angeles in 1924 became a pretext for public authorities to cordon off immigrant quarters, post guards to ensure that people remained confined to their homes, and ban public gatherings. The 'decision to quarantine Macy Street and Belvedere Gardens', writes Mark Honigsbaum in *The Pandemic Century*, 'appears to have had little to do with infection control and everything to do with racism and prejudice' (2020, p. 53). In an essay on public health concerns and immigration policy in the US, Howard Markel and Alexandra M. Stern show how foreigners have been denied entry on the suspicion of harbouring contagious disease, most often 'motivated by, and closely intertwined with, ideologies of racialism, nativism, and national security rather than substantiated epidemiological or medical observations' (2002, p. 781).[5] When the HIV/AIDS epidemic broke out in India the state responded by raiding brothels, forcibly testing inmates and detaining them if they tested positive; Pyari Bai, an HIV-positive sex worker in Kolkata was kept by the city police

[5] I discuss this in greater detail in chapter five.

in a jail till the high court ordered them to release her (Shetty, 1990a; Shetty, 1990b; Singh, 1995; Puri, 1986, p. 24). In Quilon and Jabalpur, African students who tested positive for HIV were deported (Singh & Pillai, 1987), while in Manipur HIV-positive IV-drug users were arrested and isolated in jails and remand homes (Ali, 1991). In 1989, Goa police arrested an HIV-positive gay man under the Goa, Daman and Diu Public Health Act, and detained him for more than two months till Bombay High Court ordered his release (Dube, 2015, pp. 141–145). 'Cultural margins and national borders are often summoned, if not articulated, through the figure of specific contagious diseases' (Wald, Tomes & Lynch, 2002, p. 619). The lockdown following the COVID outbreak in India in 2020 disproportionately affected migrant workers who lost their livelihoods and were prevented by the police and the local administration from returning to the safety of their villages. They were forced to take long and hazardous journeys on foot, evading police check-posts on highways and main roads, and many of them lost their lives in the process (Rajan, 2020; Kapri, 2021). The decision to impose a lockdown was taken without considering its effect on them, which reveals how migrants employed in informal sectors of production are effectively rendered invisible in governmental calculations of health safety (Naregal, 2021). While any social crisis leading to moral panic triggers boundary policing, it is especially true in epidemic times. In an essay on accusations of witchcraft and disease as techniques of social control, Mary Douglas writes: 'Attributions of occult injury and hidden infection informally entrench the hierarchy of social categories and warn well-placed persons against indiscriminate social intercourse' (1994, p. 87). It is not necessary for the accusation to be proved: in targeting already-vilified persons the proof is taken for granted by both those who make social decisions and those who approve of them, that is, the dominant social groups.

To conclude the three sections on Rosenberg, therefore, disease is a social construct even as it is a biomedical fact.[6] On this view an outbreak of infectious disease signifies a crisis that is, at once, recurrent and without precedent. As recurrent crisis, it is understood in conventional ways that draw from cultural memory and its repertoire of meanings. As unprecedented, however, the memory of how similar outbreaks had declined over time provides little consolation; for each new outbreak is perceived as unique in itself.[7] The fear that an outbreak triggers can be managed only by finding an appropriate explanation. There are broadly two ways in which outbreaks have been explained—one drawing on religion and the other on science. Once a plausible explanation is found, it frames collective responses that, being already coded, take on the form of ritual. Ritual is performed on the belief that it will work, and the performance in turn produces and reinforces that belief. This circularity is characteristic of the form and function of the performative, and it guarantees for those who participate in it the efficacy of the rite. The explanations of outbreak and the practices undertaken in response to it together constitute its social understanding in their dialectical relation to each other. Finally, epidemic outbreaks provide occasions for the shoring up of dominant norms, intensifying already existing antagonisms against those held to be socially or morally suspect. As such, they signify the breakdown of a social order that can

[6] 'Beliefs about sickness, the behaviors exhibited by sick persons, including their treatment expectations, and the ways in which sick persons are responded to by family and practitioners', writes Kleinman, 'are cultural constructions, shaped distinctly in different societies and in different social structural settings within those societies' (1980, p. 38).

[7] In a different context, Christos Lynteris explains how an epidemic outbreak is situated on two different temporalities: the time taken by long-term biological, ecological, demographic, political and economic processes interacting to culminate in an outbreak, and the phenomenological experience of the outbreak as a unique event of crisis. The long-term processes that crystallise in the outbreak follow a recurrent pattern, so much so that they can be predicted using tools of surveillance and infection-tracking. As unique events, in contrast, outbreaks are experienced as 'ruptures in social, political and economic life' constituting 'short-term catastrophic events' (Lynteris, 2014, p. 25).

only be restored by excluding those who threaten it. This is what Rosenberg means when he writes that epidemic outbreaks foreground relationships between 'ideology, social structure, and the constitution of particular selves', which are not quite so evident in normal times (1989a, p. 2).[8]

1.5. Social Construction/Framing of Disease

Let us take a closer look at the social reality of disease. My argument thus far has been that epidemic outbreak is framed or constructed in one of two alternative ways—one scientific and the other religious. Now, 'framing' and 'construction' both refer to the way we represent and attribute meaning to reality, but a construct is generally held to be more or less arbitrary whereas a frame is not. In 'Disease in History: Frames and Framers' Rosenberg argues that the concept of construct is that it tends to assume a degree of arbitrariness in the way it assigns meaning to social reality, while the frame is more firmly anchored in the 'biological' or organic reality of disease (Rosenberg, 1989b, p. 1). Further, constructionist theories tend to focus on a few diseases that have no evident organic cause, like homosexuality, hysteria and neurasthenia. Finally, they belong to a particular moment in cultural criticism that viewed with suspicion any claim to truth. While I agree with the last two arguments, I think the first—that constructionism tends to assume a degree of arbitrariness—needs to be more carefully thought out. There are two kinds of constructionism: social and linguistic. Social constructionism holds that the understanding of reality is produced by the functioning of a structure of beliefs and practices. As Peter Berger and Thomas Luckmann explain in *The Social Construction of Reality*, the 'world of everyday life is not only taken for granted by the ordinary members of society in the subjectively meaningful conduct of their lives. It is a world that originates in their thoughts and actions, and is maintained

8 Epidemic outbreaks 'enable us to see, at one moment in time, the configuration of values and attitudes that, in less-stressful times, are so fragmented or so taken for granted that they are not easily visible' (Rosenberg, 2008, p. 6).

as real by these' (Berger & Luckmann, 1967, pp. 19–20). Social reality is multiply constructed, in which the reality of everyday life is 'paramount' and serves as the norm against which all other 'finite provinces of meaning' are defined (p. 25). To explain what the reality of everyday life means, Berger and Luckmann take recourse to phenomenology. Our consciousness of the world we inhabit is of an objective reality comprising of things, persons, places and times that are relatively independent of how we apprehend them. It is a consciousness that is simultaneously personal and collective, subjective and intersubjective, that we designate as 'common sense' and take for granted. The reality of everyday life, thus, 'does not require additional verification over and beyond its simple presence. It is simply *there*, as self-evident and compelling facticity. I *know* that it is real' (p. 23, italics in original). It is what defines and delimits all other 'provinces of meaning' such as those of dreams and of religious as well as scientific and artistic representations.[9] As we apprehend these finite provinces of meaning, checking them against everyday reality that acts as their point of reference, we become conscious of the complexity and multiplicity of the world as a whole. The social consciousness of reality is constituted in the traversal of meaning through these 'provinces', in 'moving through different spheres of reality' (p. 21). Crises like natural disasters and epidemics unsettle the stability of this consciousness by revealing its underlying vulnerability to realities that it cannot assimilate: '*All* social reality is precarious. *All* societies are constructions in the face of chaos. The constant possibility of anomic terror is actualized whenever legitimations that obscure the precariousness are threatened or collapse' (p. 103, italics in original). It is precisely in such a crisis of comprehensibility that we turn to the two orders of meaning that augment our consciousness of the world—science and religion: one concerned

[9] Clifford Geertz identifies four major points of view that people use to 'construe the world': 'religious', 'common-sensical', 'scientific' and 'aesthetic' (1973, pp. 111–112). However, unlike Berger and Luckmann, he does not examine how they function together in constituting an ethos or world-view.

with natural laws and the other with cosmological. As we can see, Berger and Luckmann do not assume that the meanings we assign to reality are entirely arbitrary, even as they argue that reality is socially constructed.

Linguistic constructionism holds that the understanding of reality is constructed in the signifying structure of language. It derives from Ferdinand de Saussure's definition of the sign in *Course in General Linguistics*. 'The linguistic sign', writes Saussure, 'unites, not a thing and a name, but a concept and a sound-image' (1959, p. 66). He calls the former the signified and the latter its signifier. The distinctive character of the sign is that the relation between signifier and signified is arbitrary, that is, the signifier 'actually has no natural connection with the signified' except that dictated by convention (p. 69). It is not arbitrary in the sense that one can choose to associate any sound with any concept, but that the association conventionally accepted is random. Language does not re-present an extra-linguistic reality but actively constructs it—that is, it constructs the meaning that reality comes to bear. And it does this through a signifying function that is wholly internal to language as a system. In drawing on Saussure's theory of the sign, linguistic constructionism, unlike social constructionism, brackets out reality as a source of meaning. While it does not deny the existence of a reality outside of language, it asserts that our only way of accessing it is through signs. On this view of language, the reality of disease comes to be constituted in the way discourse about disease signifies it. Rosenberg's charge that constructionist accounts of disease emphasise the sign's arbitrariness thus seems to be warranted, if we begin from the theory of the sign. In practice, however most constructionist accounts do not hold that the representations of disease are purely arbitrary, with little correspondence to its lived experience. Paula Treichler, for instance, in an essay on the discursive construction of AIDS states: 'the notion of cultural construction is not a matter of arbitrarily envisioning an unknowable material reality but one of engaging in highly *non*arbitrary ways with the material world'

(1999, p. 173, italics in original). AIDS is thus '*simultaneously* an epidemic of a lethal transmissible disease and an epidemic of meanings or signification' (p. 11, italics added). Treichler's argument is not that disease can be reduced to whatever meanings we choose to attribute to it but that these meanings, which derive from both representations and practices, shape the way we know reality even as they are shaped by it themselves. Sander Gilman, similarly, argues that the social reality of disease is constructed not just on 'specific pathological signs or symptoms' but equally on the meanings attributed to them: 'Like any complex text, the signs of illness are read within the conventions of an interpretative community that comprehends them in the light of earlier, powerful readings of what are understood to be similar or parallel texts' (1988, p. 7). At the same time, Gilman cautions, 'the palpable signs of illness, the pain and suffering of the patient, cannot be simply dismissed as a social construction, even though this pain may be understood by patient and healthcare practitioner alike in a socially determined manner' (p. 10). Disease, in other words, is socially constructed, but it would be wrong to hold that the construction is arbitrary. There is a triadic relation between the material reality of disease, its construction in discourse and practice, and the meaning that 'common sense' gives to it, such that disease is experienced and understood as coherent and real. In other words, the difference between 'frame' and 'construct' does not seem to be significant, as the following statement by Rosenberg implies: '*In some ways disease does not exist until we have agreed that it does*—by perceiving, naming, and responding to it' (1989b, pp. 1–2, italics added). Whether we consider the social reality of disease as constructed or framed, the important fact is that such construction/framing materially affects the way we experience and respond to it as reality. I will, therefore, modify Rosenberg's terminology, to use 'frame' as a broad conceptualisation of an event and 'construct' to refer to specific images, ideas and representations within that frame.

1.6. Biomedical–Naturalistic and Cosmological–Magical Paradigms of Epidemic Disease

Scientific and religious ideas of disease constitute two distinct paradigms, biomedical–naturalistic and cosmological–magical, based on different theories of what causes it. The first assumes that diseases are natural phenomena caused by the body's constitution and/or its relation to the physical and microbial environment. This is the aetiological theory underlying the public health approach to disease. Till the first-half of the nineteenth century the dominant view was that it involved the body's constitution in relation to the local soil and climate. Mark Harrison quotes an 1835 report by a British army surgeon stationed in India that may be taken as a good example of this view. Dr Hunter's argument is that cholera is contagious in India 'if by contagion we mean a morbid poison, generated in one body, which when conveyed to another, excites a like disease in it, *provided the person is predisposed, and the epidemic constitution of the season or the locality favours it*' (as cited in Harrison, 1999, p. 188, italics added). In a medical topography of Bengal that he published two years later, James Ranald Martin states that the 'soil and the inhabitants ... always react on each other'. The main argument in *Notes on the Medical Topography of Calcutta* is that the 'industrious' races (by which he meant Europeans) could improve even 'a district overrun with noxious weeds and timber, and fast degenerating into a morass', making it salubrious and disease-free; while in the hands of a race that is 'idle and intemperate' (by which he meant Indians) a district thus improved would lose its salubrity and rapidly degenerate: 'the weeds will re-appear, the drains will become obstructed, and the edible products of the earth will lessen in quantity, and diminish in their nutritive value' (Martin, 1837, p. 45). Martin, who headed the East India Company's medical board, wrote the book as a report on the sanitary condition of Bengal Presidency with two objectives in mind: to improve public health and to establish the racial and civilisational superiority of the British. In other words, a scientific model of disease was made to serve an ideological function in validating Europe's right to rule.

After the advent of germ theory in the second-half of the nineteenth century, however, causal explanations of epidemic focused on the role of pathogenic agents rather than physiological and environmental conditions. Alfred Reed, in a disease travelogue on Asia published nearly a hundred years after Martin's *Notes*, describes how temples in India are veritable breeding sites of disease: 'Moisture, heat and darkness make them ideal culture beds for bacteria, fungi and animal parasites' (1930, p. 202). Like Martin, Reed was a public health officer and a specialist in tropical medicine, and medical observations were for him, as they were for Martin, an occasion for stigmatising non-European cultures. Hindu religion, he claims, 'deeply sunk in the depravities and perversions of phallicism', acts as a serious 'hindrance to health education and the development of a hygienic conscience in India' (p. 200). Ideology apart, public health in both Europe and its colonies was firmly based on a biomedical understanding that was founded on environmentalist or contagionist theories, naturalistic in their aetiology.[10]

The second paradigm of disease, cosmological–magical, assumes that epidemic is either caused by supernatural agents like a deity or ancestral spirit, or that its effects can be mitigated by them. It is magical in that it presupposes the role of hidden or occult forces. The domain of magic, writes Mauss, 'is a realm of the occult and of spirits, a world of ideas which imbues ritual movements and gestures with a special kind of effectiveness, quite different from their mechanical effectiveness' (1972, p. 25). According to Tambiah, magic is a mode of analogical thinking that links causes and effects on the basis of their resemblance. The Azande of central Africa, for instance, treat ringworm in children by applying ashes of dried fowl droppings on the infected area

[10] The naturalistic theory of disease causation is not restricted to biomedicine, but forms the basis, also, of other systems like ayurveda and unani. However, for reasons that have mainly to do with the history of public health as an apparatus of state in Europe's colonies, these have not played as significant a role in the modern understanding of epidemic.

because they resemble the scabby patches caused by the disease, the Zande word for which literally means 'fowl house sickness' (Tambiah, 2017, pp. 463–464). Because of this resemblance, the droppings are held to be both cause and cure of disease. Analogy also forms the basis of scientific thought, but in a way that is very different from magical thinking. In scientific explanation, as Tambiah elaborates, analogy serves a predictive function that must then be ascertained through empirical observation, while in magical explanation analogy serves a persuasive function. To explain the difference, let me take the example of Jennerian vaccination and ritual variolation as techniques of preventing smallpox. When vaccination was first introduced in Europe in 1800, it was based on an analogical transfer of meaning from the disease to its prevention, so that inoculating a healthy person with diseased tissue could possibly protect him from disease. This flew in the face of medical wisdom at the time (Foucault, 2007, p. 58), and seemed more like the axiom of 'like cures like' in magical thinking. But the prediction proved to be empirically true, when germ theory provided its theoretical justification half a century later. The practice of ritual variolation or *tika* had long existed in India, performed by professional variolators called *tikadars*. Variolation began by ritually invoking Sitala, the goddess of smallpox, to persuade people to believe in its efficacy: 'For both practitioners and observers, variolation was "practically a religious ceremony", and without Sitala its success and the safety of the person inoculated could not be guaranteed' (L.S.S. O'Malley, *Bengal District Gazetteers*, 1907, cited in Arnold, 1993, pp. 132–133). Fabrizio Ferrari argues that the rites of Sitala had not originally been a part of variolation but began sometime in the early-nineteenth century when the colonial government promoted Jenner's cowpox vaccine and actively discouraged the traditional method. *Tikadars*, fearing that they might lose their clientele, introduced Sitala into their practice as a way of persuading people of its divine authority and winning back their confidence. The invocation, therefore, began as an outcome of the conflict 'between the authority and power of different classes of health specialists' but became so widespread that by mid-nineteenth century it was 'inextricably associated with *Sītalāpūjā*' (Ferrari, 2015, p. 136). Though variolation and vaccination were essentially similar in effect because both used an attenuated form of the pathogen, their use of analogy was different. In one, analogy took the form of the '*scientific predictive*', in the other, of the '*conventional persuasive*' (Tambiah, 2017, p. 458, italics in original).

The worship of Sitala was based on an analogical transfer of meaning between disease, deity and dietary prescription. Smallpox was understood as a disease of excessive heat, since outbreaks generally occurred in summer and declined with the coming of rain. Sitala's power lay essentially in cooling the body, whence her name (from *sital* in Sanskrit, meaning 'cool'); and her dietary regimen consisted of cooling foods like curds. On the eve of her annual worship, it was believed that Sitala visited the homes of her devotees to lie down in the hearth, which must be left unlit and cold to receive her. In other words, the series of correspondences that constitute the magical aetiology of smallpox and its therapy is structured by the symbolic likeness and difference between heat and cold (Wadley, 1980). The effect of this was to persuade patients to follow a dietary regime that was held to be therapeutic.

Medical anthropologists often refer to such belief as 'personalistic' rather than 'magical.' In Strathern's and Stewart's terminology, for instance, 'personalistic' theories attribute disease to the 'actions of malevolent agents such as sorcerers or punitive ones such as ancestors' (2010, p. 11). While the term personalistic may well apply to certain aspects of epidemic deities in India, it does not apply to other aspects. Sitala, for instance, has the power to inflict smallpox if she is angered by lapses in her ritual worship, but she is also seen as a benign goddess who protects her devotees from disease instead of causing it. Ferrari points out that it is only in Bengal, in the *mangalakavyas* or devotional songs, that she is imagined as 'a dangerous, infecting goddess' (2015, p. 34). In other textual traditions, she is generally portrayed as a caring mother who alleviates suffering (Wadley, 1980, p. 54;

Nicholas, 1981, p. 21; Jash, 1982, p. 190). Similarly, in south India, the smallpox goddess Mariamma is seen as simultaneously dangerous and benign, capable of inflicting disease as well as protecting her devotees from it. Such goddesses are generally worshipped as *gramadevatas* or village deities, whose duty is to guard the village against evil coming from outside, like disease and natural calamities, and their shrines are most often set up at its entrance (Whitehead, 1921, pp. 28–33; Bhattacharyya, 1999, pp. 70–76; Wadhera, 2015). I think that the term 'personalistic' fails to account for the ambiguity underlying representations of disease goddesses in India, since malevolence is only one, and not the most prevalent, aspect of their characters. In preferring to call such beliefs 'magical' I shift the focus from the characterisation of the agent (malevolence/benignity) to the explanatory form, which is non-naturalistic in the way it attributes disease or its alleviation to supernature. My emphasis, in other words, is not on who or what causes disease but on how causation comes to be understood in the first place—this being the fundamental distinction between the two paradigms.

In South Asia, the reality of epidemic outbreak has been historically constituted in contexts defined by an opposition between the biological–naturalistic and cosmological–magical modes of thought. The former emphasises processes that govern the individual's biological existence in microbial transactions with other individuals in the social order, while the latter emphasises processes that position the individual within dense linkages of human and non-human, natural and the supernatural, secular and religious life in a cosmic order. In *The Sacred and the Profane*, Mircea Eliade explains the meaning of cosmos and its relation to religious belief. Cosmos refers to the lived world, the 'inhabited territory' created and consecrated by the gods, as distinguished from what surrounds it, 'the unknown and indeterminate space' of chaos. Cosmos is thus originally a religious notion: 'a universe within which the sacred has already manifested itself' and within which we orient ourselves in relation to other beings that inhabit it. 'The sacred reveals absolute reality and at the same time makes orientation possible; hence it *founds the world* in the sense that it fixes the limits and establishes the order of the world' (Eliade, 1959, pp. 29–30, italics in original). Cosmology re-enacts the founding of this cosmos every time a collective calamity threatens to disrupt it, in the performance of rituals that may not, strictly speaking, belong to the sacred but which take their origin and significance from it. According to Rappaport, rituals pertaining to this-worldly matters derive their performative force from 'ultimate sacred postulates' such as the existence of god. The postulates 'do not themselves provide the *logical* ground upon which the usages and rules of social life are established, they provide the ground, deeper than logic and beyond logic's reach, upon which cosmological structure can be founded' (Rappaport, 1979, p. 119).[11] The incantations with which rites of healing begin, for instance, reiterate the cosmogonic myth from which they draw their symbolic sustenance: the 'therapeutic efficacy of the incantation lies in the fact that, ritually uttered, it reactualizes the mythical time of origins' (Eliade, 1959, p. 85), both that of the cosmos and that of the malady for which healing is sought. This is the symbolic meaning of the incantations invoking Sitala in ritual variolation that I have mentioned above.

Biomedical–naturalistic and cosmological–magical comprise, therefore, paradigmatic ways of thinking that shape the

[11] Tambiah offers a broader definition of cosmology that includes secular as well as religious views, pertaining both to the social and supernatural orders of life:

> By cosmology I mean the body of conceptions that enumerate and classify the phenomena that compose the universe as an ordered whole and the norms and processes that govern it. From my point of view, a society's principal cosmological notions are all those orientating principles and conceptions that are held to be sacrosanct, are constantly used as yardsticks, and are considered worthy of perpetuating relatively unchanged. As such, depending on the conceptions of the society in question, its legal codes, its political conventions, and its social class relations may be as integral to its cosmology as its 'religious' beliefs concerning gods and supernaturals (1980, p. 121).

To the extent that scientific conceptions are also a part of this broad sense of culture, they can be considered cosmological, though not in the sense in which Eliade and Rappaport define cosmos. A scientific cosmology as an explanation of the world presupposes a naturalistic cause–effect logic, which is what distinguishes it from cosmological beliefs that are magical.

understanding of epidemic in radically different ways. For someone who subscribes to the former, the latter seems blind faith; for someone who subscribes to the latter, the former holds no assurance. I think this is what explains both the insecurity that impelled some people to worship Corona Devi ignoring COVID-safety norms, as well as the skepticism of those who denounced the worship as superstitious practice that risked spreading disease. A paradigm in this sense is what Thomas Kuhn defines as 'the entire constellation of beliefs, values, techniques, and so on shared by the members of a given community' (1996, p. 175).[12] Like Berger and Luckmann's 'finite provinces of meaning', paradigms are more or less well-defined sets of meanings and modes of experience that constitute phenomenological reality for those who subscribe to them. But paradigms, whether in science or elsewhere, never come unmixed. Multiple paradigms, like medical pluralisms, crisscross each other, contest each other and yet overlap. Biomedical–naturalistic and cosmological–magical are therefore not static binaries but constitute the two ends of a spectrum along which particular social realities of epidemic outbreak are ranged.

1.7. Epidemic Narratives: A Preview

Let me turn now to the final part of Rosenberg's schema, the 'epilogue'. Epidemic outbreaks eventually flatten out and come to an end as the number of new infections decrease and then begin their course anew as a part of cultural memory. The recapitulation of outbreak 'provides an implicit moral structure' (Rosenberg, 1989a, p. 9), as didacts, policymakers and scholars reflect on the lessons learnt from it. How did the community respond to it? What did all that suffering signify? Did the community forget the lessons it taught, did it revert to its old ways as if it had never happened, to repeat the very same mistakes that had led to the spread of disease? In the way they end, epidemics 'have always

[12] Kuhn provides this definition, which he calls 'sociological', in response to criticism of his use of the term in explaining how revolutions in scientific theory happen. See Bryant, 1975.

provided occasion for retrospective moral judgment' (ibid). That is the moment when the social reality of epidemic calls for narrative, factual or fictional, historical, scientific or literary, in print, in oral or cinematic renderings, across different media. Narratives both draw on the collective memory of past outbreaks and what they signified, and in turn preserve their memory and perpetuate it. Why narrative? Narratives are essentially about actions and happenings, how events unfold and how different characters respond to their unfolding, creating the norms on which value judgments are founded as well as the way they come to be transformed. In recounting past events, narratives constitute them in specific ways: if epidemics are always framed, as Rosenberg argues, it is narrative that shapes, recycles and reshapes these framings. And in the process narratives reconstitute epidemic as social reality, revealing and resolving, as Berger and Luckmann eloquently put it, its precariousness and the perpetual possibility of it yielding to chaos. It is in this reordering of the world that the moral import of epidemic as memory lies. Far from being an incidental part of the unfolding of an epidemic event, thus, the epilogue in its multiple narrations is what provides its key. The chapters that follow examine the various ways in which epidemic narratives serve this function.

References

Ali, S. (1991 December 30–January 5). Epidemic!. *Sunday*.

Althusser, L. (2001). *Lenin and philosophy and other essays* (B. Brewster, Trans.). Monthly Review Press.

Austin, J.L. (1962). *How to do things with words*. Clarendon Press.

Berger, P.L. & Luckmann, T. (1967). *The social construction of reality: A treatise in the sociology of knowledge*. Doubleday.

Bhattacharyya, N.N. (1999). *The Indian mother goddess*. 3rd ed. Manohar Publishers and Distributors.

Bryant, C.G.A. (1975). Kuhn, paradigms and sociology. *The British Journal of Sociology*, *26*(3), 354–359.

Das, D.K. (2021). Corona Devi: Epidemic and the disease goddess tradition. *Sambalpur Studies in Literatures and Cultures*, *6*, 11–24.

Douglas, M. (1994). *Risk and blame: Essays in cultural theory*. Routledge.

Dube, S. (2015). *No one else: A personal history of outlawed love and sex*. HarperCollins.

Eliade, M. (1959). *The sacred and the profane: The nature of religion* (W.R. Trask, Trans.). Harcourt Inc.

Fear of COVID-19 has a new name! Now, 'Corona Devi' emerges in Bihar. (2020, June 6). *National Herald*. https://www.nationalheraldindia.com/national/fear-of-covid-19-has-a-new-name-now-corona-devi-emerges-in-bihar

Ferrari, F.M. (2015). *Religion, devotion and medicine in North India: The healing power of Śītalā*. Bloomsbury.

Foucault, M. (2007). *Security, territory, population: Lectures at the Collége de France, 1977–1978* (M. Senellart, Ed.; G. Burchell, Trans.). Picador.

Geertz, C. (1973). *The interpretation of cultures: Selected essays*. Basic Books.

Gilman, S.L. (1988). *Disease and representation: Images of illness from madness to AIDS*. Cornell University Press.

Global News. (2020, March 20). *Coronavirus outbreak: A timeline of how COVID-19 spread around the world* [Video]. YouTube. https://www.youtube.com/watch?v=ST-cn2JQ31M

Guha, R. (2009). The small voice of history. In P. Chatterjee (Ed.), *The small voice of history: Collected essays* (pp. 304–317). Permanent Black.

Harrison, M. (1999). *Climates and constitutions: Health, race, environment and British imperialism in India, 1600–1850*. Oxford University Press.

Harrison, M. (2020). A dreadful scourge: Cholera in early nineteenth-century India. *Modern Asian Studies*, *54*(2), 502–553. https://www.researchgate.net/publication/335209109_A_Dreadful_Scourge_Cholera_in_early_nineteenth-century_India

Helman, C.B. (1981). Disease versus illness in general practice. *Journal of the Royal College of General Practitioners*, *31*, 548–552. PMID: 7328537; PMCID: PMC1972172. https://www.ncbi.nlm.nih.gov/pmc/articles/PMC1972172/pdf/jroyalcgprac00105-0038.pdf

Honigsbaum, M. (2020). *The pandemic century: A history of global contagion from the Spanish Flu to Covid-19*. W.H. Allen.

Jash, P. (1982). A note on the cult of Sitala. *Proceedings of the Indian History Congress*, *43*, 189–197. https://www.jstor.org/stable/44141230

Just one devotee for 'Corona Devi'. (2020, June 13). *The Hindu*. www.thehindu.com/news/national/kerala/just-one-devotee-for-corona-devi/article31816062.ece

Kapri, V. (2021). *1232 km: The long journey home*. HarperCollins.

Kleinman, A. (1980). *Patients and healers in the context of culture: An exploration of the borderland between anthropology, medicine, and psychiatry*. University of California Press.

Kuhn, T.S. (1996). *The structure of scientific revolutions*. 3rd ed. University of Chicago Press.

Light candles, diyas at 9 pm this Sunday to mark coronavirus fight: PM Narendra Modi. (2020, April 4). *India Today*. https://www.indiatoday.in/india/story/pm-narendra-modi-on-coronavirus-lockdown-1662747-2020-04-03

Lynteris, C. (2014). Introduction: The time of epidemics. *The Cambridge Journal of Anthropology*, *32*(1), 24–31. http://www.jstor.org/stable/43612893

Markel, H. & Stern, A.M. (2002). The foreignness of germs: The persistent association of immigrants and disease in American society. *The Milbank Quarterly*, *80* (4), 757–788. http://www.jstor.org/stable/3350445

Martin, J.R. (1837). *Notes on the medical topography of Calcutta*. Bengal Military Orphan Press.

Mauss, M. (1972). *A general theory of magic* (R. Brain, Trans.). Routledge.

Ministry of Home Affairs, Government of India. (2020, March 24). Order No. 40-3/2020/-DM-I(A).

Naregal, V. (2021). Labour 'invisibility' during COVID-19 times. *Economic and Political Weekly*, *56*(34), 37–43.

Nicholas, R.W. (1981). The Goddess Śītalā and epidemic smallpox in Bengal. *The Journal of Asian studies*, *41*(1), 21–44. http://www.jstor.org/stable/2055600

Puri, N. (1986, December 1–27). AIDS in India. *Sunday*, pp. 24–30.

Rajan, S.I. (2020). COVID-19 led migrant crisis: A critique of policies. *Economic and Political weekly*, *55*(48), 13–16.

Rappaport, R.A. (1979). *Ecology, meaning, and religion*. North Atlantic Books.

Reed, A.C. (1930). Medical sketches in the Orient. *The Scientific Monthly, 31*(3), 193–216. https://www.jstor.org/stable/14970

Rosenberg, C.E. (1989a). What is an epidemic? AIDS in historical perspective. *Daedalus, 118*(2), 1–17. http://www.jstor.com/stable/20025233

Rosenberg, C.E. (1989b). Disease in history: Frames and framers. *The Milbank Quarterly, 67*(Suppl. 1), 1–15. http://www.jstor.org/stable/3350182

Saussure, F.D. (1959). *Course in general linguistics* (W. Baskin, Trans.; Charles Bally, Albert Sechehaye & Albert Reidlinger, Ed.). Philosophical Library.

Singh, N.K. (1995, March 16–31). Fury over the flesh trade. *India Today.*

Singh, N.K. & Pillai, S. (1987, January 16–31). Campus jitters. *India Today.*

Shetty, K. (1990a, February 16–28). AIDS carriers: In custody. *India Today.*

Shetty, K. (1990b, June 16–30). Prostitutes: Sad ending. *India Today.*

Strathern, A. & Stewart, P.J. (2010). *Curing and healing: Medical anthropology in global perspective.* 2nd ed. Carolina Academic Press.

Superstitions galore: After Bihar, women in UP worship 'Corona Mai', offer 'laddoos' to appease her. (2020, June 9). *India.Com.* www.india.com/viral/after-bihar-women-in-up-worship-corona-mai-offer-ladoos-to-appease-her-4052883/

Tambiah, S.J. (1980). A performative approach to ritual. *The British Academy: Radcliffe-Brown lecture in social anthropology.* https://ia801000.us.archive.org/32/items/aperformativeapproachtorituraltambiahstanley/A-performative-approach-to-ritual_Tambiah-Stanley.pdf

Tambiah, S.J. (2017). Form and meaning of magical acts: A point of view. *HAU: Journal of Ethnographic Theory, 7*(3), 451–473. https://www.journals.uchicago.edu/doi/epdf/10.14318/hau7.3.030

Treichler, P. (1999). *How to have theory in an epidemic: Cultural chronicles of AIDS.* Duke University Press.

Wadhera, R. (2015). Benign goddess, terrible gaze: Gender, power and agency in the cult of Nalla Pochamma. *The Indian Journal of Political Science, 76*(3), 619–622.https://www.jstor.org/stable/26534899

Wadley, S.S. (1980). Śītalā: The cool one. *Asian Folklore Studies, 39*(1), 33–62. https://www.jstor.org/stable/1177516

Wald, P., Tomes, N. & Lynch, L. (2002). Introduction: Contagion and culture. *American Literary History, 14*(4), 617–624. http://www.jstor.org/stable/3568018

Welch, J.S. (2003). Ritual in Western medicine and its role in placebo healing. *Journal of Religion and Health, 42*(1), 21–33. https://www.jstor.org/stable/27511652

Whitehead, H. (2020). *The village gods of south India.* 2nd ed. Gyan Publishing House.

2

Pandemic Nation[1]

'[I]t is in the self-definition of the national', wrote Thomas E. Yingling, 'to reject not only disease but the very notion of embodiment it recalls' (1997, p. 29)[2]. The AIDS pandemic broke out in the US in 1980, and the government's response to it served to confirm his comment: it was only after six years, in 1986, that Surgeon General C. Everett Koop broke his long silence on AIDS and published a report that finally called for concerted state action. It took the death of Rock Hudson, America's star actor and close personal friend of President Reagan, for the government to admit that AIDS was a national emergency. (Shilts, 1987, p. 587–588) By then, twenty-seven thousand Americans were dead or dying, most of them gay persons who fell victim not to the pandemic but state-sponsored homophobia. In deciding which lives need to be protected and which sacrificed, national responses to infectious disease outbreak open up existing fractures in society. During COVID lockdown of 2020 the Indian government promoted pandemic nationalism in rituals of clapping and lamp-lighting, even as thousands of hapless migrant workers lost their livelihoods and hundreds lost their lives (Rajan, 2020; Naregal, 2021; Kapri, 2021a).

Yingling's point is about embodiment and the ideology of the nation. The 'national body' must be healthy, to defend the nation's territory and contribute to the nation's economy. When

[1] This is a revised version of the sixteenth Anita Baruah Sarmah Memorial Lecture that I gave at Gauhati University on 31 October 2022.

[2] This was in a paper that he presented at Columbia University, New York, in January 1992, a few months before his death from complications due to AIDS. It was posthumously published in an anthology titled *AIDS and the National Body*, edited by Robyn Weigman.

Indian soldiers tested positive for HIV in significant numbers, the Border Security Force produced, in collaboration with UNAIDS, a health awareness video titled *Saavdhaan*. Its objective was to promote voluntary testing, but it also addressed other issues like the risks of contracting infection, living normally if infected, and AIDS-related stigma. The video opens with shots of BSF jawans laying down their lives to protect the borders, in a plot that shifts from the norm of risk-taking in times of conflict to that of risk-avoidance in a pandemic. The real battleground, as the subtitle announces, is the body rather than territory: 'It's a battle against HIV/AIDS.' The film ends with scenes from an actual voluntary testing-camp in which A.K. Mitra, the then director-general of the BSF, urges soldiers to test in the name of the nation: 'you are the soldiers of the Border Security Force. You have a responsibility towards this country. You can fulfill this responsibility only if you are perfectly fit. … let no one say that the Border Security Force is lagging behind anywhere as far as the country's responsibility is concerned' (UNAIDS & BSF, 2007, 39:21–40:43).

The concept of risk and prudence that *Saavdhaan* invokes—its title means 'caution'—is core to national discourses of pandemic. Like acts of terrorism, pandemics are construed as a security risk for the nation; or, to be more precise, national imaginaries conflate contagion and terror as synonymous. In Aashique Abu's film *Virus*, an outbreak of Nipah disease in Kerala is investigated by a central health ministry team for links to Islamic terror outfits, though this possibility is dismissed when transmission patterns prove otherwise. *Virus* is based on an actual outbreak in 2018, in the districts of Kozhikode and Mallapuram, when there were indeed speculations of bioterrorism (Arora et al., 2018; Pulla, 2018). 'Concerns with security', writes Carlo Caduff, 'are not new, to be sure. In fact, infectious disease research has always been politically charged in many respects, but it is even more so now, and in a very particular way' (2012, p. 338). This particularity is the fear of pathogens being used in bioterrorism and biowarfare, as a most effective way of destroying the nation. This was the fear articulated in a National Intelligence Estimate report in 2000: 'As a major hub of global travel, immigration, and commerce, along with having a large civilian and military presence and wide-ranging interests overseas, the United States will remain at risk from global infectious disease outbreaks, or even a bioterrorist incident using infectious disease microbes' (NIC, 2000, p. 53; see also King, 2002, p. 763). Similarly, in the first wave of the COVID pandemic there were allegations and counter-allegations of military conspiracy on the part of both the US and China (Knight, 2021). There is a fundamental link between pandemic and the nation-state that bears scrutiny, for the insights it yields into the dynamics of pandemic control. The next two sections focus on the link between contagion and national self-definition. In the third section I discuss the implications of this link for public health policy at both national and international levels, in the way it has been unfolding in the last few decades.

2.1. Contagion and National Self-Definition

Social theorists Hans Kohn and Liah Greenfeld have proposed two forms of nationalism, ethnic and civic. Ethnic nationalism defines itself in terms of presumed commonalities of language, culture and ethnicity, which was what the term 'nation' meant prior to the eighteenth century. Etymologically, nation is linked to the concept of *natio*, or birth. One is an ethnic national by birth. As Greenfeld puts it in *Nationalism: Five Roads to Modernity*: 'one can neither acquire [ethnic nationality] if one does not have it, nor change it if one does; it has nothing to do with individual will, but constitutes a genetic characteristic' (1992, p. 11). It was with the emergence of nation-states in Europe and especially the French 'Declaration of the Rights of Man and Citizen' (1789), that the term 'nation' acquired a more republican valence—it meant a polity of citizens with equal rights irrespective of ethnic descent, and ruled by popular consent. Civic nationalism, therefore, emphasises citizenship over ethnicity, rights over *natio*, and 'is at least in principle open and voluntaristic; it can and sometimes must be acquired' (Greenfeld, 1992, p. 11). Kohn argues in *The Idea of Nationalism* (which preceded Greenfeld's *Five Roads to Modernity* by about fifty years) that ethnic or 'cultural' nationalism privileges people over territory, while civic or 'political' nationalism privileges territory over people (1946, pp. 13–18). Ethnic/cultural and civic/political are, of course, conceptual schemas, and no nation is wholly either one or the other; rather, national self-definition is constituted through elements drawn from both schemas. The Constitution of India, for instance, recognises both birth and territory. Article 5 accords citizenship at the commencement of the Constitution to a person (a) who was born in the territory of India, (b) either of whose parents was born in the territory of India, or (c) who has lived for at least five years in the territory of India.

The difference between ethnic and civic nationalisms is key to understanding the link between pandemic and nation. My argument is that they play different roles in the social understanding of pandemic as national danger, the former leading to fear of 'foreign' people and the latter to fear of breached territory. The International Epidemiology Association defines a pandemic as 'an epidemic occurring worldwide, or over a very wide area, crossing international boundaries and usually affecting a large number of people' (as cited in Singer, Thompson & Bonsali, 2021). Pandemic outbreak threatens the presumed integrity of borders, both territorial and ethnic, laying them open to contagion. In *AIDS and Its Metaphors*, Susan Sontag comments that '[d]isease inevitably comes from somewhere else', establishing 'a link between imagining disease and imagining foreignness' (1988, pp. 47–48). This is specifically true of pandemic: for the countries to which it subsequently spreads it *literally* originates on 'foreign' soil. This is why contagion's place of origin is crucial to the national imagination of pandemic, as the long list of toponymous disease indicates: Asiatic cholera, Spanish flu, West Nile virus, Middle Eastern Respiratory Syndrome, Zika, Nipah, Ebola. Former US President Donald Trump's derogatory use of the term 'Chinese virus' for SARS-CoV-2 is, ironically, in conformity with this scientific practice. Toponymy, however, is rarely neutral science: most often, it is made to ideologically prefigure a foreign land and its people as pathogenic. Nationalist and imperialist disease mapping, thus, constitutes what I have called elsewhere a 'patho-geography of blame', most often structured by a binarism of Europe versus Asia and Africa, West versus East, global North versus South (Das, 2022, p. 19, fn. 6). It was for this reason that the World Health Organisation declared in 2015 that new infectious diseases should not be named after geographic locations like 'Cities, regions, continents' (WHO, 2015a). As the assistant director-general for health security stated: 'This may seem like a trivial issue to some, but disease names really matter to the people who are directly affected' (WHO, 2015b).

The prejudicial linking of disease and place is a form of pandemic nationalism that is ethnic in its nature. It is not just the place that becomes synonymous with disease but, more importantly, its *people*, who signify in their ethnic difference pathogenicity, or the property of causing disease. Pandemic nationalism, thus, follows the logic of what Hayden White calls 'the technique of ostensive self-definition by negation', or defining the self by negating the other (1978, p. 151–152). Ethnic difference is, of course, not the only factor: to be effective in accusing another nation as source of disease, it must be bolstered by geopolitical differences. In an epidemiological report on pandemic cholera published in *The North American Review* in 1892, William G. Eggleston traces its origin to 'its home in Bengal', and its transmission along Hindu and Muslim pilgrim routes that carry it to Christendom. Imagined as an 'Asiatic' contagion, cholera infiltrates not only geographical boundaries between Asia, Europe and America but religious and civilisitional ones as well:

> It is beyond human possibility to put India in good sanitary condition in any reasonable time, and to make the pilgrims observe the commonest rules of hygiene and cleanliness would require two soldiers for each pilgrim. The most riotous imagination could scarcely exaggerate the filth of India and Egypt and of the Hindoo and Mohammedan pilgrims, for when people use the same water for bathing, washing soiled

> clothes, and drinking, they are scarcely ripe for moral suasion. So long as the pilgrimages continue Europe and this country will be endangered and will be visited by cholera. (Eggleston, 1892, p. 128)

Eggleston's report is a good instance of the ethnocentric inflection of a presumably scientific epidemiology, contextualised in the geopolitics of colonialism. A more striking instance is Alfred C. Reed's 'Medical Sketches in the Orient', published in 1930. In castigating the Orient in general, Reed specifically targets Hindu India in a conflation of hygienic and moral outrage. Of the Meenakshi Temple in Madurai he writes in a passage that I must quote in full:

> Inside is a howling, shouting pandemonium, a jostling, crowding melange of pilgrims, priests, ascetics, holy men, fakirs, beggars, soothsayers, thieves, panderers, children and aged—all mixed up together with sacred animals and birds. From elephants and camels down to the leprous dogs and sleek rats that scuttle about in the semi-darkness, all is filth, vileness and obscenity. The myriads of shrines and images divide the worshipers among them. The countless butter lamps sputter and glow in the liquid darkness and coat the images with greasy soot. Doubtless no viler sect of men ever trod this earth than the rabble of the Hindu priesthood. They debauch a race and trade on ignorance and fear in order to make an easy living and perpetuate the evil system of which they are the center. The gross obscenity of the images is exceeded only by the teachings and practices of this filthy herd. (Reed, 1930, pp. 201–202)

Contagion, as Mary Douglas argues in *Purity and Danger*, was originally a moral idea recast in the scientific language of hygiene: 'we find that certain moral values are upheld and certain social rules defined by beliefs in dangerous contagion' (1966, p. 4). Perceived in hygienic terms, moral lapse translates as dirt and disease, and signifies the breakdown of a medico-moral order that is founded on the idea of cleanliness as virtue. When dirt and disease are used to accuse another people perceived as different, therefore, what we see is not strictly science but ethnocentric bias fuelled by geopolitical interests. Reed's and Eggleston's accounts are excellent instances of this.

In the early days of the COVID pandemic, China became the target of accusations by Western nations, specifically the US. While it is true that the pandemic first broke out in the city of Wuhan, which has a 'wet market' as well as an institute of virological research, the accusations served a function that cannot be reduced to merely tracking the source of contagion. That function has been too well rehearsed for me to elaborate; but, briefly, it involved countering China's emergence as a new superpower that could challenge US hegemony. The main charge against China, openly expressed by the US and supported by other mostly Western nations, was conspiracy to wage biological warfare against its opponents: Wuhan Institute of Virology, it was alleged, was actually a secret defence laboratory to develop viral weapons. The other charge concerned the dirty eating habits of the Chinese, which included bats that were suspected to be the original reservoir of coronavirus.[3] Both charges, as Christos Lynteris writes, worked in tandem: one denigrating China 'as a barbaric place, where the common people disregard modernity and consume inappropriate animals or animals in inappropriate ways', and the other depicting the Chinese government as 'a secretive tyranny hellbent to destroy the West' (2020, p. 26). The point is not whether the charges were true, but that they were founded, as Hayden White says of imaginary self-definitions, on 'stipulation rather than empirical observation and induction' (1978, p. 151).

Pandemic outbreak provokes two kinds of vulnerabilities in the nation: territorial vulnerability and vulnerability to the vile *ethnos* of the other. Territorial vulnerability leads to the fear of breached national security, as national responses to the COVID pandemic show. The conflation of contagion and bioterrorism that I mentioned above is typically a territorial response, which pandemics provoke given the very real possibility of weaponising

---

[3] This hypothesis was later questioned, as it was found that the SARS-CoV-2 virus in bats, though genetically similar to Human SARS-CoV-2, cannot directly infect human cells. At best, bats may be an intermediary host. But it was widely circulated in the media as an established fact, leading to widespread chiroptophobia, or fear of bats. (Lu et al., 2021)

microbes. In the territorial imagination, the pathogen is an 'enemy' and pandemic a 'war'. A *Hindustan Times* story titled 'India's war against Covid-19' states: 'If we have to fight a war against the pandemic, then we might as well follow the ten principles of war', which it then goes on to list (Raman, 2021). When the pandemic broke out in India, the first state to be affected was Kerala; but thanks to a surveillance mechanism successfully developed by the state's Health Minister Shailaja in the 2018 Nipah epidemic it was soon brought under control. A May 2020 issue of *Vogue* dubbed her 'Vogue warrior' and 'commandant of the coronavirus battle' (Rajan, 2020). The metaphor of COVID as war is so ubiquitous nowadays that we hardly recognise it as metaphor any longer. If war becomes a metaphor for disease, as Sontag states (1978, pp. 65–76), disease also, in a curious inversion, becomes metaphor for war. In 1946 when America's Cold War had just begun George F. Kennan, who was then ambassador to Russia, sent a telegram on Soviet policy to the secretary of state. 'World communism', wrote Kennan, 'is like malignant parasite which feeds only on diseased tissue' (1967, p. 559).

Ethnic vulnerability, in contrast, lends itself to cultural rejection and othering. In 'Witchcraft and Leprosy' Mary Douglas observes that accusations of causing 'occult injury and hidden infection informally entrench the hierarchy of social categories and warn well-placed persons against indiscriminate social intercourse' (1992, p. 87). Such accusation, she further states 'can be completely outrageous; it will be credible essentially if the political system on whose behalf it is made is accepted'. It is not, therefore, necessary for the allegations against China and the Chinese people to be factually true: it will produce its effects nonetheless, depending on the ideology that is dominant. In the first year of the pandemic, when the Republicans ruled, incidence of hate crimes against Asian Americans in the US increased to a very high extent, such that when the Democrats came to power in 2021 they introduced a new law to stop the witch-hunting. The COVID-19 Hate Crimes Act, which was passed in May 2021, began by noting that 'there were nearly 3,800 reported cases of anti-Asian discrimination and incidents related to COVID-19 between March 19, 2020 and February 28, 2021, in all 50 States and the District of Columbia' (COVID-19 Hate Crimes Act, 2021).

Rejection and othering necessarily target already-vilified minorities, as it happened in India in March 2020. The Tablighi Jamaat, a transnational Deobandi Islamic mission, organised a congregation at Banglewali Masjid in Nizamuddin, South Delhi shortly before the nationwide lockdown was announced. The pandemic spread to different parts of the country when the Jamaatis returned to their homes, leading to a sudden rise in new COVID cases. The government took immediate steps to trace and quarantine those infected, and the situation was eventually brought under control. Yet mass media networks and the social media blew it out of proportion, accusing the Jamaatis of conspiracy against the nation. Dubbed 'Corona Jihadis', they became the target of an Islamophobia that held *all* Muslims suspect. TFIPOST, a right-wing social media platform, stated: 'It seems clear that the organisation is pursuing a nefarious goal—spreading the Coronavirus throughout entire regions and countries' (Narang, 2020). It accused them of intentionally distributing infected sweets to fellow passengers on trains and spitting on doctors and nurses to spread infection, switching off their mobile phones to evade the authorities, and attacking policemen and health workers who tried to detain them. For the author, this provided unquestionable proof of 'their clear decision to keep passing on the virus' (Narang, 2020). In a news telecast on 31 March 2020, Republic TV anchor Arnab Goswami accused the jamaatis of 'conspiracy against India' and stated: 'They have broken every law of this country. They have been spreading hate against the lockdown, and they have told their followers to do everything possible to defy and defeat the national lockdown.' (Republic World, 2020, 00:25–00:41) In both inter- and intra-national contexts, therefore, ethnocentrism tends to define the nation against its perceived others in pandemic times.[4]

[4] For more on this, see Woods et al., 2000.

2.2. Contagion and the Nation-State's Public Health Policy

Pandemics always begin as local epidemics. COVID-19 first broke out in Wuhan before it spread to the rest of China and other countries. Spanish Flu first broke out perhaps in Camp Devens, a cantonment of the Seventy-Sixth Division of the US Army located in a village in rural New England called Ayer (Honigsbaum, 2020, pp. 1–9).[5] This obvious fact points to three things. First, public health governance to control disease outbreaks happens at three levels: the local, the national and the international. In Albert Camus' novel, plague broke out in the town of Oran but the local authorities managed to control it before it spread to the rest of Algiers and France (Camus, 1960). In Ananthamurthy's *Samskara*, it broke out in Shivamogge but the colonial government failed to take notice and it spread to Durvasapura and other places rapidly (Ananthamurthy, 1976). We will shortly see the implication of these dynamics, when we go to the concluding section on internationalism in health policy. The second thing it points to is that epidemic outbreaks necessitate public health efforts first at the national level, given the biopolitical obligation[6] of modern nation-states to protect the lives of their citizens. Thirdly, these efforts can have unforeseen consequences that both strengthen the nation and weaken its legitimacy. I will elaborate these last two points in the paragraphs that follow.

Epidemic events, as Rosenberg states, have a three-part

[5] It did not originate in Spain, though it was called *Spanish* Flu. Rather, Spain was the first country to announce its outbreak while the other countries, which were engaged in a world war, suppressed information.

[6] 'Biopolitics' refers to the duty of states to provide necessary conditions for the well-being of their subjects, such as food, housing, healthcare, education, employment and protection against accident and natural disasters. For a brief summary of the concept, see Foucault, 2003, pp. 243–249. In the Indian Constitution, it is part of the right to life under Article 21 and codified in the Directive Principles of State Policy. Based on this, the Supreme Court ruled in a judgment of 1987 that the state must 'enforce creation and sustenance of good conditions of health' (*Vincent Panikurlangara v Union of India* AIR 1987 SC 990).

structure in the way they unfold: official acknowledgement of outbreak, attempts to make sense of it through already existing explanatory frames, and efforts to control it based on these frames. 'The peculiar texture of any epidemic reflects continuing interaction among incident, perception, interpretation, and response' (Rosenberg, 1989, p. 3).[7] An outbreak of epidemic demands explanation for two reasons. First, it is an aleatory event: that is, it is random or unpredictable. Even predictive health information systems with advanced surveillance and modelling techniques would not be able to detect every contingency in time to forestall it. Secondly, it leads to a triple crisis in the social order: it puts unprecedented strain on healthcare resources, it causes untold death and suffering, and it intensifies discrimination against those perceived to spread disease. It is, therefore, necessary to understand what causes it and what it signifies. Historically speaking, there have been four major explanatory frames that can be linked to the policy imperatives of the nation-state: a supernatural thesis, a contagion thesis, an environment thesis and a personal behaviour thesis (Tesh, 1982). In the supernatural frame, a deity either causes the outbreak or protects people against it. It sometimes influences national response, as it did at the turn of the nineteenth century in the US. Sylvia Tesh provides historical evidence of how such belief was widely prevalent, with people seeking relief from disease through fasting, prayers and repentance. These practices served to underline the association between sin and death in Biblical literature,[8] and they did have an impact, however short-lived, on public health policy. 'Respect for the supernatural theory, or at least respect for its adherents had prompted Presidents Washington, Adams and Madison to

[7] Rosenberg, of course, is not referring to the biological event of outbreak per se, but the way it is configured as a social phenomenon. It is important to bear this in mind, for policy responses are shaped by the logic not of biology but of social understanding, which (as discussed in the earlier chapter) need not conform to scientific reasoning. Political and economic imperatives play a far greater role in it than science.

[8] Cf. the Epistle of James: 'Then when lust hath conceived, it bringeth forth sin: and sin, when it is finished, bringeth forth death' (King James Bible, 2001, James 1:15).

proclaim fast days to combat disease' (Tesh, 1982, p. 330).[9] The contagionist frame assumes that disease comes from elsewhere. At the level of national policy, it leads to curbs on travel, mass surveillance and testing, identification of containment zones and mandatory isolation of those infected. To these already existing mechanisms of public health COVID has added a third: nation-wide lockdowns.[10] The environment thesis has had two forms historically: miasma theory till the mid-nineteenth century and currently the theory of environmental accident. Miasma theory, which was put to rest when germ theory gained prominence, held that disease was caused by noxious vapours emanating from decaying animal and vegetable matter. The environmental accident theory holds that emerging zoonotic outbreaks like Nipah, Ebola, SARS and possibly COVID are caused, among other things, by 'urbanization and destruction of natural habitats, leading to humans and animals living in close proximity' (WHO, 2014, p. 1). National policy in both cases addresses the need to intervene in environmental degradation. Finally, the personal behaviour thesis holds that people engaging in risky behaviours infect both themselves and others and thereby cause the spread of disease. National policy includes campaigns targeting high-risk groups to change their behaviour patterns. In response to the HIV/AIDS epidemic in India, for instance, the National AIDS Control Organisation conducted behaviour change campaigns for truck-drivers and sex-workers. The nation-state may at times use more coercive methods, as in the Goa, Daman and Diu Public Health Act, 1985 which provided for mandatory testing of individuals suspected to be HIV-positive and their forced

[9] Another instance of supernaturalism, though not an official public health measure, is the South Asian tradition of worshipping epidemic goddesses like Sitala, Mariamma, and currently Corona Devi, which I have discussed in the previous chapter.

[10] Since lockdowns and quarantines have negative effects on the economy, states are reluctant to impose them, preferring instead to persuade individuals to adopt risk-prevention practices like using masks and social distancing.

isolation if found to be so, under Sections 53(vi) and 53(vii).[11] Onir's 2005 film *My Brother ... Nikhil* was based on an actual case under this law—the custodial detention of Dominic D'Souza in an abandoned sanatorium for sixty-three days.

Social response to epidemic draws on all four paradigms outlined by Tesh, with one or two being in dominance. Thus, response to COVID-19 includes the worship and appeasement of Corona Devi; quarantines, masks, lockdowns and social distancing to prevent contagion; epidemiological studies on animal hosts and animal-to-human transmission dynamics; and pedagogic measures to teach people how to protect themselves from infection. National public health policy in the pandemic gave priority to the contagionist paradigm followed by personal behaviour and environmental risk, while the supernatural paradigm informed popular practices.

Public health strategies do in fact succeed in curbing epidemic spread, but they also lead to the suspension of basic civil rights like free movement or the freedom to choose whether to vaccinate or not, whether to wear a mask or not. In India these are a part of fundamental rights, under Articles 19(1)(d) and 21 of the Constitution. Factually speaking vaccination is voluntary, but when airports and railway stations demand vaccination certificates from travellers to permit them to travel it is no longer a matter of free choice. During the lockdown in 2020 in India, one got to see innumerable YouTube videos of the police beating or shaming 'lockdown violators' and imposing heavy penalties on those who did not wear masks. Common sense tells us that such impositions are necessary for the good of all, even if personal liberty is at stake. What common sense *conceals*, however, is the fact that in epidemic crisis the nation-state arrogates to itself immense and unprecedented power over the lives of its subjects.[12]

---

[11] These two sections were introduced by an amendment to the Act in 1987, when there was a significant increase in HIV incidence in the state of Goa. Section 53(vii), mandatory isolation of HIV-positive individuals, was subsequently removed by another amendment in 1995.

[12] This was evident in the Dominic D'Souza case mentioned above. For a critical discussion of the case, see Das, 2019, pp. 121–124.

It is well-known that Foucault departed from the theory of power as repressive, emphasising instead its productive functions. Biopolitics, on such view, is a positive exercise of power in the modern state. But Foucault also pointed to its negative underside when the state, in the name of preserving life, takes the very life it is committed to preserve. The effect of the lockdown on migrant workers in India is an apt instance: suddenly left without jobs in the cities to which they had migrated, thousands were forced to return home on foot, bicycles or by hitching rides on trucks. Not only did many die in tragic accidents or due to exhaustion and hunger, the return migration also resulted in new COVID cases in the rural hinterlands. Vinod Kapri made a documentary titled *1232 KMs* on a group of returning migrants who cycled all the way from Ghaziabad to their village in Bihar, and followed it up with a book—*1232 kms: The Long Journey Home*. Kapri recounts the precarious condition of the migrants who received little government support, though they were promised much. It was the outcome not just of the callousness of a few government officials, but equally of larger structural inequalities in a neoliberal state that uses informal labour for its infrastructural projects but without the protections that it guarantees to formal labour. (Rajan, 2020; Naregal, 2021; Sammadar, 2016)

In elaborating Foucault's 'biopolitical enigma', or the paradox of a state that takes life to save life, Giorgio Agamben advances the concept of a 'state of exception'. Conditions of emergency, such as war or pandemic, require an exception to the biopolitical rule that life and personal liberty must be protected. That is, this rule is not cancelled but temporarily suspended till order is, hopefully eventually, restored. As he puts it, '*The rule applies to the exception in no longer applying, in withdrawing from it*' (1998, p. 18, italics in original). Agamben's thesis is that in contemporary biopolitics the state of exception has itself become the rule, and the imposition of emergency measures that had once been exceptional have now become more generalised. Thus, in 'The Invention of an Epidemic', he argues that the COVID lockdown makes manifest 'the tendency to use a state of exception as a normal paradigm for government' (2020). It is a drastic measure that puts in peril the very lives it is supposed to save, by ratcheting up fears that it paradoxically tries to mitigate. As numerous studies of the lockdown have shown, it failed to significantly reduce loss of life and created instead conditions under which people, especially the poor, lost their livelihoods. What, then, did the lockdown achieve? It brought to the fore the state's prerogative to use illiberal force in what is formally a liberal political order. In Kapri's account of the lockdown the migrants were first deprived of their livelihood and then prevented from returning to their own villages where they could survive the crisis. The governmental exercise of power, as Foucault points out, targets both individuals and populations. Surveillance, testing and self-isolation are techniques that deal with individuals, while containment zones and lockdowns are population-oriented. Thus, outbreaks of contagion serve to extend state authority over the everyday lives of citizens, in a form of political rationality which integrates individual bodies into a totalised national body. It 'results from a constant correlation between an increasing individualization and the reinforcement of this totality' (Foucault, 1988, p. 162). Under epidemic conditions its practical form is public health strategy, while its ritual form is the lighting of lamps and clapping from balconies—what Rosenberg calls 'the visible acting out of community solidarity' (1989, p. 7).

Public health response to epidemic crisis does not necessarily entail consolidation of state authority; its effects are contingent upon the context. In the context of colonialism in India it served to intensify nationalist struggle, as popular reaction to the plague measures of 1897 shows. When bubonic plague broke out in Bombay Presidency, Poona's Plague Commissioner Walter Charles Rand instituted extreme measures that included forced hospitalisition of the infected and segregation of their contacts, house-to-house searches, fumigation and destruction of articles of daily use. Popular resistance to these measures soon took the form of anti-colonial resistance, leading to the assassination of Rand by Damodar Hari Chapekar and his brothers on 22 June

1897 (Arnold, 1987, pp. 57–68; Kidambi, 2007, pp. 49–51)[13] If colonialist public health measures provoke nascent nationalism, national health measures call into question the legitimacy of the state. In 'Community Spaces in India: Constructing Solidarity during the Pandemic', Suparna Banerjee shows how local community efforts like providing food and medicines to the needy during the COVID-19 lockdown constituted 'acts of resistance, acts of building solidarities against the inherent inequality of the neoliberal order' (2022, p. 124). In *1232 km: The Long Journey Home*, Vinod Kapri narrates an incident in which migrant workers detained at a quarantine centre in Bihar rose in protest against the lack of food and water, lack of proper habitation and official apathy—in short, the precariousness of their condition in the camp. Precarity, it has been argued, is caused not just by personal factors like ill-health or adversity, but equally by structural factors like inegalitarian and unjust politico-economic regimes (Ettlinger, 2007; Puar, 2012; Harris & Nowicki, 2018; Muñoz, 2018; Prakash & Borker, 2022). Acts of solidarity like helping the needy in a lockdown or the migrants' protest show how pandemics occasion agential resistance to the hegemony of the nation-state.

The politicisition of pandemic outbreaks, therefore, has had uneven effects on nations and nationalism. If in colonial India the plague outbreak led to the intensification of anti-colonial resistance and the birth of a new nation-state, COVID in postcolonial India has called into question the legitimacy of that nation-state's policy. While the construction of pandemic as a national problem is necessary for controlling it, there are clearly limits to its effectivity.

2.3. Conclusion: Nation, Internationalism and Pandemic Response

In this concluding section, I will briefly outline the need to move beyond nationalism in resolving pandemic crises. Shortly after

[13] The Marathi film *22 June 1897* is based on this event. Released in 1979, the film was directed by Jayoo and Nachiket Patwardhan. I discuss the assassination of Rand in greater detail in the next chapter.

the formation of the United Nations in 1945, Hans Kohn made a prediction in *The Idea of Nationalism*: 'With the transformation of social and economic life, with the growing interdependence of all nationalities on a shrinking earth, with a new direction to education, the circumference may widen to include supranational areas of common interest and common sympathy' (1946, p. 21). By 'circumference' he meant the kind of social order that people preferred, which from the nineteenth to the early-twentieth century had been the nation-state. Kohn's view was that the privilege of nation-states would decline with the emergence of the new international order. Pandemic crisis provides an apt testing-ground for this prediction.

Pandemics are driven primarily by the movement of people across national borders, a phenomenon that has been intensified in contemporary times. As Stephen Morse observes: 'Human population movements are of obvious importance for disseminating viruses' (1991, p. 398). It was probably with such a view that the UN, soon after it was formed, created a *World* Health Organisation. But supranationalism in pandemic control is possible, as Cindy Patton points out, only if member-nations 'relinquish their sovereignty over disease (and in essence, over their own populations) to the WHO' (2011, p. 109). The recent history of pandemics shows that this has not always happened. During the H1N1 pandemic, the European Union accused WHO of catering to the needs of the pharma industry rather than global health. More recently, the US accused the WHO of being 'China centric' in dealing with the COVID pandemic, and threatened to withhold its funding (Gostin et al., 2020). 'The implication that the WHO, with its carefully managed global image, did not stand above country pressures and outside capitalist interests was potentially devastating for the organisation' (Patton, 2011, p. 107). Patton's argument is that the 'incomplete sovereignty' of the WHO in global decision-making makes it very difficult for it to broker partnerships between nations. Under these circumstances, Kohn's prediction of supranationalism and interdependence between nations seems unlikely, unless there is a more balanced relation between WHO and its member-states.

'The interest behind nationalism and its institutions (e.g., nation-state)', writes Liah Greenfeld in the context of COVID-19, 'is alive and well….It is transnational institutions, rather than the nation-state, that are likely to fall victim to the pandemic' (Woods et al., 2020, p. 813). To prevent this and to achieve a more equitable and comprehensive policy of disease control, therefore, we need a paradigm shift from security concerns tied to the nation-state, to human security in general and the security of life as such—be it human, animal or vegetal, animate or inanimate. It remains to be seen how and when this happens, as the world recovers from COVID-19 and prepares for the next microbial assault on its nations.

References

Agamben, G. (1998). *Homo sacer: Sovereign power and bare life* (D. Heller-Roazen, Trans.). Stanford University Press.

Agamben, G. (2020). The invention of an epidemic. *European Journal of Psychoanalysis*. https://www.journal-psychoanalysis.eu/articles/coronavirus-and-philosophers

Ananthamurthy, U.R. (1976). *Samskara: A rite for a dead man* (A.K. Ramanujan, Trans.). Oxford University Press.

Arnold, D. (1987). Touching the body: Perspectives on the Indian plague, 1986-1900. In R. Guha (Ed.), *Subaltern Studies V: Writings on South Asian History and Society* (pp. 55–90). Oxford University Press.

Arora, A., Dogra, A., Dogra, A., Goyal, B. & Sharma, A.M. (2018). Nipah virus: An outbreak of deadly paramyxvirus. *Biomedical and Pharmacology Journal, 11*(3). https://biomedpharmajournal.org/vol11no3/nipah-virus-an-outbreak-of-deadly-paramyxvirus/

Banerjee, S. (2022). Community spaces in India: Constructing solidarity during the pandemic. In B. Bringel & G. Pleyers (Eds.), *Social movements and politics during COVID-19: Crisis, solidarity and change in a global pandemic* (pp. 120–127). Bristol University Press.

Caduff, C. (2012). The semiotics of security: Infectious disease research and the biopolitics of informational bodies in the United States. *Cultural Anthropology, 27*(2), 333–357. http://www.jstor.org/stable/23252424

Camus, A. (1960). *The plague* (S. Gilbert, Trans.). Penguin.

COVID-19 Hate Crimes Act, S.937 (2021). https://www.congress.gov/bill/117th-congress/senate-bill/937/text

Das, D.K. (2019). *Teaching AIDS: The cultural politics of HIV disease in India*. Springer Nature Singapore.

Das, D.K. (2022). Epidemic narratives: Two paradigms. In S. Venkatesan, A. Chatterjee, A. D. Lewis & B. Callendar (Eds.), *Pandemics and epidemics in cultural representation* (pp.13–27). Springer Nature Singapore.

Douglas, M. (1966). *Purity and danger: An analysis of concept of pollution and taboo*. Routledge.

Douglas, M. (1992). Witchcraft and leprosy: Two strategies for rejection. In *Risk and blame: Essays in cultural theory* (pp. 83–101). Routledge.

Eggleston, W.G. (1892). Oriental pilgrimages and cholera. *The North American Review*, *155*(428), 126–128. http://www.jstor.org/stable/25102418

Ettlinger, N. (2007). Precarity unbound. *Alternatives: Global, Local, Political*, *32*(3), 319–340. http://www.jstor.org/stable/40645223

Foucault, M. (1988). The political technology of individuals. In L.H. Martin, H. Guttman & P.H. Hutton (Eds.), *Technologies of the self: A seminar with Michel Foucault* (pp. 145–162). University of Massachusetts Press.

Foucault, M. (2003). *'Society must be defended': Lectures at the Collège de France* (D. Macey, Trans.). Picador.

Greenfeld, L. (1992). *Nationalism: Five roads to modernity*. Harvard University Press.

Gostin, L.O., et al. (2020). US withdrawal from WHO is unlawful and threatens global health and US health and security. *The Lancet*, *396*(10247), 293–295. https://www.thelancet.com/journals/lancet/article/PIIS0140-6736(20)31527-0/fulltext

Harris, E. & Nowicki, M. (2018). Cultural geographies of precarity. *Cultural Geographies*, *25*(3), 387–391. https://www.jstor.org/stable/26497911

Honigsbaum, M. (2020). *The pandemic century: A history of global contagion from the Spanish Flu to Covid-19*. Penguin Random House.

Kapri, V. (2021a). *1232 km: The long journey home*. HarperCollins.

Kapri, V (Director). (2021b). *1232 KMS* [Film]. Bhagirathi Films.

Kennan, G.F. (1967). *Memoires: 1925–1950*. Little, Brown.

Kidambi, P. (2007). *The making of a metropolis: Colonial governance and public culture in Bombay, 1890–1920*. Ashgate.

King, N. B. (2002). Security, disease, commerce: Ideologies of postcolonial global health. *Social Studies of Science, 32*(5/6), 763–789. http://www.jstor.org/stable/3183054

Knight, D. (2021). COVID-19 pandemic origins: Bioweapons and the history of laboratory leaks. *Southern Medical Journal, 114*(8), 465–467. https://www.ncbi.nlm.nih.gov/pmc/articles/PMC8300139/pdf/smj-114-465.pdf

Kohn, H. (1946). *The idea of nationalism: A study in its origins and backgrounds*. Macmillan.

Lu, M. et al. (2021). Does public fear that bats spread COVID-19 jeopardize bat conservation? *Biological Conservation, 254* . https://www.ncbi.nlm.nih.gov/pmc/articles/PMC7837179/pdf/main.pdf

Lynteris, C. (2020). The imperative origins of COVID-19. *L'Homme, 234/235*, 21–32. https://www.jstor.org/stable/27123018

Morse, S.S. (1991). Emerging viruses: Defining the rules for viral traffic. *Perspectives in Biology and Medicine, 34*(3), 387–409. https://pubmed.ncbi.nlm.nih.gov/2067933/

Muñoz, S. (2018). Precarious city. *Cultural Geographies, 25*(3), 411–424. https://www.jstor.org/stable/26497913

Narang, A. (2020, April 10). They distributed sweets to strangers. Many are still hiding. Did Tablighi Jamaat spread Coronavirus knowingly? https://tfipost.com/2020/04/they-distributed-sweets-to-strangers-many-are-still-hiding-did-tablighi-jamaat-spread-coronavirus-knowingly

Naregal, V. (2021). Labour 'invisibility' during COVID-19 times. *Economic and Political Weekly, 56*(34), 37–43.

National Intelligence Estimate. (2000). *The global infectious disease threat and its implications for the United States (NIE-99-17D).* https://www.dni.gov/files/documents/infectiousdiseases_2000.pdf

Patton, C. (2011). Pandemic, empire and the permanent state of exception. *Economic and Political Weekly, 46*(13), 103–110.

Prakash, A. & Borker,H. (2022). Life, livelihood, and death in the time of pandemic. *Economic and Political Weekly, 57*(5), 40–45.

Puar, J. (2012). Precarity Talk: A Virtual Roundtable with Lauren Berlant, Judith Butler, Bojana Cvejić, Isabell Lorey, Jasbir Puar, and Ana Vujanović . *TDR*, *56*(4), 163–177. http://www.jstor.org/stable/23362779

Pulla, P. (2018, June 2). Nipah virus: Anatomy of an outbreak. *The Hindu*. https://www.thehindu.com/news/national/kerala/anatomy-of-an-outbreak-how-kerala-handled-the-nipah-virus-outbreak/article61642466.ece

Rajan, M.S. (2020, May 7). Vogue warriors: Meet Kerala's health minister who is taking the state out of the pandemic. *Vogue India*. https://www.vogue.in/culture-and-living/content/vogue-warriors-kk-shailaja-kerala-health-minister-covid-19-response

Rajan, S.I. (2020). COVID-19-led migrant crisis: A critique of policies. *Economic and Political Weekly*, *55*(48), 13–16.

Raman, R. (2021, April 21). India's war against Covid-19. *Hindustan Times*. https://www.hindustantimes.com/opinion/indias-war-against-covid19-101618913917918.html

Reed, A.C. (1930). Medical sketches in the Orient. *The Scientific Monthly*, *31*(3),193–216. http://www.jstor.org/stable/14970.

Republic World. (2020, March 31). Arnab Goswami's lead story—Markaz lockdown violation: How can one group put all at risk? [Video]. YouTube. https://www.youtube.com/watch?v=564jlHlzfNE

Rosenberg, C.E. 1989. What is an epidemic? AIDS in historical perspective. *Daedalus*, *118*(2), 1–17. http://www.jstor.org/stable/20025233

Sammadar, R. (2016). Migrants and the neo-liberal city: An introduction. *Economic and Political Weekly*, *51*(26/27), 52–54.

Shilts, R. (1987). *And the band played on: Politics, people, and the AIDS epidemic*. St Martin's Press.

Singer, B.J., Thompson, R.N., & Bonsali, M.B. (2021). The effect of the definition of 'pandemic' on quantitative assessments of infectious disease outbreak risk. *Scientific Reports*, *11*(2547). https://www.nature.com/articles/s41598-021-81814-3

Sontag, S. (1978). *Illness as Metaphor*. Farrar, Straus and Giroux.

Sontag, S. (1988). *AIDS and its metaphors*. Penguin.

Tesh, S. (1982). Political ideology and public health in the nineteenth century. *International Journal of Health Services*, *12*(2), 321–342. http://www.jstor.org/stable/45130380

UNAIDS & BSF. (2007). *Saavdhaan—It's a battle against HIV/AIDS* [Film]. India.

Vincent Panikurlangara v. Union of India AIR [1987] SC 990.

Wald, P. (2008). *Contagious: Cultures, carriers, and the outbreak narrative*. Duke University Press.

White, H. (1978). *Tropics of discourse: Essays in cultural criticism*. Johns Hopkins University Press.

World Health Organisation Regional Office for South Asia (2014). *A brief guide to emerging infectious diseases and zoonoses*. https://iris.who.int/handle/10665/204722

World Health Organisation. (2015a). *World Health Organisation best practices for the naming of new human infectious diseases*. https://apps.who.int/iris/bitstream/handle/10665/163636/WHO_HSE_FOS_15.1_eng.pdf

World Health Organisation. (2015b). WHO issues best practices for naming new human infectious diseases. https://www.who.int/news/item/08-05-2015-who-issues-best-practices-for-naming-new-human-infectious-diseases

Woods, T., Schertzer, R., L. Greefeld, L., Hughes, C. & Miller-Idriss, C. (2020). COVID-19, nationalism and the politics of crisis: a scholarly exchange. *Nations and nationalism*, *26*, 807–825. https://onlinelibrary.wiley.com/doi/10.1111/nana.12644

Yingling, T.E. (1997). Wittgenstein's tumor: AIDS and the national body. In R. Wiegman (Ed.), *AIDS and the national body*. Duke University Press.

3

Militant Nationalism and Narratives of the Poona Plague Outbreak

In the summer of 1896 an epidemic of bubonic plague broke out in different parts of Bombay Presidency, claiming within the first three years more than two million lives. It rapidly spread to other parts of India, causing untold suffering and tragedy. Entire families were wiped out in a matter of a few weeks or left behind orphans with no one to take care of them. A report in *The British Medical Journal* of 27 October 1900 narrates one such pathetic story. In a village in Kumaon, an entire family of seven was wiped out save a nine-year-old girl named Danauli. First the father died, followed a week later by his wife and, subsequently, three of their children. When Colonel Hutchinson, a British army officer, chanced upon them only Danuali and a seven-year-old boy were left alive. He found Danauli holding her brother wrapped in a blanket. 'The girl explained how all the rest had died; how the people all ran away; how the body of the little brother who had set fire to the house had been carried away by jackals in the night; how she herself had buried the year-old baby, taking the body in a basket and digging a trench for it with a pick; and how for several days she had cooked rice for herself and the boy, and slept with him in her arms' ('Pandemic plague', 1900, p. 1250). What makes this story of nine-year-old Danauli so exceptional is its insertion in a report otherwise written in the impersonal style proper to scientific writing.

The outbreak of plague in India was part of a sequence of pandemic events that is believed to have begun in the Chinese province of Yunan in the 1850s, from where it was carried to Hong Kong in the 1890s and then to other parts of the world

(Benedict, 1988, p. 108). This was the third pandemic of the bubonic type of the disease[1] in world history, the first being in sixth-century Mediterranean and Middle Eastern regions and the second, popularly known as the Black Death, in fourteenth-century Europe. Myron Echenberg traces the origin of the third pandemic to the foothills of the Himalayas. 'Emerging from its wild rodent reservoir in the Himalayan borders between China and India soon after 1855, and traveling this time not west but east, bubonic plague infected the densely populated provinces of south China before attacking Guangzhou (Canton) and then the British colonial port of Hong Kong in 1894' (Echenberg, 2002, p. 431). Maritime trade carried the disease from there to different parts of the British Empire within a few short years. It seems plausible that the outbreak in Bombay in September 1896 was an importation from Hong Kong, where there had been an increase in mortality the same year. 'For most of the twentieth century', writes Ian J. Catanach, 'the consensus ... was that plague had come to Bombay in 1896 with rats in the cargo of a ship from Hong Kong' (2001, p. 135). In partial support of this theory he cites the work of bacteriologist R. Devignat, who found similarities between the Hong Kong and Bombay plague bacilli. There was also another theory proposed by Ernest H. Hankin, a government bacteriologist appointed to the United and Central Provinces, that plague was carried to Bombay Presidency by itinerant fakirs or ascetics from Garhwal and Kumaon in the north. In July–August 1896, a large number of them had camped at Walkeshwar Temple in Bombay on their way to Nasik, where the Kumbh festival was held every twelve years. During the day they begged alms in the quarters of the banias or grain-dealers of Mandvi, and the first cases of plague appeared there shortly thereafter. Plague was believed to be endemic to the Garhwal–

[1] There were primarily two types of plague outbreaks in India at the time, bubonic and pneumonic, 'the "bubonic" type being very little contagious, while the "pneumonic" is justly dreaded as one of the most virulent contagious maladies we have any acquaintance with' (Bannerman, 1906, p. 179). Bannerman was director of the Plague Research Laboratory set up in Bombay during the 1896 outbreak.

Kumaon region, breaking out in epidemic form from time to time.[2] Nasik had been the focus of two earlier outbreaks of plague, both severe, when Garhwali fakirs attended the Kumbh Mela there in 1860 and 1884. The outbreak in 1896 was the third in the sequence. 'It is at least a striking coincidence that of the eight twelve-yearly festivals held during the nineteenth century at Nassik, three should have coincided with outbreaks of plague, and these the only outbreaks that happened' (Hankin, 1905, p. 54).[3]

Whatever the origin of the Bombay outbreak, it certainly caused severe panic, owing both to the ravages of disease as well as the methods adopted to check it. Most of the anti-plague measures were derived from earlier European experience of epidemics in general and of plague in particular. They were based primarily on two different theories of disease causation, one holding that diseases were caused by insalubrious conditions in specific localities and the other that they were caused by germs. Localist approaches to plague control emphasised sanitary measures such as complete or partial evacuation of people from plague-affected sites, while contagionist approaches emphasised isolation of the diseased in plague hospitals, inoculation of the healthy and house-to-house searches to detect new cases. Since these were mostly carried out in British-occupied territories of India by military officers or administrators aided by soldiers, most of whom had little knowledge of the caste and gender sensitivities of Indians and had little sympathy for them even if they did, the anti-plague measures led to popular discontent that often broke out in violent clashes and riots (Klein, 1988). Adding to the confusion was the lack of specific knowledge about plague, and the failure on the part of the plague administration to convince the public of the need for sanitary measures.

[2] 'At the present time there are believed to be three endemic haunts of plague. The first in Mesopotamia; the second in Garhwal and Kumaon at the foot of the Himalayas in the North-West Provinces; the third in Yunnan in China' (Condon, 1900, p. xii).

[3] Hankin bases his theory on the report of the German Plague Commission in Bombay (1905, p. 53).

Rumours were rife about the government's intentions behind these measures, ranging from interference in religious and caste norms, conversion to Christianity, poisoning people to eliminate surplus population, to extracting oil from the bodies of those admitted in hospitals (Arnold, 1993, pp. 218–223).

3.1. The Bombay Plague Epidemic

Prior to the appearance of plague in Bombay there had been two severe outbreaks in western India, one in Cutch in 1812 that claimed half its population and the other in Pali between 1836–1838 in which an estimated hundred thousand people died (Condon, 1900, pp. xiii–xv). In August 1896, the first cases appeared in Bombay, but it was only on 23 September that a private practitioner, Dr Viegus identified and reported it officially to the Municipal Commissioner. Condon divides the epidemic into three periods: the first beginning from 23 September 1896 to 4 June 1897, the second from 4 June 1897 to 3 June 1898, and the last from 3 June 1898 to 2 June 1899. In the first phase, severe outbreaks occurred in Bombay, Bhiwandi, Cutch, Mandvi, Daman and Poona, spreading northwards and claiming almost thirty thousand lives. There was a slight lull in the epidemic in the second phase, but it came back with renewed vigour in September. Cases appeared in places that had hitherto escaped it, like Ahmednagar, Aundh, Sholapur, Belgaum, Dharwar and Khandesh, causing more than sixty thousand deaths. In June–July 1898 it again subsided and in some places altogether ceased, to return once again in its severest intensity, causing more than hundred and fifteen thousand deaths, by May 1899. The worst-affected was Dharwar district (now part of Karnataka), which alone accounted for more than thirty thousand deaths (pp. 1–9). Plague did not disappear altogether after the third period, but continued sporadically as either endemic or epidemic in different parts of the country till well into the twentieth century.

The plague pandemic of 1896 became the focus of intense scientific research in bacteriology. Ever since the advent of germ theory in the last quarter of the nineteenth century, following the work of Louis Pasteur, Robert Koch and Joseph Lister, bacteriology had grown in prestige. The plague outbreak provided a timely opportunity for testing its methods. A month after plague made its first appearance in Hong Kong, two microbiologists arrived to study its causative agent. Japan sent Shibasaburo Kitasato, who had trained under Robert Koch, and France sent Pasteur's student Alexandre Yersin. 'Thus a pupil of Koch and a pupil of Pasteur began to apply the newly invented bacteriological techniques to the solution of the age-old problem of the etiology of plague' (Hirst, 1953, p. 107). Though Kitasato was the first to see the bacillus, having arrived in Hong Kong three days before Yersin, it was to the latter that the credit for the discovery was given, presumably because he had identified it correctly. The bacillus causing plague, which was at the time called *Pasteurella pestis*, was later renamed *Yersinia pestis*. By 1897, three years after the isolation of *Y. pestis*, researchers in Bombay established the connection between rats and plague, but there were still a number of questions left unanswered. How exactly was it transmitted to human beings? How were personal articles like clothes pivotal in the transmission though microscopic examination failed to show any bacilli in them? Why was it unsafe to handle a rat that had just died of plague, but perfectly safe to do so a couple of hours later? When an infected traveller introduced plague to a place where it had not existed earlier, why did it take several weeks for it to appear in the local population? In 1898 Paul-Louis Simond discovered through his study of the Bombay cases that the actual vector for *Y. pestis* was not rat but rat flea, a blood-sucking insect that infested the bodies of rats (pp. 152–157). In 1903 William Glen Liston discovered the exact mode of transmission of plague from rats to humans. An Indian Medical Service officer and scientist at the newly set-up Plague Research Laboratory at Parel, Bombay, Liston learnt that the flea left the body of an infected rat when it died, in search of a new host. If its natural host was no longer available either because all the rats had died or fled the premises, it turned to humans. Liston and his colleagues established the transmission dynamics of plague through numerous laboratory experiments as well as field observations (pp. 170–174). Condon had begun his 1900 report on the epidemic in Bombay with the observation that plague 'has baffled alike the investigations of science and the observations of the most perspicacious' (1900, p. ix). By 1908 most of the baffling questions about the disease had been answered, thanks to the efforts of the scientists at Hong Kong and Bombay, and all that remained was a vaccine to prevent its recurrence. In 1886, soon after the outbreak in Bombay, the government requested the bacteriologist Waldemar Haffkine, who had successfully produced an anti-cholera vaccine, to find a vaccine for plague. Haffkine arrived in Bombay on 7 October 1896, and within three months he developed a vaccine which he first tested on himself (p. 113). In a letter dated 16 January 1897, he informed the Bombay government that his plague vaccine was ready and could safely be used without adverse effects. It was first administered to the inmates of Byculla Jail, where plague had broken out in the same month. Of the 147 who had volunteered to take the vaccine only two went on to contract plague and no one died, while among the 172 who did not take it there were twelve cases and six deaths. It was then introduced to the general public and by October 1897 more than eight thousand had been vaccinated (pp. 35–36). Haffkine's laboratory, which had started with a staff of one clerk and three peons in a single room in Grant Medical College, was expanded with time and on 10 August 1899 it was shifted to a large building, the old Government House at Parel. The Plague Research Laboratory now had a staff of forty-two of whom eight were doctors. By the time Condon wrote his report on 30 November 1899, it had a production capacity of ten thousand doses per day and had already dispatched a hundred thousand. In his speech on the day he visited the laboratory, the Governor of Bombay Lord Sandhurst said: 'when the time comes for the history of this plague to be really written, it cannot be doubted that the name, from the point of view of science, of Professor Haffkine will occupy the foremost place' (pp. 113–118).

What prompted this flurry of scientific activity around the pandemic? One factor was the rapid advance in bacteriology made by the time it broke out in Hong Kong. Pasteur and Koch had already laid the groundwork for the procedure of isolating germs, which was successfully applied to a range of different infections. The other factor that spurred the work of Yersin, Simond, Liston, Haffkine and their colleagues was that the places where it broke out, Hong Kong and Bombay, were major seaports of colonial trade. Comparable progress had not been made, for instance, in the numerous outbreaks of cholera across the empire throughout the nineteenth century. In Bombay, the government generously supported the efforts of the scientists, with Sandhurst himself inaugurating the laboratory newly set up at Parel and eulogising its work (Condon, 1900, pp. 116–117). Faced with international pressure in the tenth International Sanitary Conference held at Venice on 16 February 1897, the colonial government had little option but to step up its efforts to control the epidemic. The main objective of the Conference was 'to devise means for preventing the bubonic pest, now prevailing in India, from reaching Europe' (Jones, 1897, p. 453). Among the means proposed were ship inspections, quarantine of suspected ships, and everything short of an actual embargo on all vessels coming from India. The decision to prohibit the merchandise they carried or accept it after thorough disinfection was left to local authorities (p. 458). The general tone of the resolutions was to warn the colonial government against any lapses. In the sanitary reports of the time, therefore, the reality of plague was framed in scientific terms as well as those of the political and economic imperatives of empire. A dispatch from the governor of Bombay to the secretary of state for India, which was read out in the 1897 Sanitary Conference, stated that all efforts were being made by the Bombay Municipal Corporation to curb the outbreak, such as evacuating houses of infection and disinfecting them, cutting off water connections in order to force people to leave containment zones, destroying the bedding and clothing of infected persons, and 'strict medical inspection of all passengers' at railway stations (p. 458). The municipal commissioner was given extensive powers under the newly-drafted Epidemic Diseases Act.

The Bombay Municipal Corporation, however, proved unequal to the task and was soon superseded by a special Plague Committee set up for the purpose. Newspapers responded to the supersession either by supporting it outright, as did the *Times of India*, or by rallying in support of the Corporation. The *Rást Goftár*, in its issue of 10 January 1897, held the corporation 'morally, if not legally, responsible for the present most pitiable and abject condition of the city, where plague predominates and death is knocking at the doors of despairing and disconsolate citizens' (India Office Library and Records 1897b, p. 14). The *Kaiser-e-Hind*, on the other hand, wrote: 'We make bold to say that there is no Corporation in India which goes through a larger amount of work of a practical and important character all through the year than the Municipal Corporation of Bombay; and it is simply discreditable to those who, like the *Times of India*, churlishly attack it when, on the contrary, it should be encouraged and sympathised with' (p. 15).

If city corporations were a little tardy in their efforts to curb the outbreak, the plague committees often proved to be overzealous. What people found most irksome were not the measures in themselves but the manner in which they were carried out. The '*men* entrusted with the carrying out of the beneficent measures, admirable in every way', wrote the *Champion* on 2 October 1898, 'have in the insolence of their power and authority worked them to the great annoyance and vexation of the people. It need not be said that in some notable localities the men appointed to carry out the plague measures were themselves veritable pests —moral plagues of an infinitely worse character than the physical plague they were called upon by their Government to suppress' (India Office Library and Records, 1898f, p. 11, italics in original). The *Indian Spectator* criticised, in its 18 April 1897 issue, 'the forcible deportation to plague hospitals of people whom no reasonable man could suspect having the plague', an oppression 'not rare in Poona, Surat and Kalyan, nay, even in Bombay itself' (India Office Library and Records, 1897d, p. 10). When mortality due to plague increased in Dharwar in September 1898, the *Gurákhi* and the *Loka Bandhu* reported that people preferred death to forced hospitalisation and some even committed suicide (India Office Library and Records, 1898f, p. 14–15). The *Champion* of 6 February 1898 claimed that fear of removal to plague hospitals killed people 'more efficiently' than plague itself: 'There are cases of patients, we are told, who have died soon after hearing the order of their removal to hospital; some have died on their way to hospital and some immediately after their admission into hospital' (India Office Library and Records, 1898b, p. 13). As Arnold points out, fear of hospitalisation was triggered by rumours that doctors cut up bodies of those admitted or extracted from them a magical curative called *momiai.* [4] A more realistic fear, however, was that of caste pollution in hospitals (Arnold, 1993, pp. 219–221). People tried to evade hospitalisation by concealing the ill, thereby increasing the spread of plague. To prevent this, the plague committees carried out house-to-house searches with the help of medical officers, police constables or soldiers who were almost invariably European and therefore had little knowledge of the sensitivities of the people they dealt with. In most cases the services of local volunteers were not used, despite public demand that at least some of the search party members must be from that locality. Some plague committees, however, were more sympathetic and sought the help of volunteers, but from newspaper reports it appears that these were more the exception than the rule. The *Mahrátta* of 25 April 1897 wrote: 'It is all very well to say that Government is doing all this for the welfare of the people; but that is hardly a justification for taking undue liberties with or offending the feelings of the people in every possible

[4] *Momiai* was in fact a traditional preparation in Persian herbal medicine, and was quite well-known in Europe. In India, it was wrongly believed to be extracted from the bodies of young boys. In an article in *Nature*, the Himalayan topographer and surveyor Henry Godwin-Austen mentions that he first learnt of this substance during a survey in April 1857, on the eve of the Sepoy Mutiny. His informant told him that 'children were kidnapped, hung up by their heels, head downwards, and an incision was made in the breast from which flowed the wonderful substance which gave us such power' (Godwin-Austen, 1920, p. 241). Arnold cites William Crooke who states that it was a magical balm that could cure wounds and make people invulnerable, believed to be derived from embalmed mummies (1993, p. 316).

way' (India Office Library and Records, 1897e, p. 10). Adding to public resentment was the discriminatory nature of anti-plague policy. The *Dnyán Prakásh* of 13 and 20 December 1897 protested against the 'distinction between Europeans and Indians with regard to exemption from quarantine and disinfection', which, it said, 'must be attributed to a lack of common sense or an overdose of patriotic bias on the part of those who framed it' (India Office Library and Records, 1897i, p. 12). Apart from house searches, measures adopted by railway authorities were also a cause for concern. Travellers from infected locations were detained and subjected to medical examination and disinfection. Here, too, a discriminatory policy was adopted that exempted European travellers from such treatment. A frequent complaint in the newspapers was regarding the disinfection of women railway passengers, who were ordered to bathe and change clothes in public (India Office Library and Records, 1898a, p. 13).The measures adopted to control plague disproportionately affected the poor, and their reaction often found expression in acts of violence. In February 1898, rioters at Sinnar in Nasik district burnt down sheds constructed for a plague hospital and killed the hospital assistant and the plague committee chairman. The *Indu Prakásh* of 10 February 1898 wrote: 'The riot at Sinnar has shown to what a stage of desperation the ordinarily quiet people like the Kunbis[5] can go when they are once roused from their lethargic state' (India Office Library and Records, 1898b, p. 14). Plague thus came to be politicised as a crisis of public health governance in the way it came to be reported. While the epidemiological and sanitary reports framed it from the perspective of the colonial government, the native newspapers framed it from that of the governed. These contrasting perspectives, as we will see in the following sections, shaped the social understanding of the Bombay plague epidemic as a watershed moment in the narrative of Indian nationalism, its focus being the incidents that unfolded in the years 1897 and 1898 in Poona.

[5] The Kunbis are a peasant community living in parts of Gujarat and Maharashtra.

3.2. Native Newspaper Reports on the Poona Outbreak

Plague reached Poona in January 1897. On 3 January the *Vyápári* reported nearly ten cases, and two weeks later the *Dnyán Prakásh* reported nineteen cases and twelve deaths (India Office Library and Records, 1897a, p. 19; India Office Library and Records, 1897b, p. 17). Anti-plague measures were soon put into effect by a plague committee headed by Walter Charles Rand of the Indian Civil Service. By the middle of March rumours of oppression by the committee were rife, and many people fled the city. In April newspapers carried reports of harassment by soldiers forcibly entering houses, misbehaving with inhabitants, looting and destroying property. The *Dnyán Prakásh* of 19 April wrote that they 'are said to put into their mouths whatever eatable they happen to find there, to pocket other things that are portable and handy, to assault and ill-treat persons who have the audacity to protest against their conduct, and lastly to insult and behave disgracefully towards Native ladies' (India Office Library and Records, 1897d, p. 12). It published a letter wherein the author alleged that soldiers stripped his old servant naked and danced about him, indulging all the while in 'peals of laughter'. The same issue carried another story describing the conduct of soldiers during the house-searches.

> One of the soldiers picked up flowers from the idols of a Brahman and was going to offer them to the gentleman's young daughter-in-law; the old man protested only to receive blows on his face. Another party burnt a few images from a shrine; a third party demanded milk and other things for a drink. There are other complaints of a different nature: the soldiers seem to be highly pleased when they see people dancing naked, and they indulge in this diversion occasionally to chase away the fatigue caused by breaking open boxes and safes of other people (p. 11).

Even if we grant that some of these reports were exaggerated, the frequency and uniformity with which they protested against the plague measures suggest that there must have been some grain of truth. In any case, they reflect how the city's public perceived the anti-plague measures. In marked contrast to these reports were those on measures carried out in Bombay city, where the plague committee was headed by Lieutenant-General William Gatacre. 'His kindly and genial disposition and his suave manners and mature judgment and tact have stood him in good stead', wrote the *Rást Goftár*, 'and it is now hoped on all sides that he will soon be able to vanquish the much dreaded foe of the plague' (India Office Library and Records, 1897c, p. 12). 'Bombay passed through her trial during the days of plague without the slightest friction', wrote the *Champion*, 'but Poona has been filled with lamentations ever since the plague authorities began their work. Why is this? The answer is simple. General Gatacre relied upon civil help, Mr. Rand upon military help. Tommy Atkins is a fine fellow as a fighting machine, but he is a dangerous individual to admit into the house of an Indian family in search of plague-stricken people' (India Office Library and Records, 1897g, p. 24).

Of the various charges levelled against soldiers accompanying search parties the most serious was their conduct towards women. For both Hindus and Muslims alike women's spaces or zenana were prohibited to outsiders, and the honour of the householder depended on his ability to protect his female kin. The forced entry of soldiers into these spaces, physical examination of women by male doctors and their removal to camps were perceived as an assault on the householder's esteem as well as that of the community as a whole. Arnold cites a kazi who protested in anger, 'How could a husband be expected to tolerate the sight of his wife's hand being in the hand of another man?' Any instance of the outrage of women's modesty, therefore, 'provoked the fiercest resistance and the most vehement opposition' (Arnold, 1993, pp. 213–214). On 4 February 1897 the colonial government passed the Epidemic Diseases Act enabling the use of extraordinary measures in arresting the outbreak. It proved to be so severe that all people, Hindus and Muslims alike, viewed it as an unwarranted intrusion on their privacy and, as the *Phoenix* of 17 April put it, 'a direct oppression on them and an insult to them and to their women' (India Office Library and Records, 1897d, p. 8). The *Sudhárak* of 19 April wondered whether Rand himself would sit quietly if his wife were dragged out of her bed and into the street (p. 12).

Rand took charge of the Plague Committee in Poona in March 1897, when deaths were mounting and there was panic in the city. In Rand's view it was a difficult situation that presented many challenges. A large part of the city's inhabitants had deserted it, among them several municipal commissioners and honorary magistrates as well as shop owners and labourers. Those of the leading citizenry who remained proved unsupportive of any government operations and even seemed to actively work against them. 'It was of the utmost importance', he wrote in an early report, 'to crush the epidemic with the least possible delay, both to stay the great mortality that was taking place in Poona and to prevent the spread of the disease to the other towns of the Deccan, in none of which had it so far attained epidemic proportions' (as cited in Condon 1900, p. 224). It seems unlikely that he was himself bent upon harassing the city's native population, but he was indirectly responsible for it to the extent that he ignored the reports of the newspapers and the petitions of the people. The Poona newspapers, as we saw above, gave ample indication of popular discontent with the way search operations were carried out. A few days after his assassination the *Gujaráti* wrote: 'Government must consider whether they acted wisely in ignoring the loud and universal chorus of disapproval that the action of the Plague Committee in Poona called forth in contrast with the expressions of unstinted praise the admirable tact, magnanimity and forethought of General Gatacre evoked in Bombay' (India Office Library and Records, 1897f, p. 14). Petitions alleging harassment by search parties went unheeded. 'If any one takes a complaint to Mr. Rand orally', wrote the *Dnyán Prakásh*, 'he simply laughs and sends the applicant away in disappointment. If any one presents a written application he gets a stereotyped reply that his allegations are false and that the soldiers did not at all behave improperly in his house' (India Office Library and Records, 1897e, p. 13).

The Poona newspapers were critical primarily of Rand's tactlessness and lack of consideration for the people. Shortly after he took charge, a correspondent of the *Champion* described him as 'a military martinet who looks at everything only from a drum-head court-martial point of view' (India Office Library and Records, 1897c, p. 12). The *Mahrátta* wrote that he cared little about the customs or the feelings of those he subjected to his harsh measures. 'His supreme contempt for the suggestions made to him in a spirit of co-operation, his laconic and curt replies to any queries put to him, his indifferent and very often sullen bearing, and, above all, extreme distrust in the work of Native agency have made him more than a tyrant at a time when people are suffering from the double scourge of plague and famine' (India Office Library and Records, 1897e, p. 10). 'He is acting like the Sultan of Turkey', wrote the *Dnyán Prakásh*, 'and there is not a single Native who does not remark that Mr. Rand has brought discredit upon the British name' (p. 12).

On the night of 22 June 1897, when Poona was celebrating the Diamond Jubilee of Queen Victoria's reign, Plague Commissioner Rand and Lieutenant Ayerst were attacked as they were returning from Government House. Ayerst died on the spot, and Rand, who was fatally injured, died two weeks later, on 3 July. The Bombay bi-weekly *Native Opinion* expressed the view that the assassin was likely someone who had suffered at his hands, and that Rand 'perhaps brought on the misfortune on himself by his tyrannical and arrogant administration during the last four months' (India Office Library and Records, 1897f, p. 18). Clearly, Rand was extremely unpopular with the Poona public, but that someone could go to the extent of killing a British officer of his rank seemed incredible to the government and its supporters, the editors of Anglo-Indian papers. The *Times of India* accused the Poona brahmins of conspiracy and the Poona newspapers, most of which were run by brahmins, of carrying seditious and inflammatory reports against the administration. In his speech to the city's leading members Collector Richard Lamb threatened strong action unless they helped find Rand's and Ayerst's killers, and a punitive police force was imposed on the city. The burden of funding the police force, which the *Native Opinion* reported to be two hundred and thirty thousand rupees over two years, fell to the Poona municipality and the public (India Office Library and Records, 1897f, p. 22). In 1898 the government passed M.D. Chalmers's anti-sedition bill, which made it seditious to publicly express disaffection with the government even without directly inciting subversive acts. Actually most native newspapers, including the *Kesari*, did not openly challenge the authorities or use inflammatory language, but preferred more peaceful methods like writing open letters to the governor of Bombay Presidency and urging the public to send petitions. The anti-sedition law was clearly an overreaction to the assassination of Rand and Ayerst, its chief motive being to find a scapegoat for what seemed to be the outcome of the government's own apathy and disregard of public opinion. In a confidential report to the secretary of state dated 29 July 1897, the Bombay government submitted that the double murder was most probably 'inspired by the peculiarly violent writing of the Poona papers regarding plague administration' and the outcome of 'a political plot emanating from a section of the Poona Brahmins' (Maharashtra State Gazetteers, n.d., p. 340). Police arrested Bal Gangadhar Tilak, editor of the Poona weeklies *Kesari* and *Mahrátta*, for allegedly seditious writing, and the Natu brothers Balwantrao and Hari for participating in political activities.

The charges against Tilak and the Natus were subsequently proved false when Damodar Hari Chapekar was arrested on the basis of evidence supplied by Ganesh Shankar Dravid and his brother Ramchandra. Chapekar made a full confession of his and his brother Balkrishna's roles in the murders of Rand and Ayerst on 8 October, in the presence of the chief presidency magistrate of Bombay. Though he subsequently retracted it he was convicted and sentenced to hang by the sessions court, Poona, and the verdict was confirmed by the high court (Maharashtra State Gazetteers, n.d., pp. 347–359).

The story of the events following the assassinations of Rand and Ayerst as told in the native newspapers reveals how the colonial government's plague operation and popular resistance to it played out in press rivalries and the politics of race, caste, religion and locality. The charges made in the Anglo-Indian newspapers against the brahmins and the press in Poona led to an exchange of accusations and rebuttals in the native papers. The *Rást Goftár*, an Anglo-Gujarati weekly from Bombay founded by Parsi leaders Dadabhai Naoroji and Kharshedji Cama, wrote that 'the cowardly and murderous attack was the result of inflammable writings which appeared in the Deccan papers for some time past against plague officials', and that Poona was 'a hotbed of sedition' which the government must suppress without delay (India Office Library and Records, 1897f, pp. 10–11). The *Dnyánodaya*, another Bombay periodical run by a Protestant missionary group, wrote that the attacks on Rand and Ayerst were 'without doubt the fruit of the seditious spirit that has been smouldering underneath a certain portion of Poona society' (p. 11). The *Káthiáwár News*, an English-Gujarati bi-weekly published from Rajkot, accused the Poona newspapers of 'indulging in a perfect orgy of sedition' and the cowardly 'clique of Brahmans' in Poona of lacking 'any sense of duty in the whole class', incapable of anything but mischief and conspiracy. It even went so far as to claim that the mutiny of 1857, too, was 'the result of such a conspiracy' (pp. 11–12). The English daily *Káthiáwár Times*, also published from Rajkot, came to the defence of the Poona brahmins and categorically rejected such views: 'The Deccan Brahmans are a highly educated community, who fully realize their relations with the delegated authorities of Government. We think, therefore, that they would never stoop to such folly and baseness.'(p. 12). Many of the Bombay papers came out in support of the Poona scribes and the brahmins. The *Native Opinion* wrote that charges made by the Anglo-Indian press were 'a deliberate attempt to prejudice the authorities against certain people, whose utmost offence has been nothing beyond laying popular grievances before the authorities' (p. 13). 'Our Anglo-Indian contemporaries ... and some of their Native toadies', it wrote in another issue, are 'indulging in reckless charges against the Poona Brahmans *et hoc omne genus* and the Poona newspapers in particular' (p. 17). The *Gujaráti* wrote that the papers merely expressed the views of the people, and that the brahmins had little reason to conspire against Rand as they suffered less than the other communities. 'Those who are so inclined might indulge with impunity in vituperation against both; but we must say that it is not fair to shift the whole responsibility on other peoples' shoulders in a moment of panic and angry excitement' (p. 14). The *Indu Prakásh* held that it was unreasonable to blame the Poona scribes or the brahmins for what were genuine grievances on the part of the public. Such grievances had been expressed both informally and in formal petitions by the entire populace of Poona, Hindus and Muslims alike, cutting across caste and religious divides (pp. 14–15).

The Poona papers rebutted the charges against them outright. The *Sudhárak* wrote: 'The populace here, no doubt, suffered at the hands of the officials entrusted with anti-plague operations, and the Native papers as their spokesmen wrote about the sufferings with expressions of indignation commensurate with the suffering, but none wished such a thing as this—a brutal assault by murderous villains on high Government officials' (India Office Library and Records, 1897f, p. 16). The protests had been made on lawful and constitutional grounds, and the charges against them were wholly false. The *Dnyán Prakash*, too, emphasised that both the newspapers and the people of Poona, while appreciating the need for sanitary measures adopted by Rand, followed constitutional ways of expressing grievance. The *Kesari* wrote that the libellous charges against the brahmins and the press were unwarranted and more wicked than the murder itself. The *Udyoga Vriddhi* challenged the *Times of India* to furnish any evidence of sedition against the government on the part of the Poona brahmins in the past, and retaliated by accusing it of prejudice, hatred and malice against the community (pp. 10–20). With suspicion directed against the brahmin public and press of Poona, other communities tried to distance themselves from anti-plague sentiments. The Muslims of Poona sought to express their loyalty to the government by stating that they did not find the plague measures oppressive, despite having signed petitions to the contrary (India Office Library and Records, 1897h, p. 18). A correspondent of the *Rást Goftár* called upon all Parsis, especially those of Poona, to condemn the murders and to express their solidarity with the British government (India Office Library and Records, 1897g, p. 25). Counter-allegations were also levelled against groups other than the brahmins. The *Deshabhakta*, a Baroda weekly, hinted that the crime may have been committed by the lower castes, who had suffered the most from the plague operations: 'Instead of trying thus to mislead the police and the public the *Times* would do a great service to the public if it put them on the right scent and allowed the police to search for the culprits in the community which is notorious for the quality and number of criminals it annually turns out' (India Office Library and Records, 1897f, p. 18). The *Mahrátta* pointed to 'other classes' that are 'lawless and fanatical': 'It is therefore amongst this class of *badmashes* that we must look for the authors of this murderous attack' (pp. 15–16, italics in original). The *Kalpataru* of Sholapur suggested that it could have been the work of a soldier who had had easy access to arms and whose feelings Rand had offended (p. 20).

Controversy marked not only the question of possible suspects, but equally the character of Damodar Chapekar when he was apprehended and during his trial and execution. The Poona papers felt vindicated by the arrest of Chapekar, and demanded the immediate release of Tilak and the Natu brothers. The *Champion* asked: 'Will the Anglo-Indian press apologize for the falsehoods they uttered concerning Poona? And will the Government first set them a good example by releasing Mr. Tilak and the Natu brothers, and by withdrawing the punitive police force?' (India Office Library and Records, 1898b, p. 17). Some reports represented Chapekar as a misguided fanatic who put everyone at risk of reprisal for his act. 'In the attempt to serve his people', wrote the *Indian Spectator*, 'the wretch has done an immense harm to the whole country; for to him we have to trace a string of calamities, the last of which up to date is Mr. Chalmers' Sedition Bill'. The *Dnyán Prakásh* wrote: 'The wretched youngster, with his mischievous notions of patriotism, hardly knew what he was about when he conceived the dastardly plan of murdering Mr. Rand. Being found guilty of the foul crime on the night of 22nd June last, we can only say he has but got his deserts in getting the extreme penalty that the law could give'. The *Rást Goftár* went even further, and when Chapekar was hanged on 18 April 1898 it wrote: 'Altogether the man proved himself to be a despicable creature, and the world will be the wiser and better for his removal from amongst us' (India Office Library and Records, 1898e, p. 10). However, such views were not unanimous. The *Mahrátta*, which had reservations about the way Chapekar was tried and convicted, expressed the view that he deserved death if he was in fact guilty of the murders, but nobody deserved more pity than him if the confession was wrongly extracted and he was actually innocent. Even if he were guilty, it was his fate and not his personal character that was to be blamed. Chapekar had tried several times to join the army, but was turned down because he was a brahmin and the British Indian military did not recruit brahmins: 'only think what a fine fellow he would have turned out if the rules of Government had been more liberal and made it possible for Chapekar to make his fortune as a soldier in the service of Her Majesty' (p. 11). In his autobiography, as we will see shortly, Chapekar had mentioned this as a main reason for his animosity towards the British. The *Dnyán Prakásh* wrote that while his conviction was just, it must be admitted that 'he possessed excellent parts, and had the way been opened for him into the British army he would have made a fine soldier' (India Office Library and Records, 1898d, p. 13). Like the *Mahrátta*, it blamed his fate that made him take 'a different turn and at last brought him to the gallows'. When Chapekar was led to the gallows to be hanged, wrote the *Indu Prakásh*, he had a copy of the *Bhagavad Gita* in his hands, and reminded one of the honest and upright Charudatta sentenced to be hanged by King Palaka on a trumped-up charge of killing his mistress Vasantasena. In the myth Vasantasena appears at the last minute to save her lover. This allusion to the epic *Mrichhakatika* presented Chapekar as a hero unjustly wronged, in contrast to the negative views in other papers.

While many newspapers commended the judiciary for convicting Chapekar and sentencing him to death, some expressed doubts as to its legality. The *Mahrátta* questioned the cross-examination and doubted whether 'the verdict obtained in this way would be wholly valid' (India Office Library and Records, 1898b, p. 18). The *Native Opinion* questioned the evidence: 'Apart from the question whether Damodar was rightly convicted or not on his withdrawn confession, no man of any judicial experience can help saying that the evidence adduced against him was a mere travesty. There are important gaps and no attempt was made to fill them up' (p. 19). At the time of Chapekar's trial, a British soldier called Piper had been tried and acquitted for the murder of an Indian with whom he had picked up a quarrel. Piper had shot the man dead in full view of witnesses, but pleaded self-defence. Commenting on this the *Native Opinion* observed: 'Piper's trial inevitably suggests a contrast with Chapekar's trial. Here a man is acquitted although all the main facts are undisputed; there a man is found guilty and sentenced to be hanged on the barest of all circumstantial evidence' (p. 20). It concluded with the ironic remark that 'it would be advantageous to all the parties concerned if another Penal Code is enacted for the benefit of European culprits'. Other papers that noted the contradiction between the two judgments were the *Indu Prakásh* and *Kesari* (pp. 20–21). The trial and execution of Damodar Chapekar as it was recounted in the native papers served to bring to the fore a gap between the colonial government of Bombay and those it governed, seriously challenging its legitimacy and carefully-crafted image of benevolent rule.

Prior to the assassination of Rand, Governor Sandhurst had endeared himself to his Indian subjects due to his sense of fairness and sympathy especially for the poor. In March 1896, for instance, he had personally visited the slums of the city to acquaint himself with the conditions there instead of deputing a committee. Many newspapers viewed this as a rare gesture on the part of the highest representative of the empire in the presidency. 'This was probably the first time, within living memory', wrote the *Indian Spectator*, 'that a Governor of Bombay has condescended to visit its slums, the gullies, alleys and places of darkness on which the sun never shines—the haunts of life-long suffering and the breeding ground of current epidemics.' The *Kaiser-e-Hind* praised him in the following words:

> His Excellency Lord Sandhurst is nothing, if not very active. Animated with the most laudable desire to make himself personally acquainted with the condition of his poorest subjects, he has deemed it desirable to devote nearly two hours in walking through some of the most congested parts of Bombay City, and there can be no manner of doubt that the knowledge of the condition and the wants of the people that he has been able to acquire for himself will stand him in good stead in dealing with the various questions affecting the sanitation of the city that may be brought before his Government (India Office Library and Records, 1896a, p. 10).

Even during anti-plague operations that led to a riot in Bombay in March 1898, the public trusted their governor to be humane. Sandhurst had called a public meeting to explain certain modifications in the sanitary policy so as to cause the least inconvenience. 'His Excellency', wrote the *Native Opinion*, 'will earn the gratitude of thousands of poor and ignorant people by the modifications in the plague regulations which were announced' (India Office Library and Records, 1898c, p. 12). The imposition of a punitive police force in Poona and the arrests of Tilak, the Natus and others for sedition shattered this trust.

The moment of Rand and Ayerst's assassinations is important in that it marks a rupture in the narrative of benevolent imperialism that Sandhurst's popular acts had constructed. In 'Disrobing Colonialism, and Making Sense of it', B. Surendra Rao outlines this narrative and its critique in nationalist discourse. Acts and speeches of colonial authorities like Sandhurst served to legitimise their rule and to promote it, not only among the 'educated' elite in India but equally among those who questioned its legitimacy in England. 'That accounts for a long list of the benefits of colonial rule, from peace and order and rule of law which, they said, the Mughals did not provide, to the larger material and moral advancement of the colony, including trusting those who had come under their rule to participate in the administration' (Rao, 2010, p. 17). Colonialism in India as elsewhere followed what Abdul JanMohamed calls a 'Manichean' logic: in the first or 'dominant' phase it asserted itself through military coercion, while in the second 'hegemonic' phase it established its legitimacy through indoctrination and the manufacture of consent rather than the use of force (JanMohamed, 1985, pp. 61–62). Its Manicheanism lay in the way it oscillated between these two phases, depending on contingencies of rule, that is, whether it needed force or consent. In the Poona outbreak this oscillation in Sandhurst's rule took the form of a swing from benevolence to ruthlessness in imposing a punitive police force and arresting, on charges of sedition, the scribes and community leaders of Poona.

An argument from Michel Foucault's critique of European modernity can help illuminate the inconsistencies of colonial governance that Rao and JanMohamed outline. Political modernity, Foucault argues, was formed in the shift from the rule of the sovereign with his 'right to take life', to that of the state with its 'right to make live' (2003, p. 241). The sovereign's authority derived from a show of power over the lives of its subjects, as in ritualised public executions of those who dared to offend it. The state's authority, in contrast, derived from the way it exercised what was literally a paternalistic concern for its subjects, taking care of their health, wealth and happiness to improve their productivity and thus the prosperity of the state. In the treatises on government in the sixteenth and seventeenth centuries, the model for the state was *oikos nomos* or economy, the norm of the family.

> The art of government essentially appears in this literature as having to answer the question of how to introduce economy—that is to say, the proper way of managing individuals, goods, and wealth, *like the management of a family by a father who knows how to direct his wife, his children, and his servants, who knows how to make his family's fortune prosper, and how to arrange suitable alliances for it – how to introduce this meticulous attention, this type of relationship between father and the family, into the management of the state*? (Foucault, 2007, pp. 94–95, italics added)

Though this was greatly modified over the centuries, with changes in the meaning of economy from managing a household to governing a population, it remained as the basic principle of the state, its *raison d'État*. Alongside and opposing it, however, was another principle that the treatises called *coup d'État*, or a temporary suspension of *raison d'État* in response to an emergent crisis that put the state's survival at risk. The assassinations of Rand and Ayerst on Jubilee night, the very night that spectacularly staged the sovereignty of Queen Victoria as the symbolic power of the colonial state, was such a moment of risk. The *coup d'État* reveals briefly but violently the dark underside of *raison d'État* and its hegemonic function. 'The usual, habitual exercise of *raison d'État* is not violent precisely because it readily avails itself of laws as its framework and form. But when necessity demands it, *raison d'État* becomes *coup d'État*, and then it is violent. This means that it is obliged to sacrifice, to sever, to cause harm, and it is led to be unjust and murderous' (Foucault, 2007, p. 263).

Another aspect of *coup d'État* that Foucault implies but does not elaborate is that, in its display of power the state also reveals its deepest anxieties. As I have remarked above, the colonial state's immediate reaction to the assassinations was somewhat excessive and unwarranted. Misled by the Anglo-Indian press, it feared sedition and this fear triggered the memory of 1857. 'Sedition', wrote *Native Opinion*, 'is the word that is now bandied about from day to day, and if these writers are to be believed, the whole atmosphere of Poona, or even of the whole Deccan, would seem to be permeated with sedition!' (India Office Library and

Records, 1897f, p. 17). Allusions to the 'mutiny' [6] often appeared in newspaper reports of the outbreak, either as prefiguring the assassinations or as proof that the two events were connected, however remotely and fancifully. A correspondent of the *Kalpataru* predicted in April 1897, two months before Rand was killed, that the scenes of 1857 would be re-enacted at Poona if Rand's *zulum* was not stopped (India Office Library and Records, 1897d, p. 13). On 3 July, soon after Rand's murder, the *Áryávarta* wrote that it was a small-scale version of the mutiny. Listing the wild charges made in the Anglo-Indian press, the *Native Opinion* of 4 July wrote: 'the *Indian Daily News* of Calcutta caps all by asserting dogmatically enough that the Poona murder was connected by a long concatenation of circumstances with the mutiny of 1857, and even the deposition of the Peshwa in 1818. The only thing that will surpass this will be a hint that Nána Sáheb, the leader of the mutiny, has come into the world again for the sole purpose of murdering Messrs. Ayerst and Rand!' (India Office Library and Records, 1897g, pp. 11, 24).

Collector Lamb's speech to the Poona public soon after the murders reveals the tensions that marked British rule in this moment of crisis. Lamb's threats, commented the *Indian Spectator*, 'must have struck the hearers as indications of weakness' (India Office Library and Records, 1897g, p. 13). The *Champion* reported parts of the speech, which began with Lamb censuring the Poona papers and the public for failing to demonstrate their loyalty by remaining silent about the crime instead of condemning it, and ending with an open threat of 'stern measures' if they continued in their seditious activities. 'Could folly go further than this?' asked the *Champion* (p. 15). Lamb was known to be a mild-mannered man, and the tone of his

[6] The term 'Sepoy Mutiny' has been contested by historians, who have argued that it was not solely the outcome of a conspiracy among the sepoys of the East India Company, but a struggle against Company rule in general that involved native chiefs and talukdars as well. It was more in the nature of a legitimate revolt against colonial authority rather than mutiny, a term that precasts it as already illegitimate. Some historians have gone further to claim that it was a war of independence. See Majumdar, 1957, pp. 180–242, for a detailed discussion of the arguments against the use of the term.

speech shocked his audience. The *Indian Spectator* commented with sarcasm that 'the lamb roaring like a tiger was a sight for gods and men!' (p. 13). The *Hindu Punch* commented that Lamb, who by disposition was like a lamb, behaved like a wolf that day. It is pitiable, wrote the *Native Opinion*, 'when officers of a high and mighty Government like the British descend to street billingsgate or behave like old dames thrown out of their wits' (India Office Library and Records, 1897f, pp. 21–22). The tone of these reports shows that Lamb's performance, which was intended to display the might of empire, actually had had the opposite effect: it exposed the insecurity beneath the posturing of power. 'The rhetoric of colonial aggression', writes Caroline Levine in a different context, 'is always haunted by the threat of impending decline' (2006, p. 638). That the murders took place on the very night when Government House was celebrating the sixtieth year of Victoria's rule in England and its thirty-ninth in this most prized colony, was deeply unsettling for the imperial establishment.

If Condon's report on the Bombay plague tells the triumphal story of colonial bacteriology and sanitary science, the reports in the native newspapers tell a different story—that of a plague administration which exceeded the bounds of necessity and good sense in intervening in the lives of its subjects, of a government that in displaying its vengeful might revealed instead its cowardice, and, on the other side, of a subject population and its pressmen divided by caste, religion and community differences. Framed by these contrary storylines, the Bombay plague outbreak appears as a complex socio-political and cultural event, the meanings of which surpass its biological reality. In the rest of the chapter I will discuss two narratives of the plague and its aftermath in terms of these meanings, the first being Chapekar's autobiography and the second, a film on the assassination of Rand.

3.3. *Autobiography of Damodar Hari Chapekar*

Damodar Hari Chapekar, the main accused in the murders of Rand and Ayerst, was hanged at Yerawada Central Jail, Pune on

18 April 1898. His autobiography, which he wrote in jail, was subsequently translated into English and published in the *Bombay Police Abstracts*. In its sixty-odd pages Damodar recounts his life and the events that led up to Rand's assassination. It opens with a long preface on why one should tell the story of one's life, what kind of life story deserves to be told, and what lessons may be drawn from it: 'If the story of one's life does not contain anything that is not to be found in the lives of the generality of men, if the perusal of one's good or bad career does not arouse in the minds of the people any pleasure or pain, or, if one's righteous conduct is barren in its effect in inculcating a wholesome moral or in gratifying the public taste, then of what avail is such a treatise?' (Chapekar, n.d., p. 955) At the same time, he is acutely conscious of the ordinariness of his life: 'But of what worth am I? I am only an insignificant individual among those ignorant men who are to be found in this vast world. … Because those warriors and statesmen wrote, should even an imbecile, who has not wit enough to manage his domestic affairs, write a story of his feeble life?' (p. 956) Read together, the goals of his self-writing and the expression of self-doubt convey an urgent need to attribute to his life, at this moment of reckoning, a significance that would make it worthy of public acclaim. He finds this significance in his patriotic zeal. 'I shall relinquish all happiness and sacrifice *my life for my country*. … Hence a life so full of joy and sorrow as mine will probably be interesting to the public mind in some measure at least.' The rest of the narrative is framed by this preface, which he signs 'Well-wisher of the country, DAMODAR HARI CHAPEKAR, Patriot' (p. 958, italics in original).

Damodar was born on 25 June 1869 to an impoverished brahmin family in the village of Chinchwad in Poona district, Bombay Presidency. His grandfather Vinayak was a 'liberty-loving' man who relinquished government service and spent all his wealth in various enterprises that failed, including a 'grocer's shop, a printing press, a sweetmeat stall, and a loom' (Chapekar, n.d., p. 959). His father, too, preferred to be self-employed, and became an itinerant singer of religious songs or *kirtans*. He taught his three sons how to compose verses and play musical instruments so that they could join him in his performances. Damodar seems to have been deeply influenced by his grandfather and father, since he too valued liberty, however beset by difficulties, over an easy life in servitude. The entire family took up minstrelsy as its profession and travelled to different places in search of patrons (p. 963). He recalls a pilgrimage to Benaras that the family undertook when he was a child: 'In my tender years I had an opportunity of drinking the water of the Ganges, bathing in it, and giving alms and seeing and touching (the image of) Kashivishveswara' (pp. 959–960). The *kirtan*s and the visit to Benaras inculcated in Damodar and his brother Balkrishna a deeply religious outlook and respect for Hindu tradition that in his view played a role in his patriotism. He writes, 'That man is learned indeed who performs the various duties prescribed by the Shastras' (p. 964).

Chapekar narrates these childhood experiences as formative of his personality as he grew up. The profession of *kirtan*-singing did not bring in much money, for not many patronised it, and the family faced many hardships. They were often compelled to seek alms and to eat in *annasatras* where food was distributed free to brahmins and mendicants. What would have been a humiliating experience for anyone else became for Damodar a mark of his self-esteem: 'I … not only do not regret these occurrences, but on the contrary contemplate with a feeling of pride that the Chapekars, though beset with such difficulties, did not even care to seek the help of their well-to-do relatives and friends, but that, as suited to their unbending haughtiness, they tided over these (hard) times by simply uttering the name of God and without sacrificing their independence or accepting bondage.' Begging, he asserts, 'is a hundred times better than subjection to others' (Chapekar, n.d., p. 961). The family's itinerant lifestyle disrupted his schooling, and whatever meagre learning he picked up was either from his father or self-taught. Perhaps because of this he developed a hatred for formal education, which, he writes, emasculates a person. 'We are of the opinion that the loss of our physical strength is partly to be laid at the door of this Mlechha[7] education. The entire society has devoted itself to education and become too much thoughtful, and thereby has lost manliness.'[8] The British introduced 'the vice of education' in order to kill the spirit of Hinduism, as a result of which 'Brahmins destroyed their religious observances, caste, families, morality and immorality, manliness and impotence' (pp. 1002–1003). Especially abhorrent is English education:

> So strange is the influence of the study of English that if one simply intends to study that language, or if a child learns by heart only the first two or three letters of its alphabet, he begins at once to look upon his elders as fools and despises his good and ancient religion. If the mere odour of English education has this effect, where is the wonder if any righteous person who fully tastes it should turn an Englishman from top to toe and an earnest votary of the bottle? (p. 964)

Hatred of English ways became so deeply ingrained in him that he often turned on boys playing cricket and disrupted their game: 'We intensely hated the boys who, laying aside our one thousand games, had shown a predilection for that game' (p. 976). As he grew up he became increasingly orthodox and intolerant of any deviation from what he narrowly defines as Hindu religion and culture.

The targets of Damodar's orthodoxy were those who attempted to reform Hindu tradition. He recounts a number of incidents that exemplify this. They include breaking up a marriage procession because the groom and bride are over the age prescribed by the shastras, and harassing a native missionary and two Europeans who pass by the training ground of a club that the brothers establish to protect Hinduism. A group of religious reformers frequented the site on which the club was located, and the self-styled defenders of religion disrupted their meetings

---

[7] *Mlechha* in Sanskrit means a foreigner who lacks caste and is therefore held to be a source of ritual pollution; here, it means polluting, and refers primarily to the education imparted by the British.

[8] As we will see later, he seems to have been deeply impressed by the ideal of manliness.

(Chapekar, n.d., pp. 972–977). The club, which the brothers created in 1895, was called 'Rashtra Hitechhu Mandali', with the god Maruti or Hanuman as its patron deity (Majumdar, 1966, p. 85; Chapekar, n.d., p. 976). Its motto: 'Better to stick to our own religion until the end; the religion of others is full of peril' (Chapekar, n.d., p. 974). The activities of the club were, however, hardly in keeping with its grand objective of defending Hinduism against its detractors. Its zeal to fight for its faith could find outlet only in sundry acts of mischief—a situation that Damodar and his brother must have found disappointing.

Shortly thereafter the brothers quit the club because of petty internal rivalries, and continued their mission against reformers in earnest with the support of their friend Dattatraya Bhuskute. There were at this time two factions in the Congress, with Tilak leading the orthodox faction and Mahadev Govind Ranade, the reformist. The three friends turned against Ranade and his group, though they did not support Tilak either and bore little respect for him. They were critical of Congressmen as a whole, because the latter held meeting after meeting without taking any direct action against the British. The Chapekar brothers and Bhuskute attempted to burn down a pavilion where Ranade and his Social Conference met, but were unsuccessful. They attacked Patwardhan, editor of the reformist paper *Sudhárak*, and another reformer called Kulkarni who taught in a local school. They harassed European missionaries, and set fire to a building where they met in Poona. They attacked Velankar, a professor at Wilson College who had converted to Christianity, and a schoolteacher called Thorat, who they suspected to be a paedophile and who consumed meat and alcohol and abused the Hindu religion. They composed songs against a reformist lawyer called Khare, 'because this vilest of Brahmins had eaten beef' (Chapekar, n.d., pp. 979–977).

Damodar and Balkrishna next turned their attention to the British, and planned a move that would 'fill the British with sorrow, and put upon us the indelible brand of treason'. But all that they did was secretly smear with tar a statue of Queen

Victoria in Bombay and garland it with a string of old shoes, in a symbolic act of defying imperial power: 'This woman', Damodar writes in his autobiography, 'after the Mutiny of 1857, acquired the universal sovereignty of India by making fair but deceitful promises. She alone is the real enemy of our people. Other white men are our enemies only in so far as they are her subjects' (Chapekar, n.d., p. 999). They wrote an anonymous letter to a Marathi paper with a request to forward it to the *Times*, in which they claimed to have formed a secret society to protect morals—the disfiguring of the statue being its first warning to all those who encourage 'immorality', including the queen (p. 1001).

Plague broke out in Poona shortly thereafter, and Bhuskute was taken ill and died. There were rumours that the government would impose harsh measures to check its spread, and the Chapekar brothers decided to oppose it. They followed the search parties to observe the atrocities committed by them. 'Every day saw new modes of oppression. Temples were desecrated in one part of the city, in another women were outraged and idols broken. The poor and the helpless were the greatest sufferers at the hands of these marauders' (Chapekar, n.d., p. 1009). Since Rand directed the operations himself, they decided to punish him and set an example for the others. They kept a close watch on his movements, and planned for an opportune moment to strike. To exasperate the British at the moment of their highest glory, the Diamond Jubilee celebrations of Victoria's rule, they procured old shoes, stuck pictures of the Queen on the soles and put them on display on a main road of Poona city (p. 1013). It was on the same night that the brothers set upon Rand and Ayerst as they were returning from the celebrations at Government House.

In his autobiography, Damodar recounts the preceding incidents as signs of his patriotism, the assassination being its ultimate proof. How and when does this patriotic sentiment emerge, transforming his religious intolerance into desire for freedom from imperial rule? Early in their life the two brothers had developed a fascination for acts of outlawry. During one of the family's travels in search of patronage, they had come across a wooded hilly tract that seemed to them an ideal refuge for outlaws: 'Since then we began to meditate upon such terrible deeds.' To carry out this mission they vigorously took up bodybuilding, formed the club and trained its members in the arts of war. 'We knew that physical strength and a sufficiency of men were indispensable for overpowering and expelling the powerful brigand and pretender who had entered and taken possession of our house' (Chapekar, n.d., p. 966). Their ideal, however, seemed to be the soldier rather than the revolutionary, as evidenced by their repeated attempts to get themselves enlisted. We will shortly see the reason for this. They approached various officials of the colonial army and of native states like Hyderabad, Gwalior, Indore, Baroda and Sangli and even Nepal and Portuguese Goa. The response in all cases was more or less the same: brahmins are not fighting men. In his confession of 8 October 1897, Damodar states: 'I petitioned the Commander-in-Chief [of the British Indian army] at Shimla and got a reply that I could not be employed. I was told that the Risala was divided into companies of different castes and as there were not enough Brahmans there was no company of Brahmans and I could not be employed. I offered to collect 400 Brahmans and form a company but they would not accept the proposal' (Maharashtra State Gazetteers, n.d., p. 347). The brothers made one last attempt and were once again rejected. 'This was the last disappointment suffered by us and we strongly reviled the English as follows: "A system of administration so cruel as that of the English cannot, if search be made, be found, in any region of this globe"' (Chapekar, n.d., p. 998). The Chapekars' patriotic zeal, therefore, was not unmixed: their love for land and resentment against subjugation required a trigger, and that trigger was their repeated failure to join the army. 'This was the first and most potent cause of the enmity between the English and ourselves' (p. 992). Why did the brothers so wish to become military-men? From the autobiography it is clear that brahmins, generally, and the Deccan brahmins, in particular, were held in low esteem. A popular view was that Deccan brahmins were selfish and were responsible for the downfall of the Maratha kingdom. Baji Rao II, who was the last peshwa of the Maratha confederacy, lost his kingdom to the British because he spent his time 'by feasting Brahmins and by indulging in vicious habits' (p. 987). Though Damodar agrees to this charge, he cites the case of Nana Saheb, the adopted son of Baji Rao II who fought against the British in the revolt of 1857: 'Dhondopant Nana, as if with a view to wipe off the stigma cast on his father's name, distinguished himself on the battlefield and departed to the other world along with his friends Bala Saheb, Rao Saheb, Tatya Tope and Lakshmibai of Jhansi' (p. 988). Concluding that brahmins are the true revolutionaries, Damodar declares: 'In 1857, Nana Saheb, (showed himself to be a Brahmin of this type), then Wasudev Balwant, and after that we two brothers Damodar and Balkrishna Hari Chapekar' (p. 989). Another slur was that brahmins as a caste lacked manliness and were unable to endure hardships. The Subedar-Major of the Fourth Infantry Regiment, a Maratha, rebuked him: '[H]ow will you be able to observe the customs of your caste in the regiment? A regiment is not a place for eating sweetmeat balls. Look at my feet and see how bronzed they have become. This is the way we are required to move about (from place to place); we alone can do that'. By enlisting in the army at all costs, the Chapekar brothers hoped to prove that this bias against the brahmin caste was undeserved. Their wish to join the army resulted from an overvaluation of military manliness, to counter the charge that brahmins were unmanly and lacked integrity. Thus, their determination to enlist cannot be due solely to military ambition, but also indicates their need to restore caste prestige.[9] When Damodar and Balkrishna failed in their efforts to join the army, they worked hard to develop bodily strength and endurance and acquire martial skills and dedicated themselves to the cause of religion and country. The assassination of Rand was, thus, the outcome of a complex of subjective factors including loss

[9] It is significant that two of the prominent native newspapers that wrote in defence of Damodar were run by upper-class educated brahmins. The *Mahrátta* and *Dnyán Prakásh*, as I have already stated, wrote that he would have made an excellent soldier in the service of Her Majesty's army had he been given the opportunity to do so.

of personal pride and caste esteem and the desire to overcome it through acts of courage and manliness, religious zeal and the zeal to acquire public fame as revolutionaries.

Decades later, the assassination came to be viewed as a significant event in anti-colonial nationalism in India. In *Militant Nationalism in India* Biman Majumdar cites a patriotic song that the Chapekar brothers sang at a Ganapati festival in Bombay:[10] 'Here we find a clear proof of the nationalist spirit of Damodar Hari Chapekar. Though religion was his primary motive, yet the influence of nationalism was not less strong on his mind' (Majumdar, 1966, p. 87). In recent years there has been a renewed interest in the Chapekar brothers' role as revolutionaries, partly sponsored by the state. Their family home at Chapekarwada in Pune was renovated in 2005 and is now a museum dedicated to the brothers, all three of whom were hanged in connection with the assassination plot.[11] In 2009, National Book Trust published a book for children titled *Hanged for Their Patriotism*, which includes a chapter on them. 'The sacrifices of these young men, almost a century ago, are still fresh in the mind of the people of India and we all salute these young patriots, who were idols for the Indian revolutionaries' (Tandon, 2009, p. 56). The question is not whether Rand's assassination constitutes a patriotic act, for acts do not have meanings immanent in themselves. Rather, meaning is the outcome of how they are *interpreted* and *framed* as meaningful acts.

Culture provides interpretative cues that shape the meaning of an act. Culture, as Clifford Geertz writes, is the 'imaginative universe' within which our 'acts are signs' (1973, p. 13). Geertz gives as an example the difference between a wink and a twitch. A wink can signify, depending on the context of action, a sexual advance, a conspiracy, or even a parody of someone

[10] The song is given in full in the autobiography (Chapekar, n.d., p. 993).

[11] The youngest brother, Vasudeo Hari was not implicated in the assassination itself, for he was not present at the scene of crime. He was convicted and hanged for the murder of the Dravid brothers, who had testified against Damodar and Balkrishna (Maharashtra State Gazetteers, n.d., pp. 365–368).

who has an uncontrollable twitch. A twitch, in contrast, bears no significance—or, putting it more precisely, its significance is that it signifies nothing. A 'stratified hierarchy of meaningful structures in terms of which twitches, winks, fake-winks, parodies, rehearsals of parodies are produced, perceived, and interpreted, and without which they would not (not even the zero-form twitches, which as a cultural category, are as much nonwinks as winks are nontwitches) in fact exist, no matter what anyone did or didn't do with his eyelids' (p. 7). In other words, the cultural codes that make an act meaningful pre-exist the act itself, and are internalised by the actor in the process of socialisation.

On this view, patriotism is a meaning that interpreters attribute to an act which, under a different scheme of interpretation, may signify other things. Thus, the Sedition Committee stated that the Chapekar brothers 'had no definite political aims' other than composing patriotic songs and indulging in childish pranks like burning pavilions and desecrating Victoria's statue (as cited in Majumdar, 1966, p. 89)—even while it held that there 'can be no doubt that the Chapekar Association was a criminal conspiracy connected with the revolutionary movement in India' (Sedition Committee, 1918, p. 4). This does not imply that one can attribute any meaning whatsoever, for the culturally accepted codes on which interpretative acts are based restrict the play of meaning. As Stanley Fish argues, the activity of decoding is governed by an 'interpretative community' that authorises certain interpretations as intelligible and acceptable, irrespective of whether they are valid objectively or merely subjective impressions: 'they will not be objective because they will always have been the product of a point of view rather than having been simply 'read off'; and they will not be subjective because that point of view will always be social or institutional' (1980, p. 335). When we turn to narrative as a signifying practice, the same principles hold good: an act becomes plausible in a story to the extent that it draws on the codes that define human action. Cultural norms underlying narration, as Geertz says of interpretation, constitute the act as 'sign' and attribute to it a meaning and value that are consensual.

Interpolating Geertz's argument into his theory of narrative, Paul Ricoeur writes: 'the composition of the plot is grounded in a pre-understanding of the world of action, its meaningful structures, its symbolic resources, and its temporal character' (1984, p. 54). Let us see how this works out in the plot of Damodar's autobiography.

In narrating the story of his life, Damodar arranges the events in a chronological sequence beginning with his birth and closing with his assassination of Rand. The various incidents of his childhood and youth are retrospectively interpreted as leading up to this closure. His early fascination for 'dreadful deeds', exercises of strength and endurance, founding a club to defend Hindu religion and culture, punishing reformers, missionaries and those who deviate from shastric conduct, desecrating the queen's image—all these are imbued with a latent significance made manifest in the murder of Rand, the significance of which is in turn anticipated by the preface signed by the 'Well-wisher of the country' and 'Patriot'. Damodar's narrative is emplotted, thus, not simply chronologically but causally as well, in a narrative process that integrates discrete events into a totality that Ricoeur calls 'configuration'. The events of a story follow a chronological order, which the plot rearranges to constitute them into a united sequence that can be grasped as a whole by the reader. Ricouer calls the chronological order 'the episodic dimension' of the narrative, and its emplotment as a coherent unity, its 'configurational dimension' (1984, p. 66). In plotting the events of the past as a cause-and-effect sequence, however insignificant they may seem in themselves, Damodar's narrative configures them as a sign of patriotism.

This technique of emplotment is as central to historical narratives as it is to fictional ones. History, writes Hayden White, makes events 'into a story by the suppression or subordination of some of them and the highlighting of others, by characterization, motific repetition, variation of tone and point of view, alternative descriptive strategies, and the like—in short, all of the techniques that we would normally expect to find in the emplotment of a novel or play' (1978, p. 84). *Hanged for Their Patriotism* comprises a series of historical sketches of martyrs who laid down their lives for the country, in order to edify its young readers. The chapter on the Chapekar brothers closely follows the autobiography in its selection and highlighting of events like their failed attempts to join the army, the creation of a private army of 'true patriots', the attacks on the British and the desecration of Victoria's statue, the distribution of pamphlets against the colonial government, and the killing of Rand and Ayerst (Tandon, 2009, pp. 53–54). What it leaves out are the many instances of Damodar's religious intolerance and the harassment of social reformers, missionaries and those who converted to Christianity, presumably because these seem irrelevant to his more patriotic deeds. Perhaps, too, these incidents would likely not be well-received by a young readership taught to be secular in its outlook and tolerant of religious difference. History and autobiography, or rather history as a re-reading of autobiography, construct the meaning of Damodar's life as what he partly was and what he aspired to be—a true patriot—from a series of heterogeneous events that do not readily submit to such a singular meaning. The Chapekarwada Museum in Pune consolidates and archives this meaning as the authoritative view of history.

To return to the autobiography, the brothers planned to waylay Rand at Ganesh Khind when he returned from the celebrations at Government House. Uttering the word 'Gondiya', which was the signal for attack, Damodar fired at Rand as his carriage passed by him. Ayerst, who was following in another carriage, saw this, and, before he could raise alarm Balkrishna shot him at point-blank range. The only witness to the crime was Mrs. Ayerst, but she failed to identify the killers. When news of the double-murder spread in the city, the people were jubilant and celebrated by distributing sweets. 'I leave it to my readers to imagine what gratification we must have felt when the universal feeling of joy was so great' (Chapekar, n.d., p. 1014). Yet Damodar admits that he bore no personal grudge against Rand. On the contrary, during the three-and-a-half months that he observed Rand 'we came to entertain a very good opinion of him':

> He was a proud man like ourselves and we believe that he was not addicted to any vice. There was no meanness in his character. We had seen him playing lawn-tennis at the Gymkhana. He would never play with ladies, and from this (we inferred) that he disliked associating with the wives of others. (p. 1014)

His only reason for taking Rand's life was that he took no notice of the way his soldiers conducted the house searches in utter disregard of the peoples' religious sentiments: 'As he made himself an enemy of our religion, we deemed it necessary to take revenge upon him'. After he was arrested on the testimony of the Dravid brothers, he made a voluntary confession admitting his role and that of Balkrishna in the assassination. He concludes the autobiography by expressing his gratitude to the two officers in charge of the case, who treated him with kindness and respect: 'I have entirely forgotten my long cherished hatred of the English owing to the intercourse I subsequently had with Superintendents Kennedy and Brewin' (p. 1015).

Damodar Chapekar's autobiography narrates the story of the plague outbreak in terms of socio-political meanings that it evoked in the minds of a people subjected to the excesses of colonial power. It is written from the point of view of the main actor in this drama of thwarted ambition, hurt self-esteem, and an almost obsessive need to restore it through acts of martyrdom in the cause of religion and nation. In telling the story of his decision to kill Rand, Damodar dredges from memory random experiences, both profound and trivial, and weaves into them significances that make what begins as an epidemic crisis into a momentous event in the history of his people. As he tells his reader in the preface, he was initially reluctant to record his story; but 'the dictate of conscience' compelled him to write it so that those patriots who came after him may take inspiration from it (pp. 957–958). In its subsequent retellings, the story acquires an iconic significance that surpasses the event at its core. *Hanged for Their Patriotism* and the museum at Chapekarwada are two such retellings; we will now look at a third.

3.4. *22 June 1897*

22 June 1897, directed by Nachiket and Jayoo Patwardhan and released in 1979, won a Golden Lotus for the best film on national integration and for art direction in the National Film Awards, 1980. It tells the story of the assassination of Plague Commissioner Rand during the outbreak at Poona. In this section, I will attempt to read the film alongside Damodar Chapekar's autobiography, the story of the Chapekar brothers in *Hanged for Their Patriotism* and government records in Maharashtra State Gazetteers.

22 June 1897 recounts the story of the assassination from a triple perspective: religion, anti-colonial politics and the military aspiration of Damodar and Balkrishna. It weaves these perspectives into separate storylines dealing with each of the Chapekar brothers and the family as a whole. The film opens with a voice-over in which Damodar expresses their determination to undertake the 'fateful task' despite the danger it entails. This is followed by the credits sequence in which we hear the sound of prayers, the galloping of horses and gunshots. The title of the film and the opening sequence thus serve to establish the murders of Ayerst and Rand as the narrative centre of the film. The plot can be divided into two sections—the first leading up to this event which occurs approximately at the film's midpoint and the second, its unfolding.

The first part of the film selectively recounts events from Damodar's life that explain why he and his brothers kill Rand, and can roughly be grouped into those that concern their religious beliefs, their anti-colonial politics and their ambition to join the army. It begins with the baptism of Vishnu Keshav Velankar and his punishment by Damodar, Balkrishna and Bhuskute. The Chapekar brothers and their friends meet and discuss the event, and declare their opposition to Christianity, the English language and British rule. 'Muslims rampaged our country, they raped our women, but the English are worse. These white-faced hellhounds are thieves who are steadily engulfing our country and will swallow us up with their language and religion' (Patwardhan, 1979, 0:04:44–0:05:30). They attack a missionary who passes by the field where they are training. The next sequence deals with their attempt to join the British Indian army. They are told that the army does not recruit brahmins, whose work is to offer prayers and not fight. Besides, brahmins have no loyalty for they 'ruined the Peshwa's kingdom'. 'Go home', they are told, 'go back to your begging bowls' (0:06:20–0:07:20). This insult to their caste also plays an important role in their decision to oppose the British. As symbolic of their anti-British stance they disfigure a photograph of Queen Victoria, garland it with shoes and hang it in a public place. This sequence thereby draws into focus the different motives behind the assassination of Rand, as we have seen recounted in the autobiography. This is in contrast to Tandon's chapter on the Chapekar brothers that emphasises only their patriotism. The sequence is followed by a shot of Hari Vinayak Chapekar's disapproval of his sons' bodybuilding exercises in the name of defending their faith: 'Gymnastics and hooliganism, is that your religion?' (0:08:29–0:09:03) Hari is shown performing a *kirtan* on the story of Usha and Aniruddha, with his three sons providing accompaniment. Such scenes, which are quite frequent, focus on the family that the other accounts we have seen (including the autobiography) leave out. The film deftly weaves these scenes of domesticity into the public story of the assassination. More importantly, however, they set up a counter-narrative that complicates what would otherwise read like a straightforward story of patriotism.

The next sequence begins with a montage of shots showing the outbreak of plague in Poona: a rat dying beside a corpse, a funeral procession and people evacuating the city (Patwardhan, 1979, 0:12:47–0:14:00). A public announcement is made from Government House proclaiming the enactment of the Epidemic Diseases Act and the imposition of martial law in Poona, empowering the Plague Committee to search houses and fumigate them. Rand is appointed as its head and whoever disobeys his orders is to be severely punished 'without right of appeal' (0:15:42–0:16:33). Soldiers forcibly enter a house in which there is a corpse, take into custody its occupants, including women, and march them into a quarantine camp. The house is fumigated and lime-washed to sanitise it.[12] One of the women refuses to go and implores Rand, who is supervising the operations, to let her stay: 'Don't drag me into quarantine … let me die in my house' (0:18:34–0:18:44). Worried residents make a representation to meet Rand, but he refuses them. Meanwhile, in the Chapekar house Hari decides to leave for their ancestral home at Chinchwad village but Damodar refuses: 'Leaving town when we are needed would be cowardly … we want to work for Mr Tilak' (0:14:54–0:15:11). The three brothers are next shown ambushing and beating two soldiers, in reprisal for the atrocities on innocent people. Damodar meets Tilak, who admonishes him: 'What will you achieve by beating up poor soldiers? They only obey orders, the real culprit is elsewhere. He should be taught a lesson' (0:21:40–0:21:58). The film thus accords Tilak a primary role in the conspiracy against Rand. Later in the film when Damodar retracts his confession on the ground that the police forced him to do so, it is Tilak who dictates the petition he submits to the High Court. In reality, Damodar himself was actually quite critical of Tilak's brand of patriotism and made no mention of his role in the conspiracy either in the autobiography or in his recorded confession. A possible reason for this may be that he wished to protect Tilak, but it seems unlikely as he had named others who had helped him.

To prepare for the murder of Rand, the Chapekar brothers and their friends practise shooting. Bhuskute dies of plague, and Damodar vows to avenge his death: 'Datta, we'll complete our task as planned. Rand will not remain alive. Only then will your soul rest in peace' (Patwardhan, 1979, 0:24:21–0:24:33). Meanwhile, the plague epidemic abates, martial law is lifted in Poona and people return to their homes. They celebrate by singing songs. In a deep-focus shot a family is seen putting things back in their places, bustling about their home and sanctifying it (0:25:44–0:26:15). It is then that Damodar decides to kill Rand. 'But why

[12] Repainting houses of infection with a fresh coat of lime was standard sanitary practice at the time. Lime is alkaline, and destroys micro-organisms.

kill Rand now?' asks one of his friends. 'He has controlled the plague. Everything is normal now!' Damodar replies: 'Have you forgotten his atrocities? Women molested at Shanipur. God and temple defiled. And who will avenge Datta's death? Rand will be killed' (0:28:22–0:28:50). They plan to carry out the assassination on Jubilee night, and send a letter of warning to Rand.

The assassination sequence is the longest in the film, almost eighteen minutes in length (Patwardhan, 1979, 0:29:40–0:47:25). It opens with the invocation of Goddess Durga (also known as Amba and Bhavani), as they sing 'Goddess Amba lead us to victory in our righteous path, give me strength Goddess Bhavani, to crush our enemy' (0:29:45–0:30:03). They choose a lonely spot on Ganesh Khind Road, and decide that Vasudeo would follow Rand's buggy as he returns from the party at Government House, and shout 'Gondiya *ala re*' (Govinda is coming), which would be the signal for Damodar and Balkrishna to get ready. In the confusion, Balkrishna mistakes Ayerst for Rand and kills him. Mrs Ayerst is also in the buggy, but is not able to get a good look at the killer. When Rand's buggy comes, Damodar springs on it and shoots him. Ayerst dies on the spot while Rand is mortally wounded and dies a few days later. In the autobiography, however, they shoot Rand first and then Ayerst to make sure there is no witness.

The assassination sequence provides the turning point when the story shifts from the plot to kill Rand to the investigation, conviction and execution of Damodar, Vasudeo, Mahadeo Ranade and Balkrishna. It performs a symbolic function in the narrative of patriotism, for Rand's assassination on the Diamond Jubilee of Queen Victoria's reign is not just about the atrocities committed in the search operations or about avenging the death of Bhuskute, but a direct attack on the empire: 'Britishers are killed and England is insulted', Brewin tells Damodar when he visits him in jail. 'Walter Charles Rand represented the British empire when he was shot. The empire was shot at' (Patwardhan, 1979, 1:10:16–1:11:17). The film visually evokes this in a shot that shows the Union Jack flying over Government House at the time of the assassination. It thus serves to bring into focus one meaning, patriotism, from among the several others that the film constructs.

The government announces a reward of twenty thousand rupees for information leading to the arrest of the culprits and Brewin starts his investigation. Ganesh Dravid and his brother Ramchandra testify that they had seen Damodar and Balkrishna hiding guns in their uncle Govinda's well the day after the assassination. Ganesh, who is in jail for forgery, is promised a remission of his sentence and both brothers are promised the reward money. The information given by the Dravids leads to Damodar's arrest in Bombay and his remand to jail custody in Poona on 29 September 1897. Brewin persuades him to confess his crime by working on his patriotic sentiments and promising him a commutation of sentence from death penalty to imprisonment for four years, a job after his release and pension for his family, as well as the reward money that he had already promised to the Dravids. For a martyr, he tells Damodar, it is the 'pride of nation, self-respect, that is uppermost'. The true martyr does not hide his act but 'comes into the open, bares his chest and says I did it, come on, punish me' (Patwardhan, 1979, 1:10:54–1:11:56). Does Brewin play a trick on Damodar by enticing him with false promises? On 22 April 1898, Brewin had actually submitted a report to the Commissioner of Police, Bombay, urging the government to remit the rest of Ganesh's jail sentence and give the entire reward money to him and his brother: 'Unless this is done, an impression will get abroad that the Government do not uphold the pledges of their officers, to the detriment of public interest' (Maharashtra State Gazetteers, n.d., p. 344). Thanks to his intercession, Ganesh was released and a part of the money was given to the brothers, the rest being given to the Hyderabad police for their help in arresting Balkrishna,[13] and the film shows this. However, in the case of Damodar who trusted him so much that he mentioned it in his autobiography, there is no historical record that Brewin did indeed try to intercede on his behalf.

[13] This decision was taken by the government and Brewin had no role in it.

Later scenes in the film show Brewin trying to lure Vasudeo into revealing Balkrishna's hideout and testifying against him, on false promises of money and security. Why does the film show him in this unfavourable light insofar as his conduct with the Chapekar brothers is concerned? Its purpose seems to be to portray him (and his government by implication) as wily and unscrupulous, a charge not found either in the newspapers or Damodar's autobiography. It gives credibility to the view that the assassination was a patriotic act against unjust rule, which is further strengthened when Vasudeo confesses to the murder of the Dravids. The Chapekars, Vasudeo says, 'will be loyal to their country, not to strangers. Chapekars kill those who are traitors' (Patwardhan, 1979, 1:50:11–1:50:18).

If the film presents the character of Brewin negatively, it presents that of Tilak in more favourable light than Damodar does in his autobiography. It is Tilak who suggests that Rand must be punished, it is to him that Damodar goes after killing Rand, and it is he again who dictates to Damodar his petition retracting the confession. There is no mention of these incidents in the autobiography, nor do the native newspapers suggest the possibility; they had stated, on the contrary, that Damodar's confession proved Tilak's innocence. By altering history thus, the film foregrounds the theme of patriotism, for Tilak has been widely acclaimed in history as a patriot and nationalist.

22 June 1897 is a fictionalised retelling of history. It often departs from archived history of the Poona episode, though conforming to it in the main. It reconfigures the events of that history differently from the way they are represented in media reports, colonial records and Chapekar's autobiography, to attribute a specific set of meanings to it. It is a very good instance of what White figuratively calls 'fictions of factual representation' (1978, p. 121)—that is, emplotting real events using techniques generically associated with fiction. In disguising its fiction as history, the film adds a complex layer of significance to both the objective rendering of past events in the newspaper reports and colonial records and the subjective account of these events in

Chapekar's autobiography as well as Tandon's allegory of militant nationalism. It interprets the history of the Jubilee night murders as well as the murders of the Dravid brothers as the outcome of loyalty to country first, and then, secondarily, to thwarted ambitions, desire for fame, the need to restore caste esteem and religious intolerance. It combines objective events and the subjective response of the Chapekar family, especially the father, to these events. This is poignantly expressed in the film's closing sequence. As we hear the sound of the trapdoor falling under Balkrishna's feet when he is hanged, the camera focuses on Hari Chapekar trying to control his grief (Patwardhan, 1979, 1:53:26–1:53:48). Like Brewin and Tilak, Hari's role is emphasised, too, in the film, to underline the emotional cost of the brothers' patriotism. These departures from archived history constitute what Ricoeur calls the 'iconic augmentation' of meaning that fiction adds to history, in 'the *interweaving* reference between history and narrative fiction' (1984, p. 82, italics in original). Whether we consider history and fiction as generically different (as Ricoeur does) or as essentially the same (as White does), our reading of *22 June 1897* clearly shows how the two are inseparably linked in reconstructing the past.

3.5. Conclusion

When plague broke out in Bombay in August 1896, the colonial government hastily adopted extraordinary measures to check its spread, partly triggered by the threat of sanctions on trade by other European nations. On 4 February 1897, when the disease ravaged the city of Poona, the government of India passed the Epidemic Diseases Act which made it mandatory for the public to submit to house searches, physical examination and removal to quarantine camps and plague hospitals. To carry out these measures without any possibility of resistance it imposed martial law and made any act of non-cooperation a cognisable offence. Instead of forestalling resistance, as the authorities had hoped, it actually triggered massive protests and even riots. There were two reasons for this. On the one side was Rand's failure to check the conduct of the soldiers who forcefully intruded on the privacy of families, humiliated the men and misbehaved with the women, desecrated places of worship, ransacked houses and engaged in pillage. When representations were made to him by the public and the newspapers, he dismissed them as false without inquiring into them. On the other side were the rumours that the government's hasty action provoked, that plague was merely a pretext for violating religious and caste norms, converting people to Christianity, forcibly removing people to hospitals to administer poison and to extract *momiai* from their bodies. While these rumours may have been wild and unwarranted, they expressed popular distrust of the colonial government and its motives. The Poona newspapers highlighted the excesses of the plague operations and urged people to protest against them. It was in this volatile context that the decision to kill Rand was taken and carried out by the Chapekar brothers.

The story told in the newspaper reports reveals how a disease event was configured as social and political disorder and the breakdown of governance. What had caused the government to impose harsh penalties for the murder of Rand and Ayerst, at the cost of risking whatever public loyalty it had achieved through liberal reforms? The revolt of 1857 was still fresh in the minds of the administration, and comparisons to it in the newspapers renewed fears of a recurrence. The excessive nature of the government's reaction to the murders—the imposition of punitive police force in Poona and the passing of Chalmers' anti-sedition bill—was due partly to fear of popular uprising and partly to what the killing of Rand symbolised. Rand and Ayerst were killed on the night of the Diamond Jubilee celebrations of Queen Victoria's reign, and for the British it meant a direct attack on the rule of empire.

Damodar's autobiography and *22 June 1897* bring out further significances of the assassination. While the newspaper reports and colonial records represent this event in terms of public acts, these two narratives emphasise its more personal and subjective dimensions. As Damodar recounts his life from his birth into a poor brahmin family of minstrels to the killing of Rand, what unfolds is a story of thwarted ambition, religious intolerance, loss of caste pride as well as of personal self-esteem and the attempt to restore both through an act of martyrdom for nation and faith. In his version of the story, these various strands of meaning shape its central narrative of patriotism. It is this narrative that subsequent retellings of the story of the assassination take up. In *Hanged for Their Patriotism*, Tandon makes it a core event in the story of militant nationalism in India. This meaning is what the museum of Chapekarwada in Poona archives. *22 June 1897* tells the story in a much more nuanced manner, emphasising not just patriotism but the complex factors that motivate Damodar and his brothers to kill Rand. It interweaves history and fiction to construct a credible explanatory paradigm of the Poona outbreak and its consequences.

Damodar's autobiography, Tandon's chapter on the Chapekar brothers and *22 June 1897* reveal the way in which narratives reconstruct the past. In *Framing History*, Virginia Carmichael shows how this reconstruction is never simply an alternate version of the past, but one that is embedded in relations of power. Carmichael reads the story of Julius and Ethel Rosenberg, executed for treason against the US government in 1953, from historical records, films and television serials of the 1950s that promote the official version, and two revisionary narratives of the event written in the 1970s—E.L. Doctorow's *The Book of Daniel* and Robert Coover's *The Public Burning*. In a changed political climate, Doctorow's and Coover's novels interpret the execution of the Rosenbergs as an outcome of Cold War anti-communist hysteria in the McCarthy era. '[I]n any political society', she concludes, 'that group with the greatest power over the uses and distribution of meaning also has the power to represent—and fashion—our perception of a specific reality according to a protocol of linguistic and political splitting and projection that is neither primary, natural, nor inescapable' (Carmichael, 1993, p. 200). At the time of Rand's assassination, Damodar's act was interpreted variously as a planned conspiracy against the colonial government, a despicable crime for which the perpetrator was justly hanged, and a deed inspired by a misguided notion of patriotism. The report of the Sedition Committee interpreted it as a 'criminal conspiracy' linked to the nascent anti-colonial movement. Against these versions, Damodar's autobiography may be read as a counter-narrative that inverts the meanings attributed to the assassination by the colonial government and those who supported it. In postcolonial representations of the event—in Tandon's account, the film and the Chapekarwada Museum—the story comes to be reframed from the opposite perspective, stabilising the interpretation that Damodar gives to it and mainstreaming it as militant nationalism. A critical reading of the texts, therefore, shows how the outbreak comes to be configured at different moments in response to differing political imperatives and power structures. In the next chapter we will look at another story of plague in which it is used to signify a crisis of religious faith and premonition of cosomological disorder.

References

Arnold, D. (1993). *Colonizing the body: State medicine and epidemic disease in nineteenth-century India*. University of California Press.

Bannerman, W.B. (1906). The spread of plague in India. *The Journal of Hygiene*, *6*(2), 179–211. http://www.jstor.com/stable/3858816

Benedict, C. (1988). Bubonic plague in nineteenth-century China. *Modern China*, *14*(2), 107–155. http://www.jstor.org/stable/189268

Catanach, I.J. (2001). The 'globalization' of disease? India and the plague. *Journal of World History*, *12*(1), 131–153. http://www.jstor.org/stable/20078880

Carmichael, V. (1993). *Framing history: The Rosenberg story and the Cold War*. University of Minnesota Press.

Chapekar, D.H. (n.d.). *Autobiography of Damodar Hari Chapekar*. Bombay Police Abstracts of 1910 (pp. 955–1016). https://gazetteers.maharashtra.gov.in/cultural.maharashtra.gov.in/english/gazetteer/VOL-II/ autobiography.pdf

Condon, J.K. (1900). *The Bombay plague, being a history of the progress of plague in the Bombay Presidency from September 1896 to June 1899*. Education Society Steam Press.

Echenberg, M. (2002). Pestis redux: The initial years of the third bubonic plague pandemic, 1894–1901. *Journal of World History, 13*(2), 429–449. http://www.jstor.org/stable/20078978

Fish, S. 1980. *Is there a text in this class? The authority of interpretative communities*. Harvard University Press.

Foucault, M. (2003). *'Society Must Be Defended': Lectures at the Collège de France, 1975 – 76* (M. Bertani and A Fontana, Ed., D. Macey, Trans.). Picador.

Foucault, M. (2007). *Security, territory, population: Lectures at the Collège de France, 1977–1978* (M. Senellart, Ed.; G. Burchell, Trans.). Picador.

Geertz, C. 1973. *The interpretation of cultures: Selected essays*. Basic Books.

Godwin-Austen, H.H. (1920). Momiai. *Nature, 106*, 241.

Hankin, E.H. (1905). On the epidemiology of plague. *The Journal of Hygiene, 5*(1), 48–83. http://www.jstor.org/stable/3858730

Hirst, L.F. (1953). *The conquest of plague: A study of the evolution of epidemiology*. Clarendon Press.

India Office Library and Records. (1896a). *Report on native papers for the week ending April 04, 1896*. https://www.jstor.org/stable/saoa.crl.25636120

India Office Library and Records. (1897a). *Report on native papers for the week ending January 09, 1897*. https://www.jstor.org/stable/saoa.crl.25636160

India Office Library and Records. (1897b). *Report on native papers for the week ending January 16, 1897*. https://www.jstor.org/stable/saoa.crl.25636161

India Office Library and Records. (1897c). *Report on native papers for the week ending March 20, 1897*. https://www.jstor.org/stable/saoa.crl.25636170

India Office Library and Records. (1897d). *Report on native papers for the week ending April 24, 1897*. https://www.jstor.org/stable/saoa.crl.25636175

India Office Library and Records. (1897e). *Report on native papers for the week ending May 01, 1897*. https://www.jstor.org/stable/saoa.crl.25636176

India Office Library and Records. (1897f). *Report on native papers for the week ending July 03, 1897*. https://www.jstor.org/stable/saoa.crl.25636185

India Office Library and Records. (1897g). *Report on native papers for the week ending July 10, 1897.* https://www.jstor.org/stable/saoa.crl.25636186

India Office Library and Records. (1897h). *Report on native papers for the week ending August 21, 1897.* https://www.jstor.org/stable/saoa.crl.25636192

India Office Library and Records. (1897i). *Report on native papers for the week ending December 25, 1897.* https://www.jstor.org/stable/saoa.crl.25636210

India Office Library and Records. (1898a). *Report on native papers for the week ending January 01, 1898.* https://www.jstor.org/stable/saoa.crl.25636211

India Office Library and Records. (1898b). *Report on native papers for the week ending February 12, 1898.* https://www.jstor.org/stable/saoa.crl.25636217

India Office Library and Records. (1898c). *Report on native papers for the week ending March 19, 1898.* https://www.jstor.org/stable/saoa.crl.25636222

India Office Library and Records. (1898d). *Report on native papers for the week ending April 23, 1898.* https://www.jstor.org/stable/saoa.crl.25636227

India Office Library and Records. (1898e). *Report on native papers for the week ending April 30, 1898.* https://www.jstor.org/stable/saoa.crl.25636228

India Office Library and Records. (1898f). *Report on native papers for the week ending October 08, 1898.* https://www.jstor.org/stable/saoa.crl.25636251

JanMohamed, A.R. (1985). The economy of Manichean allegory: The function of racial difference in colonialist literature. *Critical Inquiry*, *12*(1), 59–87.

Jones, W.S. (1897). International Sanitary Conference. *Public Health Reports (1896–1970)*, *12*(19), 452–459. http://www.jstor.org/stable/41437123

Klein, I. (1988). Plague, policy and popular unrest in British India. *Modern Asian Studies*, *22*(4), 723–755. http://www.jstor.org/stable/312523

Levine, C. (2006). Strategic formalism: Toward a new method in cultural studies. *Victorian Studies*, *48*(4), 625–657. http://www.jstor.org/stable/4618909

Maharashtra State Gazetters. (n.d.). *The revolutionaries 1: The Chapekar brothers*. https://gazetteers.maharashtra.gov.in/cultural.maharashtra.gov.in/english/gazetteer/VOL-II/REVOLUTIONARY_I.pdf

Majumdar, B. (1966). *Militant nationalism in India and its socio-religious background (1897–1917)*. General Printers and Publishers Private Ltd.

Majumdar, R.C. (1957). *The Sepoy Mutiny and Revolt of 1857*. Firma K.L. Mukhopadhyay.

Pandemic plague. (1900). *The British Medical Journal*, *2*(2078), 1247–1255. https://www.jstor.org/stable/20266180

Patwardhan, N. (Producer). (1979). *22 June 1897* [Film]. Sanket/FFC.

Rao, S.B. (2010). Disrobing colonialism, and making sense of it. *Social Scientist*, *38*(7/8), 15–28. http://www.jstor.org/stable/27866720

Ricoeur, P. 1984. *Time and narrative*, vol. 1 (Kathleen McLaughlin & David Pellauer, Trans.). University of Chicago Press.

Sedition Committee. (1918). *Report*. Superintendent Government Printing, India. https://www.thehinducentre.com/resources/65642999-Sedition-Committee-1918-Report.pdf

Tandon, R.K. 2009. *Hanged for their patriotism*. National Book Trust, India.

White, H. 1978. *Tropics of discourse: Essays in cultural criticism*. Johns Hopkins University Press.

4

Plague as Ethical Crisis in U.R. Ananthamurthy's *Samskara*

Set in the fictional village of Durvasapura in the mid-1940s, U.R. Ananthamurthy's *Samskara* opens with the death of Naranappa, who contracts bubonic plague during one of his frequent visits to the town of Shivamogge. Until his cremation is carried out according to the rites, no one in the agrahara can partake of food or perform sacred duties. Naranappa has repudiated his community's caste norms by consuming meat and alcohol, living openly with a low-caste concubine and befriending Muslims. Is he any longer a brahmin and can one cremate him without losing caste purity? Since he has not been excommunicated he is technically a brahmin. If he is to be given a ritual cremation, who shall cremate him? He has no children and has long since antagonised Garuda and Lakshmana, his only relatives in the agrahara. The agrahara turns to Praneshacharya to find in the scriptures an answer for this dilemma. Pranesharcharya, who has studied at Kashi and has been crowned 'Crest-Jewel of Vedic Learning' (Anathamurthy, 1976, p. 7), knows the ritual norms of his community and has practised them all his life. But even he fails to find an answer, either in the scriptures or as a sign from the god Maruti. In a moment of weakness, he cohabits with Naranappa's concubine Chandri, and is no longer in a position to guide others as he considers himself defiled. The word *samskara* has several meanings—one of which refers to cremation rites and another to the cultural tradition of a community (Ramanujan, 1976, p. 119). By giving his English translation of the novel the subtitle 'A Rite for a Dead Man' Ramanujan links the two meanings: unless the *samskara* of Naranappa is performed in accordance with the rules of ritual purity, the *samskara* of the community cannot be upheld. Thus, the outbreak of plague leads to a moral crisis that the community must resolve in order to maintain its caste integrity.

Samskara has been read predominantly as a critique of caste and religious orthodoxy in the context of brahmin society. This is borne out by Ananthamurthy's own comments on how he came to write the novel. It was inspired by his childhood memory of an outbreak of plague in Shivamogge, which broke out when he was 'barely 13 years old' (Ananthamurthy, 2005, p. 69)—that is, in 1945. 'In my village only the pariahs died. That was because, I had realized, the orthodox doctor had not gone to inoculate against plague–they were untouchables. Although I was surrounded by all these people, something in me was stirred against all these superstitious people'. When people in his village said that plague was god's way of punishing the untouchables who, inspired by Gandhi, had entered and desecrated temples, he told them that 'this was a stupid and immoral reasoning, for, those who died were not inoculated, because they were untouchable'. 'Ever since', Ananthamurthy writes, '"touch" has become one of my themes.' He also mentions another incident that had a deep impact on him, when a young man of their agrahara who had joined the army in protest against his parents' orthodoxy eloped with a harijan girl. 'When the girl ran away I wrote a story' (Ananthamurthy, 2007, p. 121). The story, titled 'Tharangini' (The Wavy Lake), treated the issue of caste obliquely: 'I had to do this metaphorically for I did not want the elders to know what I knew. Metaphors serve as hiding places for writers in all ages' (ibid., see also Ananthamurthy, 2005, p. 70). His father, however, was more modern in his attitudes, had read Gandhi's writings against caste in the *Harijan*, and was a source of encouragement for him. The themes of caste discrimination, orthodox tradition and modernity that *Samskara* expresses were, therefore, nurtured quite early in his life.

It was during an outbreak of plague, therefore, that Ananthamurthy became sensitised to the oppressive nature of caste orthodoxy. The other source of inspiration for the novel that he mentions is Ingmar Bergman's film *The Seventh Seal*, also about a plague outbreak (Ananthamurthy, 2005, p. 70). He saw it with Malcolm Bradbury, and was so impressed by it that he thought of rewriting the story of the harijan couple he had written earlier. Bergman's film is about an outbreak of plague in medieval Europe that leads its protagonist, who has just returned from the Holy Crusades, to question his faith in the existence of god. As Bergman himself summarised it: '*The Seventh Seal* is an allegory whose theme is very simple: man, his eternal search for God, with death as the only certitude' (as cited in Mambrino, 1959, p. 89). In short, the theme of caste and religion was linked by circumstances to the theme of plague, which provided Ananthamurthy both the inspiration and the point of departure for his novel. The novel begins with the outbreak, which happens in Shivamogge as it did in Ananthamurthy's childhood; and its questioning of religious codes is inspired by Bergman's depiction of Antonius Block's crisis of faith during a plague epidemic. Yet interpretations of the novel do not address the plague story, and most do not even mention it. My view in this chapter is that the story of the outbreak is not incidental to the plot of *Samskara*, but serves to *focalise* the issues of brahmin tradition, caste and religion that form its broader themes.

4.1. Critical Reception of *Samskara*

Before I elaborate this view, let me summarise some of the key arguments in the critical literature on the novel. Ever since its publication in Kannada in 1965, *Samskara* has been subject to controversy even as it has received wide acclaim.[1] Views on the novel have ranged from praise for its bold presentation of

---

[1] Its publication sparked off protests against it by orthodox brahmin groups, and when Ananthamurthy died on 22 August 2014 protestors celebrated his death with firecrackers (Prabhakara, 2014, p. 27). *Samskara* 'has been widely praised by the critics, but it has also been harshly attacked by fanatical brahmins who went so far as to try to block the release of the film' (Gupta, 1976, p. 20). The film version of the novel, which was made in Kannada by Pattabhirama Reddy in 1970, was at first banned by the Censor Board on the ground that it 'would hurt the sensibilities of a "particular community"'. When there was public reaction against the ban, the Ministry of Information and Broadcasting revoked it ('Film and its censorship', 1970, p. 10).

caste and religious orthodoxy and its attentiveness to social and philosophical issues, to criticism for its defective and biased understanding of brahminism, caste and the Hindu way of life. The interpretations of *Samskara* have focused predominantly on three aspects: its critique of brahminism, its depiction of tradition and modernity, and its allegorical structure and dialectical form.

V.S. Naipaul reads *Samskara* as a satire on a 'barbaric civilization' that is crippled with 'the crudest ideas of pollution and caste and power' (Naipaul, 1977, pp. 104, 109). In Krishnamoorthy Aithal's view, the author does satirise the brahmins, but also expresses empathy for them: 'Though he is critical towards the *brahmin* community, he is not lacking in imaginative sympathy for the community. Superficially viewed, the portraits of *brahmins* may seem to be simple caricatures. But if these are carefully examined, one will note that the author gives us various aspects of the character and shows a deep insight into the working of the mind of the character, unlike an ordinary caricaturist' (1981, p. 88, italics in original). Vijay L. Sharma reads it as a story that begins with criticism of brahmin orthodoxy, but subsequently develops into 'a conflict between faith and heresy, between the spiritual and materialist, idea and experience, asceticism and eroticism' (Misra, Sharma & Kaul, 1982, p. 104). Others disagree with this view, arguing that critique of brahmin orthodoxy is not the novel's main concern. Meenakshi Mukherjee writes that such readings of the novel 'limit it severely' (2005, p. 85), a view that Ananthamurthy himself expresses in an interview he gave to Susheela Punitha: 'to study the novel as a caste and religious text is to diminish it, to underrate its metaphysical dimension' (Punitha, 1976, p. 143). Mukherjee's essay, too, mentions its metaphysical concern, though she does not elaborate it (2005, p. 85). R.K. Gupta's view is that criticism of brahmin society may be present in *Samskara*, but 'is only one of its aspects, and perhaps not the major one.... The novel does not satirize brahminism as such (as many people mistakenly assume) but only a decadent and perverted form of it, which is local and topical in nature' (1980, p. 21). In a more detailed examination of its anti-brahminical passages, R. Radhakrishnan argues that it barely succeeds as critique. If the character of Naranappa is the sole focus of this critique, it does not constitute a real challenge to brahminical norms. Naranappa is 'a mere troublemaker with no independent truth claims of his own: a truant adolescent whose only wish is to shock and scandalize the orthodox Brahmins. He does not constitute any substantive antagonism or a real and critical counterpoint to the axiology of Brahmanism' (Radhakrishnan, 2005, p. 140). The character of Naranappa is founded on a logical contradiction: on the one hand he is no longer a brahmin because he does not observe the norms of brahminhood, yet on the other he continues to be a brahmin on the simple logic that only a brahmin can be accused of not observing the norms. The contradiction, therefore, cancels out any critical force that the character may have had, so that 'the work does not live up to the level of the critique that it initiates' (p. 148).

A close look at the text shows how brahminism as a way of life is not what it actually targets. The novel is critical only of the brahmins of the agarahara, who are portrayed as cupidinous and crafty. To avoid performing Naranappa's last rites, Garuda and Lakshmana use the pretext of a long-standing quarrel, but when Chandri offers gold for this purpose they vie with each other over what they now consider their claim as kin. Others grossly exaggerate Naranappa's sins, lest they are called upon to cremate him and thereby risk being excommunicated. Dasacharya, who survives entirely on the occasional free meal that he gets during ceremonials and 'would walk ten miles' for it (Ananthamurthy, 1976, p. 9), is worried about not being invited to a ritual feast if he performs the cremation; yet if they do not cremate Naranappa, they cannot touch food as per caste norms. The Madhava brahmins of Durvasapura are arrogant about their presumed superiority over the Smarta brahmins of neighbouring Parijatapura and refuse to accept food from them. Yet Dasacharya cannot pass up the *smarta* Manjayya's offer of a meal when he visits him on the pretext of discussing the cremation: 'I don't really mind eating in your house. But if those rascals in our agrahara hear about it, no one will invite me to a ceremony again' (p. 49). The brahmins look at the low-caste women of the village with lust, because their wives deprive them of sex, but are scared of being defiled by their touch. They look ugly and grotesque, their houses are full of dirt, cockroaches and rats and their wives are emaciated and sexually unappealing. 'Their moral deviance and impoverishment', comments Sharon Pillai, 'find an eloquent marker in their physical deformity and decrepitude' (2014, p. 108). They are illiterate and lack understanding of the ritual norms that they nevertheless espouse because they are conditioned to do so by tradition. Compared to them, Naranappa appears far more dignified because he has the courage to challenge the traditions and values he no longer believes to be true. The sole exception to the un-brahminical conduct of the Durvasapura brahmins is Praneshacharya, who, in his learning, his compassion and the virtues that he both preaches and practises, is the true brahmin. The novel's caricature of the brahmins' conduct is restricted to those of Durvasapura only and does not extend to the Parijatapura brahmins. In other words, as Gupta contends, it cannot strictly speaking be taken as an indictment of brahminism in general, but of the particular set of individuals it holds up to ridicule.

In the afterword to his translation of the novel Ramanujan states that in Praneshacharya's moral crisis 'brahminism questions itself in a modern existentialist mode ... and the question leads him into new and ordinary worlds' (1976, p. 121). Many critics have followed this lead in reading *Samskara* as a story about tradition versus modernity. Suresh Raval locates this theme in the plot's setting in a traditional village in modern times and in a protagonist who represents both traditionalist and modern existentialist views of the human condition. Like Roquentin in Jean-Paul Sartre's *Nausea*, Praneshacharya attempts to resolve his crisis by taking responsibility for his acts though he has not chosen them of his own accord. Unlike Roquentin, however, Praneshacharya feels no guilt for his acts—sleeping with Chandri and partaking food in the temple feast at a time when he is ritually unclean. Instead, in the new mode of thinking his experience leads him to, fixed distinctions between right and wrong—and hence the concept of guilt itself—are transcended. 'Roquentin is in revolt against a world that has revealed its relative nature in opposition to the absolute postulates he holds about reality, existence, experience, and so on. Praneshacharya is in no such revolt. His experience of the world calls into question his absolutist postulates in terms of which he has functioned as a priest in his community' (Raval, 2005, p. 122). In Raval's view, therefore, while the novel seems at first to be about modernity versus tradition, it actually proceeds to attempt some form of reconciliation between them; this despite the fact that it is not easy, as the inconclusive ending of the novel suggests. 'In avoiding an ending that might be prematurely affirmative or optimistic, the narrative leaves the reader pondering the consequences of a tradition that has become a monstrous deadweight on a people who have not thought about whatever syncretist elements and flexibility there might be within that tradition' (p. 124). Nalini Natarajan links the question of modernity with the novel's representation of caste and gender, to argue that it reveals some of the historical tensions that made colonial modernity an incomplete project in India. *Samskara* is set in a key moment of this project, marked by Gandhi's anti-colonialism, the secularism of the Congress Party and the new consumerism that brought products like the gramophone to the Indian middle class. While these may seem at first to break with tradition, they actually continue to serve traditional norms. In her analysis of the novel, she foregrounds the way in which its representation of modernity lies only on the surface while deeper down the old social disparities and erasures of caste and gender, which are 'constitutively connected to the emergence of the Brahmin modern', continue unchallenged (Natarajan, 2005, p. 151). Natarajan's argument is that, since the sources of brahmin modernity, as seen in Naranappa and Praneshacharya, are already complicit with a tradition they are posed to confront, 'the text's meanings cannot be understood by recourse to unchanging "traditional" meanings' of caste and gender (p. 172). Sharon Pillai, too, questions the thesis that the novel is about tradition and modernity. The 'central dialectic in *Samskara* is not between tradition and modernity but between two varieties of traditional thinking: namely, desire for the Good, identified with the Upanishadic concept of *shreyas*; and desire for the Pleasing, identified with the Upanishadic concept of *preyas*' (Pillai, 2014, p. 98, italics in original). The first refers to the idea of the human being as combining spirituality and morality in an ideal of virtuous life, while the second holds pleasure to be a primary good, realised in a life of sensual engagement. While this may seem to coincide with the Western binary of asceticism/hedonism, Pillai traces it through texts in the Hindu tradition. Praneshacharya, who leads a 'life commendably lived' according to an ideal of 'ascetic purity', (p. 99), stands for *shreyas*; while Naranappa, with his 'prodigious appetite for the three Ms of conservative brahmin horror, as it were—*madira* (wine), *mamsa* (meat), and *maithuna* (copulation)' (p. 104, italics in original), stands for *preyas*. Unlike Natarajan, Pillai argues that it is not modernity, either in its European or incomplete Indian colonial form, which is central to the novel's world-view but two contending forms of traditional thinking that derive from a dialectics of *tyaga-bhoga* and *deva-asura*. Like Raval, she argues that this dialectic enables the author to think through the traditional if it 'is to survive and become revitalized' (p. 115)

Critics have noted, too, the allegorical structure of the novel. *Samskara* is a 'contemporary re-working of ancient themes', writes Ramanujan, and is allegorical in its allusions to mythology and its characterisation. 'The characters come in sets: eg. Praneshacharya v. Mahabala-Naranappa-Shripati; their lower caste mistresses v. the brahmin women. Neatly, schematically, the opposites are mediated. Praneshacharya merges with his opposite number through Chandri, the latter's lover; the Acharya's erotic description of a classical heroine rouses Shripati, and he makes love to an outcaste woman on the riverbank' (Ramanujan, 1976, pp. 122–124). But the setting of the novel is realistic in its representation of the way of life in a south Indian village of pre-independence times. In its theme, characterisation and use of allegory and realism, the novel shows a dialectical form, a point that other critics agree with. Thus, for Gupta the novel 'dramatizes a conflict between two extreme ways of life, the ascetic and the hedonistic', (1980, p. 20) one represented by the ideal brahmin, Praneshacharya, and the other by his antagonist, Naranappa. In Mukherjee's view the principal opposition is between '[a] direct involvement in the sensuous aspects of life and a detachment through the denial of the senses' (2005, p. 86), at first externalised in the contrast between Naranappa and Praneshacharya and later internalised in the dualities of Praneshacharya's experience. Pillai argues that the theme of *Samskara* is the reconciliation of *shreyas* and *preyas*, desire for the Good and desire for the Pleasing, first signified in the contrast between Praneshacharya and Naranappa and later in Praneshacharya's irresolvable dilemma.

Critical discussion of *Samskara*, therefore, has been framed by the novel's use of realism and allegory and its dialectical form, its critique of caste and religious orthodoxy, and the theme of modernity versus tradition. Can a reading of the novel as outbreak narrative throw any light on how it works these into the plot? Ananthamurthy's comments on how he wrote *Samskara* and the fact that the outbreak remains pervasive all through the text, suggest that plague is not just circumstantial or incidental to it. In the rest of the chapter, I will try to bring out the way the theme of plague connects with the broader social and metaphysical concerns of the novel. I will start with the history of plague in south India at the turn of the twentieth century, as a context for reading *Samskara*.

4.2. Plague Outbreaks in Mysore State

As it spread from Bombay to Madras after 1897, the epidemic was not marked by such incidents as in Pune, though anti-plague operations did cause occasional inconvenience. First, the outbreaks in the South, which recurred almost every year, were not as severe as that in the west, and could therefore be managed by less stringent methods. Secondly, popular resistance in Bombay Presidency and especially the assassination of Plague

Commissioner Rand led the colonial government to choose a more cautious and conciliatory approach to control its spread. 'As a consequence of the resistance encountered and the resulting reappraisal of its political priorities and administrative limitations', notes David Arnold, 'the Government of India made a series of compromises and concessions in its plague policy in 1898–99' (1993, p. 233). Coercive measures like the use of soldiers to carry out house inspections, body searches and forced removal to hospitals and segregation camps were either abandoned or carried out by consulting the local leaders and with their help. Plague in the South, therefore, came to be framed in vastly different ways from that in Bombay presidency. This may be one reason why the colonial context never appears in *Samskara*; the other being that Mysore was not officially ruled by the British but was an independent state.

Plague entered the south through Bangalore on 12 August 1898. The servant of an employee of the Madras and Southern Maratha Railway who had been infected with the bacillus was the index case, and he passed on his infection to others in Bangalore's British-ruled Civil and Military Station. The CSM authorities immediately started surveillance, isolation of the diseased, and disinfection of their habitations, but the response in the princely-ruled parts of the city were slower (Dhanpal, 2023, pp. 467–468). Plague spread to Madras for the main part from Mysore state. In Madras city alone by 31 March 1899, 382 cases were reported to have come from Mysore (Madras Presidency, 1899, p. 208). The Census of 1911 noted that the most striking feature was the 'terrible mortality caused by the plague in Karnátak', with 148,000 deaths in Belgaum district and 144,000 in Dharwar (Census of India, 1912, pp. viii, 26). Thanks to timely action by the Madras administration and that of Mysore state, the spread was soon arrested. The plague operation was headed by municipalities with local representation, unlike that in Bombay, and the measures included eradication of rats besides the more usual steps to evacuate people from affected areas, disinfect premises, remove infected cases to plague hospitals and vaccinate the rest. Local leaders and members of the municipalities ensured the cooperation of the public in these measures. 'In the 1920s South India', writes Vempalli Raj Mahammadh, 'prominent measures including rat destruction, sun-disinfection of grain, use of cyanogas, calcium cyanide used as an effective rodenticide, and cleaning of houses, drains, grain stores and railway stations were adopted in the Presidency' (2020, p. 335). Over the next fifty years plague mortality in the South fell sharply, from 174,192 deaths in 1901–1921 to 52,297 in 1922–1942 and 8,267 in 1943–1945. In 1951, the number of reported deaths was only fifty-one (Mahammadh, 2020, pp. 329, 333, 337). The princely state of Mysore, which was headed by the Wadiyars under Commission Rule by the colonial government, was not far behind in its efforts to control the spread. Krishnaraja Wadiyar IV and his successor Jayachamaraja Wadiyar, who reigned from 1895 to 1947, were progressive-minded rulers and took all efforts to modernise their administration. By the 1940s, they had set up a well-organised public health system with a Bureau of Epidemiology and Communicable Diseases to control epidemics (Swamy, 1942, pp. 55–56). When the British constructed Fraser Town, a model plague-free locality, in Bangalore in 1910, Krishnaraja (who had supported its construction) carried out similar improvements in Mysore city. 'The Princely State of Mysore contested colonial authority by setting itself up as a centre of "modernisation" as a countermeasure to British paramountcy to prove that modern Indians could rule themselves better than any colonial state. This was achieved through advances in industry, engineering, and technology and when concerns for public health and hygiene arose from the plague, through municipal institutions.'[2] In recognition of such efforts the colonial government awarded Mysore the title 'best administered native state in India' (Dhanpal, 2023, pp. 490–491). When the plague outbreak that inspired Ananthamurthy to write *Samskara* occurred in Shivamogge in 1945, therefore, the situation was far different from what it had been in Mysore in 1898–99 or in Bombay in 1896–97.

[2] Krishnaraja Wadiyar IV appointed as his diwan the architect of modern India, Sir M. Visweswaraya in 1912, and the control of Spanish flu when it broke out in Mysore in 1918 has been largely credited to the latter's efforts.

The social understanding of plague at the time was largely constructed by three frameworks of meaning: (i) it was caused by a pathogen, *Yersinia pestis*, transmitted by rat fleas; (ii) it was caused by the action of supernatural agents like a goddess or a malevolent spirit; and (iii) it was a cosmological crisis resulting from moral transgression. The first was a modern biomedical explanation, the latter two traditional and cosmological. Plague operations in colonial Madras and princely Mysore illustrate the biomedical, in that they were founded primarily on preventing the effects of a natural agent. By the opening years of the twentieth century, as I have shown in the last chapter, a considerable amount of scientific information had been gathered regarding the cause, symptoms, prognosis and prevention of plague. By the 1940s the municipalities in Mysore state were well-equipped to deal with the disease, as the town-crier's announcement at Melige in *Samskara* shows (Ananthamurthy, 1976, p. 108). Alongside this biomedical frame, which was adopted mostly by the government and its public health agencies, there were other more traditional and popular explanations. A goddess variously known as Bombai Mai, Uramma and Plague-amma found worship in the regions that were most affected (Bhattacharyya, 1999, p. 56). Henry Whitehead reported in 1921 that temples of Plague-amma had been established in the South 'during the last ten years, as a result of the prevalence of plague', while Uramma (literally 'village-mother') found worship as a plague and cholera goddess mainly in Bellary district of Karnataka (Whitehead, 2020, pp. 21, 71). There was already in existence a centuries-old tradition of disease goddesses, like Sitala and Mariamma associated with smallpox and Ola Bibi/Ola Chandi with cholera, and when new epidemics broke out they were easily incorporated into it (Das, 2019, pp. 189–222; Das, 2021). When plague broke out in Bangalore and later Mysore city, Mariamma acquired new form as a plague goddess, with temples being dedicated to her worship (Ushadevi, 2001, p. 849). At Halasur village in Bangalore, for instance, a shrine was built for her in the name of Shri Plague Maheswari (Soman, 2016); while a similar shrine stands even now outside

Mysore Palace near Gun House (Satya, 2020). Significantly, both temples continue to draw devotees even if plague outbreaks have now become a thing of the past.[3] During the outbreak in Bombay Presidency at the end of the nineteenth century, there were rumours of plague as a divine visitation. The *Gujaráti* of 21 February 1897 carried an article which stated that it was the result of increasing immorality and disbelief in god, and that a 'holy ascetic living on the Himalayas' had written that it 'will spread to the whole country and continue to rage for three years, that after chastening the sinful, correcting the irreligious, guiding the mistaken and infusing religious zeal into the hearts of the atheists, it will vanish and cease to exist' (India Office Library and Records, 1897, p. 13).

4.3. Plague in *Samskara*

My purpose in recounting the social history of plague as a context for reading *Samskara* is not to show how closely *Samskara* approximates that history, but to show how the outbreak is integrally connected to the themes that the critical literature on the novel has emphasised. Let us first look at the three aetiological frameworks mentioned above. The lower-caste people living in the huts outside the agrahara believe that it is caused by a demon who must be appeased. 'If Pilla gets the Demon on him today', says Belli, 'we must ask about this. I'm quite scared, Chinni. What's all this, rats coming like an army to our poor pariah huts! Chowda and his wife popping off, snap! Like that! And now papa and mama trodden all over by the Demon' (Ananthamurthy, 1976, p. 51). She sacrifices a cock to the 'Demon' and promises a sheep next, 'yet both Belli's parents died the same night' (p. 91). The town-crier in Melige announces that there is an 'epidemic of Mari' in Shivamogge, naming it after the goddess Mariamma (p. 108). In contrast to this view of the disease as caused by a malevolent spirit or goddess, the brahmins of the agrahara see

[3] The last major outbreak was in Surat, Gujarat, almost three decades ago in 1994. It claimed more than fifty lives. Only two localised outbreaks have since been recorded in Shimla, Himachal Pradesh (in 2002, causing four deaths) and Uttarkashi, Uttarakhand (in 2004, causing three deaths).

it as punishment for transgression. When vultures alight on the rooftops, they take it as a sign of impending cosmic disaster. 'The orthodox brahmins were distraught, as if nothing in the lives to come would wash the filth of their day' (p. 53). These events are 'due to Naranappa's untimely death' and their 'dereliction of duty in not performing his final rites' (p. 89). The birds of carrion, the dead rats and the desolation of their agrahara are a sign to them that 'their protecting gods had left them to their own devices.' Their 'very life-breaths quaked' and they 'seemed to become one shapeless mass, hugging each other and shivering in the dark' (p. 65). Finally, there is Manjayya for whom the death of rats is sign of an outbreak of plague. Instead of being 'bound to some blind belief', he thinks, immediate steps should be taken to stop its spread. 'In his very practical brain, the decisions were well-formed already: one, to tell the municipality and get the dead body removed; two, to call in doctors and get everybody inoculated; three, to get rat exterminators and pumps, fill the ratholes with poison gas and stop them up; four, if necessary, to evacuate the people from the agrahara' (pp. 89–90). These, it will be recalled, were the steps taken by the public health authorities in Madras and Mysore to curb the outbreak. In fact, it is not Naranappa with his secular ideas and opposition to orthodoxy who is the novel's most representative modern character, it is Manjayya. Naranappa's iconoclasm, as Pillai argues, is 'a malignant outgrowth of tradition': all his acts of transgression are simply reactive inversions of that tradition and bear no significance without reference to it (2014, p. 115). While being outwardly respectful of traditional norms, Manjayya knows how to deal with the times when tradition fails and a more modern outlook is called for: 'Experienced in affairs as he was, in the exchanges, the markets, the law courts and the offices of Shivamogge, he'd just laughed at the other brahmins' explanations' (Ananthamurthy, 1976, p. 89). In short, it is the theme of plague that provides a focal point for the theme of modernity versus tradition in these passages, not Naranappa's heresies nor Praneshacharya's quasi-existentialism.

Plague also serves to focalise the juxtaposition of allegory and realism in *Samskara*. The accounts of plague in the novel bear strong resemblance to events in actuality such as the signs of impending epidemic, symptoms of disease and measures adopted to control the spread, based as they are on the outbreak in Shivamogge in 1945. Yet there are significant departures from realism that one can hardly fail to notice.[4] No one in Durvasapura is able to figure out why rats and vultures suddenly appear in the village, which seems strange for a people who had lived through recurrent, almost annual, outbreaks of plague. During the plague epidemic in Mysore city, writes Gouri Satya, the sight of dead rats falling from the roof would at once trigger fears of an impending outbreak: 'People would scream "rat has fallen, rat has fallen" (ili biddide, ili biddide) in the little town within the Palace Fort where resided most of the city's population' (2020). High fever and buboes were well-known symptoms of the disease by the 1940s, and it seems odd that no one in the agrahara could guess what these meant. In fact, the word 'plague' is not even mentioned in the novel till well into the plot, in Part III, when Manjayya alone makes the connection. Till this moment when the real cause of the deaths and the presence of vultures and dead rats is revealed, the narrative allows for the play of meanings that link the ominous events at Durvasapura to the theme of spiritual crisis. It is in these gaps in the novel's realistic texture that symbolisation takes place, to reconfigure it as allegory.

Finally, there is the temporal coincidence between the appearance of rats and vultures on the one hand, and Praneshacharya's ethical dilemma on the other, a fact that has not been noted in critical discussions of *Samskara*. This is what connects the plague story to the novel's critique of caste and religious orthodoxy. The rats and vultures appear at *more or less exactly the same time* as the Acharya's fall when, having failed to elicit Maruti's guidance, he has sex with Chandri

[4] In discussing realism and allegory in the novel, Ramanujan points to this fact: '"Realistically" speaking, there are many things wrong with the story' (1976, p. 124).

(Ananthamurthy, 1976, pp. 44–55).[5] This is followed in rapid succession by deaths in the pariah quarter and the deaths of Bhagirathi, Dasacharya, Padmanabhacharya and Gundacharya. The crisis in Durvasapura brought on by the rats, vultures and deaths does not simply parallel Praneshacharya's crisis; it serves as an analogue for it, or, in T.S. Eliot's now-unfashionable phrase, its 'objective correlative'—an artistic technique by which a character's inner emotion finds its exteriorised equivalent in an image. Eliot defines the objective correlative as 'a set of objects, a situation, a chain of events which shall be the formula of that *particular* emotion; such that when the external facts, which must terminate in sensory experience, are given, the emotion is immediately evoked' (1934, p. 145, italics in original). Praneshacharya's ethical crisis, which is so deeply subjective that it can only be rendered in internal monologue and free indirect discourse,[6] finds its analogue in the shock of sudden inexplicable deaths and the visceral sensation of vultures tearing into dead rats in the agrahara, the din of gongs and conches, and the stench

[5] The film version of *Samskara* conveys this simultaneity much more explicitly than the novel.

[6] The term 'free indirect discourse' refers to a mode of third-person narration that is midway between direct and indirect speech. It is generally used 'to present vividly the flow of thought through a character's mind' (Leech & Short, 2007, p. 270). It is somewhat like stream-of-consciousness narration, as the character's thoughts are not mediated by the voice of the narrator. A good example is the following passage that shows Praneshacharya looking at the sky and thinking of eventide in the agrahara:

> Praneshacharya looked up. The long evening of a summer day. Streaks of red on the west. Line after line of white birds returning to their nests. Down below, at the edge of the tank, a stork is gurgling. It's almost time for lighting the lamps. How many days ago was it that the lamps were lit in the agrahara, that the returning evening cows and calves were tied up and milked, and the milk offered to the Lord? (Ananthamurthy, 1976, p. 115)

Praneshacharya has just left the temple feast and is washing his hands at the tank. The passage expresses his thoughts without either quotation marks, as in direct speech, or an introducing clause, as in reported speech. The reader is invited to see the evening through Praneshacharya's eyes, hear the sounds through his ears, and ruminate along with him. Free indirect discourse is a rhetorical technique that is used to foreground a character's subjectivity within the overall structure of objective narration.

of a rotting corpse. The function of this analogical link is to make more *immediate* what is otherwise distanced and mediated by the Acharya's philosophical reflections. Relief from the crises can only be sought by cremating Naranappa's plague-ridden corpse. For the Acharya this seems to be the only solution: 'Maybe when the fire leaps and dances around Naranappa's dead body, there'll be a certain consolation.' He thinks of the 'torches lit for the night service' in Durvasapura (Ananthamurthy, 1976, p. 115); a little later, he hears from the temple the 'noises of gongs beaten, conches blown for worship' (p. 117), echoing an earlier moment when vultures alighted on the agrahara in the dawn: 'Downhearted, the brahmins blew their sacred conches and beat their gongs' (p. 65). The total effect of these sights and sounds is to merge in a surrealistic image the dualities of lamp-flame and cremation fire, the auspicious blowing of a conch in a temple and its inauspicious blowing to drive away vultures. It is at this enigmatic moment that Praneshacharya finally decides to return to Durvasapura, with Putta tagging along if he must (p. 117). But Naranappa has already been cremated, not by his caste-members but a Muslim and a low-caste prostitute. The novel, as Ramanujan puts it, ends 'without the usual climax or closure' (1976, p. 122). It brings no consolation either in resolving the crisis or offering respite from the epidemic, which possibly still rages on to claim more lives. The close connection between ethical crisis and epidemic crisis with which the novel had opened is thus maintained right till its end.

The film version of *Samskara* brings this out more explicitly. I will focus on a seven-and-a-half minute sequence that occurs in the middle of the film, from the shot of the vultures descending on the agrahara to that of Praneshacharya and Chandri making love (Reddy, 1970, 0:39:24–0:46:55). Several lines of action are presented in this brief sequence: the Acharya visiting the temple to seek guidance from Maruti and Chandri following him in the hope of a decision; Dasacharya visiting Manjayya's house to sate his hunger without others knowing; rats dying in the agrahara, vultures alighting on the rooftops to eat the dead rats and the brahmins trying to shoo them away; Maruti's silence and the

Acharya's hopelessness, Chandri's sympathy for him and their desperate lovemaking. The sequence rapidly crosscuts between these lines of action, to condense them into an integrated whole that juxtaposes the crisis of the outbreak with that of the agrahara following Naranappa's death and Praneshacharya's personal crisis of faith. These are presented as disparate events happening in discrete times and spaces in the novel because of the temporal structuring of its story, a limitation that all verbal narratives admit. Film, in the way it combines story, image and sound, is able to overcome this limitation by juxtaposing and merging time and space through the technique of montage. In reconstructing the verbal into the audio-visual, film adaptations reorganise, reconfigure and edit their stock to render visible and explicit spatio-temporal linkages that are obscure in the verbal medium. They do not simply translate an originally verbal text into cinema; they are interpretations that bring out meanings implicit in the original.

Samskara the film follows, more or less closely, *Samskara* the novel in terms of its plot trajectory but departs significantly in its ending. In the film, Naranappa's corpse has not been cremated till Praneshacharya returns. Chandri tries to persuade Seshappa, the cartman, to help her cremate Naranappa but he refuses because he cannot touch a brahmin body. There is no Ahmad Bari, the fish merchant, who performs the cremation in the novel. The novel ends with Praneshacharya getting into the cart that will take him to his village, but the film extends the story beyond this to his arrival at Durvasapura and meeting with Chandri. The final shot is of flames going up, implying that together they have cremated Naranappa.[7] Why does it provide a resolution that the novel refuses, closing off what in the original is an open ending? There may be several reasons for this. One, it may be because a

[7] There is another change, too: Praneshacharya confesses to Putta that on the very night his wife died he had sex with a prostitute, and that he has polluted the temple feast by partaking of it. Upset by this, Putta decides not to tarry with him any longer and sets off elsewhere. In the novel, no such confession happens, and Praneshacharya's secret remains with him. In my view, the film makes this change to show how even the pleasure-loving Putta, who has no compunction introducing Praneshacharya to

film that ends without resolving its crisis does not appeal to most viewers, who are not looking for metaphysical conundrums but emotional satisfaction.[8] Two, because the story has been building up to this ending as its most logical closure. It has emphasised the need to cremate Naranappa as the original issue that leads to the crisis and it must be resolved, not disposed off midway. The third, and in my view the most plausible, reason is that in resolving the plot it brings together the two central themes of the story—the outbreak of plague and the crisis of *samskara*. As Praneshacharya is on his way to his village, the cartman tells him: 'We left the fair when we heard that plague has broken out in Shimoga. Is that why you are also leaving? Haven't you heard that in Durvasapura also there is plague? Nobody will be there.' 'There is somebody there, waiting for me', replies Praneshacharya (Reddy, 1970, 1:42:11–1:42:25). When he enters the agrahara, a dying Gundacharya sees him and calls out for help. In the penultimate shot a bird flies and settles down on an abandoned hut. These scenes indicate that the plague is still raging, thus keeping the epidemic theme in focus while closing the theme of moral crisis.

4.4. Outbreak and the Autoimmunitary Function

Let me now turn to the only essay I found on the theme of plague in *Samskara*, Ganaa Jayagopalan's 'Spatial Pathologies: The Biopolitics of Disease, Death, and the Caste-Body in Ananthamurthy's *Samskara*: *A Rite for a Dead Man*'. Her argument is that the link between caste and religious orthodoxy on the one hand and the outbreak of plague on the other can

the prostitute Padmavati, conforms to orthodox moral norms. It thereby intensifies the Acharya's sense of moral isolation from the rest of the community.

[8] This was what prompted Vijay Anand in his adaptation of R.K. Narayan's *Guide* to change the ending of the novel. Narayan's novel ends ambiguously, implying but not showing the death of Raju the protagonist, while Anand's film ends with his death and cremation. Narayan, who was aggrieved by this change, wrote in his autobiography that it was solely for financial reasons, 'to placate eleven financiers who saw the final copy of the film tightly clutching the money bags and would not part with the cash unless a satisfactory mourning scene was added' (1974, pp. 174–175).

be best understood through the concepts of social immunity and autoimmunity. Briefly, immunity refers to a defensive function of a body, biological or social, that protects it from invasion by an 'other'. In the immunology of disease the 'other' is a microbe that enters the body, bypassing its defences. Autoimmunity is a dysfunction of the immune apparatus by which it turns, not against the invading microbe, but against its own cells to destroy them from within. In the sociological metaphor of immunity, the 'other' is the outsider who stands for everything that is antithetical to the norms of society—political, ethical, religious, cosmological—which the social body must neutralise and expel in order to maintain its integrity and protect itself from risk. Social autoimmunity occurs when this function turns against those within society and ends in a crisis that disintegrates the very norms that guarantee social integrity. The paradox of autoimmunity results from what Roberto Esposito calls a 'hypertrophy' of the immunitary apparatus[9] that is supposed to secure the body/society against risk: 'Instead of adapting the protection to the actual level of risk, it tends to adapt the perception of risk to the growing need for protection—making protection itself one of the major risks' (Esposito, 2011, pp. 15–16). An instance of this is the witch-hunting of marginal populations by the state in the name of national security during times of political instability or epidemic crisis. Etymologically 'immunity' is the reverse of 'community', thus providing a link between the biological concept and its social metaphor. Both terms derive from the Latin root *munus*, which variously refers to a gift, an obligation or a duty. Community is established when all its members acknowledge and bear responsibility for the common *munus* in mutual exchange of gifts (objects, labour, knowledge, etc.), in sharing collective obligations and duties. Immunity is that which exempts some of its members from the cycles of mutual

[9] By 'immunitary apparatus' Esposito means the function by which a community excludes or ex-communicates those perceived to threaten it. It is coterminous with the social impulse that binds people together in the community: 'there is no community without some kind of immunitary apparatus' (Esposito, 2011, p. 16).

exchange and sharing. In political terms, for instance, it refers to the privilege that a sovereign enjoys in being exempted from the rule of law that applies to all others in a country. But that is its positive valence: negatively it can mean the breaking of all ties to the community. 'Whereas *communitas* opens, exposes, and turns individuals inside out, freeing them from their exteriority, *immunitas* returns individuals to themselves, encloses them once again in their own skin' (Esposito, 2013, p. 49).

Jayagopalan arrives at the concepts of immunity and autoimmunity by way of a different route, to argue that the immunising mechanism of the agrahara and its caste-body by which it excludes all that is foreign and polluting turns against itself in the figures of Naranappa and Praneshacharya. Naranappa brings into the agrahara not only an actual pathogen but equally 'pathogenic' acts that threaten to undermine its integrity—drinking alcohol, consuming meat, cohabiting with a low-caste prostitute, entertaining Muslims, killing the sacred fish of the temple pond, and instigating the young men of the agrahara to flout its norms. He triggers the autoimmune function 'by ushering the outside into the community, affecting its immunity' (Jayagopalan, 2022, p. 144). Praneshacharya, on the other hand, triggers the autoimmune function by questioning from within its ethical codes, thus providing 'the body politic an opportune moment to turn inward' (p. 141). In the one case autoimmunity is inflected towards a self-destructive negative pole, in the other towards a transformative positive pole. For Jayagopalan, the novel's transformative potential lies in the latter. Jayagopalan derives this 'bipolar' character of autoimmunity from Jacques Derrida's arguments, especially in his interview with Giovanna Borradori on the World Trade Centre attack on 11 September 2001. Osama bin Laden, who was responsible for the attack, was trained by the security apparatus of the US, and Derrida reads it as an instance of the autoimmune function that both turns against the secular democratic ethos and yet contains the possibility of rethinking its politics, towards a social order that no longer casts out the 'other' but includes it unconditionally: 'Without this thought of pure hospitality … we would not even have an idea of the other, of the alterity of the other, that is, of someone who enters into our lives without having been invited' (2003, p. 129). Derrida concedes that this is perhaps idealistic and may not be possible in practice, but the only way out of such ethical aporia is to think in terms of what he calls the 'impossible' possibility (p. 134).

While the conceptual framework of Jayagopalan's essay is persuasive, some of her core arguments on *Samskara* could have been developed further. First, immunity and autoimmunity are functions of the system (in this case, the social order) and not of particular individuals: to establish that Naranappa and Praneshacharya bear autoimmune significance in the narrative, one needs to first examine what makes them do so. Why does Naranappa turn against the social body? Was it merely because he was hedonistic by nature and valued pleasure above everything else? Are hedonism and ethical restraint parts of the same system, as Pillai contends? The novel provides a clear explanation of Naranappa's contempt for brahminism. His closest relatives in the community, Lakshmanacharya and Garudacharya, exploit him by manipulating the system to grab his inheritance. He was once a 'good' brahmin, married to Lakshmana's sister-in-law and abiding by the rules of the agrahara. 'If I were still a brahmin, that Garudacharya would have washed me down with his *aposhana* water. Or that Lakshmana—he loves money so much he'll lick a copper coin off a heap of shit. He will tie another wilted sister-in-law round my neck, just to get at my property. And I'd have had to cut my hair to a tuft, smear charcoal on my face, sit on your verandah and listen to your holy-holy yarns' (Ananthamurthy, 1976, p. 22, italics in original). In other words, Naranappa turns against the community in reaction to its rigid immunitary codes and becomes, as Pillai puts it, its 'malignant outgrowth' (2014, p. 115). Unlike Naranappa, Praneshacharya does not turn the immunitary code against the community (except when he partakes of the temple feast in his polluted state), but questions its legitimacy. And he does so because the code fails him in not providing an answer to the problem of Naranappa's cremation and in prejudging his relation with Chandri as ethically wrong. In the latter case, it is significant that he is in a conflict between the sense of wrongdoing that the code imposes on him and a countering sense of release from this imposition. In brief, if Naranappa and Praneshacharya bear autoimmunitary meaning it is not because of their personal characters but as a result of the immunitary system itself in its hypertrophic rigidity.

Secondly, it is not clear in the novel that autoimmune reaction causes the destruction of the community. In fact, it is not clear at all that the agrahara is destroyed and not rendered temporarily unstable till the epidemic declines. Mahabala's abandonment of the brahminical code leads to his own alienation from the community and not that of the community from itself. Naranappa for all his antigenic threat remains a brahmin still, even after death. In the novel this is kept deliberately ambiguous if we take his cremation by Ahmad Bari as signifying, in some sense, the end of his brahmin identity. But the film removes any such ambiguity for he is given a proper brahmin cremation by none other than Praneshacharya, the community's highest embodiment of brahmin virtue. While the immunitary paradigm is certainly a productive way to read the novel's anti-brahminism, there is a limit point beyond which the corpus regains its balance. This point, which is hinted at though never actually shown, is a transformed brahminism or what Radhakrishnan calls 'trans-brahminism' (2005, p. 141). Jayagopalan's argument would have been more convincing if she had pursued this idea.

My final reservation concerns Jayagopalan's insistence that the outbreak's 'cosmological significance overwrites any possible scientific explanation to the event' (Jayagopalan, 2022, p. 148). What about Manjayya's view of the outbreak, and his practical approach to its control? This is not an insignificant question for it means that, if the cosmological overwrites the scientific, Ananthamurthy is actually reinforcing the cosmological schema and its immunitary apparatus even as he tries to dismantle it. My view is that *Samskara* pushes that schema to think beyond its limits, just as it does with norms of brahmin conduct. The novel does not subscribe to the supernatural view of the outbreak, but neither does it wholly embrace Manjayya's naturalistic explanation. By juxtaposing the two paradigms, one biological–naturalistic and the other cosmological–mythic, it brings them into critical conjuncture and compels us to think beyond a reductive reading of either. This is analogous with Praneshacharya's internal conflict during the liminal phase that he passes through on the road to Melige, before he decides to return to the agrahara and cremate Naranappa. His ruminations in the last part of the novel do not reassert the authority of the brahminical code but neither do they reject it. The novel does not end with a clear resolution, but the film does. In returning the code to its place, the film makes it clear that it still retains relevance but is in need of transformation. The transformation happens when Praneschacharya, the true brahmin, and Chandri, the low-caste prostitute, together cremate Naranappa, the apostate brahmin. To better understand Praneshacharya's '*rite de passage*' as Ramanujan puts it (1976, p. 122), let me turn to the anthropology of liminality and social change.

In *Dramas, Fields, and Metaphors*, Victor Turner discusses the process by which religious culture transforms itself from within by an internal dialectic. His argument is that in any society there are two tendencies at work. One is the tendency of the structure to consolidate itself, to close itself off against the outside. By structure, he means the hierarchical arrangement of 'mutually dependent institutions', religion and caste being two of these in the Indian context, and the 'institutional organisation of social positions' in accordance with social norms. Structures 'tend to produce distance and inequality, often leading to exploitation' of one group by another (Turner, 1974, p. 172). The other tendency is what he calls 'anti-structure' or 'communitas'—a radical openness that goes beyond institutional and social roles. It is 'spontaneous' and 'immediate' without norms and institutions to mediate and regulate it. 'Structure, or all that holds people apart, defines their differences, and constrains their actions, is one pole of a charged field, for which the opposite pole is communitas, or anti-structure, the egalitarian "sentiment for humanity"' (p. 174). Social transformation happens when communitas opens up relationships in a temporary passage from one kind of structural arrangement to another—a more liberatory one. Borrowing the term from Arnold van Gennep's theory of initiation, he calls this temporary phase 'liminality'. In van Gennep's account of the initiatory rite, the liminal stage is metaphorically described as a 'death' and 'rebirth'—death marking the separation from the old social role and rebirth, the entry into the new. During initiation, the child undergoes a ritual death symbolised by bodily mutilation such as scarring or circumcision, after which follows a symbolic rebirth: 'Where the novice is considered dead, he is resurrected and taught how to live, but differently than in childhood' (van Gennep, 1960, p. 75). In adapting this ritual structure to the context of social change, Turner stresses its symbolism: 'Symbols and metaphors found in abundance in liminality represent various dangerous ambiguities of this ritual stage, since the classifications on which order normally depends are annulled or obscured' (Turner, 1974, p. 173). If we take Ramanujan's cue that *Samskara's* 'story moves very much like a *rite de passage*' (1976, p. 122), one cannot fail to see the resonance that Gennep's and Turner's words have with Praneshacharya's 'Trishanku' state, when he finds himself 'hung suspended between two truths' (Ananthamurthy, 1976, p. 85); his symbolic rebirth in the lap of Chandri; and his intiation into communitas in the Melige temple festival where all rules and distinctions are temporarily flouted.[10] Far from rejecting the social code, therefore, *Samskara* anticipates its transformation, which is how its film adaptation ends.

The concept of immunity need not necessarily follow the logic that a particular theory of the immune system lays down for it,

[10] Putta, the malera who is half-brahmin and half-low-caste, acts as the master of initiation. In the film, as I have pointed out in footnote seven above, he turns away from Praneshacharya when he learns of his deeds, thus showing how the brahminical code continues to have its hold on even those who are ambiguously placed within it.

in which immunity is that which necessarily excludes the 'other'. Can we find an instance of a body that reverses the immunitary logic and is *inclusive* of 'otherness' instead of excluding it? In *Bios*, Esposito gives the example of childbirth. What is inside the mother's womb is simultaneously its own and foreign, in the sense that the foetus carries her germ cells as well as those of its father. Childbirth is based on an enigmatic relation between the maternal immune system and the foetus that is both the same and the other. It dissolves the difference between sameness and alterity, so that the foetus is both part of the mother and yet outside her. The uterus in which it lies separated from the rest of the mother's body, is itself within the latter. Gestation suppresses the immunitary apparatus by a natural process, without the immunosuppressants that organ transplant needs, in order to *incorporate* that which is not the corpus. As Esposito writes: 'Once again it is the "norm of life" that is in play, but according to an order that, rather than circumscribing life within the limits of the norm, opens the norm to the infinite unpredictability of life' (2008, p. 190). It is pertinent that Praneshacharya's self-transformation is figuratively presented as a rebirth, as he lies cradled in Chandri's lap: 'It felt as though he'd turned over and fallen into his childhood, lying in his mother's lap and finding rest there after great fatigue' (Ananthamurthy, 1976, p. 59). In the metaphor of birth the two poles of the body's relation to what is not itself—immunity and community, or the social code that closes it and that which opens it—converge, become indistinguishable, and life responds affirmatively to its unforeseen possibilities.

The paradigm of immunity in this positive inflection finds uncanny parallel in the science of the microbe–host interrelationship. Microbial theory explains how the entry of a microbe into the host's body results in one of four basic outcomes: colonisation, commensality, elimination and disease. Colonisation refers to an outcome in which the microbe's presence in the host's body does not produce any specific immune reaction or infection—that is, the 'other' neither destroys the 'self' nor is destroyed in its turn. Commensality refers to the outcome in which host cells and the microbe adjust to each other—that is, the 'self' and the 'other' learn to coexist. Elimination refers to the overpowering of the microbial 'other' by the immune system of the 'self', while disease refers to the reverse process in which the 'other' overpowers the 'self'. (Casadevall & Pirofski, 2000). Thus, microbe and host coexist in the first two outcomes, while they are antagonistic in the last two. If antagonism is one pole of the microbe–host relation, coexistence is its other. Translated into social terms, its implication is a radical openness in which the polarity of 'self'/'other' is dissolved and transcended. Biology, therefore, provides an apt example for a dialectical model of social order based on immunity that is more inclusive of difference than the exclusionist model. Reading *Samskara* from this perspective invites us to explore the dialectic in Praneshacharya's reflections as an opening up of the moral code that may ultimately lead to its transformation.

4.4. Conclusion

The plot of *Samskara* was inspired by an outbreak of plague in Shimoga in 1945, which Ananthamurthy witnessed when he was a child. While writing the novel he watched Bergman's *The Seventh Seal*, an allegorical film about spiritual crisis set in plague-ravaged Europe. These two events, as he later recounted, provided the point-of-departure for the novel.

Critical reception of *Samskara*, however, has by and large ignored the plague story and has focused almost entirely on its portrayal of the brahmins of Durvasapura, the character of Naranappa and the ethical crisis that Praneshacharya undergoes after he has sex with Chandri. In this chapter I have argued that the story of the plague outbreak not only inaugurates the narrative, providing its motive force, it also provides a perspective from which we can develop new insights on the novel. In the way the characters respond to the outbreak, the two different explanatory paradigms—one biomedical and the other cosmological—that have framed the social understanding of epidemic disease in India are revealed. In the novel these are polarised as modern and traditional, thus serving to contextualise the broader dialectic of modernity versus tradition that structures the narrative. Ananthamurthy deploys two contrasting styles, the realistic and the allegorical, in constructing the significance of the outbreak and the events that follow it. Broadly speaking, his account of plague in *Samskara* tends to follow closely the history of the epidemic as it unfolded in south India. There are, however, significant departures from this, and it is in these departures, in the gap they create between the realistic texture of the narrative and its symbolic structure, that allegory finds itself at play. Plague, in other words, provides the ground on which *Samskara* constructs its allegorical form. Finally, there is in the story's emplotment an important link between the outbreak and Praneshacharya's crisis of faith. Signs of the outbreak such as rats dying and vultures descending on the agrahara appear at almost the same time that Praneshacharya makes love to Chandri. Soon after this people start dying with shocking rapidity and seemingly without reason. The plague story thus provides an image that correlates with the deeply subjective conflicts that Praneshacharya undergoes as he re-examines his faith in the brahminical code and his identity as a true brahmin. They serve to concretise the abstract theme of brahmin ideology and its immanent contradictions, as Praneshacharya questions the ethicality of the life he has led and the virtues he has practised. This correlation is brought out explicitly in the film version of *Samskara*, in a montage sequence that occurs at its middle and links spatially and temporally the signs of impending plague outbreak, the crisis of the agrahara and Praneshacharya's fall. The ending of the film, which differs from that of the novel, also brings into convergence the two central themes of the story: the epidemic crisis and the ethical crisis of its protagonist.

Another insight that the plague story opens up is the immunitary inflections of the caste–religion code in Naranappa and Praneshacharya, one tending to destroy the social order and the other to transform and revitalise it. It is the systemic rigidity of the code that impels each of them to adopt a different course in response to it. The metaphor of immunity, however, emphasises its negative function. Esposito gives it a positive inflection using the metaphor of childbirth that suppresses the mother's immunitary apparatus to receive the foetus as both its self and other. This is borne out by recent thinking in immunobiology, where antagonism between the self and the other is only one of two alternative relationships, another being coexistence. By drawing on these ideas, the chapter argues that the characterisation of Praneshacharya envisages the second alternative. Praneshacharya's difficult passage from orthodoxy to, what verges on, ethical flexibility is an immunitary logic that preserves rather than destroys, anticipating an inclusive social order. Treating the outbreak in *Samskara* as a focaliser, thus, enables a perspective that illuminates the novel's broad social concerns.

References

A film and its censorship. (1970, January 3). *The Indian Express*, p. 10. https://news.google.com/newspapers?nid=P9oYG7HA76QC&dat=19700103&printsec=frontpage&hl=en

Aithal, S.K. (1981). Of culture and cadaver: Anantha Murthy's *Samskara*. *Journal of South Asian Literature*, *16*(2), 83–88.

Ananthamurthy, U.R.(1976). *Samskara: A rite for a dead man* (A.K. Ramanujan, Trans.). Oxford University Press.

Ananthamurthy, U.R. (2005). How I wrote *Samskara*. In K.C. Baral, D.V. Rao & S.P. Rath (Eds.), *U.R. Anantha Murthy's Samskara: A critical reader* (pp. 69–71). Pencraft International.

Ananthamurthy, U.R. (2007). Samvatsar lecture: Five decades of my writing. *Indian Literature*, *51*(5/ 241), 112–135.

Arnold, D. (1993). *Colonizing the body: State medicine and epidemic disease in nineteenth-century India*. University of California Press.

Bhattacharyya, N.N. (1999). *The Indian mother goddess*. 3rd ed. Manohar Publishers and Distributors.

Casadevall, A. & Pirofski, L.A. (2000). Host-pathogen interactions: Basic concepts in microbial commensalism, colonization, infection, and disease. *Infection and Immunity*, *68*(12), 6511–6518.

Census of India. (1912). *Census of India, 1911. Volume VII. Bombay, Part I: A report, by P.J. Mead and G.L. Macgreggor*. Government Central Press.

Das, D.K. (2019). Teaching AIDS: *The cultural politics of HIV disease in India*. Springer Nature Singapore.

Das, D.K. (2021). Corona devi: Epidemic and the disease-goddess tradition. *Sambalpur Studies in Literatures and Cultures*, *6*, 11–24.

Derrida, J. & Borradori, G. (2003). Autoimmunity: Real and symbolic suicides. In G. Borradori (Ed.), *Philosophy in a time of terror: Dialogues with Jürgen Habermas and Jacques Derrida* (pp. 85–136). University of Chicago Press,.

Dhanpal, S. (2023). The making of a model town: Planning in a princely city and the all-India sanitary conferences. *Planning Perspectives*, *38*(3), 467–497.

Eliot, T.S. (1934). *Selected essays*. 2nd ed. Faber and Faber Limited.

Esposito, R. (2011). *Immunitas: The protection and negation of life* (Z. Hanafi, Trans.). Polity Press.

Esposito, R. (2013). *Terms of the political: Community, immunity, biopolitics* (R.N. Welch, Trans.). Fordham University Press.

Esposito, R. (2008). *Bios: Biopolitics and philosophy* (T. Campbell, Trans.). University of Minnesota Press.

Gupta, R.K. (1980). The 'fortunate fall' in U.R. Anantha Murthy's *Samskara*. *The International Fiction Review*, *7*(1) 20–23.

India Office Library and Records. (1897). *Report on native papers for the week ending February 27, 1897*. https://jstor.org/stable/saoa.crl.25636167

Jayagopalan, G. (2022). Spatial pathologies: The biopolitics of disease, death, and the caste-body in Ananthamurthy's *Samskara*: *A rite for a dead man*. In S. Venkateasan, A. Chatterjee, A.D. Lewis, & B. Callender (Eds.), *Pandemics and epidemics in cultural representation* (pp. 137–150). Springer Nature Singapore.

Leech, G. & Short, M. (2007). *Style in fiction: A linguistic introduction to English fictional prose*. 2nd ed. Pearson Education Limited.

Madras (India : Presidency). (1899). *Report on the Administration of the Madras Presidency, during the year 1898-99*. Part II. Departmental Chapters. Government Press. https://jstor.org/stable/saoa.crl.34294709

Mahammadh, V.L. (2020). Plague mortality and control policies in colonial south India, 1900–1947. *South Asia Research*, *40*(3), 323–343.

Mambrino, J. (1959). The seventh seal. *CrossCurrents*, *9*(1), 89–91.

Misra, N., Sharma, V.L., & Kaul, R.K. (1982). Sanskara: Three critics on Anantha Murthy's novel. *Indian Literature, 25*(5), 98–122.

Mukherjee, M. (2005). *Samskara.* In K.C. Baral, D.V. Rao & S.P. Rath (Eds.), *U.R. Anantha Murthy's* Samskara*: A critical reader* (pp. 82–99). Pencraft International.

Naipaul, V.S. (1977). *India: A wounded civilization.* Penguin Books.

Narayan, R.K. (1974). *My days.* Indian Thought Publication.

Natarajan, N. (2005). Gender and caste: Modernity in U.R. Anantha Murthy's *Samskara.* In K.C. Baral, D.V. Rao & S.P. Rath (Eds.), *U.R. Anantha Murthy's* Samskara*: A critical reader* (pp. 151–178). Pencraft International.

Pillai, S. (2014). Back to the future: Tracking the moral imperative in, of, and through 'Samskara'. *College Literature, 41*(2), 97–119.

Prabhakara, M.S. (2014). U.R. Ananthamurthy: Writer, iconoclast, public intellectual. *Economic and Political Weekly, 49*(36), 26–27.

Punitha, S. (1976). 'Samskara does not exist in free space … it exists in my context': In conversation with U. R. Ananthamurthy. In U.R. Ananthamurthy, *Samskara: A rite for a dead man* (A.K. Ramanujan, Trans.; pp 135–143). Oxford University Press.

Radhakrishnan, R. (2005). *Samskara*: A reading. In K.C. Baral, D.V. Rao & S.P. Rath (Eds.), *U.R. Anantha Murthy's* Samskara*: A critical reader* (pp. 135–150). Pencraft International.

Ramanujan, A.K. (1976). Afterword. *Samskara: a rite for a dead man.* (A.K. Ramanujan, Trans.; pp. 119–125). Oxford University Press.

Raval, S. (2005). Interpreting cultural impasse in Anantha Murthy's *Samskara.* In K.C. Baral, D.V. Rao & S.P. Rath (Eds.) *U.R. Anantha Murthy's* Samskara*: A critical reader* (pp. 114–127). Pencraft International.

Reddy P. (Producer). (1970). *Samskara* [Film]. Rama Manohar Chitra.

Satya, G. (2020, March 27). Time to take a look at bubonic plague of 1896. *The star of Mysore.* https://starofmysore.com/time-to-take-a-look-at-bubonic-plague-of-1896/

Soman. S. (2014, August 14). Something could be plaguing Bangalore. *The Times of India.* https://timesofindia.indiatimes.com/city/bengaluru/something-could-be-plaguing-bengaluru/articleshow/53701526.cms

Swami, G.L. (1942). *Handbook series: Mysore state.* Mysore.

Turner, V. (1974). *Dramas, fields, and metaphors: Symbolic action in human society.* Cornell University Press.

Ushadevi, M.U. (2001). Famine in folklore: The case of the state of Mysore. *Proceedings of the Indian History Congress, 2000–2001, 61*(1), 848–851.

Van Gennep, A. (1960). *The rites of passage* (M.B. Vizedom & S.T. Kimball, Trans.). University of Chicago Press.

Whitehead, H. (2020). *The religious life of India: The village gods of south India*, 2nd ed. Gyan Publishing House.

5

Narratives of the Spanish Flu Pandemic

> Everybody knows that pestilences have a way of recurring in the world; yet somehow we find it hard to believe in ones that crash down on our heads from a blue sky.
>
> Camus, *The Plague*, 1948

In June 1918, close to the end of the First World War, a mysterious fever suddenly appeared in Bombay mostly in and around the dock area. Initially it did not claim many lives, but from September onwards it spread very rapidly throughout the country and the death toll increased sharply. Within the space of a few months an estimated number of fifteen to twenty million people died in India, a fifth of the total deaths across the world.[1] The disease, which possibly emerged in the United States and France, was subsequently named Spanish flu—not because it originated in Spain but due to the fact that Spain was the first country to declare it.[2] Countries engaged in the war did not

[1] Estimates of mortality due to Spanish flu in India vary widely. The first official report on the epidemic by the Sanitary Commissioner of India, F. Norman White, mentions it as 4,899,725 deaths, while more recent accounts mention a much larger figure. Siddharth Chandra, Goran Kuljanin and Jennifer Wray estimate it to be 13.88 million, and medical historian Mark Honigsbaum estimates a total of 18.5 million deaths (White, 1919, p. 4; Chandra, Kuljanin & Wray, 2012, p. 861; Honigsbaum, 2020, p. 27). These variations are due to the fact that records of mortality were not well-maintained at the time, and calculations had to be based on other sources of data.

[2] 'The Spring wave of influenza was first recorded in epidemic proportions in a US military camp in Kansas in early March 1918. It spread to the eastern seaboard and was then carried by US troops across the Atlantic to France in April. At about the same time the virus was taken to eastern China on trans-Pacific ships from the western coast of the USA. By May 1918 the virus reached neutral Spain to gain the popular but inaccurate soubriquet

report the outbreak because of the fear that it might demoralise their troops. By early 1920 it had claimed an estimated fifty to hundred million lives globally, turning out to be one of the most devastating pandemics in recorded history (Johnson & Mueller, 2002, p. 115). Curiously, though, it was also one of history's least remembered pandemics, as Pei-Chen Liao notes: 'the 1918 influenza was deemed a pandemic because of its global spread, but despite its heavy death toll, the influenza was quickly forgotten' (2022, p. 123). Five years after the pandemic, Andrew Balfour and Henry Scott devoted a brief chapter to it in *Health Problems of Empire*, but it was only in the 1970s with the publication of Alfred Crosby's *Epidemic and Peace, 1918* that the Spanish flu pandemic came to be studied in its own right and not just as an adjunct to the war. There are several reasons offered for this: preoccupations of the war, the abruptness of the outbreak and its decline, suppression of reports by the governments at war, and, as Catherine Belling argues, the psychological incapacity to process a trauma of such colossal dimensions: 'The First World War gave the West a lesson in the bleak meanings of human cruelty and destruction; the pandemic caused more physical damage but seemed to convey no meaning at all, overshadowed by the story of the war, with its enemies, its weapons of mass destruction, its battles, and its jubilant armistice' (2009, p. 56).

Collective apathy characterised the immediate response to the pandemic not only in the West but equally in India, at least insofar as its British administrators were concerned. In what was part reflection and part apology for the lapses of the colonial government, Assistant Health Officer of Bombay Municipality E. Selby Phipson wrote a few years after the pandemic:

> The preoccupations of a world war, the engrossing problems which have followed in its wake, and the epidemic prevalence of influenza on a considerable scale within British shores have so fully occupied our attention that the calamitous happenings

"Spanish flu"' (Killingray, 2003, p. 32). Mark Osborne Humphries (2014) cites three possible origins of the pandemic: the military camps in England and France, the Haskell County in the US and the seaport of Weihaiwei in China from where the Chinese Labour Force was recruited into the war, arguing that the last was the most likely origin.

> in India during 1918 may well have been somewhat obscured. Our minds, inured as it were, to the gigantic events of the past ten years, may have failed to appreciate fully the magnitude of the scourge which in 1918 swept over the length and breadth of India and, within the space of two months, slew at the latest computation no fewer than eight million of her people (1923, pp. 509–510).

For the Indian subjects of empire, there were other preoccupations as well: the financial burden of fighting a war that was not their own, food scarcity and rising prices, protests against the Rowlatt Committee's proposal to pass a draconian sedition act, popular dissatisfaction with the Montagu–Chelmsford report on reforms, demand for Home Rule, and, in November, the armistice and its implication for India's freedom. Reports on the pandemic had to share space with public debates on these issues, overshadowing its significance. Newspaper coverage largely concerned the failure of the colonial government in dealing with the influenza outbreak and the famine that coincided with it.

5.1. Epidemiological Reports

In what follows I give an account of the Spanish flu pandemic in India based on estimates provided by Phipson and F. Norman White, who was the sanitary commissioner of India, and not on revised estimates published later. My purpose is to examine how it was reported by those who observed it first hand and how they made sense of it. The pandemic broke out in India in two waves, the first in June and the second in September. In the first wave, 'the disease ran a mild course and the case mortality rate was almost insignificant' (White, 1919, p. 1). In the second wave, it caused severe respiratory tract infections that in most cases proved fatal. Within 'the space of four or five months', White notes in his report, the pandemic 'was responsible for the death of 2 per cent of the total population of British India' (p. 5).[3] While the first wave originated in Bombay, carried by sea from the war

[3] The total population of British India (which included India, Burma and Ceylon but excluded states like Mysore that were not directly administered by the British) was 238,026,240 in 1918, and the total deaths from influenza was 4,899,725 (White, 1919, p. 4).

zones of Europe, the second wave spread from the Deccan to the rest of the country (Phipson, 1918, p. 441; Phipson, 1923, p. 515). Mortality in Bombay Presidency peaked in October 1918, with 6 October accounting for 768 deaths, the highest per day mortality rate (Phipson 1923, p. 515). In the Central Provinces, nearly all of the total mortality of 791,000 deaths occurred during the second wave in October–November (White, 1919, p. 6). In Delhi province the total mortality was 23,175, with Delhi city recording on 26 October the highest number of deaths per day (418 deaths), while in Punjab the mortality for October and November exceeded eight lakhs (pp. 7–8). In Madras Presidency the total number of deaths attributed to influenza was 509, 667, with Madras city alone accounting for 3,481 deaths. During the three months between September to November the number of deaths in the province of Assam was estimated at 69,113, while in Bihar and Odisha it was 359,482 from July to November, and in Bengal for the corresponding period it was 213,098. The peak mortality in Bengal, however, was in December, but since the full data was not available by the time White compiled his report he did not include it (pp. 10–11). The Central Provinces suffered the worst with a death rate of 56.8 per thousand, followed by Delhi (56.6) and Bombay (45.9). The corresponding figures for the eastern and southern regions were comparatively lower, at 19 for Coorg, 12.7 for Madras, 11.4 for Assam, 10.3 for Bihar and Odisha, and 4.7 for Bengal (p. 4). In Mysore state, which was not directly administered by the British, the pandemic claimed 127,651 lives, at a rate of 22.37 deaths per thousand (p. 5). Despite these regional differences, however, influenza was widespread and spared no part of India.

Statistics of the influenza pandemic, however, fail to express the large-scale suffering that it caused, which can only be gauged from the subjective perceptions and interpretations inserted within the factual reports by Phipson and White. In his retrospective account of the pandemic in 1923, Phipson concludes with the following passage:

> It has been said that there is a soul of good in things evil, and if the experiences of 1918 have brought home to those

> voluntary workers, especially educated Indians of all classes who rendered such splendid service in a time of unprecedented stress, the distressing conditions under which the poor of Bombay continue to exist, it may be that Bombay may have in store for her a brighter history in the future than she has known in the past. In whatever hands her future destinies may lie, let us hope that the lessons of 1918, so hardly learnt, will not be easily forgotten. (1923, p. 519)

White, reporting on the mortality in various parts of the country, emphasises the plight of those who lost their kin: 'In Delhi Province, as in other parts of India, the disposal of the dead was a matter which tried the resources of all concerned. The heart-rending scenes witnessed by all who took an active part in endeavouring to combat the influenza outbreak in India in 1918 will never be forgotten' (1919, p. 7). White also quotes a paragraph from a report by the provincial sanitary commissioner of Punjab on the suffering of the people:

> The hospitals were choked so that it was impossible to remove the dead quickly enough to make room for the dying; the streets and lanes of the cities were littered with dead and dying people; the postal and telegraph services were completely disorganised; the train service continued, but at all the principal stations, dead and dying people were being removed from the trains; the burning ghats and burial grounds were literally swamped with corpses, while an even greater number awaited removal; the depleted medical service, itself sorely stricken by the epidemic, was incapable of dealing with more than a minute fraction of the sickness requiring attention: nearly every household was lamenting a death, and everywhere terror and confusion reigned. (pp. 8–9)

These words, the authors of which were government bureaucrats tasked with the job of producing factual data, provide an index to the scale of human tragedy they witnessed and the depth of feeling it aroused in them. 'Suffering', writes Belling, 'must be reconstituted within a story told by a narrator who can inhabit and convey the experience of the sufferer' (2009, p. 57). Stories like those in the reports cited above translate and transfigure numerical data into affective perceptions and meanings that numbers fail to express.

5.2. Newspaper Reports

Newspaper reports of the epidemic in India illustrate more clearly how narratives reconfigure representations of suffering from statistical abstractions into concrete human experience. 'Never within the memory of the oldest man living in Bombay', wrote the *Gujaráti* of 6 October 1918, 'has this city witnessed so many persons stricken down with fever and so many of them dying in a helpless condition' (India Office Library and Records, 1918d, p. 26). The *Praja Mitra and Pársi*, wrote the anonymous compiler of the *Report on Native Papers*, 'describes the present visitation of influenza in Bombay as a dismal calamity upon the city and remarks that the heavy toll of daily mortality it claims is nothing if not staggering' (India Office Library and Records, 1918c, p. 16). Obituaries of individuals who fell victim to the pandemic served to personalise mortality figures, often including touching details. *The Khalsa Advocate* of 8 October 1918, while noting that the flu was 'raging in a virulent form' in Amritsar and was 'exacting a very heavy toll of mortality', condoled the death of Sunder Singh Giani's wife on 4 September: 'She leaves behind 2 sons, 2 daughters, the youngest a son of only 3 months. She was a very accomplished lady quite in the prime of her youth about 28 years' (October, 1918).[4] In many of the newspaper stories the epidemic symbolises not only the personal tragedy of lives cut short by disease, but the disruption of community as well. The migration of the poor from rural districts into Bombay, the *Jam-e-Jamshed* wrote on 15 October 1918, spreads contagion in the city: 'The districts have let loose the famine-stricken over the city

[4] Obituaries are a conventional form of public announcement of death, one of their functions being to offer condolences to the family of the deceased. The other functions include personal information of the deceased, such as name, occupation, age, time and place of death as well as its cause, and details of the bereaved family (Fries, 1990). *The Khalsa Advocate* obituary cited above includes all these details except name, referring to the deceased woman as the wife of Sunder Singh Giani who is an assistant traffic superintendent, daughter-in-law of Jhanda Singh Giani, an advocate, and the daughter of Shamsher Singh, inspector general of police of Jodhpur state—in other words, the names of the men to whom she was linked by birth or marriage. It thus reflects a cultural norm under which women do not have a personal identity but are known by their relation to men.

of Bombay and the town become congested has become a hot-bed of disease and death' (India Office Library and Records, 1918f, p. 12). The panic caused by epidemic disease characteristically triggers accusations against marginal groups as carriers of infection, and migrants, especially those who are poor, often bear the greatest blame. At the same time, epidemic also serves to bring together people in relations of solidarity and support, thus rebuilding the very same community that it places at risk. Stories of epidemic outbreak, writes Priscilla Wald, frame disease as that which simultaneously threatens bonds of community and serves to restore them, in a chiasmatic intersection of human communication and communicable disease: they 'simultaneously forecast the imminent destruction and affirm the enduring foundations of community' (Wald, 2008, p. 10). On 12 November 1918, when the pandemic was on the wane, the *Kesari*, referring to the volunteers who did 'commendable work' in providing relief to the ailing, asked: 'Who are the real well-wishers of the masses? Is there love or hatred between the different communities in India? Who looked after the backward classes?' (India Office Library and Records, 1918h, p. 28) 'The philanthropic people of Guru Ram Das's Nagri', noted the *The Khalsa Advocate*, 'have done much in the way of affording relief to the poor and needy' (November, 1918). Even White and Phipson, representing a government whose failure to provide food and medicines to the needy became a contentious issue in the media, ungrudgingly acknowledged the work done by volunteer groups and charitable organisations. 'The appeal for public co-operation', wrote Phipson, 'met with such a wonderful response, and so whole-hearted was the devotion of all the workers in carrying out the various relief measures adopted, that it is probably safe to say that there was hardly a house in the city or a unit of the population that

Observing this convention in English newspapers of the Victorian era, Udo Fries writes that women are 'seen only in relation to their families: a woman might be a daughter, a mother, a wife, a relict, or a widow, all terms which were used throughout the 19th century' (p. 65). It is likely that *The Khalsa Advocate* obituary draws on this template, which conforms to the gender norms of early-twentieth century India as elsewhere.

did not have a chance of relief; hundreds of lives must have been saved by the efforts of these organisations … and in thousands of homes much must have been done to mitigate the horrors of the epidemic among the poor and more ignorant classes in the city' (1923, pp. 515–516). White, too, applauded the services provided by 'non-officials, both medical and lay, philanthropic societies, educational establishments, and a host of philanthropic workers' (1919, p 12). 'Never before, perhaps, in the history of India', he added, 'have the educated and more fortunately placed members of the community, come forward in such large numbers to help their poor brethren in time of distress. The one bright feature in the long record of misery and death, afforded by a perusal of the provincial influenza reports, is to be found in the appreciations of philanthropy and private charity which were in evidence in most parts of the country'. In such recitals of praise a wholly different picture of the outbreak emerges that constitutes a part of its total significance for those who witnessed and lived through it.

The accounts of the influenza epidemic in the newspaper and public health reports, thus, weave together a story of human suffering, vulnerability, and the simultaneous collapse and resurgence of community bonds that lies beyond the register of a demographic discourse. Theoretically, the story of epidemic can be told in two distinct ways corresponding to two different genres of narration[5], what we may call the biomedical and the cultural. The biomedical genre includes all narratives that recount an epidemic event in scientific or epidemiological terms, and represent it through figures, charts and graphs to generalise it at the level of the population as a whole. The cultural, in contrast, includes all narratives that are about how people respond to

[5] In genre theory, the term 'genre' refers to a conventional form of communication used in specific social situations and contexts. It is founded on the premise that language is primarily social in its form and function. As Gunther Kress and Peter Knapp explain, 'in any society there are types of texts of particular form: because there are recurring types of social encounters, situations, events, which have very similar structures. As these are repeated over and over and over, certain types of texts appear over and over and over. They become recognisable and recognised in a society by its members, and once recognised they become conventionalised. When they

it collectively and individually, foregrounding the subjective dimensions of an epidemic—as it is experienced and understood. They include fictional as well as non-fictional writings such as autobiographies, memoirs and local histories, fiction films and documentaries as well as stories in social media. This typology, however, is only schematic and does not correspond to the way stories are actually told (Das, 2019b, p. 41; Das, 2022, p. 18.). First, the distinction between 'biomedical' and 'cultural' collapses the moment we see biomedical discourse itself as a way in which culture attributes meaning to disease outbreaks. If we take culture to be a meaning-making system characteristic of human societies, the scientific and the lay, the objective and the subjective, are already parts of it—each providing meanings that add to those created by the other. The generic structure of biomedical and cultural narratives may differ, but taken together they constitute the total meaning of the reality that epidemic signifies. Second, as we have seen in the quotations from Phipson and White above, the biomedical or epidemiological report may also include, what serves as, subjective gloss on data that are presented numerically or graphically. The point is that while epidemics are the outcome of objective natural processes they are also experienced subjectively by those who live to tell their stories, irrespective of whether they are public health officials, journalists, historians or litterateurs. Under these circumstances, therefore, the generic oppositions between biomedical/cultural and objective/subjective blur. For the purpose of analysis, however, I will continue to retain in the following sections the distinction between biomedical and cultural narratives while keeping in mind its limitation.

5.3. Chronotopes of Contagion

Epidemics signify a break in the everyday life of individuals and communities. They accelerate and foreground the time and space of events, which the routines of daily living obscure. One of the

have become conventionalized, they appear to have an existence "of their own", with recognisable rules' (1992, p. 5).

things that both Phipson and White note about the Spanish flu pandemic is the speed and extent of its transmission. Emerging in the Bombay Docks, writes Phipson, the disease '*rapidly* became general' and within a few months '*swept over* the length and breadth of India' (1923, pp. 512, 509, italics added). A distinctive feature of the 1918 outbreak, notes White, 'was the extreme rapidity with which the disease spread over the globe, *a rapidity so great that modern increased facilities for rapid human intercourse fail to supply an altogether adequate explanation*' (1919, p. 2, italics added). Both authors record the unprecedented intensity of the outbreak and the speed with which it advanced globally, revealing thereby an acute consciousness of its time-space dimension.

Mikhail Bakhtin coins the term chronotope to signify this dimension, combining the concept of time as *chronos* and space as *topos*. 'We will give the name *chronotope* (literally, "time-space") to the intrinsic connectedness of temporal and spatial relationships that are artistically expressed in literature' (Bakhtin, 1981, p. 84, italics in original). We perceive the world from our embodied location in time and space, not as a disembodied consciousness that observes it from 'elsewhere' and is able to categorically separate the two dimensions. Spatio-temporal perception of the world is simultaneously personal and collective, and constitutes the 'world-view' shared through culture. Narratives, whether literary or scientific, draw upon this collective perception. 'Out of the actual chronotopes of our world (which serve as the source of representation) emerge the reflected and *created* chronotopes of the world represented in the work (in the text)' (p. 253, italics in original). In drawing upon the actual chronotopes, in other words, narratives do not simply reflect them but recreate or configure them in conventionally meaningful ways. In representing phenomena, narratives combine time-space with its correlates of meaning: 'We somehow manage ... to endow all phenomena with meaning, that is, *we incorporate them not only into the sphere of spatial and temporal existence but also into the semantic sphere*' (p. 257, italics added).

Bakhtin's main argument about time-space representation is its role in structuring genres: 'it is precisely the chronotope that defines genre and generic distinctions' (1981, p. 85). Though his focus is primarily on the novelistic genres, the argument is equally valid for other genres of narrative such as those that I have called biomedical and cultural. To illustrate my point as well as to show how the influenza pandemic of 1918 came to be understood across these genres, I will take two extracts that I must cite in full to demonstrate how they construct their chronotopes of contagion. The first is from Phipson's report on the outbreak in Bombay.

> The earliest cases among the civil population appear to have occurred in the Indian ranks of the City Police. On June 10th a group of seven police sepoys, one of whom was employed at the docks, was admitted to the Police Hospital with what appeared to be influenza. By the 19th, fourteen more cases were admitted, of whom four were from the Docks. … after the Police the next group to be attacked, on the 15th of June, were the employees of Messrs. W. and A. Graham's shipping firm. Next day the men of the Government Dockyard succumbed, followed on the 17th of June, by the first of a very large number of the employees of the Bombay Port Trust and the Hong Kong and Shanghai Bank. On the 18th the Government Telegraph Department was affected and on the 19th the Mint. It may be observed that the latter institution abuts on the harbour between the Government Dockyard and the Ballard Estate of the Port Trust. By the following day the disease had spread to the mill area in the centre of the island and thereafter rapidly became general. (1923, p. 512)

Phipson focuses only on the onset of outbreak, limiting it to the period 10–20 June, and limiting its space to the docks where it first broke out. The second extract is from *A Life Misspent*, a memoir by the Hindi poet Suryakant Tripathi, better known by his pseudonym 'Nirala':

> I received a telegram: 'Your wife is gravely ill. Come immediately.' I was twenty-two. I became aware of the intensity of her love just as she was ready to take leave of life. The newspapers had informed us about the ravages of the epidemic.

> I travelled to the riverbank in Dalmau and waited. The Ganga was swollen with dead bodies. At my in-laws' house, I learned that my wife had passed away. My cousin had come over from my ancestral village to help with my wife's illness, but he had taken ill himself and returned home. I left for our ancestral village the very next day. As I was walking towards my house, I saw my cousin's corpse being carried to the cremation site. My head grew dizzy; I sat down on the ground to take a hold of myself.
>
> At home I found my cousin's wife lying ill on a pallet. 'How far has the funeral procession travelled?' she asked. I had nothing to say. They had four sons and a baby girl who was still nursing. The oldest child lived with me in Bengal and went to school there. My uncle was the head of the family. He, too, contracted influenza. 'What madness brought you here?' he said to me.
>
> Words cannot describe how pitiful the scene was, how helpless, how tender. But I had no tenderness left after the death of my wife and my cousin. I said in a dry voice, 'Get well and I will take the whole family to Bengal.'
>
> This was my first attempt to serve those who were ill. Since then there has been no dearth in my life of calls for such service. Sister-in-law passed away on the third day after my cousin's death. The nursing child was also sick. I slept that night holding her. She, too, passed away in the morning. I buried her in the riverbank. Then Uncle died. One more corpse to cart to the Ganga. Sister-in-law's three sons contracted fever. Somehow I was able to nurse them back to health. This was the strangest time in my life. My family disappeared in the blink of an eye. All our sharecroppers and labourers died, the four who worked for my cousin as well as the two who worked for me. My cousin's eldest son was fifteen years old, my young daughter a year old. In whichever direction I turned, I saw darkness. (2016, pp. 53–54)

The two extracts are about the same event—the outbreak of Spanish flu—and both are factual, but they narrate it quite differently. Phipson's story is objective, written without the use of personal pronouns in a style appropriate to the genre of science writing. He gives no personal details of the individuals affected by the outbreak, who they were and how they contracted infection, mentioning them only as 'cases'. Nirala's story is deeply subjective, leaving out objective information about the outbreak, its extent of spread or morbidity and mortality data and mentioning only in passing the newspaper reports. It focuses solely on people with whom he has close personal ties as family or farmhand, who are not 'cases' for him. It describes *his* frenetic travels between Dalmau and his ancestral village, *his* view of the river 'swollen' with corpses, *his* grief, *his* inner 'darkness'—in short, his personal experience of the event.

Let us first examine how the two extracts represent time. Phipson gives us a detailed chronology of the outbreak in Bombay, a day-by-day account of its spread from 10 to 20 June. Nirala, in contrast, gives no dates or durations, but represents the passage of time as it is recollected in memory and expressed in shifting tenses between past and present. The passage predominantly uses past tense forms (I receiv*ed*, I travell*ed*, the newspapers *had* inform*ed*, my cousin *had* come, etc.), shifting abruptly to the present progressive to show how the past is linked to a present that it shapes: 'This was my first opportunity to serve those who were ill. *Since then* there *has been* no dearth in my life of calls for such service.' To understand the difference between the two extracts, let me turn to Paul Ricoeur's theory of how time is represented in narrative. Time-consciousness takes two forms. One is linear, recording the passage of time in days, months and years—that is, horological or clock time. This is what we see in the extract from Phipson, which uniformly employs the past tense. The other is a consciousness that combines past, present and future in causal relationships that prefigure memory, attention and anticipation. This is how the extract from Nirala represents the passage of time, from his first attempt at serving those who were ill, to its anterior projection in the innumerable calls for such service, up to the moment when he tells the story. In recalling the tragic incidents in his village and how they shape his course of life, Nirala merges chronology and causality. Can the sentence 'Since then there has been no dearth in my life of calls for such service' imply, as well, a future extending beyond the moment when he narrates it? I assume that it does, for in writing about his life after the outbreak Nirala also presents a self-transformation founded on that first time he learns to care for others. The 'strangeness' of this moment would then imply not just the fact that his 'family disappeared in the blink of an eye' but equally the fact that it led to a new consciousness in which past, present and future coexist as also do the transience and eternity of life. It is a moment of epiphany, as the paragraph following the extract expresses:

> After I had attended to the affairs of my household, I went to my in-laws'. In spite of the suffering, I was able to keep my mind steady. I would go sit on a mound by the Ganga and watch the file of corpses brought to the river. It is impossible to describe my feelings. The mound of sadhus in Dalmau is famous for its height. The Ganga made a sharp turn below it. The corpses were laid together. *Sometimes I would think of the ascetic sadhus, sometimes of the ephemerality of the world.* (Tripathi, 2016, pp. 54–55, italics added)

What lesson do the ascetic sadhus teach him? A few lines later, Nirala recalls the words of his friend Kulli Bhat as the latter tries to console him: 'Those who are dead have found peace already … Those who have beheld death seek peace as you do. This mound of sadhus is far from the town and, in feeling, far from the cremation grounds. It is as if an ascetic sadhu had settled *here after he died*. His *immortal* presence makes it an abode of peace' (Tripathi, 2016, p. 55, italics added). The sadhus signify the immortality of the soul, just as the corpses on the riverbank signify the ephemerality of the body. This 'strangest time' in Nirala's life marks, as I have said, a moment of epiphany in which all time is merged in a transcendence of temporality and an intuition of eternity. It marks, too, the passage from the profane to sacred time and space that, as Mircea Eliade explains, inaugurates cosmology: '*the world becomes apprehensible as world, as cosmos, in the measure in which it reveals itself as a sacred world*' (1959, p. 64, italics in original).

Building on St Augustine's rumination on time in Book 11 of *The Confessions*, Ricoeur posits that lived experience of time is not a linear flow of discrete moments organised in terms of past/present/future, but a merging of all three in the consciousness. Augustine's problem is to determine whether time exists. Whatever exists can be measured, and we do measure time as in expressions like 'a short while ago or 'a long time hence'. Yet time cannot exist because the past *no longer exists*, the future *does not yet exist*, and the present *is always fleeting*. If we still hold that time exists, where does it exist? Augustine's answer is that it exists in the mind as a 'three-fold present': the past exists as *present* in memory, the present as *present* in attention, and the future as *present* in anticipation. It is in this sense that all time is present to the consciousness. Ricoeur quotes a line from Augustine: 'The present of past things is the memory; the present of present things is direct perception; and the present of future things is expectation' (1984, p. 11). It is the simultaneity of past, present and future that constitutes the temporal structure by which we become conscious of our actions and happenings, their causes, effects and the meanings they bear. Ricoeur then interprets Augustine's meditation on eternity, with which the book opens and closes. In framing the rumination on time, the meditation on eternity provides a different consciousness of time in which eternity does not abolish temporality but deepens it (pp. 29–30). That is precisely what we see in Nirala's epiphanic vision from the mound of sadhus as he looks down on the corpses on the riverbank.

How do we characterise the concept of temporality in the two extracts? Phipson's account depersonalises time, corresponding to his detached and impersonal observation of the events he narrates. It brackets out his personal experience of the outbreak, with which he had been 'intimately associated' as health officer (Phipson, 1923, p. 510)—intimately enough to be distressed by what he observed and yet found in them 'a soul of good'. Nirala's account is deeply engaged with time, reflecting not just on its passage but equally eternity. He recalls each moment as he had lived through it in what he did, thought and felt, anticipating the promise they held for his future, in that phenomenological consciousness of time that Ricoeur, following Augustine, calls 'three-fold present.'

The representation of space in both extracts follows a similar pattern. Phipson traces in cartographic fashion the passage of the virus from its emergence in the docks, through W. and A. Graham, Government Dockyard, Bombay Port Trust, Hong Kong and Shanghai Bank, the Government Telegraph Department and the Mint, to the mill area and thence to the rest of the city. Along with figures, charts and graphs, the cartographic representation of disease transmission forms a staple device in biomedical narratives of epidemic outbreak. Perhaps the most well-known example of modern medical cartography is John Snow's map of the transmission of cholera in the 1854 edition of *On the Mode of Communication of Cholera*. On a map of Soho district in London, Snow plotted the locations of houses where deaths had occurred, tracing the epicentre of the spread to a single public water pump in Broad Street (Koch, 2005, pp. 95–101). The Soho map established mapping as a standard visual technique of epidemiological practice, of which Phipson's account of the Bombay outbreak is a textual equivalent. The medical map represents spaces as homogeneous locations of disease. The streets of cholera-stricken Soho are differentiated only by black lines that mark and quantify the houses in which people have died and their proximity to the Broad Street pump: 'all the deaths from cholera which were registered in the six weeks from the 19th August to 30th September within this locality, as well as those of people removed into Middlesex Hospital, are shown in the map by a black line in the situation of the house in which it occurred, or in which the fatal account was contracted' (Snow as cited in Koch, 2005, pp. 96–97). The various places that Phipson mentions are, similarly, equivalent to each other insofar as they are sites of disease, differentiated only on the basis of the timeline of incidence. This is a characteristic in general of cartographic representation of space, which bears an instrumental relation to the places it maps. Cartography reduces all places to coordinates, positions and distances in an abstract Euclidean representation, which, as Henri Lefebvre says of geometric space, 'is defined by its "isotropy" (or homogeneity), a property which guarantees its social and political utility' (1991, p. 285). The utility is based on economic, political, governmental or public health calculations that each reduces space quantitatively to a single parameter. 'How many maps', Lefebvre asks rhetorically, 'might be needed to deal exhaustively with a given space, to code and decode all its meanings and contents?' (p. 85).

The representation of space in the Nirala extract is not cartographic: each space signifies meanings that are clearly the outcome of his personal and embodied relation to it in the present context. The Ganga is not just a river running through Dalmau; it is a flow 'swollen with dead bodies' as viewed from the bank where he waits, or a cremation ghat as viewed from the mound on which he sits to calm his disturbed mind. The street in his village is not just the familiar path he takes to his home but also the route taken by the funeral procession carrying his cousin to the cremation ground. The mound of sadhus is an elevated site that signifies, as Kulli puts it, 'an abode of peace'. Spaces for Nirala are heterogeneous, invested with meanings that derive from his bodily and emotional relation to them—a river of death, the road to home as well as to a final resting-place, a mound that consoles even as it reveals death. They signify a qualitative as opposed to quantitative space. To explain this difference Lefebvre imagines the way a nomadic shepherd relates to the space he inhabits: 'He does not envisage himself in space as one point among others in an abstract milieu. That is a type of representation belonging to a much later period, and is contemporaneous with the space of "plans" and maps' (1991, p. 194). The 'networks of paths and roads' that make up the shepherd's space are 'just as concrete as that of the body—of which of which they [are] in fact an extension' (p. 193). Our primary relation to space, Lefebvre argues, is bodily, not cognitive. 'When "Ego" arrives in an unknown country or city, he first experiences it through every part of his body—through his sense of smell and taste, as … through his legs and feet. His hearing picks up the noises and the quality of the voices;

his eyes are assailed by new impressions. For it is by means of the body that space is perceived, lived—and produced' (p. 162).

Fundamental to Lefebvre's analytics of space is the idea that space is not a given, but is produced in our relation to it. This thesis derives from Marx's theory of production. Space is produced by human economic activity—factories and industrial complexes as well as agricultural fields—but unlike other products it is also linked to the productive forces: 'Though a *product* to be used, to be consumed, it is also a *means of production*; networks of exchange and flows of raw materials and energy fashion space and are determined by it' (Lefebvre 1991, p. 85, italics in original). Lefebvre then moves from this economic sense of production to one that is cultural: space is also produced in the representations we make of it. He distinguishes broadly between two types of cultural production: 'representation of space' and 'representational space'. Instances of the former are the 'homogeneous, clearly demarcated space with horizon or vanishing point' of landscape painting, and 'the homogeneous and isotropic space of classical (Euclidean/Cartesian) mathematics' and cartography (pp. 79, 86). Space becomes, in such representations, an object viewed from nowhere, suppressing the viewer's location in it. Representational space, in contrast, is derived from one's lived experience. It holds 'a special significance for each individual: *his* house, *his* land, as also *his* church and the graveyard which received *his* dead' (p. 79, italics added).

In the Phipson extract, therefore, what we see is an abstract 'representation of space', while in Nirala we see space as it is inhabited and lived in, a 'representational space'. Let me now return to the chronotope, with which I began this section. I have examined the representation of time and space separately for analytic reasons, but they are fused in both extracts to constitute two different chronotopes of contagion. Phipson's report maps not just the spaces of disease but equally the temporal dimension of this spread. This is fundamental to the epidemiological study of disease outbreak, serving the function of tracing and intervening in chains of transmission. In Nirala's memoir, time and space together shape his remembrance of those fateful events that left him bereft of wife and kin at the age of twenty-two, with a four-year old son, an infant daughter and four nephews to look after. What prompts his rumination on human time is a landscape viewed from his embodied location on the mound of sadhus: it would not have been possible outside of this particular conjuncture of time, space and event. 'Time', writes Bakhtin, 'as it were, thickens, takes on flesh, becomes artistically visible; likewise, space becomes charged and responsive to the movements of time, plot and history' (1981, p. 84). The Phipson extract represents time-space in its objective dimension as a generic template for biomedical narrative, while the Nirala extract represents time-space in its subjective dimension as a template for cultural narrative. Yet, as I have stated, neither genre wholly excludes the chronotopic perception of the other. Nirala's remembrance of the deaths in his cousin's house is, after all, a day-to-day account, showing how the phenomenological consciousness of time does not entirely banish its horological structuring: 'Sister-in-law passed away *on the third day* after my cousin's death. The nursing child was also sick. I slept *that night* holding her. She, too, passed away *in the morning*. I buried her in the riverbank. *Then* Uncle died' (Tripathi, 2016, p. 54, italics added). As a corollary, Phipson is barely able to suppress his subjective response to the events that he objectively records: 'we can at least devise measures to mitigate the *horrors* of its progress and in some degree, perhaps, to curtail its *ravages*' (1923, p. 519, italics added). Even more revealing is the report of the sanitary Commissioner of Punjab (cited in section 5.1), which describes the spaces of disease: hospitals 'choked' with the dead, streets 'littered with dead and dying bodies', funeral sites 'swamped with corpses', households lamenting the departed and the reign of 'terror and confusion' everywhere. These are not words expressing the objective view of the scientist studying a natural phenomenon, but words charged with an emotion that must be prised out of the dispassionate surface of the biomedical report. Contagion and death on the scale of the influenza outbreak of

1918 provoke the imagination to find suitable verbal equivalents to convey not only the magnitude and timeline of spread but equally that of their emotional impact on those who have to bear witness to them—which only figurative language can do.

5.4. Contagion and Cosmological Disorder

Narratives of epidemic are framed by two alternative explanatory paradigms, as I have explained in chapter one. The biomedical paradigm is part of a broader explanation that understands disease as the outcome of natural factors such as pathogens, the body's constitution and environment, and it derives from a naturalistic aetiology or theory of disease causation. Other medical systems included in this aetiological category are ayurveda, homeopathy, siddha and unani. The cosmological paradigm holds that supernatural agents like deities, spirits, dead ancestors and sorcerers can either cause disease or protect against them. Unlike malevolent agents, however, gods and ancestral spirits do not capriciously spread disease; they do so only when people violate the ritual or cosmological order. Disease on this view is a form of retribution for the non-performance of duties appropriate to that order. In contrast to the naturalistic, supernatural explanations of disease outbreak are based on a theory of magical causation. Quite often, as Rosenberg states, both explanations exist side by side notwithstanding their differences (1989, p. 5). In South Africa, for example, lay explanations of the Spanish flu outbreak ranged from germs, insanitary conditions and overcrowding in slums to divine retribution and spells cast by witches or wizards (Phillips, 1987). Howard Phillips cites the instance of a bishop who combined both explanations, in claiming that the outbreak was punishment for disregarding God's command that people follow rules of good health such as 'fresh air, cleanliness, and nutrition' (1987, p. 81). Pluralistic understandings of the pandemic in many societies, especially those that had been colonised, take the form of both scientific and religious explanations unhindered by the obvious contradictions between them.

In India, however, the pandemic of 1918 either did not give rise to religious explanations or they were not reported. I could find no reference to a goddess assigned to it in the newspaper stories or the literature I accessed. I can think of only three reasons for this: one, that it was a new disease outbreak unlike smallpox and cholera, which had long been associated with goddess figures; two, it did not in the first wave lead to large-scale mortality or panic; and three, the second wave that proved more fatal than the first did not last for more than a few months. But there were other epidemic diseases that under the same conditions came to be assigned new deities or were incorporated into existing deific frameworks. Plague, which broke out with exceptional virulence at the end of the nineteenth century, was a new disease, as were HIV/AIDS and COVID-19. The plague goddess was worshipped in different parts of India where she was known under various names such as Plague-amma, Uramma and Bombai Mai (Bhattacharyya, 1999, p. 56). The total deaths caused by COVID in India till 20 April 2020 was 826 ('Coronavirus India lockdown', 2020), which was far below the ten to fifteen million attributed to Spanish flu, yet a new goddess called variously as Corona Devi or Corona Mai found worship in widely scattered parts of the country. In *Making Virtuous Daughters and Wives: An Introduction to Women's Brata Rituals in Bengali Folk Religion*, Judith McDaniel mentions an account of the worship of Sitala as the goddess of AIDS. Patua singers and scroll-painters of Bengal tell stories of Sitala 'travelling to different countries and spreading the disease … AIDS was brought by Shitala because people were neglecting her worship, and this was her divine revenge upon irreligious and secular people' (cited in Ferrari, 2015, p. 154). In 2017, I visited a shrine to AIDS-amma in a village in south Karnataka, its function being not to seek the intervention of the deity but to help create awareness of HIV (Das, 2019a, pp. 189–222). AIDS-amma, writes Ferrari, 'was born in anomalous context. On the one hand, there is no supporting myth. On the other, she just borrowed elements from the local plague-goddess (Māriyamman)' (2010, p. 164).[6] What Ferrari fails to see is that the vernacular tradition of disease goddess worship has rarely followed the taxonomic rules that Indologists lay down for it, reassigning the functions of existing deities and incorporating new deities in capricious and contingent ways. It is pointless, therefore, to look for a reason why Spanish flu had no goddess, just as it is pointless to expect that AIDS-amma needs a supporting myth to be consistent with tradition.

Public discourse on the 1918 influenza outbreak seems to have favoured the biomedical paradigm, frequently emphasising the need to scientifically ascertain its cause and transmission. The *Bombay Samachar*, for example, lent support to a proposal requesting 'the Government to appoint a committee composed of scientists and medical men to inquire into the causes of the influenza epidemic' (India Office Library and Records, 1918g, p. 19). With regard to cause, there was speculation on whether the microbe was a bacillus, bacteria or some other agent.[7] With regard to transmission, it was generally agreed that it was brought into India by returning soldiers who had contracted it abroad. *Young India* reported on 2 October 1918: 'There is a wide-spread rumour that it has been caused by the influx of a large number of troops

[6] Ferrari refers to a particular incarnation of the goddess, called Plague Mariamma. Mariamma, however, was worshipped in south India primarily as the goddess of smallpox (Whitehead, 1921, pp. 31–32; Bhattacharyya, 1999, p. 55; Srinivasan, 2019). Her name derives from the Tamil word for water (*mari*), and she is also worshipped as the goddess of rain. According to Paul Younger, she has many powers for ensuring the well-being of her worshippers: she protects from disease, drought, adversities and enemies, grants offspring and bounteous harvest, and helps withstand oppression (1980, pp. 504–509).

[7] The general theory was that it was either bacillus or bacteria. Phipson believed that Pfeiffer's bacillus or *Bacillus influenzae* was the most likely agent, in co-action with pneumococci and streptococci (1918, p. 444; 1923, p. 511). White expressed doubts about this, and suspected 'a germ so infinitely minute that the highest powers of the microscope are unable to demonstrate it' (1919, p. 2). As it turned out later, White was correct. Jeffery Taubenberger and his group at the US Armed Forces Institute of Pathology identified it in antibodies preserved from survivors in the 1930s as 'an H1N1-subtype virus, probably closely related to what is now known as classic swine influenza virus, which may have emerged from an avian reservoir before the 1918 outbreak' (Taubenberger et al., 1997, p. 1793).

suffering from it. It is said …that the military authorities told the Municipal Health authorities that they were disembarking only three persons affected by it but actually brought in three ship loads or 900 men in all' (India Office Library and Records, 1918d, p. 26). It reiterated this in its 16 October issue, pointing to the lapse on the part of the government: 'It is extraordinary … that Government has remained indifferent to the rumour, so widely current, which ascribes the present evils to the negligence of the military authorities' (India Office Library and Records, 1918f, p. 11). Coinciding with the outbreak of influenza was an acute food crisis, and that was held to be a reason for its high mortality rate. The *Praja Mitra and Pársi* of 28 September stated that 'the virulence of the existing visitation of influenza is, to a considerable extent, due to the want of stamina among the people to resist all disease brought on by heavy prices of foodstuffs' (India Office Library and Records, 1918c, pp. 16–17, translated from the original Gujarati by the compiler of the report). In other words, the social understanding of Spanish flu in India was predominantly naturalistic and not associated with the supernatural.

The absence of a deity and the preponderance of a scientifically-inclined media discourse do not, however, rule out cosmological interpretations. Any fearsome event that kills people on an unprecedented scale is often imagined as cosmic disorder. Cosmology, broadly defined, refers to a 'body of conceptions that enumerate and classify the phenomena that compose the universe as an ordered whole and the norms and processes that govern it' (Tambiah, 1980, p. 121). It is composed of axioms that are held as sacrosanct, and do not require empirical validation. While it may include relationships between humans and gods or ancestral spirits, it is not reducible to them as such. On this view, Nirala's musings on mortality and immortality on the mound of sadhus is as much a part of cosmology as the worship of Sitala, Plague-amma and AIDS-amma. Let me now turn to another cosmological narrative of the Spanish flu outbreak, Ahmed Ali's novel *Twilight in Delhi* (1940).

Twilight in Delhi is about the passing away of a cultural tradition due to colonisation and the modern ways of living it ushered in. In an interview that he gave to the *Journal of South Asian Literature*, Ali stated:

> What I had in mind when I wrote the novel was the awareness or the consciousness of the past, the sadness and the agony of suffering and of sacrifice. Also, a certain feeling for the glory that was gone, the failure of the people of India, and of the Muslims especially, to have held on to life, to have been able to look at things in terms of cause and effect. And behind this sadness and sorrow was the reason for the disappearance of this glory: the *bêtes noires*, British imperialism and the British people themselves. (Ali & JSAL, 1998, p. 154).

Set in the by-lanes and neighbourhoods of old Delhi in the early-twentieth century, the novel recounts the declining fortunes of Mir Nahal and his family, ending in his growing disillusionment and death. The chapter on the Spanish flu pandemic stands out in this respect: it is the only one in the novel that is not about the central character or his family. Ali was only eight years old when the pandemic struck Delhi, and perhaps had little personal remembrance of it. He does not mention it in the interview cited above nor does he mention anyone else telling him about it; yet he considered it important enough to include it as a major event in the story. This may possibly be because it did exist in public memory of the city in 1938, when he began working on the novel. In just two months, October and November, there were 7,044 deaths in the city, with a maximum of 418 on a single day, 26 October. The scale of mortality was so huge that the disposal of the bodies of one's dead kin proved daunting, and there were many 'heart-rending scenes' as Sanitary Commissioner White himself wrote (1919, p. 7). Ali walked about Delhi collecting material for the book, observing people and places, and talking to people who may have remembered the pandemic: 'I went and met as many old people as I could … I would try to meet as many people in the muhalla [neighbourhood] as possible, as many members of my family as I could' (Ali & JSAL, 1998, p. 153).

The Spanish flu chapter, though it makes no mention of Mir Nahal's family, mirrors its decline as also the general decline of the community. It seems significant that, in the interview, Ali uses the metaphor of death to describe this decline: 'A society was dying. ... I showed that it was moving towards death, yet living, marching on, for it did continue to live right down until 1947–1948' (Ali & JSAL, 1998, p. 155). The story of the pandemic serves, in other words, as an allegory for this collective 'dying'. While the style of the novel in general is realistic, the account of the influenza outbreak is replete with metaphor, pathetic fallacy and personification. Every evening as Shams sat by the grave of his wife, for instance, he saw 'the day die and night spread her veil of darkness and gloom over the grief-stricken earth' (Ali, 1940, p. 229).

The chapter opens with a description of Delhi in the summer of 1918 that presages the fateful events to follow:

> The summer of 1918 was more terrible than the summers of the previous years. The sky was of a coppery hue throughout the day, and at night the stars were hidden behind the sand which rained down from the sky, and the loo did not stop. It howled more fiercely than before as the City Walls had been demolished, and the wind could blow free from the mountainous wastes outside the city. The dogs moaned and wept at night as if afraid of death, and the cats, whose numbers had surprisingly decreased, were quiet and subdued. (Ali, 1940, p. 229)

In this chronotope of looming calamity, Ali compares the glorious past of the Muslims of old Delhi to their present decadence. The Walled City was built in 1648 by Shahjahan as the capital of his empire. After the British quelled the Revolt of 1857, they pulled down, over the years, large sections of this wall. By 1906, a total of 1466 yards of the wall had been demolished (Gupta, 1971, pp. 66-68). Ali links the ruined wall metonymically to the moral defeat of the Muslim community, for it had been within the walls that its elites had lived before 1857.[8] In the aftermath of the revolt, the British drove them out of the Walled

[8] Ali traced his roots to the time when Shahjahan settled several families of

City, confiscated their property, looted their treasures and desecrated their holy shrines (Lahiri, 2003, pp.38–42). Ali traces the downfall of the community to those times. Earlier in the novel, Mir Nihal remembers the martyrs of the Revolt when he attends the coronation of King George V in Delhi. 'There were those men of 1857, and here were the men of 1911, chicken-hearted and happy in their disgrace' (Ali, 1940, p.147). He meets there Mirza Nasirul Mulk, the youngest son of Bahadur Shah the exiled emperor of Delhi, who has now been reduced to begging (p. 150). All of these nuances find expression in the spatial image of the ruined city walls that recall the past and presage the future.

To return to Ali's story, the war in Europe took countless Indian lives and the pandemic was set to take many more: 'Influenza broke out in epidemic form, and from the houses in the mohallah all around, heart-rending cries of lamentation and weeping began to rend the air. There was hardly any house where a death did not take place' (1940, p. 229). So many people died in so short a time that their last rites could not be carried out properly: 'In life they had no peace, and even in death there seemed no hope of rest. … Yet in death it was immaterial whether you were naked or clothed or burnt or thrown away to be devoured by vultures and jackals' (p. 230). The moral debasement of the community is witnessed in the avarice of grave-diggers, shroud-sellers and the *ghassal*s, who washed the bodies of the dead before burial. The grave-diggers charged exorbitantly for the graves they dug improperly, marked with the cheapest gravestones, and dug up old graves for stones, to sell them at high rates. The banias in the city raised the price of winding-sheets on the pretext that costs were high because of the war. The *ghassal*s charged heavily for washing the bodies of the dead before burial, besides pocketing any valuables they found on them, all the while muttering God's name and massaging 'their bellies with satisfied yet greedy hands' (p. 232). People prayed to God in their misery, but God either did not exist or was too far away to hear their pleas. The chapter closes

*imam*s and *ulama*s, or Islamic scholars, in Delhi. He descended from one of those families, so his nostalgia for the Walled City was as deeply personal as collective (Ali & JSAL, 1998, pp. 117–118).

with a dismal image of unbearable suffering, the precariousness of life in the epidemic, and the desperation with which the dying clung to it:

> Death walked with hurried strides through towns and cities, devastating them, taking her fat and unending toll of lives, stalking among the dead. And Izrael, the angel of death, had not a moment to spare. From house to house he rushed, from door to door, snatching souls away from human beings burning with fever yet hungry after life, wanting to live on in a world which did not care about them at all. (Ali, 1940, p. 233).

Ahmed Ali's chronotopic representation of the influenza outbreak is similar to that of Nirala, in that both are symbolic and express subjective meanings rather than objective facts of contagion. Yet there is an important difference: Ali's account is about the suffering of the community as a whole, while Nirala's is about individual suffering. This follows from the way the two narratives differ in their focus, the former being a novel about a community—it is not Mir Nahal on whom the 'twilight' descends, but 'Delhi'—and the latter a memoir. As such, Ali's account is more amenable to cosmological framing than Nirala's. If cosmos refers to the moral order that binds all beings, humanity in *Twilight in Delhi* violates this order in the cupidity of those who live off of the misery of their fellow-beings. Influenza, Ali's omniscient narrator states, is a retribution for these iniquitous acts: 'Nature herself ... seemed angry with the people of Hindustan. ... filled with anger against the inhumanity of man, Nature wanted to demonstrate her own callousness and might' (1940, p. 229). Of course this is not the only explanation, for the epidemic was also assumed to be 'the outcome, perhaps, of the gases used in the European War' (p. 230)[9]; but the cosmological view is what dominates all through the account.

A goddess, therefore, may not have been assigned to Spanish flu but it nevertheless carried cosmological overtones. It signified a disorder of the cosmos in the way it led to the collapse of just

[9] In South Africa it was held that 'the indiscriminate use of poison gas' in the war was a factor in the spread of Spanish flu (Phillips, 1987, p. 88). Such a view may also have been circulated in India, though I could find no evidence of it except for this sole mention in the novel.

and ethical relations between people, even as it was punishment for that disordering. Ahmed Ali's framing of the outbreak in Delhi may be fictional, but it expresses a social reality for those who lived through the outbreak and, perhaps, spoke to Ali about it when he went round gathering material for the book. It is in the nature of epidemics, in the suffering they cause, that they call for metaphysical beliefs about order, disorder and the human condition.

5.5. Contagion, Food Scarcity and Colonial Biopolitics

The disastrous consequences of the Spanish flu outbreak in India were partly due to lapses in public health governance. Phipson, as we have seen, did not hesitate to admit this though he offered a justification for the same: it was an exceptional time marked by preoccupations of the war and deaths back home in England, and the minds of the colonial administrators had been numbed by these 'gigantic events' (Phipson, 1923, p. 509). White, too, admitted that the public health infrastructure was inadequate to meet an emergency of this scale, even as he claimed that the most efficient arrangement could not have prevented it. There was no specific cure or vaccine for influenza, and the spread was so rapid that 'medical science [could] do but little to check its incidence' (White, 1919, p. 3). Part of the blame, White claimed, lay with the Indian masses: 'With a population as uneducated as is that of India to-day, and with the relatively low standard of living pertaining, the control of so virulent an epidemic is completely outside the present scope of human endeavour' (1923, p. 12). Both White and Phipson, in other words, were searching for excuses to lay the blame elsewhere. This section examines the opinions expressed in newspapers regarding the colonial state's dereliction of its biopolitical duty.

Michel Foucault may not have been the first to coin the term 'biopolitics', but he certainly gave it its present meaning.[10] It refers to the way states take the life of their subjects as a central factor of

[10] One of the first to use the term 'biopolitics' was Rudolph Kjellén in his *Outline of a Political System* (1920), where he elaborates the idea of the

statecraft. In *Security, Territory, Population*, Foucault argues that when the state-form emerged in early modern Europe it differed radically from the rule of the monarch in the way it exercised power. While both the state and the monarch extracted wealth from subjects by levying taxes, the state enabled them to increase their productivity by providing the conditions necessary for it. These conditions included opportunities for developing their skills and resources, infrastructure to transport their produce to the market, and trade regulations to ensure that they get a fair price for it. They included also factors that enhance life,—like housing, healthcare, adequate food supply and other amenities necessary for happiness and well-being. The apparatus to ensure these conditions was the 'police', not in its current sense of a law-and-order authority, but an agency with a broader purview, to foster the life of subjects: 'the objective of police is everything from being to well-being, everything that may produce this well-being beyond being, and in such a way that the well-being of individuals is the state's strength' (Foucault, 2007, p. 328). By biopolitics, Foucault means the political calculation that links the power and wealth of the modern state to the life and well-being of its subjects: 'the attempt, starting from the eighteenth century, to rationalize the problems posed to governmental practice by phenomena characteristic of a set of living beings forming a population: health, hygiene, birthrate, life expectancy, race ... We know the increasing importance of these problems since the nineteenth century, and the political and economic issues they have raised up to the present' (p. 317).

Two of the key biopolitical duties of the state, that Foucault discusses elaborately, are protection of public health and prevention of famine, which the colonial state, according to the view expressed by Indian newspapers, failed to fulfill. The concept of public health emerged in seventeenth-century Europe as a technique for improving the life and productivity of the population

state as an organism that follows the laws of *bios* or biological life. By the time Foucault developed his theory of biopolitics, there had existed several versions of the concept, from which his usage both derives differs. For a more detailed account, see Esposito 2008, p. 16.

as a whole, in the interests of increasing the state's wealth. It began with recording statistics of births and deaths, to which healthcare and health surveillance came to be added later. The functions of the 'medical police' in the eighteenth century included: (i) creating 'a system of observation of sickness', both endemic and epidemic; (ii) ensuring 'standardization of medical practice and knowledge'; (iii) setting up an 'administrative organization for overseeing the activity of doctors'; and (iv) appointing 'medical officers … who would take responsibility for a region' (Foucault, 2000, pp. 140–141). This was the structure on which sanitary governance and medical education and practice in colonial India was also founded. The state established colleges for the training of doctors and a system of licensed or registered practitioners to regulate their services, introduced systems to collect and compile data on annual morbidity and mortality, and appointed local health officers and sanitary commissioners for each region and a sanitary commissioner for the country as a whole to oversee them (Jeffery, 1988, pp. 75–102; Harrison, 1994, pp. 6–35). With regard to food scarcity and famine, governance in modern European states devised a number of mechanisms to foresee and forestall it. Food scarcity occurs primarily due to climatic conditions, but it can also be man-made. In times of scarcity, traders tend to hoard grains in the hope of selling them at higher prices when scarcity increases; when scarcity is localised and not overall, they tend to buy grain from regions where it is cheaper, to sell it where it is dearer, thus creating new areas of scarcity. Governments in Europe dealt with this situation, deriving from both climate and human cupidity, by utilising a range of legislative, disciplinary and security mechanisms (Foucault, 2007, pp. 30–47, pp. 341–348). In a mercantilist economy these included price control, laws to prevent hoarding and export of grain, setting up of a system of surveillance and supervision to ensure that people follow these laws, and punishing them for any violation. In a liberal economy the policy held to be most effective in preventing scarcity was non-interference in the market: allowing traders the freedom to decide the price of food, when to hoard or to release their stocks, and whether to import or export grain—in short, the principle of *laissez-faire*. In dealing with famines the colonial state in India broadly followed the latter policy, deviating from it only when conditions warranted intervening in the free trade of grain—which, as the report of the Indian Famine Commission appointed in May 1878 notes, were not entirely absent. 'At the same time that we recommend the general principle of abstention from interference with private trade in the supply of food to any tract suffering from scarcity, we admit that there are exceptional cases in which the Government may find it necessary to intervene' (1880, pp. 51–52). To mitigate the distress caused by scarcity, for instance, it may import grain to be sold at prices less than that of the market or to distribute it free to the needy. The Commission also recommended the creation of an agricultural department headed by a director of agriculture to oversee food production, and the appointment of a famine commissioner and special officers of the rank of deputy collector 'to take charge of all matters connected with the economic condition and well-being of the people' (p. 41).

The biopolitical principles pertaining to public health and food supply, therefore, were broadly the same in colonial India as in Europe. Then why did these mechanisms fail in 1918, when both epidemic and famine broke out at the same time? More importantly for the purpose of this chapter, what kind of story of the influenza epidemic did the newspapers tell in their criticism of colonial governance? Alleging that the public health authorities had not even bothered to find out the cause of the outbreak, the *Praja Mitra and Pársi* of 27 September 1918 asked: 'What is being done by the Government and large Municipalities like Bombay and Calcutta to investigate the disease?' (India Office Library and Records, 1918c, p. 17, translated from the original Gujarati by the compiler of the report). Linking famine and epidemic, it maintained in its issue the next day that 'instead of leaving the masses of the people to their own resources, Government should start relief funds and make arrangements on a large scale to provide them with foodstuffs and medicines at much cheaper rates than the cost price'. The *Gujaráti* of 5 October wrote: 'We should like to know what steps Government have taken to help the suffering population in the Moffussil which stands in urgent need of ready-made mixtures and medical instructions. The people at large would have been glad to be enlightened by the high medical experts in the service of Government at such a juncture.' It charged that the government had failed to address effectively both the outbreak and the famine: 'High prices have done not a little to undermine the health of the people who can buy neither sufficient food nor clothing. Costly medical drugs are beyond their reach and more than a fortnight ago we earnestly appealed to Government and Municipalities to make them more accessible to the public at large than they are at present' (India Office Library and Records, 1918d, p. 27). Commenting on the 'non-appearance of the Government in the work of combating the epidemic in the City', the *Bombay Chronicle* wrote in its 16 October issue: 'Lord Willingdon [Governor of Bombay Presidency] has, it is true, personally interested himself in work of relief; but that is absolutely no extenuation of the fact that in serious business, not to say crises, the Government are often, through their itinerant propensities, an absent item' (India Office Library and Records, 1918f, p. 11). On the same day, *Young India* commented:

> It is a pity that at such a critical juncture, the Government of Bombay should have remained absent from its proper place, which is rightly speaking at the headquarters. It would not be unjust or unfair to say that the Government which at other times has claimed to be the *ma bap* of the people, simply chose to throw the people on the hands of providence. Whereas a sense of the duties of the *ma bap* should have recalled to its proper place and required it to bestow all care and attention on the afflicted population (italics in original).

The *Sunday Chronicle* of 20 October reiterated the same criticism: 'Everything has so far been left to the Municipality and local philanthropic institutions, the paralyzing atmosphere in the Bombay Secretariat having kept the *ma-bap* of the people in a state of coma.... The policy of leaving things to take their own course, what in French they call *laissez-faire*, is most dangerous and reprehensible at this crisis, as it is nothing short of gross dereliction of duty' (italics in original). In addition to the charge of failing to ensure public health, the *Gujaráti* criticised the government for failing to provide relief from famine as well: 'What Government should have done months ago, is now being attempted in the usual style of the circumlocution department. The prices of foodstuffs and cloth would not have gone up so high, resulting in serious hardships to the people, if the Indian Government had not been so slow to recognise the gravity of the position as had been developing for months together' (p. 12). Dismissing the excuse that other countries suffered equally in the pandemic, a view expressed by the sanitary commissioner of India as well as the assistant health officer of Bombay Municipality,[11] the *Gujaráti* commented on 13 October: 'It is not enough to call the epidemic a world scourge and then sit with folded hands' (India Office Library and Records, 1918e, p. 20). With regard to the excuse of wartime preoccupations,[12] it replied that 'we too in India have to wage a formidable war against the enemies of the human race like plague, malaria and influenza, and face the misfortunes brought on by scarcity or famine'. Regarding the transportation of grains to areas affected by the famine, the *Gujaráti* wrote on 22 September: 'The shortage of railway trains for the transport of goods can, we think, be remedied, when all kinds of specials are being arranged for gamblers in horse-racing. It is little short of astonishing that the needs and requirements of the masses should not be given priority over the claims of pleasure-seekers and of those who make money by gambling' (India Office Library and Records, 1918b, p. 16). On 19 November the *Bombay Chronicle* wrote: 'the situation in this Presidency—particularly in the Northern Division [Gujarat]—is as grave as it can be and the consequent suffering and the misery of the people are aggravated by the fact that the agony of the famine

[11] 'The medical arrangements were inadequate in every severely affected country, few of the administrations of which escaped adverse criticism' (White, 1919, p. 3). '[I]t will be conceded', wrote Phipson, 'that hitherto no country and no city which has lain in the natural path of influenza in its pandemic form has succeeded' in controlling its incidence (1923, p. 519).

[12] See, for instance, Phipson, 1923, p. 509.

is superimposed on the affliction caused by the prevalence of a most virulent epidemic and continued high prices' (India Office Library and Records, 1918i, p. 21). Commenting on a cricket match organised by Lord Willingdon to raise public fund for famine relief, it added: 'He is going to play a cricket match in aid of the famine! The Government of which he is the head, have hitherto failed to declare a famine. Where is the famine Lord Willingdon is willing to aid by a cricket match but which his Government are unwilling to face by a long-delayed declaration and timely institution of proper official relief measures?' (p. 22) On 5 October, at the peak of the epidemic's second wave and when prices of food and cotton had shot up, the *Young India* wrote: 'we urge with all emphasis that we can the need of taking immediate steps for the relief of the distress of those millions that are hungry and those that are insufficiently clad and those that are in the grip of a fell disease' (India Office Library and Records, 1918d, p. 23). Food riots had broken out in Calcutta and Madras, and there was growing resentment against the government's inaction. Papers expressed mixed views on the riot at Madras, but all were more or less critical of the government. The *Justice* of 10 September disapproved of the 'mob violence' but blamed it partly on the laxity of the law-and-order apparatus: 'If constituted authority is freely allowed to be defied by mischief-makers and if the prestige of the Government is lowered in the eyes of the public in a thousand and one ways especially in the eyes of the ignorant and illiterate multitude, a state of general lawlessness is bound to follow' (Madras (India: Presidency), 1918a, p. 1373). The *Commonweal* of 6 September held the government solely responsible, warning it of more organised revolt if it did not take immediate steps to relieve the scarcity of food: 'If a hungry mob is dangerous in itself, will not its fury be far greater if educated India also should, at the same time, be forced into a sullen and bitter attitude against the bureaucracy?' (p. 1374) The food riot in Madras, wrote the *Desabhaktan* on 1 October, was due to the apathy of the government, the officials of which 'have been airing themselves at Ootacamund without paying due attention to the state of affairs in the province' (Madras (India:

Presidency), 1918c, p. 1532, translated from the original Tamil by the compiler of the report). A correspondent of the *Servant of India* of 12 September wrote: 'In ordinary times, especially during the last fifteen or twenty years, people have learnt to look up to Government to organise relief measures in anticipation of famine. This year we are in the very midst of it. And war has added its own inconveniences, miseries and horrors to increase the seriousness of the situation. With all this Government has not moved its little finger to grapple with the problem' (India Office Library and Records, 1918a, p. 12). The Madras papers also expressed discontentment with the government's inept handling of the influenza crisis, especially when it peaked in October. 'It is feared that the mortality is increasing', wrote *The Hindu* on 12 October, 'and we would ask what steps the authorities are taking to combat it and provide the public with the necessary assistance. The situation is rapidly becoming very grave and we would earnestly urge the Government to place all their resources at the disposal of the public unreservedly and at once' (Madras (India: Presidency), 1918c, p. 1519). On the same day, the *Desabhaktan* asked: 'What steps did the Madras Government take to prevent the influenza from spreading in Madras when they heard that it was committing havoc in Bombay? What have they done even now when it has visited this city and is afflicting many people?' (Madras (India: Presidency), 1918d, p. 1553, translated from the original Tamil by the compiler of the report). On 22 October the *Manorama* noted that 'it is the undoubted duty of the Government to find out ways of escape from such calamities which affect the population as a whole, and that municipalities and local boards are responsible for the health of the people entrusted to their care. But what has the Government done and what have municipalities accomplished in this matter?'(Madras (India: Presidency), 1918e, p. 1576, translated from the original Malayalam by the compiler of the report).

The influenza epidemic and the concurrent famine, therefore, occasioned a prolific discourse on the failure of governance and administrative lapses on the part of the state in colonial India, expressing a sentiment stopping short of open anti-colonialism. The 'emerging public sphere of native newspapers and periodicals of the early twentieth century', writes Madhu Singh, 'was instrumental in shaping public opinion' against the colonial government in handling these crises (2021, p. 50). When the government had the necessary public health and food supply infrastructure in place, what accounted for its failure in fulfilling its biopolitical duties and mitigating the combined effects of epidemic and food scarcity? In *Society Must Be Defended* Foucault presents another inflection of the politicisation of life, one that emphasises the right to take life *in the name of preserving life*. The two examples that come to mind immediately are capital punishment and compelling people to lay down their lives in war. These are ordinarily part of what Foucault calls the sovereign's 'right to take life or let live'. The state's right, in contrast, is 'the right to make live and to let die' (Foucault, 2003, p. 241). 'How can a power such as this kill', asks Foucault, 'if it is true that its basic function is to improve life, to prolong its duration, to improve its chances, to avoid accidents, and to compensate for failings?' (p. 254). His answer to this enigma is a 'racism' practiced by the state, in the way it decides which lives are valuable and must be protected, and which devoid of value that can be set aside or sacrificed. As Judith Butler puts it in *Precarious Life*: 'Who counts as human? Whose lives count as lives? What makes for *a grievable life*?' (2004, p. 20, italics in original). All forms of racism, whether or not they draw on presumed bodily differences, function on the attribution of differential value to people, and it is in this extended sense that Foucault calls the state's right to take life racism. In the case of the colonial state, however, it was race—narrowly defined—that formed the basis of difference. For Phipson and his fellow members of the Raj, thus, British lives lost to the pandemic were more grievable than Indian lives. Similarly, for the colonial state the poor in India could be sacrificed in a famine in order to send food to the soldiers fighting England's war in Europe. A correspondent wrote in the *Servant of India* of 12 September: 'Very large quantities of food supplies have already been exported from India, so that if the rains continue to hold off longer, all the supplies available in India may not suffice for all her needs' (India Office Library and Records, 1918a, p. 12). The rising prices of food affected mostly the poor, who were already burdened with mortality due to influenza and the high cost of medicines. The government's refusal to declare a famine and put the Famine Code into action, as recommended by the two Famine Commissions, points to a lack of administrative will, as does the reluctance on the part of the railways to make provisions for transporting grain. 'The Railways', writes the *Kesari* of 10 September, 'can afford to give all facilities for races, while they advance the plea of shortage of waggons for the transport of goods' (p. 11, translated from the original Marathi by the compiler of the report). It was the racism of the colonial state that underlay the lack of will.

The story of the Spanish flu outbreak as recounted in these newspaper reports provides a view which is quite different from that in Nirala's memoir or Ahmed Ali's novel. It is not about individual suffering or one that is caused by nature's outrage, but the suffering of a whole population due to the indifference of those who ruled it. It is about the failure of the colonial state, on the pretext of war, to implement the very safeguards against such crises that it had itself framed in various famine commissions and public health policies. The 'calamitous events' that Phipson laments in his report might very well have been averted, or at least their effects considerably mitigated, had the government paid timely attention to them. The politicisation of Spanish flu thus serves to show how the social understanding of epidemics is framed not just by biomedicine or cosmology, but equally by the structure of power relations and the logic of state racism. This was a meaning of epidemic that influenza brought to the fore in 1918, and which COVID has reiterated a hundred years later.[13]

5.6. Spanish Flu in COVID Times

On 10 May 2020, at the peak of the first wave of COVID-19, the BBC Hindi news service telecast a documentary on the influenza

[13] In chapter ten, I show how the precarious condition of migrant workers caught in the nationwide lockdown in 2020 was because of the low priority they were accorded in the public health calculations of the government.

pandemic of 1918. Though the video neither shows any scenes of the COVID pandemic nor even mentions it in the narration, its subtitle explicitly links the two: 'More deadly than COVID', it says, 'Spanish flu left corpses strewn all over the country' (BBC News Hindi, 2020, my translation). In other words, it is the COVID pandemic that frames the story of Spanish flu. The video opens with a narration from Nirala's memoir accompanied by still pictures of dead bodies floating on the Ganga and being cremated on its banks. This re-reading of Nirala's account adds retrospective significance to the 1918 pandemic if we keep in mind that similar scenes were reported in the second wave of COVID in India. Spanish flu 'took the lives of about one crore eighty-thousand Indians' and '10–20 crores' worldwide (BBC News Hindi, 2020, 01:30, 02:39, my translation). Still pictures in black-and-white show soldiers returning from the war, the docks of Bombay where Spanish flu first broke out, makeshift hospitals with rows of patients, field hospital tents, people wearing masks, cemeteries full of graves, corpses being unloaded from ambulances, animals dying in the famine, and the railways spreading the virus across the country from 'the heights of Kashmir to the villages of Bengal' (BBC News Hindi, 2020, 05:10, my translation). The video also mentions the political implication of the outbreak in India: 'because of the pandemic the anger of the people against the British government touched the skies' (BBC Hindi News, 2020, 01:46–01:50, my translation). It will not be difficult to see the resonances with COVID, which witnessed similar scenes.

A random survey of media stories linking the two pandemics reveals a number of recurrent themes. Of the five that I looked at, three cite Nirala's account of the Spanish flu outbreak: bodies piling up for cremation on the banks of the Ganga (Sreevatsan, 2020), the river 'swollen with dead bodies' and the shortage of firewood for cremation (Kapoor, 2020; Biswas, 2020); and the poet's bereavement as his family disappears 'in the blink of an eye' (Biswas, 2020). Another recurrent theme is the similarity in the way the two pandemics are shown to unfold. Both were transported to India from outside, one entering through Bombay and the other through Kerala, and spread rapidly across the country (Acharjee, 2020; Annapurani, 2021); both came in waves, the second wave proving more fatal than the first (Annapurani, 2021; Kapoor, 2020); both inflicted heavy fatalities, unprecedented in other epidemic outbreaks (Annapurani, 2021; Sreevatsan, 2020). The Spanish flu outbreak, wrote Sreevatsan, is 'a historical reservoir of experience that shows, in painful detail, what happens when an unprepared country comes in the way of a virulent pandemic' (2020). The measures to control the spread of disease—social distancing, wearing of masks, personal hygiene, quarantine—were characteristic responses to both pandemics (Acharjee, 2020; Annapurani, 2021; Sreevatsan, 2020). 'Ultimately', concluded Sreevatsan, 'irrespective of how the next few weeks play out, Covid-19 may change the world in profound ways, much like the 1918 influenza pandemic' (2020). The articles highlighted, also, the differences between the outbreaks. The 'medical realities', wrote Biswas, 'are vastly different now. Although there's still no cure, scientists have mapped the genetic material of the coronavirus, and there's the promise of anti-viral drugs, and a vaccine. The 1918 flu happened in the pre-antibiotic era, and there was simply not enough medical equipment to provide to the critically ill' (2020). 'There are many differences between 1918 and 2020', Sreevatsan noted, 'India is not ruled by a colonial government; the coronavirus is technically different from an influenza virus though they cause similar symptoms; also, much of what we have come to understand as modern medicine did not exist a century ago' (2020). My point is not that these claims of similarity between Spanish flu and COVID were either false or unwarranted: it is to show how the story of the 1918 pandemic, lost to human memory for almost a century, became remembered and rearticulated in the context of COVID. Why should it be necessary to recall and recount the history of Spanish flu in a time of coronavirus disease, so similar yet so different from the latter? Because that forgotten history, as Acharjee claimed, can serve 'as a guiding point and proof of what can happen if disease ranges out of control' (2020). 'India', wrote Kapoor in *The Economic Times*, 'has progressed a lot since the ship carrying the deadly virus docked on the shores of Bombay a century ago. But as another virus—this time from the East—wreaks havoc across the globe in 2020, India should look back to let history not repeat itself' (2020). Those who forget their past, as George Santayana famously said, are condemned to repeat it.

Historical narratives, as we have seen in chapter three, do not simply document the events of a past. As Hayden White explains, they make them into a story in accordance with conventional forms of storytelling through which both they and their readers make sense of what would otherwise be a random series of happenings. 'A historical interpretation, like a poetic fiction, can be said to appeal to its readers as a plausible representation of the world by virtue of its implicit appeal to those "pre-generic plot-structures"[14] or archetypal story-forms that define the modalities of a given culture's literary endowment' (White, 1978, p. 58). The plots of both historical and fictional narratives derive from a typology that exists in culture. The significance of an event is, thus, not intrinsic to it but is shaped by the plot-form that narrative uses in recounting it. Thus, the Spanish flu outbreak in India, as we have seen, may signify a personal or collective calamity in one rendering while in another it may signify failure of the state. In retelling the story of Spanish flu from the perspective of COVID, the BBC documentary and the media stories attribute to it a meaning that lies not in the pandemic itself, but in what it means for us now in comprehending our present crisis.

Let me now turn to a fictional representation of the Spanish flu pandemic—Sidin Vadukut's *Bombay Fever* (2017). The outbreak in the novel is *not* Spanish flu, it is Legionnaires' disease, caused by a drug-resistant mutant strain of *Legionella* bacteria; the story is set *not* in 1918 but in an unspecified time in the future; in fact Spanish flu is *not* mentioned even once in the novel. It is nevertheless the story's genesis as well as its absent referent.

[14] White borrows this phrase from Northrop Frye's *Anatomy of Criticism* (1957).

The idea of writing the novel came to him when Vadukut was working on an article on Spanish flu for the *Mint* (Vadukut, 2017, p. 366).[15] Spanish flu was dubbed 'the Bombay fever' in the newspaper reports of its time.[16] The outbreak in the novel begins, as it did in the case of Spanish flu, in Ward A of Bombay. The symptoms of the fictional pandemic include fever, persistent cough and respiratory distress, like those of Spanish flu, though it differs in its terminal stage. It kills by turning the immune system against the body's own cells, leading to a 'meltdown' in which blood spurts out of every orifice: 'Even medical practitioners and public health workers, who in their careers had seen some of the worst outbreaks of disease in the world, would watch in awe and disgust. Nothing had prepared them for this' (p. 13). The reality that *Bombay Fever* depicts may not correspond exactly to that of the Spanish flu pandemic as constructed in the epidemiological accounts, the newspaper reports, Nirala's memoir and Ali's novel, and reconstructed in contemporary media stories in the times of COVID, but it evokes the same sense of incomprehension, panic and despair. Regarding the question of referentiality in literature, Paul Ricoeur writes: 'poetic texts, too, speak *of* the world, even though they may not do so in a descriptive fashion'. Instead, they set in motion 'a more radical power of reference to those aspects of our being-in-the-world that cannot be talked about directly' (1984, p. 80, italics in original).

Bombay Fever belongs to a fairly recent genre of medical thrillers that Priscilla Wald calls 'outbreak narratives'. They are primarily about highly virulent but short-lived pandemics caused by new viruses and bacteria, mostly zoonotic, or older ones that break out in places where they had not been found earlier. The

---

[15] The article, published in the *Mint* of 28 November 2014, was titled 'Déjà View: The Bombay Fever'. At the end of the article, Vadukut writes: 'If there are any budding non-fiction writers out there, you have around four years left to come up with a perfectly timed book' (2014). 2018 marked the hundredth anniversary of the pandemic, and Vadukut did precisely what he suggested to his readers, though as fiction.

[16] See, for instance, para. 104, *Report on Native Papers in the Madras Presidency for the week ending October 12, 1918* and Madras (India: Presidency), 1918b, p. 1511.

stories are prompted by outbreaks in the late-twentieth century, starting with HIV/AIDS and SARS and continuing almost annually till date, with COVID being the latest. They are typically biomedical in content, foregrounding transmission patterns, statistics of disease and death, the investigative process that leads to the discovery of the causative agent and public health responses, and ending with a sudden decline in cases as the microbe runs out of hosts. 'The conventions of the paradigmatic story about newly emerging infections have evolved out of earlier accounts of epidemiological efforts to address widespread threats of communicable disease' (Wald, 2008, p. 2).

Bombay Fever tracks the unfolding of the outbreak from its origin in Sri Lanka to Geneva, then to Mumbai and subsequently other parts of India. Outbreak narratives, according to Wald, 'map the changing spaces, relationships, practices, and temporalities of a globalizing world' (2008, pp. 6–7). In the novel the outbreak begins in 2016 when a fertiliser factory is set up, with the help of China, on the outskirts of Jaffna. The cooling towers of the factory are the source of the bacteria. The first person to be infected is Kanimozhi Balasingham, a Swiss citizen of Sri Lankan origin who had paid a visit to her grandparents in Jaffna. She transmits the bacteria to Hormazd Patel, a journalist visiting Geneva to cover a trade show, who carries it on his return to Mumbai. Hormazd self-medicates with antibiotics, thus unwittingly producing a drug-resistant strain of the pathogen. 'Unbeknownst to anybody, Hormazd Patel became the carrier of a new, immeasurably more potent mutant strain of the bacteria that had reduced Kanimozhi Balasingham to a bloody puddle on the grounds outside the Lausanne Murugan temple' (Vadukut, 2017, p. 31). On returning to his flat in Cusrow Baug, he transmits the disease to his mother. He also transmits it to Amod Patil, the administrative manager of a newspaper office when he attends a job interview there. Amod, who was the first to die, is the 'Subject Zero' of the epidemic (p. 21). Four days later, on 'Day Zero', the epidemic breaks out in Ward A of Mumbai including the dock area, Cusrow Baug and a hotel where an international summit is to be held. The cases multiply rapidly from then on all over the city, and a lockdown is imposed to prevent its further spread. Despite this, cases appear in Pune, Nasik, Nagpur and New Delhi. There is panic everywhere and a violent mob blocks the Mumbai–Pune highway, attacking people who try to get across. Within a few days hospitals are swamped with new cases, and when a rumour circulates that antibiotics can cure the disease medicine shops are ransacked. As violence goes up, police and paramilitary forces are called in and Mumbai assumes the state of a city in war. Vadukut traces the progress of the disease from the time when Kanimozhi dies and passes it on to Hormazd, eighty-six days before the outbreak, recounting day-to-day events from the fourth day, to twelve days after it shows signs of abating. On the fifth day of the outbreak there are twelve thousand cases reported in the city and six to seven hundred deaths, and on the sixth, fifteen thousand cases and more than eight hundred deaths. The novel, thus, recounts the unfolding of the outbreak in real time-space, creating a chronotope of contagion conventionally associated with what Wald calls the outbreak narrative. On the eighth day, the cause of the outbreak becomes known: it is Legionnaire's disease in a highly virulent and drug-resistant form. 'Hormazd had been infected with a slow-acting, if devastating, bug. His medication amped it up' (p. 355). The mutant disintegrates at higher temperatures and releases toxins that cause excessive bleeding and death. When people turn off air conditioners, therefore, the death rate, which had seemed to stabilise, shoots up. Once this connection is made, all the infected are shifted to a cold environment, deaths reduce and the outbreak is contained. Eventually, it tapers off as the bacteria find no new host to infect.

The primary focus of the novel is on the epidemiological work carried out by medical officers, scientists and the team from the National Centre of Disease Control, who track the disease's transmission chains, identify its cause and bring it to a close. The 'role of epidemiology', in outbreak narratives writes Wald, 'was at once to read and to write the epidemic as a story of detection with predictive value' (2008, p. 23). Scientific procedures for tracking and detecting disease-causing organisms evolved in the 1950s, with the setting up of an Epidemiological Investigation Service of the Communicable Disease Center, later renamed as the Centers for Disease Control, in the United States. These were not available when the Spanish flu pandemic occurred, and in reframing its story in terms of disease detection *Bombay Fever* adds to the reports by Phipson and White a retrospective significance. It also adds to the newspaper accounts a political dimension by bringing into greater focus the role of the state, especially in the figure of a prime minister who runs away from the scene of contagion but closely monitors it, a chief minister who bravely takes up leadership in his absence, the NCDC team and the officers of a national plan for drug-resistant diseases called the Srivatsa programme. It adds a new element, too, to the outbreak paradigm. Vadukut narrates the story in two temporal modes: one presenting the events as they happen, and the other retrospectively, when Ayush Vajpeyi, a public health official tasked with curbing the outbreak, faces an inquiry years later. By alternating between the two modes, *Bombay Fever* is able to present the events as well as their interpretation in retrospect. It is also able to juxtapose personal stories of fear, bewilderment and loss with the official version of the outbreak, which it highlights in the retrospective narrative.

Bombay Fever was composed sometime between 2014 and 2017. It cannot, therefore, be considered a retelling of the Spanish flu outbreak in COVID times, which happened several years later. But when we read it now, as I have done, it looks back on a catastrophic past to presage a not-too-distant future, and in this prophetic act it becomes meaningful to us. It recreates the social reality of contagion, renewed and augmented with new meaning every time contagion breaks out, as it has been happening since the beginning of this century. Reading the novel in terms of COVID may not be what the author anticipated, but that is how literature works: every new reading reconstitutes the text and adds meanings that it seems to warrant. '[E]very literary work', as Bakhtin puts it, '*faces outward away from itself*, toward the listener-reader, and to a certain extent thus anticipates possible reactions to itself' (1981, p. 257, italics in original). Or, as Ricoeur puts it, 'it is the reader who completes the work inasmuch as … the written work is a sketch for reading' (1984, p. 77)

5.7. Conclusion

The 1918 Spanish flu epidemic in India, which broke out in mid-June, subsided and then returned three months later to claim fifteen to twenty million lives. Its impact was greatest in Bombay Presidency, where the brief first wave killed sixteen hundred people, followed by Delhi, Punjab, the Central Provinces and the United Provinces, and to a relatively lesser extent in the east and the south. Amplifying its impact was a famine that broke out concurrently, partly because of adverse weather conditions and partly due to the mismanagement of food supply by the colonial government. Though Spanish flu was the biggest pandemic in the recorded history of India as well as the world—it still continues to be so—it left few traces in collective memory and was not even widely reported at the time. There were several reasons for this: the preoccupations of the First World War that began in 1914 and continued till November 1918, resentment among Indians against a draconian sedition act that prohibited any form of political activity, and demand for reforms, especially Home Rule, that would give Indian leaders a more active role in their own governance. These issues took up much of the space that might have been given to the outbreak in less contentious times.

Drawing on literary accounts, epidemiological reports and newspaper articles, I have tried to reconstruct in this chapter the story of the outbreak in the way it was experienced and understood by both the rulers and the ruled. I have analysed these texts to show how they told the story variously in biomedical, social and cosmological frames of meaning, each elaborating different dimensions of the event. My main theoretical distinction is the biomedical/cosmological binary: that is, the contrast between those accounts that represented the pandemic in terms of its morbidity and mortality rates, timelines and maps of spread, and those that recounted it as a breakdown of the social, political and cosmic order. In discussing each individual text, I have tried to bring out the two broad meanings attributed to the outbreak: a public health crisis magnified by food scarcity and the failure of the colonial authorities to address both proactively, and a catastrophe on an unprecedented scale that tested the limits of human endurance.

Though the story of Spanish flu might have been forgotten for almost a century after it broke out, it came to be remembered and reconstituted from the fragments it left behind in the times of COVID-19. In 2020–2021, during the first and second waves of coronavirus disease, stories of Spanish flu began to circulate across various media. Linking its various aspects to the current pandemic, they constructed it as both a precursor to COVID and an index of how it was to unfold. In this context, I have attempted to read Sidin Vadukut's novel *Bombay Fever*, which fictionalises the Spanish flu outbreak in another time of collective disaster. Though it was written well before COVID, reading it now provides added significance to the events of 1918 as well as those yet to happen in our time.

As a way of concluding these acts of remembrance, let me cite an event that took place in Goa on 11 October 2020. It was an event that added yet another layer of meaning to the multiple significances of outbreak experience. In 1918 a large number of people in and around the village of Raia in south Goa succumbed to Spanish flu and the cemetery had to be expanded to bury them. The village head and elders built a monument to the dead with a cross and a plaque that read '[I]n memory of the victims of the flu of 1918'. In July–August 2020, when cases of COVID infection and death started mounting, 'people began flocking to the memorial, turning to it to pray for the survival of near and dear ones' (de Souza, 2020). The memorial, which had been left unattended all these years, was publicly restored and consecrated again on 11 October. 'Ever since, it has seen a steady stream of devotees and visitors who light candles and pray for the recovery of those ailing from Covid-19.' It was as if the spirits of the dead would help them survive a crisis not unlike the one that had taken them away. At the limits of our endurance, as Clifford Geertz says, we turn to the power of worship, in the belief that, while it cannot materially relieve our suffering, it can at least make it more bearable: 'As a religious problem, the problem of suffering is, paradoxically, not how to avoid suffering but how to suffer, how to make of physical pain, personal loss, worldly defeat, or the helpless contemplation of others' agony something bearable, supportable—something, as we say, sufferable' (1973, p. 104). The Raia monument, in remembering the Spanish flu dead, epitomises that belief.

References

Acharjee, S. (2000, March 19). Pandemics of the past. *India Today.* https://www.indiatoday.in/india-today-insight/story/coronavirus-pandemics-of-the-past-1656730-2020-03-18

Ali, A. (1940). *Twilight in Delhi.* Rupa Publications.

Ali, A. & JSAL. (1998). Interview: Ahmed Ali: 3 August 1975, Rochester, Michigan. *Journal of South Asian Literature, 33/34*(1/2), 117–194.

Annapurani, V. (2021, July 9). Spanish flu and Covid-19: A tale of two pandemics. *The Hindu BusinessLine.* https://www.thehindubusinessline.com/news/spanish-flu-and-covid-19-a-tale-of-two-pandemics/article34746020.ece

Arnold, D. (2020). Pandemic India: Coronavirus and the uses of history. *The Journal of Asian Studies,* 79(3), 569–577.

Bakhtin, M. (1981). Forms of time and of the chronotope in the novel. In M. Holquist, (Ed.); C. Emerson & M. Holquist (Trans.), *The dialogic imagination* (pp. 84–258). University of Texas Press.

Balfour, A. & Scott, H.H. (1924). *Health problems of empire: Past, present and future.* W. Collins Sons and Co. Ltd.

BBC News Hindi. (2020, May 10). *Spanish Flu: Corona virus se bhi khatarnak woh bimari, jisne bharat mein har taraf lashein bichhaa di thi…* [Video]. YouTube. https://www.youtube.com/watch?v=WiDGE_Zut18

Belling, C. (2009). Overwhelming the medium: Fiction and the trauma of pandemic influenza in 1918. *Literature and Medicine,* 28(1), 55–81.

Bhattacharyya, N.N. (1999). *The Indian mother goddesses.* 3rd ed. Manohar Publishers and Distributors.

Biswas, S. (2020, March 18). What India can learn from the deadly 1918 flu. *BBC News.* https://www.bbc.com/news/world-asia-india-51904019

Butler, J. (2004). *Precarious life: The powers of mourning and violence.* Verso.

Camus, A. (1948). *The plague* (S. Gilbert, Trans.). Penguin.

Chandra, S., Kuljanin, G. & Wray, J. 2012. Mortality from the influenza pandemic of 1918–19: The case of India. *Demography, 49*(3), 857–865. https://www.jstor.org/stable/23252674

'Coronavirus India lockdown day 33 updates: April 26, 2020'. (2020, April 26). *The Hindu.* https://www.thehindu.com/news/national/india-coronavirus-lockdown-april-26-2020-live-updates/article62125374.ece

Crosby, A.W. (1976). *Epidemic and peace, 1918.* Greenwood Press.

Das, D.K. (2019a). *Teaching AIDS: The cultural politics of HIV disease in India.* Springer.

Das, D.K. (2019b). Cultural narratives of epidemic: Ananthamurthy's *Samskara. Anekaant, 11* (2019–20), 41–44.

Das, D.K. (2022). Epidemic narrative: Two paradigms. In S. Venkatesan, A. Chatterjee, A. D. Lewis & B. Callendar (Eds.), *Pandemics and epidemics in cultural representation* (pp. 13–27). Springer Nature.

de Souza, G. (2020, October 14). Once forgotten, 1918 Spanish flu memorial gains following amid Covid-19 scare in Goa. *Hindustan Times.* https://www.hindustantimes.com/cities/once-forgotten-1918-spanish-flu-memorial-gains-following-amid-covid-19-scare-in-goa/story-VobuVy0yfCusX9P4OCFROM.html

Eliade, M. (1959). *The sacred and the profane: The nature of religion* (W.R. Trask, Trans.). Harcourt, Inc.

Esposito, R. (2008). *Bios: Biopolitics and philosophy* (T. Campbell, Trans.). University of Minnesota Press.

Ferrari, F.M. (2010). Old rituals for new threats: Possession and healing in the cult of Śītalā. In C. Brosius & U. Hüsken (Eds.), *Ritual matters: Dynamic dimensions in practice* (pp. 144–171). Routledge.

Ferrari, F.M. (2015). *Religion, devotion and medicine in north India: The healing power of Śītalā.* Bloomsbury.

Foucault, M. (2000). The birth of social medicine. In J.D. Faubion (Ed.); R. Hurley, et al. (Trans.), *Power* (pp. 134–156). The New Press.

Foucault, M. (2003). *'Society must be defended': Lectures at the Collège de France, 1975–1976* (M. Bertani,& A. Fontana, Eds.; D. Macey, Trans). Picador.

Foucault, M. (2007). *Security, territory, population: Lectures at the Collège de France, 1977-1978* (M. Senellart, Ed.; G. Burchell, Trans.). Palgrave Macmillan.

Foucault, M. (2008). *The birth of biopolitics: Lectures at the Collège de France, 1978-79* (M. Senellart, Eds.; G. Burchell, Trans.). Palgrave Macmillan.

Fries, U. (1990). Two hundred years of English death notices. In M. Bridges (Ed.), *On strangeness* (pp. 57–71). Gunter Narr Verlag.

Geertz, C. (1973). *The interpretation of cultures: Selected essays*. Basic Books.

Gupta, N. (1971). Military security and urban development: A case study of Delhi 1857–1912. *Modern Asian Studies*, *5*(1), 61–77.

Harrison, M. (1994). *Public health in British India: Anglo-Indian preventive medicine, 1859–1914*. Cambridge University Press.

Honigsbaum, M. (2020). *The pandemic century: A history of global contagion from the Spanish flu to Covid-19*. Penguin.

Humphries, M.O. (2014). Paths of infection: The First World War and origins of the 1918 influenza pandemic. *War in History*, *21*(1), 55–81.

India Office Library and Records. (1918a). *Report on native papers for the week ending September 14, 1918*. https://jstor.org/stable/saoa.crl.25637082

India Office Library and Records. (1918b). *Report on native papers for the week ending September 21, 1918*. https://jstor.org/stable/saoa.crl.25637083

India Office Library and Records. (1918c). *Report on native papers for the week ending September 28, 1918*. https://jstor.org/stable/saoa.crl.25637084

India Office Library and Records. (1918d). *Report on native papers for the week ending October 05, 1918*. https://jstor.org/stable/saoa.crl.25637085

India Office Library and Records. (1918e). *Report on native papers for the week ending October 12, 1918*. https://jstor.org/stable/saoa.crl.25637086

India Office Library and Records. (1918f). *Report on native papers for the week ending October 19, 1918*. https://jstor.org/stable/saoa.crl.25637087

India Office Library and Records. (1918g). *Report on native papers for the week ending October 26, 1918.* https://jstor.org/stable/saoa.crl.25637088

India Office Library and Records. (1918h). *Report on native papers for the week ending November 16, 1918.* https://jstor.org/stable/saoa.crl.25637091

India Office Library and Records. (1918i). *Report on native papers for the week ending November 23, 1918.* https://jstor.org/stable/saoa.crl.25637092

Indian Famine Commission. (1880). *Report of the Indian Famine Commission, part I: Famine relief.* Her Majesty's Stationery Office.

Jeffery, R. (1988). *The politics of health in India.* University of California Press.

Johnson, N.P.A.S. & Mueller, J. (2002). Updating the accounts: Global mortality of the 1918–1920 'Spanish' influenza pandemic. *Bulletin of the History of Medicine, 76*(1), 105–115.

Kapoor, A. (2020, April 3). An unwanted shipment: The Indian experience of the 1918 Spanish flu. *The Economic Times.* https://economictimes.indiatimes.com/news/politics-and-nation/an-unwanted-shipment-the-indian-experience-of-the-1918-spanish-flu/articleshow/74963051.cms

Killingray, D. (2003). A 'new imperial disease': The influenza pandemic of 1918–19 and its impact on the British Empire. *Caribbean Quarterly, 49*(4), 30–49.

Koch, T. (2005). *Cartographies of disease: Maps, mapping, and medicine.* ESRI Press.

Kress, G. & Knapp, P. (1992). Genre in a social theory of language. *English in Education, 26*(2), 4–15.

Lahiri, N. (2003). Commemorating and remembering 1857: The revolt in Delhi and its afterlife. *World Archeology, 35*(1), 35–60.

Lefevbre, H. (1991). *The production of space* (D. Nicholson-Smith, Trans.). Blackwell Publishing.

Liao, P.C. (2022). Outbreak narratives of the 1918 influenza pandemic: Contagion, community, and politics in Myla Goldberg's *Wickett's Last Remedy* and Thomas Mullen's *The Last Town on Earth*. In S. Venkatesan, A. Chatterjee, A.D. Lewis & B. Callendar (Eds.), *Pandemics and epidemics in cultural representation* (pp. 121–133). Springer Nature.

Madras (India : Presidency). (1918a). *Report on Native Papers in the Madras Presidency.* https://jstor.org/stable/saoa.crl.30377725.

Madras (India : Presidency). (1918b). *Report on Native Papers in the Madras Presidency.* https://jstor.org/stable/saoa.crl.30377813

Madras (India : Presidency). (1918c). *Report on Native Papers in the Madras Presidency.* https://jstor.org/stable/saoa.crl.30377814

Madras (India : Presidency). (1918d). *Report on Native Papers in the Madras Presidency.* https://jstor.org/stable/saoa.crl.30377815

Madras (India : Presidency). (1918e). *Report on Native Papers in the Madras Presidency.* https://jstor.org/stable/saoa.crl.30377817

Phillips, H. (1987). Why did it happen? Religious and lay explanations of the Spanish flu epidemic of 1918 in South Africa. *Kronos*, *12*, 72–92.

Phipson, E.S. (1918). Influenza in Bombay. *The Indian Medical Gazette*, 53(12), 441–448.

Phipson, E.S. (1923). The pandemic of influenza in India in the year 1918. *The Indian Medical Gazette*, *58*(11), 509–524.

Ricoeur, P. (1984). *Time and narrative, Vol. 1.* (K. McLaughlin & D. Pellauer, Trans.). University of Chicago Press.

Rosenberg, C.E. (1989). What is an epidemic? AIDS in historical perspective. *Daedalus*, *118*(2), 1–17.

Singh, M. (2021). Bombay fever/Spanish flu: Public health and native press in colonial Bombay, 1918–19. *South Asia Research*, *41*(1), 35–52.

Sreevatsan, A. (2020, March 12). Why 1918 matters in India's corona war. *The Mint.* https://www.livemint.com/news/world/why-1918-matters-in-india-s-corona-war-11584033795146.html

Srinivasan, P. (2019). Sprouts of the body, sprouts of the field: Identification of the goddess with poxes in south India. *Religions*, *10*(147), 1–15.

Tambiah, S.J. (1980). A performative approach to ritual. *The British Academy: Radcliffe-Brown lecture in social anthropology*, pp. 113–169.

Taubenberger, J.K., Reid, A.H., Krafft, A.E., Bijwaard, K.E. & Fanning T.G. (1997). Initial genetic characterization of the 1918 'Spanish' influenza virus. *Science*, *275*, 1793–1796.

The Khalsa Advocate. (October 8, 1918). *The Khalsa Advocate*, *16*(39). https://jstor.org/stable/saoa.crl.35194979

The Khalsa Advocate (November 5, 1918). *The Khalsa Advocate, 16*(42). https://jstor.org/stable/saoa.crl.35194982

Tripathi, S. (2016). *A life misspent*. (S. Khanna, Trans.). Harper Perennial.

Younger, P. (1980). A temple festival of Māriyammaṉ. *Journal of the American Academy of Religion, 48*(4), 493–517.

Vadukut, S. (2014, November 28). Déjà view: The Bombay fever. *The Mint*. https://www.livemint.com/Opinion/XuaCIAq7Bcy8FOPtVRoPFM/Dj-View--The-Bombay-Fever.html

Vadukut, S. (2017). *Bombay fever*. Simon & Schuster India.

Wald, P. (2008). *Contagious: Cultures, carriers, and the outbreak narrative*. Duke University Press.

White, F.N. (1919). *A preliminary report on the influenza pandemic of 1918 in India by the sanitary commissioner with the government of India*. Government Monotype Press.

Whitehead, H. (1921). *The village gods of south India*. 2nd ed. Association Press.

6

Infectious Hepatitis

Religion, Rationality and Politics in Satyajit Ray's *Ganashatru*

Satyajit Ray's 1990 film *Ganashatru*, an adaptation of Henrik Ibsen's *An Enemy of the People*, is about an outbreak of infectious hepatitis in a pilgrimage town in West Bengal. The town's doctor identifies the source of spread in the *charanamrita* or holy water of the town's temple, and tries to warn the public against drinking it. But he is opposed by his brother, who heads the town's municipality, and the temple's founder, both of whom have a vested interest in suppressing news of the outbreak. The main source of the town's economy is the money it gets from pilgrimage, and business interests overtake public concern in their minds. They first try to gag the doctor when he thinks of publishing his findings in the local newspaper, and when he calls a public meeting they disrupt it and instigate the audience against him. He loses his job, his daughter is sacked from the school where she teaches, his rented house is vandalised, and the landlord asks him to vacate. When things seem to go out of control, his future son-in-law, who leads a drama group, rallies support by mustering the town's youth and the educated public. The film ends with slogans in praise of the doctor, implying that the townspeople's faith in him will soon be restored and the temple's water supply cleaned.

Ganashatru is in many ways different from Ray's earlier films, a point that has often been noted, though it continues with his characteristically realist style. First, unlike the others which are shot mostly on location *Ganashatru* is shot almost entirely on sets.[1] Visually, its cinematography connotes the claustrophobic environment and the mindset of a small town in rural Bengal. Second, it focuses more on characters than spaces, emphasising their moods, expressions and body language in order to foreground the conflicts that animate them. Third, it explores political issues in a manner that Ray's earlier films—especially the *Apu Trilogy* and the Calcutta films, *Pratidwandi*, *Seemabaddha* and *Jana Aranya*—did not, though they too were about social reality. Finally, it is explicitly allegorical, with the two main characters, the doctor and his brother, representing opposed qualities such as honesty versus corruption, public interest versus self-interest and openness versus manipulation, and the townspeople representing reason versus blind faith in religious dogma. *Ganashatru* is an allegory of a crisis precipitated by an outbreak of viral jaundice, which a politics of self-interest and religious dogma try to suppress despite its threat to the community as a whole. In the following sections of the chapter, I will discuss the historical context of jaundice outbreaks in India that informs the film's realistic core, Henrik Ibsen's play *An Enemy of the People* which Ray adapted for his film, and its reconfiguration in *Ganashatru*.

6.1. Epidemiology of Infectious Hepatitis in India

Infectious hepatitis refers to a disease of the liver caused by a microorganism belonging to the genus *Hepatovirus*, its symptoms being fever, nausea, loss of appetite, liver enlargement, abdominal distress, and yellowing of eyes and skin caused by increased bilirubin. It was earlier known by several other names such as 'epidemic jaundice', 'infective hepatitis' and 'catarrhal jaundice', but in 1953 the World Health Organisation's Expert Committee on Hepatitis recommended the use of the term 'infectious hepatitis' and identified for the first time its causative agents: hepatitis A virus or HAV and hepatitis B virus or HBV (WHO, 1953). Subsequently, three other subtypes of the virus

[1] Ray suffered a heart attack in 1983 and was advised rest. After he had recovered, in 1988, his doctors insisted that he must restrict himself to working on sets and not outdoor locations (Robinson, 2004, p. 339).

have been identified, namely C, D and E. Hepatitis A and E are transmitted through water contaminated with faecal matter, while B, C and D are transmitted through infected blood (WHO, 2019). Most outbreaks of epidemic jaundice are caused by A and E viruses, and are localised in areas with insanitary water supply. Hepatitis B, C and D infections, in contrast, are sporadic and rarely focused in a specific locality, given that they are spread by infected blood or blood products.[2]

Historical records suggest that *hepatoviruses* may have existed for centuries. A disease called *icterus*, named after the Greek word for the golden-crowned thrush (*T. aurocapillus*), finds mention in the Hippocratic corpus. 'According to ancient Jewish and Greek beliefs, placing this bird near the umbilicus of a jaundiced person may lead to resolution of the icterus/jaundice, recovery of the patient, and death of the bird.' The term 'jaundice' comes from the Old French *jaunisse*, derived from *jaune* (yellow), which dates it at some time between the eighth and fourteenth century AD. The disease also finds mention in Chinese medical literature of the second century (Shouval, 2020, p. 14). In India, it is mentioned as *kamala* in *Caraca-Samhitā* (1996, p. 145) and in *Sushruta Samhita*, where it is described as imparting a '(deep) yellow tint' to the complexion of the patient and producing 'physical weakness', yellow stool and urine (2006, p. 270). Modern outbreaks of infectious hepatitis have often occurred in times of war, because of which it came to acquire the epithet '*jaunisse des camps*' or 'camp jaundice'. An estimated forty thousand troops died of the disease in the American Civil War, and an estimated sixteen million were affected during the two world wars (Feinstone, 2019, p. 1; Shouval, 2020, p. 14; Mirsky, 1954, p. 308).

Outbreaks of infectious hepatitis have occurred regularly in India. Satsangi and Chawla mention six such outbreaks, in Delhi

[2] An outbreak of hepatitis B infection was reported from the town of Modasa in Sabarkantha district, Gujarat, in 2009. A total of 856 persons were found to be infected with the virus over a seven-month period, and the outbreak was attributed to the use of unsterilised injection needles and syringes by local practitioners (Patel et al., 2012).

(in 1955, with 29,300 cases), Aurangabad (1961, 865 cases), Siliguri (1966, 4,287 cases), Ahmedabad (1975, 2,572 cases), Kanpur (1990, 79,091 cases) and Nellore (2008, 23,915 cases) (2016, p. 205). The Delhi outbreak, perhaps one of the biggest in India in recent times, started in the last week of November 1955, reached its peak a month later, and receded in the middle of January 1956. Like most such outbreaks in India, it was caused by the mixing of the drinking water supply with sewage water. Seepage from Najafgarh Nallah, a storm drain that had degenerated into a sewage canal, entered the nearby Wazirabad Water Works that supplied piped water to many parts of the city (Viswanathan, 1957).

Epidemic jaundice in India is caused mostly by hepatitis A and E viruses. Of the 163 outbreaks with known causes reported to the Integrated Disease Surveillance Programme (IDSP) during 2011–2013, 54 were due to hepatitis A and 78 due to hepatitis E (Kumar et al., 2015; Aggarwal & Goel, 2021, p. 169). Though the exact causative agent in the Delhi outbreak could not be ascertained at the time when it occurred, it has retrospectively been attributed to hepatitis E (Labrique et al., 1999, p. 162). An outbreak of hepatitis E epidemic was reported in Sambalpur district, Odisha in 2014, causing nearly three thousand infections and twenty-six deaths (Dwibedi et al., 2018). A random sampling of reports in medical journals reveals that outbreaks of hepatitis A and E have occurred frequently across India in the last fifteen years, from Kashmir (Kadri et al., 2018) to Palakkad in Kerala and Tiruchirappalli in Tamil Nadu (Zachariah et al., 2017; Geetharani et al. 2016); from Ahmedabad in Gujarat to Sambalpur in Odisha and Kolkata (Chauhan et al., 2010; Dwibedi et al., 2018; Das et al., 2004). In all cases the outbreaks were linked to the water supply. *National Action Plan Combating Viral Hepatitis in India*, a report published by the Ministry of Health and Family Welfare in 2019, states: 'HAV and HEV are important causes of acute viral hepatitis and acute liver failure (ALF). Due to paucity of data, the exact burden of disease for the country is not established. However, available literature indicates a wide range and suggests that HAV is responsible for 10–30% of acute hepatitis and 5–15% of acute liver failure cases in India. It is further reported that HEV 10–40% of acute hepatitis and 15–45% of acute liver failure' (sic) (p. 23). To prevent outbreaks of epidemic jaundice, the ministry has introduced a number of sanitary interventions under its Swachh Bharat Abhiyan that include providing safe drinking water, improving urban sewage systems, and installing toilets in households to prevent open defecation (pp. 25–26). In a random sampling of 494 referrals at a hospital-cum-research and diagnostic laboratory that receives samples from almost all districts in West Bengal, carried out from July 2017 to June 2018, it was found that fifty-six tested positive for hepatitis A virus and eighty-nine for hepatitis E (Chatterjee et al., 2019). An *India Today* story of 28 February 1993, three years after the release of *Ganashatru*, reported that faecal matter was found in the water supply of a large number of temples in Kolkata. Inspired by Ray's film, a doctor tested samples from twenty-four temples, of which seventeen were found to be contaminated (Biswas, 1993). I cite these references to emphasise three points that are relevant to the story of *Ganashatru*: (i) water-borne hepatitis infection has, in the last several decades, become both endemic and epidemic in India; (ii) this is primarily due to contamination of drinking water supply from leaking sewage lines; and (iii) outbreaks of infectious hepatitis have been reported from temple towns. My objective is to show how this constitutes a realistic core for Ray's allegory. Biswas's story underlines the central theme of the film, that blind faith in religious dogma often overtakes our capacity to reason. He cites a priest who insists that the holy water of a temple can never be polluted and that no one has ever fallen ill after taking it; he also cites an engineer who says: '*Charanamrita* is sacred, it is pure. It can never do you bad' (Biswas, 1993, italics in original). Read in the context of *Ganashatru*, these seem to be echoes of key dialogues in the film. In his biography of Satyajit Ray, Andrew Robinson writes that a serious outbreak of infectious hepatitis in the temple town of Tirupati had been reported in the press about a month before Ray began shooting for *Ganashatru*. 'In 1992, after Ray's death, his instinct was confirmed by a public health survey in Bengal that revealed high counts of faecal coliform bacteria (usually found in sewage) in the water of many temples' (Robinson, 2004, pp. 343–344).

6.2. Public Health in *An Enemy Of The People*

Ibsen's play, first published in 1882 and staged the next year, is about an outbreak of gastro-intestinal diseases in a southern coastal town in Norway that has recently been established as a spa centre and is making good on it. The town's doctor, who is also a member of the spa committee, traces the source of contamination to his father-in-law's tannery upstream, and decides to inform the authorities and publicise the outbreak in the local newspaper. He expects that the town would be grateful to him for this timely detection of a problem that would otherwise have affected its new-found prosperity. But it turns out that his brother, the town's mayor, the editor and printer of the local newspaper, and the townspeople by and large oppose him because of vested interests. When the doctor calls a meeting to make the matter public, he is not allowed to speak and is declared an enemy of the people. The entire town is set against him, and the townspeople try to hound him out. He is removed from his post as medical officer of the Baths, his daughter loses her job as teacher in the local school, his school-going sons are asked to stay at home, and his landlord evicts him. The only persons who support him are his family and a sea-captain, who offers them refuge in his house. The doctor determines to remain in the town, to provide his services free to the poor and open a school for their children.

An Enemy of the People has been interpreted as a critique of public opinion in defence of the Nietzschean exceptional individual who singularly confronts it. This view is based on Dr Stockmann's diatribe on 'the masses, the majority,—this infernal compact majority' in Act IV and his closing line: 'the strongest man in the world is he who stands most alone' (Ibsen, 2010, p. 95, p. 133). In Scandinavian intellectual circles of the time, the political philosophy of Nietzsche was widely discussed and debated (Gjesdal, 2014, pp. 109-110). Ibsen seems to have also had a personal reason for his attack on public opinion. He wrote the play in retaliation against the hostile reception that his earlier play *Ghosts* had received in the press (Brustein, 1962, p. 140). *Ghosts* was about a family destroyed by adultery and incest, venereal disease, and the stranglehold of the past. *Enemy* is about yet another disease that opens up latent social and familial conflicts, and looks forward to a millenarian future that can resolve them. What links the two plays is not just their critical focus on society, but their figurative coupling of biological pathogens and social pathogenesis. Bodily disease triggers moral disease in the social body, and the plays are about how both can be sanitised and what form this sanitisation would take. Ibsen, thus, frames the question of public health in allegorical terms, by joining physical and moral disease metaphorically.

In mid-nineteenth century Europe, at the time when Ibsen wrote *An Enemy of the People*, there were three predominant models of public health. The first was environmentalist, based on the classical concept of 'miasma', that is, the theory that disease was caused by poisons in the air, soil and water of a place, its 'bad air' or 'mal-aria'. Prevention of outbreak required evacuation of people from the places where it broke out. The second, deriving from the concept of contagion, was segregationist. Outbreak-prevention relied on quarantining the diseased and setting up a *cordon sanitaire* between them and those presumed to be healthy. The third was sanitary engineering: supply of safe drinking water, proper disposal of waste, elimination of disease-vectors like rats, fleas and mosquitoes, and improvements in ventilation. The sanitary model built upon the theories of both miasma and contagion, in its simultaneous focus on the body and the environment (Das, 2019, pp. 150–156).

The history of public health responses to the cholera pandemics of nineteenth-century Europe illustrates this. I take cholera as my example because it seems to be the disease that best fits the outbreak Ibsen describes but does not name in *Enemy*. In 'Choleric Fictions: Epidemiology, Medical Authority, and *An Enemy of the People*' (2008), Timothy Matos argues that the emerging field of sanitary science was what provided Ibsen his historical context. Thomas Stockmann, the public-spirited medical officer of the Baths, was modelled on the heroic figures of Louis Pasteur and Robert Koch, whose theory of germs as agents of disease, formulated partly in response to cholera, laid the foundation of sanitary science. Theodore Dalrymple (2012) suggests that the character of the doctor was based on a Dr Meissner, who was driven out of the Bohemian spa town of Teplitz-Schönau because he announced an outbreak of cholera. In an unpublished doctoral dissertation on travel-writing, Alison Hiley writes: 'Meissner evidently felt it his duty to publicise the facts, but having been grossly insulted by a crowd who surrounded his home, it became clear that Teplitz was no longer a safe place of abode for him and he was forced to escape under military protection' (1985, p. 29). Lorentz Irgens, too, links the play to cholera outbreaks in Norway: 'The fight against cholera became a public concern to the extent that it was reflected in Henrik Ibsen's (1832–1906) play "An Enemy of the People" of 1882. A Norwegian town is threatened by an epidemic caused by microscopic "infectious animals", and the hero, the whistleblowing physician, turns out to be the enemy' (2015, p. 23).

The emergence of sanitary science in the mid-nineteenth century was partly due to the pandemics of cholera that broke out in Europe and other continents from 1817 to 1899. There were six waves in all that broke out in 1817, 1829, 1852, 1863, 1881 and 1899 (Pollitzer, 1954). Cholera did not support the two existing models of disease-causation: environmentalist and contagionist. 'If cholera was contagious, why did it suddenly appear in a section of town out of touch with cholera victims? Why did it not affect medical personnel who attempted to care for the sufferers? If a miasma was responsible, why did the disease strike some people in a town and not others? Why did the disease seem to move along routes of human traffic?' (Hays, 2009, p. 138) What it did support was the new model of urban sanitation, the chief architect of which was Edwin Chadwick. Chadwick proposed in the 1840s an integrated system of water supply and sewerage. Based on his system England passed the Public Health

Act of 1848, which 'empowered local boards of health to enforce drainage, build sewers, compel the servicing of cesspools, pave and clean streets, deal with nuisances, inspect lodging houses and burial grounds, control the water supply, and raise local taxes to pay for it all' (p. 146). In the 1850s and 1860s, sanitarianism overtook the soil-water-air theory and the theory of contagion as the dominant public health response to cholera. Germ theory, which emerged at this time with the work of Pasteur, did not gain widespread acceptance till Koch's report on the comma bacillus on 2 February 1884.[3]

Cholera first appeared in Norway in the coastal town of Drammen in the autumn of 1832, during the second pandemic wave of 1829, and spread the next year to Christiania (now Oslo), Ager, Holmestrand and Moss. In August 1834 there were severe outbreaks in Frederikstaad. Moss, Soon, Krageroe, Farsund and Egersund (Hirsch, 1883, p. 400; Pollitzer, 1954, p. 438). Others followed periodically, during the second, third and fourth pandemics. In Drammen in 1832–33 and 1857, the total number of cases amounted to 544 with 336 deaths. In Bergen in 1848–1849, where it was most probably introduced by a Dutch ship, there were 605 deaths. Kristiansand in Ager County suffered three outbreaks in 1833, 1853 and 1866, but recorded only 15 deaths, possibly because of its stringent quarantine measures (Oeding, 1992; Torstveit & Vesterhus, 2005). The last outbreak in Norway, mild compared to the earlier ones, was in 1873, nine years before Ibsen wrote *An Enemy of the People* (Pollitzer, 1954, p. 448). Norway, in fact, suffered far less than its neighbours and other countries in Europe, the entire region north of Bergen being spared of any outbreak (p. 457). But the panic caused by a disease that was believed to have been confined to Asia—it was called *Asiatic* cholera at the time—and yet broke out so suddenly

[3] Pasteur's work in the 1860s and 1870s marked the beginning of what later came to be called germ theory, especially his identification of the causative agent of anthrax in 1876 and of tuberculosis in 1882, but it was Koch's isolation of the comma bacillus (*Vibrio cholerae*) that finally confirmed the aetiological role of germs and put paid to Max Pettenkofer's influential theory of soil and water (Coleman, 1987).

and so often with such devastating effects that it was enough to make it critical for Norway's public health policy. In the early decades of the nineteenth century, when Norway became self-governing, its major concern had been nation-building. Public health interventions, which were restricted to vaccination, the training of healthcare workers and the constitution of district medical boards, had received comparatively little attention. When cholera broke out in the 1830s, these interventions proved inadequate to deal with the crisis. The Public Health Law of May 1860 decentralised health services and led to the creation of boards of health for each community comprising of a health officer and local representatives (Hubbard, 2006, p. 114). The governance of the spa town in *Enemy* is an outcome of this reorganisation of public health. Many a times, as in Ibsen's play, public health decisions of the community were influenced not so much by medical priorities as by 'the economic resources and political preferences of the communal councils' (pp. 114–115).

Cholera outbreaks occurred in the spa towns of Holmestrand and Moss in the 1830s, and such places must have felt more vulnerable than others from the point-of-view of their business. 'Taking the waters', which had once been an aristocratic privilege, had become accessible to a newly-prosperous middle class that could afford the benefits of Norway's fledgling health tourism industry. 'Bathing in sea water and sea air, in general, were promoted in the nineteenth century as invigorating, and this was also the case at Sandefjord spa' (Rees, 2010, p. 55). Ibsen himself was a frequent visitor at Sandefjord, which he used as a setting for the first act of *When We Dead Awaken* (p. 41). The town's sense of vulnerability in *Enemy*, therefore, seems not uncommon for a community that had invested so much in constructing the Baths, and explains why it chose to keep the problem under wraps instead of addressing it. In 'Nietzschean Variations: Politics, Interest, and Education in Ibsen's *An Enemy of the People*', Kristin Gjesdal (2014) argues that the play is about the confrontation between two views of what constitutes the good social order: commitment to bodily health and commitment to socio-economic health. In his overweening insistence on making his discovery public, the doctor turns a blind eye to the town's larger interests. As Hovstad, the editor of the town's newspaper tells him: 'you do not realize that it involves a great many other things' (Ibsen, 2010, p. 34). In ordering him to keep it secret, the mayor ignores the consequences of an outbreak of disease that would ultimately affect the town's prospects. Each one, of course, is prompted by his own interest. For the mayor, making the outbreak public would involve financial loss if the Baths' reputation was damaged: 'There are other towns in the neighbourhood with qualifications to attract visitors for bathing purposes', he tells his brother. 'Don't you suppose they would immediately strain every nerve to divert the entire stream of strangers to themselves? Unquestionably they would; and then where should we be? We should probably have to abandon the whole thing, which has cost us so much money—and then you would have ruined your native town' (p. 45). For the doctor, it would be a boost to his vanity: 'It is a splendid thing for a man to be able to feel that he has done a service to his native town and to his fellow-citizens' (p. 28). The other characters, too, are motivated by their own interests. For Morten Kiil it would be the vindication that he seeks against the townspeople for expelling him from the council; for Hovstad, an opportunity to play the radical scribe who exposes the town's leading citizens; for Aslaksen it would improve his political standing in the Householders' Association and the Temperance Society (pp. 32, 36, 38). The self-seeking motives of Kiil, Hovstad and Aslaksen serve as a gloss on the antagonism of the two brothers, echoing their actual intentions regarding the problem that the town faces. On an abstract level, however, the doctor and the mayor represent 'different (incompatible) conceptions of society' (Gjesdal, 2014, p. 116). Terrance McConnell (2010), too, argues that the two brothers represent conflicting standpoints in a 'moral combat' centred in the principle of harm. The question before them is: which of the two options, publicising the outbreak or concealing it, would do least harm? Dr Stockmann, the Medical Officer of the Baths, must not risk the health of its patrons; his brother, the town's mayor, must not risk the financial welfare of its public (McConnell, 2010, pp. 80–81). As a problem play—a genre of realistic drama on social issues that Ibsen had inaugurated—*Enemy* does not try to resolve the conflict between these two conceptions of what is ethically right because it is irresolvable, but presents it as an enigma.

Norway, which had been under Danish and Swedish rule for four centuries, became a self-governing state with its own constitution and parliament in October 1814. In the ethos of nationalist-democratic politics that followed, two questions were uppermost: that of public good and that of public opinion. The themes that Gjesdal and McConnell emphasise in their reading of *An Enemy of the People* reflect the former, while the Neitzschean interpretations reflect the latter. The story of outbreak joins the two interpretations in the conjoined image of the microbial contamination of the Baths and moral contamination of the townspeople: 'all the sources of our moral life are poisoned and … the whole fabric of our civic community is founded on the pestiferous soil of falsehood' (Ibsen, 2010, p. 92).

6.3. *Ganashatru* as Epidemic Narrative

Satyajit Ray's concern in adapting Ibsen's play for his film was quite different. In localising the outbreak and transposing it to a small-town Indian milieu, he introduces a number of significant changes in the plot. First, the disease in question is not cholera but infectious hepatitis, which broke out with notable frequency in Ray's time. Cholera, which had caused massive devastation earlier, had become more endemic than epidemic. Second, the origin of disease is not a tannery upstream that contaminates the town's water supply but leaking sewerage pipes, a cause of water-borne infections that has been quite common in India. As we have seen in section 6.1 above, infectious hepatitis often broke out in epidemic form due to this. Third, the place where it breaks out is not a health resort but a temple town: thus, *Ganashatru* makes, what is in *Enemy*, a matter of sanitation alone a religious as well as sanitary concern. Finally, and most importantly, the whistle-blowing doctor finds support not in a lone itinerant member of the community but a significant section of the townspeople who believe in his fight against vested interests and canvass public opinion on his behalf. It ends with the doctor's closing words: 'I am not alone, Maya, I am not alone. I may be an enemy of the people, but I have a lot of friends' (NFDC, 1990. 1:38:53–1:39:00). My reading of *Ganashatru* as epidemic story explores the implication of these changes for Ray's critique of contemporary Indian society.

Ganashatru opens with a close-up of a stethoscope on Dr Ashoke Gupta's study table that establishes the film's key theme, scientific rationality versus religious dogma. It cuts to the doctor calling up Haridas, the editor of the town's daily, *Janavarta*, to inform him of a possible outbreak of jaundice, with cases also of typhoid, gastroenteritis and other waterborne infections. Haridas suspects that the source of contamination is a chemical factory on the river that supplies Chandipur's water, but Dr Gupta is sure that it is due to the leaking water and drainage lines. Soon after this, Chandipur's Tripureshwar Temple is brought up in a conversation that Haridas has with the doctor's wife Maya and brother Nisith. Haridas tells them that the temple, which was built ten years ago by the town's leading entrepreneur Bhargava, has brought in a lot of prosperity, establishing the town as an important pilgrimage centre. The number of visitors to the town has increased three-fold in the years after the temple was built. Haridas's comment introduces the other key theme: profiteering from faith. Within the first five minutes, thus, the film establishes its storyline: the way religion and vested interests oppose scientific reason even at the cost of a community's well-being.

It has been suggested that the film's criticism of religion is a veiled attack on the growing fundamentalism of the late 1980s. Andrew Robinson, while discussing *Ganashatru*'s treatment of religious dogma, notes that Ray had made a public statement 'warning Hindus against embracing religious fundamentalism' (2004, p. 340). Chandak Sengoopta, too, suggests that Hindu fundamentalism may be a context, linking the film's criticism of religion to the influence of Ray's Brahmo[4] upbringing, especially Brahmoisms's 'cosmopolitan, progressive ideology' (2023, p. 1). Ray himself made no reference to fundamentalism, Hindu or otherwise, in his own comments on the play, preferring to stress other meanings, especially corruption: 'Looking around me I feel that the old values of personal integrity, loyalty, liberalism, rationalism, and fair play are all completely gone. People accept corruption as a way of life, as a method of getting along, as a necessary evil' (Ray as cited in Robinson, 2004, p. 340). As far as the Brahmo influence is concerned, he categorically denied it in an interview that he gave to *Cinéaste* in 1981: 'I don't even know what being Brahmo means. I stopped going to Brahmo Semaj [*sic*] around the age of 14 or 15. I don't believe in organised religion anyway. Religion can only be on a personal level' (Gupta & Ray, 1982, p. 28). Ray's remarks, thus, do not suggest that the film was about fundamentalist ideology. There is no doubt that critique of religion is at the centre of *Ganashatru*'s plot, but it is about religious dogma and not religion as such. Moreover, it is not presented as the abstract polemical stance that Sengoopta and Robinson read into it, but is grounded specifically in the outbreak that provides its premise, as the opening and closing shots of the film show. My contention is that *Ganashatru*'s realistic core, which I have tried to contextualise in section 6.1 on the epidemiology of hepatitis in India, is so integrally tied to its allegorical frame that the critique loses conviction without it.

In *Ganashatru*, Dr Gupta traces the contamination to Bhuvanapulli, the most populous part of the town at the centre of which sits the Tripureshwar Temple, and intends to report it to the municipal authorities. As soon as they learn of this, Nisith and Bhargava confront him. Nisith is the chairman of the town's municipality, as well as Bhargava's business partner and the one who had first proposed the idea of a temple. Both fear that the report would adversely affect the town's financial interest as well

[4] The Brahmo Samaj, a sect of Hindu reformers established in Calcutta in the nineteenth century, advocated against the ritualisation of religion. Ray's grandfather, Upendrakishore converted to the Brahmo faith in 1883.

as their own. There is also a sense of ownership of the temple and they do not take any criticism of it kindly. Dr Gupta's suggestion that the temple be temporarily closed till the leakage is repaired finds no favour with them, as it would mean a lot of expenditure as well as loss of income from pilgrims. Like the priest and the engineer in Soutik Biswas's *India Today* story cited in section 6.1 above, Bhargava declares that *charanamrita* can never be polluted, even if the water supply is: 'This isn't just tap water. It contains water from the Ganges river, too. How else can we use it for worship? ... Then there's milk in it. There is *bael* leaf. There is sesame. And most important, there is *tulsi* leaf. Did you know that *tulsi* leaf removes all impurities?' (NFDC, 1990, 0:31:40–0:32:14). [5] Nisith, who believes in religion even as he exploits it, supports this view. [6] Bhargava leaves a bottle of *charanamrita* on Dr Gupta's study table, challenging him to prove that it contains germs, and warns him against 'giving my temple a bad name' (0:33:16–0:33:20). Nisith also cautions him not to 'spread any rumours that the temple water carries diseases' (0:35:48–0:35:50). Both imply that the consequences for him would be severe if he persists in his efforts to publicise the outbreak.

This scene, which occurs in the first-third of the film, underlines the moment of crisis and the turning point of the plot. Till this moment the doctor's story has been progressing in expected ways, with Haridas and Adhir Mukherjee the publisher and printer of *Janavarta* pledging support, and Nisith not openly opposed to his idea. In *An Enemy of the People*, on the other hand, the antagonism between the two brothers emerges quite early, almost at the beginning of the first act, when Hovstad gives credit for the Baths to Dr Stockmann. Hovstad tells his brother,

[5] *Bael* (wood apple) and *tulsi* (holy basil) are held to be sacred plants in Hindu rituals. *Bael* leaves are offered to Shiva, while *tulsi* leaves are offered to Vishnu. In mythology, *bael* is the abode of Lakshmi while *tulsi* is one of her incarnations.

[6] In an earlier scene he tells his sister-in-law Maya: 'I'm not like *dada*, I believe in religion. A week after praying in the temple, my spondylitis was cured' (NFDC, 1990, 0:08:11–0:08:19). In the public meeting held later he categorically denies that *charanamrita* can be contaminated, though this may be read as a ploy to counter his brother.

Peter Stockmann, that the Baths 'owe their existence' to the doctor, who first discovered the water's healing properties and thought of the idea of a spa. Peter retaliates: 'To him! Indeed! It is true I have heard from time to time that some people are of that opinion. At the same time I must say I imagined that I took a modest part in the enterprise' (Ibsen, 2010, p. 9). When Dr Stockmann enters the antagonism comes out in the open, at first in casual conversations about his children and the improvement in his financial condition and later, more forcefully, when he mentions the outbreak. 'You have an ingrained tendency to take your own way, at all events', Peter berates him, 'and, that is almost inadmissible in a well ordered community. The individual ought undoubtedly to acquiesce in subordinating himself to the community—or, to speak more accurately, to the authorities who have the care of the community's welfare' (Ibsen, 2010, p. 15). In the corresponding scene in *Ganashatru*, the discussion between the two brothers seems more amicable, with Nisith even assuring Dr Gupta of all cooperation in the matter (NFDC, 1990, 0:09:05–0:10:18). It is not that there is no antagonism between them, but at this stage it is much more muted than in *Enemy*. It is only in the scene with Bhargava and Nisith in the doctor's study that it flares up for the first time. Just before the confrontation, Dr Gupta tells his wife that Nisith would definitely support him because he loves Chandipur and is equally concerned about its welfare. The confrontation, therefore, comes as a shock. Visually the scene conveys this when Nisith, after trying to persuade his brother to suppress the report, threatens him with dire personal consequences. It shifts from shot–reverse shot, which is the usual editing technique for conversations, to a long shot of Nisith with his back turned to the doctor (0:34:45–0:36:42). From this scene till the sequence of the public meeting, the film focuses on the two brothers, drawing them sharply into their opposing roles. Its culmination is the scene just before the public meeting begins, when the two adversaries, Dr Gupta accompanied by Maya, Ranu and Ronen and Nisith accompanied by Adhir Mukherjee and Haridas, are shown ranged on opposite sides of the platform

(1:15:20–1:15:33). The film, thus, stages visually and thematically the opposition not just between the two brothers but the value systems for which they stand. The muting of their personal hostility and the amicability of the opening sequences serve to heighten the effect of this shift.

In scripting the public meeting Ray makes a significant departure from Ibsen's play: Dr Gupta intends to read his report on the jaundice outbreak and not, like his counterpart in the play, to admonish the 'compact majority' that 'poisons the sources of our moral life and infects the ground we stand on' (Ibsen, 2010, p. 97). In other words, *Ganashatru* is essentially about the conflict between duty and self-interest that an epidemic crisis precipitates, and not about a solitary individual ranged against the public, as in *An Enemy of the People*. Read in this light, the conflict between scientific rationality and religious faith gains both allegorical and literal resonance within the social context of *Ganashatru*. A crucial scene in the public meeting brings this into focus. Nisith asks Dr Gupta whether he has ever worshipped at the Tripureshwar Temple in the last ten years, implying that he is an atheist and his report thus motivated. The latter's reply makes it very clear that his concern is not about the religious faith or practices of the townspeople but the risk of disease:

> There are certain Hindu customs that I don't follow, because science has taught me otherwise. But that's a private matter.[7] I wouldn't dream of denigrating the faith of someone who worships at the temple and drinks *charanamrita*. The water of the temple has been found to be full of disease-causing germs, so I say it's dangerous to drink the temple water and *charanamrita* right now. This is a question of health, not religion. (NFDC, 1990, 1:24:50–1:25:25)

This position has been described as agnostic, a term that Ray himself used (Sengoopta, 2023; Robinson, 2004, p. 345), and forms the core of *Ganashatru*'s critique of religion. Dr Gupta's speech, however, makes it clear that his religious position is not agnosticism, but a personal view that has no conflict with faith

[7] This is almost an echo of Ray's perspective of religion in the 1981 *Cinéaste* interview cited above.

as such. The doctor's concern is not about holy water, but the question of drinking it when it is contaminated. Thus, the film subordinates its theme of religious orthodoxy to that of epidemic: it is 'a question of health, not religion'. This is brilliantly captured in the closing shot, a close-up of Dr Gupta's table on which lie his stethoscope and the bottle of *charanamrita* that Bhargava had given him. Certainly, the themes of science versus religious dogma and public-spiritedness versus the cynical manipulation of religion for personal gain are present in the film. But these are not presented as abstract arguments, at least insofar as the characterisation of Dr Gupta is concerned, and the context in which he insists on reason and duty is important.

The ending of the film points to the essential difference between Stockmann and Gupta in the way their characters are conceptualised. Ibsen's doctor is inspired both by public conscience and personal pride, as he anticipates with pleasure the appreciation he would receive from the public. Ray's doctor, in contrast, is modest about his discovery. When Haridas tells him that it would make him a 'national hero', he replies: 'No, Haridas, I don't want to be a hero. I want to be an ordinary citizen' (NFDC, 1990, 0:19:51–0:20:04). After the public meeting in *Enemy*, Dr Stockmann thinks of leaving the town and settling in America: 'that the common herd should dare to make this attack on me, as if they were my equals—that is what I cannot, for the life of me, swallow!' (Ibsen, 2010, p. 110). In *Ganashatru*, when Maya suggests that they should leave Chandipur, Dr Gupta refuses: 'What will happen to the contaminated water? What will happen to my patients? This is Chandipur's darkest hour. How can I run away?' (NFDC, 1990, 1:28:05–1:28:36) Though Satyajit Ray felt drawn to the Nietzschean characterisation of the doctor in *Enemy* (Robinson, 2004, p. 342), it is community and public-spiritedness rather than the heroism of the lonely crusader that his film stresses, in its characterisation of Dr Gupta and the public support he receives at the end. The crisis that *Ganashatru* foregrounds is that of the community, not the protagonist as it is in *An Enemy of the People*. The film is about the way an outbreak of disease threatens to disrupt the social harmony in Chandipur and how this harmony is restored when people realise that Dr Gupta is concerned about their well-being, for which he is ready to sacrifice his own interests. It is an allegory on the breaking and remaking of community, and epidemic jaundice provides its context.

6.4. Conclusion

Outbreaks of epidemic acquire social significance in the way they are configured as crisis. In narratives they signify humanity at its worst as well as its best. They bring to the fore conflicts that are latent in social life when personal survival gains precedence over public good, but they also foreground the selfless acts of individuals who sacrifice their own interests for the good of others. As Camus writes at the end of *The Plague*, 'what we learn in a time of pestilence [is] that there are more things to admire in men than to despise' (1960, p. 297). Satyajit Ray's *Ganashatru* is an apt instance of this. Like many other epidemic stories, it frames the reality of outbreak as allegory, investing it with meanings that are both literal and metaphorical. Literally it is about the way jaundice breaks out in a small temple town due to contaminated *charanamrita*; metaphorically it represents moral uprightness triumphing over corruption and vested personal interest in restoring the social order.

The first section of this chapter has elaborated the literal context of the film. Jaundice caused by water-borne *hepatoviruses* has broken out in epidemic form from time to time across the country, almost always due to contamination of public water supply with sewage and human waste. What inspired Ray to choose this disease over the far more serious and fearsome cholera? 'The seemingly arbitrary way in which the disease chose its victims', David Arnold writes, 'the rapidity of its advance, the high fatality among those attacked and the violent nature of their death all contributed in making cholera in India … a singularly frightening disease' 1986, p. 119). Gangetic Bengal was a reservoir of cholera in the nineteenth century, and the disease caused so much suffering that a goddess was assigned to it. But Ray chose jaundice instead because by the 1980s, when the film is set, cholera had become endemic rather than epidemic. Though infectious hepatitis was less severe in terms of mortality and therefore less fearsome, there had been several notable outbreaks reported in newspapers in Bengal and elsewhere. There were instances, too, of outbreaks in temples, which spread through the ritual use of water as *charanamrita*. As Andrew Robinson suggests, that may have given Ray the idea of the outbreak in the temple town of Chandipur. Read in this light, *Ganashatru* is not just about values but equally about the real risk that religious rituals may pose in times of infectious disease outbreak. More precisely, it is about how rituals place at risk the very thing their performance is supposed to assure: the health and well-being of those who perform them. In a review of medical literature on infectious diseases, Kiran Gajurel and Stan Deresinkski point out how this is true of any faith, and not just Hindu rituals: 'In many cultures and faiths, holy water is collected from rivers and religious shrines, and ritualistic sprinkling of holy water is believed to cure ailments. Unfortunately, bacterial contamination of water sources in religious shrines is not uncommon. And furthermore contamination due to "unholy" pathogens already present in collecting vessels can occur' (2021, p. 4). They mention, too, the spread of cholera in *kumbh mela*s through drinking contaminated holy water.

The second section of the chapter has discussed Henrik Ibsen's play *An Enemy of the People*, which Ray adapted for his film. It examines the outbreak of disease in the play in the context of public health issues in Norway in Ibsen's time. Owing to the frequent pandemics of cholera, sanitation became a major concern throughout nineteenth-century Europe. Though Norway was not as badly affected as other countries, the sudden emergence of a disease that was believed to be confined to Asia, especially India, created panic, more so because it was almost inevitably fatal. The most vulnerable were spa resorts, which were rapidly becoming popular and were a lucrative source of income across Europe. In

Norway, outbreaks of cholera had occurred in the spa towns of Holmestrand and Moss during the second pandemic in 1829. In 1830, a Dr Meissner, who reported an outbreak of the disease in the mineral water baths of Teplitz, was hounded out of town, and had to escape to Karlovy Vary. Ibsen may have based his story on this incident, though there is no historical evidence to confirm it. *Enemy* is about a courageous doctor who antagonises his town's authorities, especially his brother, the mayor, by attempting to make public an outbreak of gastro-intestinal disease in the Baths. The idea of the Baths had been his and he had actively supported it till he discovered the outbreak. The problem for the mayor and others was that they had constructed the Baths at great expense, and had made good profit. Closing the Baths in order to carry out repairs, therefore, was economically unacceptable to them. The play counterposes two polar conceptions of social order: one that ensures the life and health of all and one that ensures their economic well-being. To this it juxtaposes two corresponding concerns in the Norway of Ibsen's time: democratic values and the legitimacy of a public opinion that disregards what is good for the community as a whole. It has been read as anti-democratic in its political stance, based on the doctor's speech about the moral failure of the townspeople and his closing remark about the strength of the individual who fights the majority alone.

Ganashatru, in contrast, presents the opposite stance: public opinion when it disregards what is good for all must be changed, and people persuaded to do the right thing. In refiguring the plot of *Enemy* thus and adapting it to the Indian context, Ray changes the script. The source of infection is a temple on which the economy of the town depends, thereby superimposing the conflict between scientific rationality and religious dogma on Ibsen's theme of public duty versus private interest. Further, Dr Gupta in *Ganashatru* is not, like Dr Stockmann, a crusader alienated from the community that he tries to save, but a socially committed member who ultimately gains the support of his fellow-members in preserving the community's well-being. Though it has been read as a criticism of religious orthodoxy, its object is actually not religion as such but only religious customs which pose a risk to health. This is why it takes the contamination of the temple's water supply as its point of departure, iconically presented in the closing shot of the stethoscope and *charanamrita*. The allegory of *Ganashatru* that posits the doctor's commitment to the well-being of people against the greed, deceitfulness and cynicism of his brother, therefore, can be best appreciated when it is read with the literal outbreak as its narrative centre. In turn, the allegory constructs the social reality of outbreak as a political and ethical crisis, in addition to being a crisis of health—or, more precisely, a politico-ethical crisis to the extent that it concerns the health of the community.

References

Aggarwal, R. & Goel, A. (2021). Hepatitis E: Current status in India. *Clinical Liver Disease, 18*(3), 168–172. https://www.ncbi.nlm.nih.gov/pmc/articles/PMC8518337/pdf/CLD-18-168.pdf

Arnold, D. (1986). Cholera and colonialism in British India. *Past and Present, 113*, 118–151. https://www.jstor.org/stable/650982

Biswas, S. (1993, February 28). Charanamrita: Scientist finds holy water extremely polluted. *India Today*. https://www.indiatoday.in/magazine/living/story/19930228-charanamrita-scientist-finds-holy-water-extremely-polluted-810772-1993-02-27

Brustein, R. (1962). Ibsen and revolt. *The Tulane Drama Review, 7*(1), 113–154. https://www.jstor.org/stable/1124634

Camus, A. (1960). The plague. (S. Gilbert, Trans.). Penguin.

Caraca-Samhitā. (1997). *Caraka Samhitā, vol. 5*. 2nd ed (A. Chandra Kaviratna & P. Sharma, Trans.). Sri Satguru Publications.

Chauhan, N.T., Prajapati, P., Trivedi, A.V. & Bhagyalaxmi, A. (2010). Epidemic investigation of the jaundice outbreak in Girdharnagar, Ahmedabad, Gujarat, India, 2008. *Indian Journal of Community Medicine, 35*(2), 294–297. https://www.ncbi.nlm.nih.gov/pmc/articles/PMC2940189/

Chatterjee, S., Haldar, J. & Ray, R. (2019). Prevalence of Hepatitis A and Hepatitis E in West Bengal India—A tertiary care hospital based study. *Journal of Evolution of Medical and Dental Sciences, 8*(29), 2341–2346. https://jemds.com/data_pdf/1_raja%20ray-kru-giri-july-22-Ori-Finnal.pdf

Coleman, W. (1987). Koch's comma bacillus: The first year. *Bulletin of the History of Medicine*, *61*(3), 315–342. https://www.jstor.org/stable/44442096

Das, D.K. (2019). *Teaching AIDS: The cultural politics of HIV disease in India*. Springer Nature Singapore.

Das, D.K., Biswas, R. & Pal, D. (2004). An epidemiological investigation of jaundice outbreak in a slum area of Chetla, Kolkata. *Indian Journal of Public Health*, *48*(4), 212–215. https://pubmed.ncbi.nlm.nih.gov/15709579/

Dalrymple, T. (2012). A whistleblower's tale. *British Medical Journal*, *345*(7870), 34. https://www.jstor.org/stable/23278312

Dwibedi, B., Sabat, J., Ho, L.M., Pati, S.S., Panda, S. & Kar, S.K. (2018). An outbreak of hepatitis E virus infection caused by genotype 1 in an urban setting in eastern India: A probe into risk factors for transmission. *Virus Disease*, *29*(4), 544–547.

Feinstone, S.M. (2019). History of the discovery of hepatitis A virus. *Cold Springs Harbor Perspectives in Medicine*, *9*, 1–14. https://www.researchgate.net/publication/324851277_History_of_the_Discovery_of_Hepatitis_A_Virus

Gajurel, K. & Deresinski, S. (2021). A Review of Infectious Diseases Associated with Religious and Nonreligious Rituals. *Interdisciplinary Perspectives on Infectious Diseases*, *2021*, 1–9. https://www.ncbi.nlm.nih.gov/pmc/articles/PMC8668350/pdf/IPID2021-1823957.pdf

Geetharani, R., Kalpana, M.S., Kumar R. M., Murhekar, M. & Mehendale, S. (2016). Hepatitis A outbreak due to contaminated public water in Tiruchirappalli Corporation, Tamil Nadu, India in 2015. *International Journal of Infectious Diseases*, *455*, 223–224.

Gjesdal, K. (2014). Nietzschean variations: Politics, interest, and education in Ibsen's *An enemy of the people*. *Ibsen Studies*, *14*(2), 109–135.

Hays, J.N. (2009). *The burdens of disease: Epidemics and human response in Western history*. Revised ed. Rutgers University Press.

Hiley, A. (1985). *German-speaking travellers in Scotland, 1800–1860, and their place in the history of European travel literature*, vol. 3 [Doctoral thesis, University of Edinburgh]. Edinburgh Research Archive (ERA), Literatures, Languages, and Cultures PhD thesis collection. http://hdl.handle.net/1842/7350

Hirsch, A. (1883). *Handbook of geographical and historical pathology, volume 1: Acute infective diseases* (C. Creighton, Trans). The New Sydenham Society.

Hubbard, W.C. (2006). Public Health in Norway 1603–2003. *Medical History*, *50*(1), 113–117. pmc.ncbi.nlm.nih.gov/pmc/articles/PMC1369017/pdf/medhis5001-113.pdf

Ibsen, H. (2010). *An enemy of the people: A play in five acts* (F. Sharp, Trans.). Pennsylvania State University.

Irgens, L.M. (2015). The roots of Norwegian epidemiology—Norwegian epidemiology in the 19th century. *Norsk Epidemiologi*, *25*(1–2), 21–29. https://www.ntnu.no/ojs/index.php/norepid/article/view/1885

Kadri, S.M., Rehman, S., Rehana, K., Benetou, D.R., Ahmad, D.F., Abdullah, A. & Chattu, V.K. (2018). Hepatitis A and E Outbreak Surveillance during 2015–2017 in Kashmir, India: Is the Water to Blame? *Journal of Epidemiology and Global Health*, *8*(3–4), 203–207. https://www.ncbi.nlm.nih.gov/pmc/articles/PMC7377564/pdf/JEGH_8_3-4_203.pdf

Kumar, T., Shrivastava, A., Kumar, A., Laserson, K. F., Narain, J.P., Venkatesh, S., Chauhan, L.S. & Averhoff, F. (2015). Viral hepatitis surveillance–India, 2011–2013. *Morbidity and Mortality Weekly*, *64*(28), 758–762.

Labrique, A.B., Thomas, D.L., Stoszek, S.K. & Nelson, K.E. (1999). Hepatitis E: An emerging infectious disease. *Epidemiologic Review*, *27*(2), 162–179.https://academic.oup.com/epirev/article/21/2/162/490562

Matos, T.C. (2008). Choleric fictions: Epidemiology, medical authority, and *An Enemy of the People*. *Modern Drama*, *51*(3), 353–368.

McConnell, T. (2010). Moral combat in 'An enemy of the people': Public health versus private interests. *Public Health Ethics*, *3*(1), 80–86. https://www.jstor.org/stable/26644809

Ministry of Health and Family Welfare, Government of India. *National action plan combating viral hepatitis in India*. (2019). https://nvhcp.mohfw.gov.in/common_libs/National-Action-Plan-Combating-Viral-Hepatitis-in-India.pdf

Mirsky, S. (1954). Epidemic jaundice (Viral hepatitis). *Canadian Medical Association Journal*, *70*, 308–311. https://www.ncbi.nlm.nih.gov/pmc/articles/PMC1825697/

NFDC (Producer). (1990). *Ganashatru* [Film]. National Film Development Corporation of India.

Oeding, P. (1992). Cholera in Bergen in 1848–1849—What caused the epidemic? [Abstract]. *Tidsskrift for den Norske Laegeforening, 112*(17), 2214–2217. https://pubmed.ncbi.nlm.nih.gov/1523661/

Patel, D.A., Gupta, P.A., Kinariwala, D.M., Shah, H.S., Trivedi, G.R. & Vegad, M.M.. (2012). An investigation of an outbreak of viral hepatitis B in Modasa town, Gujarat, India. *Journal of Global Infectious Diseases, 4*(1), 55–59. https://www.ncbi.nlm.nih.gov/pmc/articles/PMC3326959/

Pollitzer, R. (1954). Cholera studies. *Bulletin of the World Health Organisation, 10*, 421–461. https://www.ncbi.nlm.nih.gov/pmc/articles/PMC2542143/pdf/bullwho00557-0108.pdf

Rees, E. (2010). Problems of landscape and representation in Ibsen's Når vi døde vågner. *Ibsen Studies, 10*(1), 37–61. https://www.academia.edu/581270/Problems_of_landscape_and_representation_in_Ibsens_N%C3%A5r_vi_d%C3%B8de_v%C3%A5gner

Robinson, A. (2004). *Satyajit Ray, the inner eye: The biography of a master film-maker*. I.B. Tauris.

Satsangi, S. & Chawla, Y.K. (2016). Viral hepatitis: Indian scenario. *Medical Journal Armed forces India, 72*, 204–210. https://www.ncbi.nlm.nih.gov/pmc/articles/PMC4982980/pdf/main.pdf

Sengoopta, C. (2023). Through agnostic eyes: Representations of Hinduism in the cinema of Satyajit Ray. *Religions, 14*(749), 1–11. https://www.mdpi.com/journal/religions

Shouval, D. 2020. History of hepatitis A. *Clinical Liver Disease, 16*(S1), 12–23.

Sushruta Samhita. (2006). *The Sushruta Samhita, vol 3*. (Bhishagratna, K.K.L, Trans.). Cosmo Publications.

Torstveit L. & Vesterhus, P. (2005). Cholera and quarantine in Kristiansand. [Abstract]. *Tidsskrift for den Norske Laegeforening, 125*(24), 3490–3493. https://pubmed.ncbi.nlm.nih.gov/16357901/

Viswanathan, R. (1957). Epidemiology. *Indian Journal of Medical Research, 45*(Suppl.), 1–29. https://pubmed.ncbi.nlm.nih.gov/13438536/

World Health Organisation. (1953). Expert committee on hepatitis. Technical Report Series, 62. https://www.infected bloodinquiry.org.uk/sites/default/files/p16%20Docs/p16%20Docs/RLIT0000215%20-%20Expert%20Committee%20on%20Hepatitis%20First%20Report%20-%2021 %20Jul%201952.pdf

World Health Organisation. (2019). Hepatitis. https://www.who.int/news-room/questions-and-answers/item/hepatitis#:~:text=Hepatitis%20A%20and%20E%20are,contact%20with%20infected%20body%20fluids

Zachariah, S.M., Sreedevi, C. Aswathy, S. Kokkayil, P. & Mathews, A.A. (2017). Investigation of Hepatitis A outbreak in Palakkad district. *International Journal of Community Medicine and Public Health*, *4*(11), 4125–4130.

7

AIDS Narratives

> With this illness, one that elicits so much guilt and shame, the effort to detach it from these meanings, these metaphors, seems particularly liberating, even consoling. But the metaphors cannot be distanced just by abstaining from them. They have to be exposed, criticized, belabored, used up.
>
> Sontag, *AIDS and Its Metaphors*, 1988

When Susan Sontag wrote these lines in 1988, India was already into the second year of the AIDS pandemic.[1] I recall the 'meanings' wildly circulating in those days: that it was an American disease, that it caused the genitals to shrivel and fall off, that people died horrible deaths and that it never happened to 'us'. Some even called it the 'disco disease', perhaps because it was rumoured to be associated with those sexually liberated by the new discotheque culture. A *Sunday* story attributed the origin of the outbreak in India to either 'white skins' or 'Negroes, Mauritians and Sri Lankans', or to Indian labourers who had 'contracted the disease in Sri Lanka, Dubai or Malaysia' and had carried it home (Pratap, 1986, p. 50). Disease, as Sontag says, is always understood as 'foreign' and is invariably projected onto a

[1] The first cases of HIV infection were detected in 1986 during a random screening of sex workers in Chennai conducted by Dr Nirmala, a microbiology student at Madras Medical College, and her supervisor Dr Suniti Solomon. Both were surprised when six of the tests turned positive, for earlier samples screened in Mumbai had all been negative. The announcement of the finding in Parliament on April 29 by the then Health Minister Mohsina Kidwai 'sent seismic waves through the country' (Venkatramani, 1986).

territorial or social 'other' (1988, p. 47).[2] Over the years people from the margins of mainstream society came to be recruited into narratives of blame, mostly on the basis of already existing social antagonisms, supported by epidemiological studies of risk: sex workers, labourers, migrant workers, truck drivers, intravenous drug users, men-who-have-sex-with-men and hijras. In media usage 'high risk' ambiguously meant both those who were at risk of contracting infection and those who posed a risk for the health of others. Media discourse and political rhetoric, writes Jan Zita Grover, translate the epidemiological concept of risk into one that is 'used to stereotype and stigmatize people already seen as outside the moral and economic parameters of 'the general population'' (1988, p. 27). The typical profile of high-risk persons, as one story put it, includes 'those who had abandoned themselves to sexual "debauchery", or had diverse sexual inclinations' (Puri, 1986, p. 25). Haemophiliacs and thalassaemics were also recruited into the narratives, but as 'innocent victims' whose suffering was caused by the moral lapse of others. When about a decade later middle-class housewives tested positive for the virus, they replaced haemophiliacs and thalassaemics, who were now considered to be relatively safe because of the new protocols of blood safety (Das, 2019, pp. 49–70).[3] As Rosenberg explains, epidemiology often serves the interests of the moral order in the face of what is perceived to threaten it. In an outbreak of a fatal

[2] Speculations about the foreign origin of infectious diseases are partly true, especially in contemporary times, for they do spread across the world through travel, but the insistence with which public health authorities and the media assert it suggests a need to lay the blame elsewhere. The partial truth of such assertions reinforces its imagined 'truth' in ideology. National self-definition requires that disease be rejected, in an ideological strategy that 'is essential to nationhood' (Yingling, 1997, p. 24). I have discussed the national construction of epidemic disease in chapter two.

[3] Ensuring blood safety was a main focus of the first phase of the National AIDS Control Policy (Rao, 2017, p. 202), but it was not strictly enforced by the authorities. In 1996 the Supreme Court issued a directive to the government to ensure safe blood supply and, for this purpose, to set up a National Council of Blood Transfusion with corresponding councils in the states and union territories. (*Common Cause*, 1996). Despite all efforts to ensure blood safety, however, transfusions still account for new infections as NACO estimates show. I cite in the text one such estimate for 2020–2021.

infectious disease, the sense of vulnerability is intensified. In such a context, calculations of differential risk that are essential for epidemic control become reconfigured in social understanding as indices of threat, and those who are more susceptible are hypothetically held to be 'sources' of disease. 'Such hypothetical schemes constituted a framework within which moral and social assumptions could be at once expressed and legitimated' (Rosenberg, 1989, p. 5).

7.1. Narrative Templates

Broadly speaking, stories of AIDS draw on two narrative templates, one representing outbreak as collective calamity[4] and the other representing disease as individual suffering. These reflect the two dimensions of the epidemic. On the one hand, large numbers of people began testing positive within a few years of the outbreak; on the other, unlike many other infectious diseases, there was a long period of debilitating illness before one's death. In both cases AIDS became moralised more than most other diseases. As a collective calamity it led to the stereotyping of certain individuals and groups in allegories of deserved and undeserved punishment, guilt and innocence. As individual suffering it became emblematic of human vulnerability, precarity of life, and the isolation of those affected by it.

[4] I use the term 'outbreak narrative' in a somewhat different sense from Priscilla Wald's usage. As I explain in the next chapter, she uses the term to refer specifically to what are called 'emerging infections'—the series of zoonotic virus outbreaks in the present century, such as SARS, Nipah, Zika, Ebola and COVID-19. Characteristically, the main events in an outbreak narrative, as she defines it, are the identification of a new pathogen and the epidemiological work of tracking and arresting its spread. Wald herself excludes AIDS narratives from her definition of the outbreak narrative. The AIDS epidemic, she writes, could not 'be directly incorporated into the mythic dimensions of communicable-disease outbreak narratives' (Wald, 2008, p. 27). I use the term 'outbreak' more generally to refer to any infectious disease, prevailing or emergent. The outbreak narrative, therefore, can include conventional constructions of outbreak as social and moral crisis, emphasising its cultural rather than biomedical dimension and its function in maintaining a symbolic order. My usage derives from Rosenberg's account of the social understanding of epidemic outbreak.

What was it that made it possible to construct such meanings? Let us take the first template: the outbreak narrative. The human immunodeficiency virus, unlike many other infectious disease agents, cannot easily be transmitted in everyday social encounters, but only those involving exchange of blood or sexual fluids. As such it came to be predominantly associated with certain lifestyles that put one at risk, unlike other diseases that seem more random. The virus is transmitted in four known ways—sexual contact with an infected person, transfusion of infected blood or blood products, use of infected injecting apparatus and from infected mother to child. In 2020–2021, more than three decades after it broke out, the transmission pattern of HIV disease in India was 85.6 per cent for heterosexuals and men-who-have-sex-with-men, 0.7 percent for infected blood/blood products, 6.3 per cent for infected syringes and needles, and 3.4 per cent for mother to child, with 3.9 per cent unspecified (NACO, 2021, p. 32).[5] In other words, the majority of cases were people who could be framed as 'immoral', indulging in illicit or 'unnatural' sex and drug abuse and therefore deserving of their fate, while a minority (mothers and their children, transfusion recipients) could be framed as 'innocent' and undeserving. AIDS narratives that are moralistic draw on this template in order to legitimise, as Rosenberg writes, dominant social assumptions about who gets disease and how.

Let us now take the second template, the illness narrative. These typically recount the experiences of HIV-positive persons or their caregivers, framed by ideas of vulnerability as well as the heroic struggle of individuals and families. The illness narrative, which has become quite prominent in the last fifty years, is premised on the distinction between disease as an objective condition and illness as subjective perception. One of the contexts for this distinction, as Arthur Kleinman argues, was

[5] I present this data primarily to give a sense of HIV's transmission patterns. In the early years of the epidemic, surveillance for HIV had not been undertaken, and no data is available for this period. Surveillance was introduced only after the formulation of the National AIDS Control Policy, in 1993 (Rao, 2017, p. 202).

the increasingly technoscientific nature of corporate healthcare. Characteristically, biomedicine has favoured the objective and verifiable information produced in the laboratory or imaging room, over the patient's story. 'Thus, the doctor is expected to decode the untrustworthy story of *illness as experience* for the evidence of that which is considered authentic, *disease as biological pathology*' (Kleinman, 1995, p. 32, italics in original). In such a situation patients need to tell their stories to whoever is willing to listen, because narrating their experience enables them to make sense of it, highlighting themes like the unpredictability of fate, alternating cycles of despair and hope, courage, endurance, and when the crisis is resolved, the patient's ultimate victory over death. The effects of illness may vary from person to person, but the meanings we attribute to the *experience* of illness are cultural and collective. 'The plot lines, core metaphors, and rhetorical devices that structure the illness narrative are drawn from cultural and personal models for arranging experiences in meaningful ways and for effectively communicating those meanings' (Kleinman, 1988, p. 49). According to Joseph Frank, the illness narrative opened 'a space for the particular experience of individuals', and patient networking contributed to its collective circulation as a new genre initially meant for other patients and subsequently addressed to a broader readership (Frank, 1993, 39–40). The most well-known narrative is perhaps Audre Lorde's *The Cancer Journals* (1980), which is about her struggle with breast cancer. In recent years a number of such narratives about cancer and mental illness have been published from India.[6] The emergence of illness narratives as a genre coincided with another phenomenon, the increasing incidence of chronic illnesses associated with lifestyles that exposed one to risks associated with professional stress, lack of adequate exercise, and consumption of tobacco, alcohol,

[6] For instance, Yuvraj Singh's *The Test of My Life: From Cricket to Cancer and Back* (2013), Reshma Valliappan's *Fallen Standing: My Life as a Schizophrenist* (2014), *I am a Survivor* (2017), a collection of cancer stories compiled by Vijay Anand Reddy, and Shaheen Bhatt's *I've Never Been (Un) Happier* (2019), which are all memoirs. Jerry Pinto's *Em and the Big Hoom* (2012), partly based on his mother's mental illness, is fiction, but it fits into the genre.

recreational drugs and high cholesterol diets. There are two factors underlying this, one being an actual increase in incidence and the other being the availability of diagnostic techniques that can detect diseases before symptoms became apparent (Beck, 1992, p. 204; McGrail, Lavergne & Lewis, 2016, p. 2). Epidemic disease declined considerably by the mid-twentieth century thanks to vaccines and antibiotics, and lifestyle disease came to replace it as the new 'epidemic', with illness being the metaphor of choice for human vulnerability. When HIV/AIDS appeared in the early 1980s it fitted well into the definition of lifestyle disease, and narratives by persons with HIV adopted the format of the illness narrative.

AIDS narratives, therefore, have broadly followed two plot lines: one building on the experience of outbreak as collective calamity and apportioning guilt and innocence, the other building on the experience of individual illness and symbolising suffering, loss and the struggle against disease and social stigma. The two templates or plot-forms bear to each other what is best described as an asymptotic relationship, approaching each other as two contrasting curves but never joining. The stigmatising of a guilty population in the outbreak plot acts as a corollary to the undeserved suffering of the innocent in the illness plot. As Morrison writes of the early AIDS narratives in mainstream American culture which typically focused on the 'innocent victim': 'The suffering children or untainted hemophiliacs of these tales are set against the (usually absent) gay man, and the sympathy elicited for the 'innocent' derives precisely from the encodement of *that which they are not*—a figure, that is, of insidious otherness whose voracious appetites and perverse rejection of the 'natural' social order have led to this logical fate' (1992, p. 170, italics in original). Narratives by gay men, who were either themselves HIV-positive or partners and caregivers of those who were positive, emphasised the suffering caused by disease and stigma. Douglas Crimp, who was a gay activist and curator of gay art, stated in a conference on AIDS in Yokohama, Japan, in 1994: 'We urgently need resources to help us cope with the consequences of losing hope for a cure for AIDS, of dealing with loss upon loss, with so much hatred directed at us, and with the simple and horrible fact, very rarely given voice, that all of us will almost certainly live with AIDS for the remainder of our lives, however long that may be' (Crimp, 2002, p. 267). Gay stories of AIDS in the US, which became prolific from the late 1980s onwards, were intended as part of those resources, and the subject of these stories was the person with AIDS as well as the entire gay community of America.

If the experience of AIDS produced a massive cultural response from the gay community in America, it was partly because of the negative representation of the community in outbreak narratives of mainstream culture. By the 1980s, gay men had become politically active in resisting homophobia and had acquired immense cultural capital as they included writers, artists, filmmakers and intellectuals. The indifference of the federal government to their plight and the renewed hostility of the heterosexual majority provoked them to retaliate through AIDS activism and cultural production.[7] In India, the situation was quite different. First, by the time the initial cases were detected the social frameworks for understanding AIDS were already in place. It had acquired a name, the causative agent was known and so too were the modes of transmission and the

[7] In *And the Band Played On*, Randy Shilts writes: '[W]ithin the executive branch of government, there seemed little excitement about launching anything like a coordinated attack on the disease' (1987, p. 586). It was six long years after the first cases were detected that President Ronald Reagan appointed a commission to assist him in controlling the epidemic. Meanwhile, gay people had set up activist networks in different cities for the care and support of persons with HIV. ACT UP, or AIDS Coalition to Unleash Power was founded in 1987 by Larry Kramer and others (Kramer, 1989, pp. 127–139). In the same year, three important cultural initiatives were launched in support of the gay community's struggle with AIDS and AIDS-related homophobia: (i) *Let the Record Show...*, a window installation curated by the New Museum of Contemporary Art; (ii) 'Art against AIDS', a gallery and sale of art works at Sotheby's in New York, curated by Robert Rosenblum; and (iii) the AIDS Memorial Quilt, made of panels in memory of those who had died of AIDS. Apart from these public initiatives, there were innumerable memoirs, novels, plays, poems, films, and painting and photographic exhibitions produced on the theme of AIDS.

communities held to be responsible for its spread. Though it was framed as a gay disease in North America and Europe, in Africa it was assumed to be predominantly heterosexual. As Paula Treichler shows, stories about 'African AIDS' in the Western media emphasised prostitution as the major cause of spread (1999, pp. 99–109). Therefore, in 1986 when the sex workers in Chennai tested positive, the media had a ready-made plot: all that was needed was either to find an African 'source' or to reconfigure the plot using Indian characters and settings. Since the targets of public blame were sex workers, migrant labourers and truck-drivers, who neither saw themselves as a community nor had the economic, political and cultural capital to fight back as the gay community could in the US, they had no way of challenging the stigmatising representations. People belonging to the middle class, who were both authors and readers of these stories, assumed that the epidemic was not their problem, till its unfolding in the latter half of the 1990s disproved this myth. It was only then, when AIDS became a reality for the middle class, that more nuanced and sympathetic stories drawing on the illness narrative template could emerge. Most such narratives, however, are not in the first person, but are reported by authors who are not themselves affected. This is in sharp contrast to the stories produced by the gay community in the US as well as the stories of other illnesses in India, especially cancer. This is most likely due to the intense stigma still associated with AIDS, making it practically impossible for HIV-positive persons or their families to come out with their own stories.

7.2. Media Construction of AIDS: The Outbreak Narrative

Stories of the outbreak in its early years focused primarily on the foreign origin theory. Nisha Puri in an article published a few months after the outbreak cited prominent public health authorities to state that 'AIDS in this country has been brought in by foreigners or Indians who have travelled abroad' (1986, p. 26). Her sources were the director-general and deputy director-general of the Indian Council of Medical Research, head of virology at the All India Institute of Medical Sciences, head of epidemiology at the School of Tropical Medicine, and a professor at the National Institute of Choleric and Enteric Diseases—in other words, people credentialled to know the 'truth' of AIDS. Dr A.S. Paintal, the ICMR chief reportedly stated: 'I am so certain that our findings in this matter are 100 per cent accurate that I no longer advance this theory as a hypothesis, but as a fact of life. If in the heading for your article, you use the title, "There is no indigenous AIDS virus in India", you would be right on the mark' (pp. 26–27). Other newsmagazine articles reinforced this view by reporting that the government had imposed restrictions on the entry of foreigners and non-resident Indians, and had carried out mandatory HIV tests on students of African origin, deporting those found to be positive (Raghunathan, 1986; Singh & Pillai, 1987). The ICMR even proposed a legislation to ban sex with foreigners (Puri, 1986, p. 29). Three stories of persons who had acquired HIV infection abroad were widely circulated, reproducing the innocent/guilty binary of the moralistic AIDS narrative: the first two were a Mumbai-based businessman and a microbiologist from Hyderabad who had received infected blood/blood product in the US,[8] and the third was a bisexual man from Srinagar who had engaged in anal sex in Germany (Puri, 1986, p. 27; Venugopal & Raghunathan, 1986, p. 22). Predictably enough, the businessman and the microbiologist were 'innocent victims', while the bisexual man was 'guilty' and deserved his fate. In short, what these stories and the government's approach to the outbreak did was construct 'AIDS in India' as simultaneously real and unreal. It was real to the extent that there were confirmed cases, and unreal in that its 'source' was not 'Indian'. It was even claimed, citing expert opinion, that the epidemic would not continue for long in the country because of its strong moral culture. Puri cited a professor at the School of Tropical Medicine

[8] B.R. Makhija, the businessman, underwent a coronary bypass surgery and was transfused with infected blood; the microbiologist, who was not named, had haemophilia and was transfused with infected anti-haemophilic factor (Puri, 1986, p. 30; Rahman & Chengappa, 1986, p. 132).

as saying: 'Ours is a sexually conservative society, and men and women still believe in marital fidelity and one sexual partner' (1986, p. 25). Thus framed in the opposition between a chaste national self and its unchaste other, American or African, 'AIDS in India' could be wished away as unreal.

Naya Zaher ('New Poison', 1991), produced by Praveen Thakar and directed by Jyoti Sarup, was the first commercially-released Hindi film on AIDS.[9] Like the media stories, it reproduces this binary logic as the 'truth' of the outbreak, authenticated by a doctor. 'If our present generation had not tried to mimic the West and had not indulged in drugs and bodily pleasures', says Dr Sapra in a dialogue that sums up the film's message, 'then we could certainly have got rid of this.' Our ideal, he adds, had once been the self-restraint of Ram and Sita, but now we are so lost in the pursuit of pleasure that for generations to come we will continue to live like walking skeletons (Thakar & Sarup, 1991, 1:59:54–2:00:33). This 'new poison', says the title song of the film, is spread by women who, influenced by Western culture, have forsaken the ideals of Sita and Savitri (Thakar & Sarup, 1991, 0:13:46–0:15:15). On the one hand, representing the negative pole, is Devyani, a politician who preaches women's liberation but runs an escort service for men, while on the other is Richa, the film's heroine who is 'as pure as Ganga *jal*' (Thakar & Sarup, 1991, 1:07:16). In between stands Mrs Dayal, who seeks Devyani's help to beget a child, but believes in the norm of *pativrata* or fidelity to her husband. It is on the woman's body that Indian tradition and Western modernity are ranged, coded in contrasting lifestyles, habits, manners and dress. In its overtly misogynist plot, therefore, women bear the burden of upholding a moral order on which is founded the national (male) self. In constructing AIDS as 'foreign' and antithetical to this order, *Naya Zaher* circulates and reinforces what became instituted as the dominant frame for AIDS in the early years of the outbreak.

[9] I am grateful to Parth Pant for bringing this to my notice. In *Teaching AIDS*, my book on AIDS pedagogy in India, I had mistakenly assumed that Mahesh Manjrekar's *Nidaan*, which I discuss later, was the first commercially-released film about AIDS.

The real theme of the film, however, is not AIDS but a love triangle beween Richa, Vikram and Avinash. Vikram, who is Richa's childhood friend, is secretly in love with her; but she is in love with Avinash, a simple country lad she meets on a trip to her native village. In trying to match up to Richa's urbanised ways, Avinash falls prey to Devyani and her escort girls, from whom he contracts HIV. The rest of the narrative is about his revenge, as he rapes and infects those who are responsible for his plight, and his attempt to unite Richa and Vikram. Meanwhile, Mrs Dayal, who had been impregnated by Avinash, gives birth to a boy and dies. In the final sequence, Avinash is killed in a fight with Devyani and her criminal accomplices, but before dying he brings Vikram and Richa together and bequeaths to them his new-born son. In keeping with the moral norms of Hindi film melodrama, Avinash cannot marry Richa because he is no longer chaste; but in punishing those who had wronged him and in uniting Richa and Vikram he absolves himself of this guilt. AIDS, therefore, is not the complication on which the plot turns, but merely a convenient way to resolve it. It uses AIDS, first, because it was at the time the most compelling metaphor for moral disorder caused by a predatorial female sexuality, represented in the figure of the sexually liberated and westernised woman. Secondly, it was also at the time the most compelling vehicle for vindicating a national ideology founded on tradition against its imagined other, Western modernity. The film actually begins with an ideologically-neutral explanation of AIDS as an incurable disease transmitted through infected blood and sexual fluids (Thakar & Sarup, 1991, 0:11:20–0:11:45), but this meaning is lost in the symbolic framing of the events as they unfold. Clearly, creating awareness about the disease was not among the film's priorities. By playing into allegories of contagion as moral disorder, stories like *Naya Zaher* served to confirm as its 'truth' the foreign origin of AIDS.

This 'truth' was, however, contrary to the findings of a national surveillance of vulnerable populations carried out by the Indian Council of Medical Research in 1986-1988, which revealed that

HIV infection was already fairly widespread throughout the country (Ramachandran, 2012, p. 15). The first high-risk persons identified for epidemic control, immediately after the formation of a national policy, were female sex workers, partly because they were the first to test positive, but more so because of the way colonial public health law (and later, its postcolonial version) had constructed the 'prostitute' as source of disease. Incidence of gonorrhoea and syphilis in the army barracks became a major issue for the British government in the mid-nineteenth century, leading to the passage of laws regulating prostitution in both England and India. These laws mandated the registration of women engaged in sexual services and their subjection to periodic medical examination. In England the Contagious Diseases Act was passed in 1864 and extended twice, in 1866 and 1869; in India the Cantonments Act was passed in 1864, followed by the Indian Contagious Diseases Act in 1868. The Indian regulations, however, were far more draconian, including in their scope virtually all native women who worked as labourers in cantonment towns as well as registered prostitutes. While the colonial state did not abolish prostitution altogether because it was held to be necessary for the troops, it maintained a close supervision on prostitutes and their sexual health, removing them to lock hospitals[10] if found to be infected (Levine, 1994). In 1956, the Indian government enacted the Immoral Traffic (Prevention) Act, which did not criminalise prostitution as such but prohibited sex workers from soliciting in public places. Government intervention in the early years of the AIDS epidemic bore the legacy of these legislations. Raids on brothels, mandatory testing of sex workers, custodial detention and the attribution of blame were thus the outcome of both surveillance and the pathologising of paid sex since colonial times. Prostitutes, one article wrote, 'are a major reservoir for the AIDS virus' (Bariah,

[10] These were hospitals set up in military cantonments for the specific purpose of isolating and treating women infected with sexual disease. The objective of this system of disease control was to protect the health of British soldiers in the colonial army (Mishra, 1999).

1997, pp. 103–104).[11] The figure of the diseased prostitute was used both to incite and to allay fears of contagion: on the one hand she threatens to spread her disease, on the other there is no cause for panic as long as the disease remains confined to her. Thus, Puri writes reassuringly that 'the prospect of a cross-over from high-risk groups to the rest of the community is dim'; yet she also claims that the sex worker poses a real risk: '[i]n the light of her profession, there is a real and urgent danger of her transmitting the virus in areas where AIDS antibodies have not yet been found and probably don't exist' (1986, p. 25, p. 24). The border between the prostitute and the 'rest of the community', in other words, is both impervious and open to transgression. The trope of the diseased prostitute was followed by the pathologisation of other groups belonging to the lower economic strata, in an ideological linkage of poverty, dirt and disease.[12] 'Research in Western countries', claimed Anita Pratap writing in *Sunday*, 'has shown that filth, insects, presence of faeces in drinking water, squalid conditions, poverty, a tropical environment, rituals and sacrifices using blood and a high rate of tuberculosis help in the spread of AIDS' (1986, p. 49), thereby recycling a colonial-era stereotype of the 'diseased tropics'.[13] According to her, 'labourers, porters

[11] *Park's Textbook of Preventive and Social Medicine*, one of the prescribed texts on public health in medical curricula in India, states: 'The prostitute acts as a reservoir of infection' (Park, 2015, p. 331). What such a statement, established as a medical fact, does is evade the question of how the prostitute came to be infected in the first place. Etymologically, 'reservoir' means a storehouse, from the Latin *servare*, 'to keep or preserve'. By implying that the prostitute 'preserves' infection to distribute it to others, it holds her directly responsible for the transmission of disease.

[12] Dirt-avoidance, argues Mary Douglas, has a long cultural history in the symbolic classification of order: dirt is fundamentally disorderly as 'matter out of place'. The association of dirt with disease, however, is of more recent origin, after the emergence of germ theory and especially sanitary science in nineteenth-century Europe; but it has become so pervasive that 'it is difficult to think of dirt except in the context of pathogenicity' (Douglas, 1966, p. 44). Of the linkage between dirt and immorality, Cindy Patton writes: 'Dirt and germs serve an important symbolic role in the social organisation of difference. Dirt is chaos, cleanliness order. Disease-stricken people are immoral, healthy people righteous' (1986, p. 11).

[13] For the pathologisation of the tropics and the complementary

and truck drivers', many of whom sold their blood for money, constituted a 'bridge population' that would transmit the disease to others by donating blood (p. 50).

What the 'national self' refers to in these stories, therefore, is the middle class, not named as such but negatively defined by excluding those outside it as sources of risk. How this is discursively achieved is revealed in the media translation of scientific concepts such as 'risk groups' and 'bridge populations' as putative sites of a 'crossover' of the virus to the 'general population'. The logic of such representations is that the self can be best validated by invalidating those who are different, its 'other'. As Hayden White explains, it is most often invoked in times of social crisis, when 'the need for positive self-definition asserts itself but no compelling criterion of self-identification appears' (1978, p. 151). In effect, therefore, 'AIDS in India' still remains a disease of the outside, except that the outside is now *inside* the nation, in its underclass, and therefore more *insidious* than that which is extrinsic to the border.

7.3. Media Construction of AIDS: The Human Interest Story

In the mid-1990s when middle-class housewives started testing positive for HIV, the 'crossover' was no longer a remote possibility but real. The 'killer that had prowled red-light areas and seedy highway *dhabas*', wrote Farah Bariah in *India Today*, 'is now stalking bourgeois neighbourhoods and beginning to attack conservative households' (1997, p. 102). Bariah recounts the personal stories of people belonging to what she calls 'the very core of Indian society' (p. 102), that is, its middle class.

tropicalisation of India see Arnold, 2005, pp. 139–142. Arnold's argument is that the trope of 'tropicality' was constituted in the intersection of multiple discourses, primarily those of travel, natural history and medicine. If the first genres to construct the 'tropics' as spatially and culturally different from Europe were travel writing and natural history, by signifying it as an exotic landscape with the abundance of nature, tropical medicine in the nineteenth century contributed to its other construction as a breeding-ground of disease. Colonialism provided the political and ideological context for this latter construct to be claimed as 'truth'.

The situation was very different from that in 1986, when it had been possible to assume that 'married couples' were 'in almost no danger of contracting AIDS' (Puri, 1986, p. 30). In the mid-1990s, new infections were being reported from among the very population that wrote and read the media stories about AIDS. The choice of the 'human interest' format, which was an established media-frame in health journalism, was therefore obvious. As a genre, it could engage readers emotionally more than depersonalised disease statistics or the stories of high-risk marginal populations. But the important question with regard to such stories is: who *now* counts as the 'human'? There had been human interest stories earlier, of persons belonging to the high-risk categories. Let us examine two such stories, for the way they construct the person with AIDS. The first is a 1990 story by Ritu Sarin about two haemophiliac brothers, Rohit and Vinit, who had been infected through transfusion of blood products. By then, as the story mentions, haemophiliacs and thalassaemics had been identified as a high-risk group. Sarin's 'The Outcast' presents a very moving account of the family's struggle to get medical care for Vinit, because hospitals were reluctant to admit HIV-positive cases. When his serostatus was known, he was refused admission to the Army Base Hospital, New Delhi where he had been taking transfusions earlier, as well as the All India Institute of Medical Sciences. Once, when he had been admitted to Jaslok Hospital for pneumonia, the hospital turned him out in the middle of the night when it learnt of his serostatus. Sarin repeatedly makes the point that Vinit had acquired AIDS 'innocently' and therefore did not deserve such treatment. He 'is not a typical AIDS patient (generally seen as either sexually promiscuous or intravenous drug users)'. Most cases of AIDS, she writes, 'have, according to one view, wrought the affliction upon themselves', but Vinit and Rohit 'have not been infected because of personal negligence' (Sarin, 1990, pp. 23–25). In order to present Vinit's condition sympathetically, thus, the story emphasises his innocence by contrasting him to those who are presumably guilty and deserve their punishment. Yet, an insert placed within the story states: 'So far, the practitioners of the world's oldest profession [sex work] have been subject to the severest surveillance—*the government has virtually ignored the threat from* homosexuals and *haemophiliacs*' (p. 25, italics added). What kind of 'threat' do haemophiliacs pose and for whom? If HIV transmission can be easily prevented by following basic sanitary procedures, as the article claims, in what sense do they pose a threat to hospital staff and the general public? Even if we concede that haemophiliacs do pose a threat, how would the government address it? By taking haemophiliacs into custody, as it has done with 'the world's oldest profession'? Would that not intensify the discrimination that Vinit has already been subjected to, and which Sarin so rightly and emphatically condemns as unjust?

The next story is 'Damned to Death' by Subhash Mishra, published in *India Today* in 2000. Mishra recounts the pathetic condition of Govind Singh, a labourer from Uttar Pradesh who had migrated to Mumbai for work. He acquires infection there, and is compelled to return to his village.

> Coursing in his blood was the virus of death and, worse, disgrace: acquired immune deficiency syndrome or AIDS. Even the mean streets of Mumbai hadn't prepared Govind for what he was about to face. News of his affliction spread like wildfire, and the villagers, including his wife, brother and other relatives dragged him into a *gote*—an enclosure where domestic animals like cows and goats are kept. Incarcerated in the cold and foul-smelling *gote* for over three months, Govind's condition worsened. (Mishra, 2000).

On 5 July, a few months after his incarceration, Govind was found dead in the *gote*. The story brings out the social ostracism that persons with HIV face due to people's lack of scientific knowledge, and Govind, his wife and many others continue to pay 'the price of ignorance'. Chucher, Govind's village in rural UP, is so backward that it lacks basic modern amenities like electricity, and is so 'primitive' that its flour mill is run by a traditional waterwheel: 'In a manner of speaking, Chucher hasn't stepped out of medieval times' (Mishra, 2000). The story includes a picture of Govind sitting huddled outside the *gote*, surrounded by dirt, his body emaciated and an abject look on his face. The story does sincerely try to elicit sympathy for Govind, yet the visual and the negative portrayal of the village actually serve to distance him from the reader, who belongs to an entirely different world where such 'medieval' thinking is presumed not to prevail. Though 'Damned to Death' admits that discrimination against HIV-positive persons exists in modern urban spaces, the overemphasis on Chucher's primitivity makes Govind's infection a typical case of ignorance and backwardness rather than a more general social concern. Besides, both the migrant worker and the haemophiliac belong to the already identified 'high-risk' categories, and readers who belong to the 'general population' would presume them to be obvious candidates for AIDS. The distance between the readers and the stories' characters can only elicit pity for the latter, which serves to compensate for the stigmatisation that underwrites it. In short, both 'The Outcaste' and 'Damned to Death' use the human interest frame, but there is a gap between the human that is the object of these stories and the human that is their subject.[14] In the stories of middle-class persons with HIV, this division of subject and object is complicated as the two coincide.

Farah Bariah's article on housewives hinges on the metaphor of the crossover of HIV from the borders within which it ought to have remained confined, brothels and highways, to middle-class populations as the virus 'stalks' them. Bariah provides two reasons for this crossover. First is the virus itself, a 'silent killer' that 'emerges from the shadows' to claim its new victims (Bariah, 1997, p. 108). The second, as we shall see shortly, is a change in the moral values of middle-class men. Thus, by imputing agency to the virus and holding middle-class husbands guilty, Bariah represents the housewives as passive victims of a predatory disease and of the moral transgression of others—as figures, in short, of pathos. Her identification with these women is evident in the way she describes the virus as 'sneak[ing] into *our* backyard'

[14] By 'subject' here I mean the persons who produce, circulate and consume the stories, while the 'object' is the person whose story they narrate.

(p. 105, italics added). Of the eleven stories recounted in the article, six are of housewives infected by their husbands, most of whom acquired infection from 'prostitutes'. The remaining five are about single men infected either by prostitutes or promiscuous women, who, like the liberated woman in *Naya Zaher*, initiate sex. Amit Dhanak and Nigel Fernandes are lured into commercial sex by a more experienced friend; Sundar Malhotra is seduced by his co-worker Marisa Jacob during an official visit out of town; and Raghuram, who is otherwise 'a married, respectable man', has an 'occasional fling with a female colleague' (pp. 103–105). Bariah attributes this growing incidence of HIV to the breakdown of 'old concepts of middle-class morality' due to 'growing affluence of the middle class and Hollywood', change in working conditions such as frequent travel, and even the recruitment of women in the workforce. Taken together, these lead to 'an increasing number of casual sexual relationships' (p. 103). In other words, what makes the middle class vulnerable to HIV is a set of structural factors—socio-cultural change, change in practices of work, gender equality—that are beyond their control and not, as in the case of the economically backward classes, sexual transgression. In place of the stigma ordinarily reserved for the marginal groups, the characters of Bariah's human interest stories deserve sympathy. 'It is a private purgatory: confiding in your family can make you a moral pariah, confiding in colleagues can cost you your job, there are virtually no professional counsellors. And the end, when it comes, is ignoble' (p. 108). For her women characters, she reserves both sympathy and admiration for an undeserved suffering that they nevertheless bear stoically: 'Betrayed by their husbands, often condemned by their in-laws for a crime they did not commit, they still find the strength to forgive, nurture and fight for their doomed families' (p. 108). Evidently, it is an admiration that Bariah has for only those women who conform to gender norms as dutiful housewives, and not those who presumably violate these norms by taking up employment. While Bariah's portrayal of these hapless housewives is genuinely compassionate without reducing them to objects of pity, this has clearly to do with the class to which they belong. Those who do not belong to this class, like the prostitutes and truck drivers cohabiting in 'red-light areas and seedy highway *dhabas*', deserve no such compassion.

It is not surprising that mainstream media narratives must either blame those 'guilty' of spreading contagion or recount the pathos of 'innocent victims', given the way AIDS is framed as a crisis of morality. As Susan Sontag explains, there is no contradiction in this double-framing of AIDS as both 'punishment for deviant behavior' and as that 'which threatens the innocent' (1988, p. 64). The two are actually complementary, in the sense that one serves as the ground for the other. All infectious diseases that come to be stigmatised, where the innocent/guilty opposition can be effectively deployed, serve as a pretext for the consolidation of dominant social and moral norms: 'they enable us to see, at one moment in time, the configuration of values and attitudes that, in less stressful times, are so fragmented or so taken for granted that they are not easily visible' (Rosenberg, 2008, p. S6). The double-framing of persons with AIDS in the outbreak narrative and the illness-as-human-interest story, one emphasising their responsibility and the other absolving them of guilt, follows from this.

7.4. Rewriting the Illness Narrative: *Ek Alag Mausam, AIDS Sutra* and *Positive Lives*

The binarism that structures the epidemic story as moral allegory is not just a characteristic of the mass media story, but is evident even in more sensitive and nuanced representations. *Ek Alag Mausam* ('A Different Season'), a film directed and produced by K.P. Sasi in 2003, tells the story of a woman infected with HIV by her husband who seeks solace in volunteering for the care of terminally-ill patients. Aparna leaves her husband, aborts the child she is carrying, and joins Jeevan Jyoti, a clinic for persons with HIV set up by the socially committed Dr Machado. Initially distressed by the suffering and death she witnesses every day, she eventually learns to cope with it and finds fulfilment in her work.

She adopts the child of a sex worker who dies of complications due to AIDS, to compensate emotionally for the child she has lost. She falls in love with George, an HIV-positive co-worker who drives the clinic's truck and assists Dr Machado, but refuses to marry him because she doubts his morals. Since George drives trucks, she reasons, he must have acquired his infection as every other truck driver did, through sexually promiscuous conduct. Much after she leaves Jeevan Jyoti, she learns from Dr Machado that he had acquired the disease by the transfusion of infected blood that he had received from the doctor's own son. The film ends, predictably, with their reunion and the beginning of 'a different season'. *Ek Alag Mausam*, however, is not the run-off-the-mill Hindi film melodrama: scripted by Mahesh Dattani and with an impressive cast that includes Nandita Das, Anupam Kher and Rajit Kapur in the lead roles, it is a narrative that portrays with equal compassion the suffering of those presumed to be guilty as it portrays that of those presumed innocent. In fact, being non-judgmental is one of the first lessons Aparna learns from the good doctor. But the force of the moral framing of disease is such that without it there can be no satisfactory closure, especially in a story that opens with the husband's infidelity. George, therefore, must be absolved of guilt and proved innocent before Aparna can accept him as life partner. Despite its conscious effort to de-moralise AIDS, therefore, *Ek Alag Mausam* ends up reinforcing it unwittingly.

As the epidemic progressed further into the current century, however, there was a noticeable shift in the way it came to be framed and imagined. Negar Akhavi's anthology *AIDS Sutra*, published in 2008, is a good example. It features a wide range of articles on persons with HIV across different groups, from sex workers, hijras, men-who-have-sex-with-men, truck drivers and intravenous drug users to middle-class couples, some in the form of illness stories of particular individuals and others in the form of general accounts. What is remarkable in these diverse representations of HIV and AIDS is their non-judgmentality. Thus, Sunil Gangopadhyay writes of the sex workers of Sonagachhi: 'They don't perceive themselves as sinners and fallen women anymore. They don't claim to be victims of a cruel destiny either. They speak of their profession, quite naturally and spontaneously, as though it was one of many' (2008, p.169). Gangopadhyay's observation is not just about how the sex workers view themselves: it reveals, too, how he views them. Similarly, Sonia Faleiro writes of Radhika, a sex worker who volunteers for an NGO: 'Sex work affords Radhika her livelihood. Outreach work, on the other hand, has given her a self respect whose value, for her, is above price' (2008, p. 92). As he stands in the room where Siami, an IV drug user, entertains clients as a sex worker to support her habit, Siddhartha Deb muses: 'Here, in this room, it became abundantly clear that there are outsiders and insiders, those who are visitors and those who make their homes and lives out of their rough, unforgiving circumstances' (2008, p. 215). In a telling reversal of the dominant stereotype, Deb portrays the sex-worker as 'insider' and the client who seeks her services as the 'outsider'. Such accounts counter moralism by focusing on the structural factors that lead to 'deviant' and 'diseased' lifestyles: poverty, lack of social support, unequal power relationships that make it impossible to negotiate safe sex. Writing about hijras in Bangalore, Mukul Kesavan reflects: 'It seemed to me that poor non-straight men in Bangalore grew into a kothi identity because their material and social circumstances were so oppressive and so intolerant of sexual difference that effeminacy (which in a more hospitable environment might have grown into a spectrum of sexual behaviours), found itself channelled into the one pariah form that traditional society tolerated: the kothi/hijra' (2008, p. 186). In his foreword to the anthology, Amartya Sen writes: 'the understanding of a complex reality not only demands facts, figures and empirical details, but also the use of our responsive imagination to interpret what is going on, so that crude facts can be transformed into informed comprehension' (2008, p. 2). The way AIDS and HIV-positive people are imagined in *AIDS Sutra* clearly displays a responsibility to tell the story with compassion without either stigmatising or sentimentalising the lives they narrate.

Let me now turn to another narrative that broadly exhibits this shift in the framing of HIV-positive persons at the time when such narratives were just emerging, Kalpana Jain's *Positive Lives* (2002). The book is an account of the author's journey through India, covering more than fifteen thousand kilometres in four months in order to get an idea of the epidemic's scale (Jain, 2002, pp. xvi–xvii). It belongs to the genre of what may be called the disease travelogue, that is, travel writing that explores landscapes of disease. A good example is Alfred C. Reed's 'Medical Sketches of the Orient', which I have discussed in chapter one. Let me take a brief detour through this text, in order to highlight Jain's perspective in *Positive Lives.* Reed takes us through various countries and regions of the 'Orient'—China, the Malay Peninsula, India, Ceylon and the Middle East—where he observes the prevalent diseases and their causes such as poverty, overcrowding and religious practices that are unsanitary and spread contagion. He records, too, the consumption of addictive substances like cannabis and tobacco, and the environmental causes of disease and death like mosquitoes and poisonous snakes. Scattered through various parts of his travelogue are lines directly addressing his audience, in statements like '[t]he medical pilgrim must approach India with a fair acquaintance with the history, ethnology and religions of this expansive subcontinent' and '[a]ll over tropical Asia the experienced traveller carries with him a well-constructed mosquito net, because in many places no net is provided' (Reed, 1930, pp. 198, 212). He also offers practical advice like carrying a 'stout flash-light' and eating 'freshly cooked food' rather than salads because they may be contaminated (pp. 212–213). Reed's essay thus constructs a pathologised Orient as complement to its other constructs such as political, sociological, ethnographic, military, ideological and scientific, that constituted 'Orientalism' as 'a style of thought based upon an ontological and epistemological distinction made between "the Orient" and (most of the time) the "Occident"' (Said, 1995, p. 2). The undertaking of this vast discursive enterprise was not just to know the Orient but equally to govern it, for 'the scope of Orientalism exactly matched the scope of empire' (p. 104). *Positive Lives* is in formal continuity with Reed's travelogue in the way it configures otherness spatially with disease. For the self that presumes itself as healthy, disease is always a property of the other. Yet there are crucial differences, which we will shortly see, in the way this configuration happens, and the perspective it assumes in relation to its object.

All forms of travel writing, state Marguerite Helmers and Tillar J. Mazzeo, imply the embodied perspective of the traveller-author: it is in moving bodily through spaces, observing and describing things and quite often photographing them that they visually produce the veracity of what they narrate.[15] But when travel writing intersects with relations of power, as in Reed, it tries to efface this. David Arnold uses the phrase 'traveling gaze' to show how it functions as 'an ordering, even disciplining, mechanism' that constructs geographical knowledge into 'meaningful shapes' (2005, p. 31). In its most politicised form it erases the fact of its embodiment, by turning to third-person narration. Though Reed refers to the 'experienced traveler' or 'medical pilgrim,' there is a total absence of any self-reference in the form of the narrating I, which is completely subsumed in the depersonalised observing eye. 'The imperial eye at its most penetrating is the disembodied organ of an unmarked white, male body that is always the subject and never object' (Helmers & Mazzeo, 2005, p. 268). What we note in *Positive Lives* is the way it refuses this mode of narration. Jain begins by dismantling the trope of the disembodied gaze, by constantly reflecting on her own inadequacies for the task she has set for herself:

> When I started this work, like almost everyone else, I considered HIV as being something distant. I must confess I too believed that it was largely a disease of the promiscuous. I, with my middle-class attitudes and years of conditioning of

[15] The photograph is 'proof' that the author has been there, even if it has been taken from some other source. It complements the descriptions in producing a reality that is scopic in origin, as in the saying 'seeing is believing'. It is not so much the referentiality of the photograph as its rhetorical function that makes it a generic feature of travel writing.

> what was right and wrong, felt secure that I, my family and my children were safe. It's only after coming to closely know people with HIV that I began to see how HIV could affect any one of us, through blood, needles or sex—the reason was not even that important. AIDS was more about our lives and the complexities that decide our actions or that of our sexual partners. (2002, xv–xvi)

Her narrative is about the people she encounters and interacts with in her journey, but it is equally about her own edification in the process and the empathy she learns to develop. This is clearly the reverse of what we see in Reed, whose contempt for the people he describes is all too evident. Observing Hindus worshipping in temples, for instance, he writes: 'Verily it makes the heart grow sick and the imagination pale to confront face to face such a degradation of human possibilities' (Reed, 1930, pp. 202–203). Jain's configuration of the topography of disease, therefore, is motivated by an empathy that is clearly absent—not even intended—in Reed. Perspectivally, therefore, the two texts are very different: Reed's is clearly judgmental and closed, Jain's open and non-judgmental.

A technique that Jain uses to transform medical topography[16] into travel writing is the juxtaposition of the sightseeing and the pathogenic gaze:

> Panchgani is a picturesque hill resort, 250 km from Mumbai, and a seven-hour-long drive away. In this serene township, nature and man seem to coexist harmoniously. Deeply inhaling its pure clean air, I headed towards my destination, the Bel Air hospital. With its buildings dotting several acres of sprawling green, the place seemed unlike any hospital I had visited.... the initial overall effect was appealing. Only later did I realize how much sickness and death lay hidden amidst this beauty. (2002, pp. 19–20)

[16] By 'medical topography' I mean a genre of scientific writing on locations of disease, based on incidence figures, bodily constitutions and environmental conditions. This was an important part of colonial public health literature, complementing disease mapping. In chapter one, I mention James Ranald Martin's *Notes on the Medical Topography of Calcutta* as an example of the genre.

> Chenamuthalapetty village, about 6 km from Namakkal wears a look of prosperity, with large, spacious houses along its metalled roads. The primary occupation of its people is building the chassis of lorries. Elders here traditionally gather near the temple at the entrance to the village, to chat and discuss issues. Of late, the discussion revolves around the latest death and whether it has been due to HIV. (p. 73)

The sudden emergence of HIV in what seems salubrious surroundings, like the natural beauty of Panchgani with its 'pure clean air' or the middle-class ordinariness of Chenamuthalapetty, produces a sense of the absolute unexpectedness and contingency of disease, the vulnerability of human life that AIDS foregrounds. The juxtaposition of scapes and signs of contagion is not just a formal strategy for writing disease through travel, but also underlies a perspective that levels ideological differences between the diseased and those presumed to be healthy. The spaces of disease are not those of dirt and poverty, nor are they seedy highway dhabas and brothels, but places we travel to or live in. Thus, even as Jain continues spatialising disease and otherness as the disease travelogue conventionally does, she questions its validity.

Jain also calls into question the discourse of epidemiology, by juxtaposing AIDS statistics with personal stories of people with HIV. She cites sentinel surveillance figures (2002, pp. 144–155), which she uses to indicate the spread of the epidemic. But such figures presented in the 'cold lexicon of statistics', she states, 'do not convey the trauma of being HIV positive: of the stigma, the loneliness and the ridicule. They do not define what happens to a human being infected with HIV, or a family coping with the infection' (p. 15). This is not how media stories commonly use the objective facts of epidemiology; by supplementing them with subjective perceptions it questions their very claim to truth. To bring out the truth that they suppress, therefore, she turns to personal stories of ordinary people whose lives have been suddenly disrupted by AIDS, as well as those who try to rebuild their lives after being affected. Sakubai's family, for instance, was self-sufficient till her son died of AIDS. Sangeeta, her daughter-in-law, had taken over the responsibility of running the home till she fell ill and had to be admitted to Bel-Air, a charitable hospital run by the Indian Red Cross. Now, Sakubai is compelled to work to take care of her grandchildren, leaving Sangeeta alone in the hospital as she cannot afford her treatment. Resigned to her fate, Sangeeta 'has no tears, no grief, and no joy either' (p. 37).

Jain's human interest stories differ significantly from those we had seen in the previous section, by recounting not only the suffering of their subjects but also their determination to restore self-dignity. When Ashok, a cadet-officer in the Navy, tests positive, he does not know how to cope with 'the stigma, loneliness, isolation, ridicule, hopelessness and the daily fear of death' (Jain, 2002, p. 8). He returns home where, with the support of his parents and sisters, he regains the courage to fight back. He meets Rama and Upendra who are also HIV-positive, and the three set up the first network of people living with AIDS, INP+. 'After a long time, he felt he was on the right path. Life was beginning to acquire a new meaning' (p. 120). In the last chapter Jain tells the stories of caregivers who undergo the trauma of their own disease but learn to cope with it. In *Positive Lives*, therefore, the human interest story does not merely express the devastation of AIDS, as such stories in the media commonly do, but equally the hope and positivity of people like Ashok, Rama, Upendra, Abraham, Kousalya, Deepak and Elango, who establish networks to support people with AIDS and fight for their right to a dignified life. The book, however, is not without its shortcomings: quite often Jain recycles some of the clichés in media reports of the epidemic, such as AIDS is 'a death sentence without appeal', it is a 'time bomb', sex is 'the most lethal and dangerous mode of transmission',[17] and 'Indian women are not promiscuous' (Jain, 2002, p. 24; p. 54; p. 17; p. 163). But given the overall effort to represent HIV-positive people without being judgmental, these do not seriously affect Jain's empathy for the lives she narrates.

[17] This is a clearly moralistic statement. It is intravenous transmission that carries the highest risk, and in a disease like AIDS all modes of transmission are equally 'lethal and dangerous'.

Ek Alag Mausam, *AIDS Sutra* and *Positive Lives* mark a moment in the history of the epidemic when civil society began to take an active role in addressing issues like awareness creation, destigmatisation, and the care and support of persons with HIV. *Ek Alag Mausam* was produced by ActionAid India, and was screened in a film festival on HIV/AIDS organised by the NGO in Bangalore, Kolkata and Chennai (ActionAid, 2006, p. 15). Seven of the sixteen chapters in *AIDS Sutra*, which was funded by the Bill and Melinda Gates Foundation, deal with non-governmental organisations, while *Positive Lives* covers extensively the work of HIV-positive networks and NGOs. The Y.R. Gaitonde Centre for AIDS Research and Education in Chennai, set up by Suniti Solomon in 1993, was one of the first NGOs to take up AIDS work. Solomon was the microbiologist who had identified the first cases of HIV in the country in 1986. 'Since its inception', she writes, 'YRG CARE's mission has been to provide an affordable, client-centred continuum of care that not only serves the changing needs of HIV positive clients through all stages of disease and treatment, but also addresses the prevention and support needs of their families and others affected by HIV/AIDS in their midst' (2005, p. 47). Radhika Ramasubban and Bhanwar Rishyasringa mention three justifications for the involvement of civil society institutions in AIDS work. First, they work much better than government institutions in that they are small-scale and based in local communities where they enjoy a high degree of trust. Secondly, they can provide services beyond the scope of government agencies, like professional as well as peer group counselling, facilities for rehabilitation by taking erstwhile clients into their employ as volunteers, and advocacy and legal services to those rendered vulnerable due to the epidemic. Finally, they have long been engaged in social issues, are flexible in their approach, and have an institutional commitment to human rights (Ramasubban & Rishyasringa, 2005, pp. 13–15). The National AIDS Control Organisation (NACO) partners with these organisations to carry out local and targeted interventions and to extend the reach of its awareness programmes. Narratives like *AIDS Sutra* and *Positive Lives* reflect this change in the social understanding of AIDS, not just in their accounts of civil society interventions but equally in their general view of HIV-positive people.

7.5. Narratives of AIDS and the Law: *Phir Milenge* and *My Brother … Nikhil*

Apart from being a medical, social and political problem, the HIV/AIDS epidemic has also involved legal issues, insofar as it concerns the discrimination against HIV-positive persons in healthcare, education, employment, access to public amenities, and their right to live with dignity. At the core of this is a perceived conflict between their constitutionally guaranteed rights and the state's duty to protect the lives of its 'other' citizens. In the absence of any legal precedent to resolve this conflict in the early decades of the epidemic, courts often ruled to set aside these rights as an exception. Thus, in *Lucy D'Souza v State of Goa* (1989), the Bombay High Court held that the isolation of persons with HIV was reasonable, procedurally correct and not violative of their constitutional rights as they posed a risk both to their own lives and those of others they interacted with (*Lucy D'Souza*,1990). The Supreme Court in *Mr X v Hospital Z* (1998) ruled that an HIV-positive person's right to marry could be placed under suspension as there was an imminent risk of transmitting the virus to the spouse (*Mr X v Hospital Z*, 1998).[18] As the Andhra Pradesh High Court in *M Vijaya v Chairman and Managing Director, Singareni Collieries* (2001) put it, there is 'the implied agreement of a member of the society that his own individual interest and welfare shall in all cases of necessity yield to that of the community and that his life and liberty under certain circumstances be placed in jeopardy or even sacrificed for the public good' (*M Vijaya*, 2001). It based this on the principle of

[18] This was reversed by the Supreme Court four years later, in hearing an interlocutory appeal seeking clarification on the ruling. The new judgment stated that the observations on marriage were 'unnecessary, particularly when there was no consideration of the said matter after notice to all parties concerned' (*Mr X v Hospital Z*, 2003).

salus populi est suprema, or 'the good of the people is the highest good'. While reasoning in favour of public good, however, *Vijaya* acknowledges the enigmatic nature of the issue: 'Can the State segregate HIV-positive patients in hospitals from others? Can the State compel high-risk groups like migrant workers, truck drivers, prison inmates and sex workers to undergo HIV-AIDS test and deny those persons normal life? Can the state deny the privileges and facilities to those persons who are tested HIV+ve (HIV-AIDS)?' The principle of public good, however, was not always applied to suspend the rights of HIV-positive persons or to place them in an exception: in *MX v ZY* (1997), for instance, the Bombay High Court ruled that HIV infection cannot be a ground for denying employment or dismissing an employee from service (*MX v ZY*). In most cases courts were left to decide the issue depending on their view of what constituted a reasonable restriction on the rights of HIV-positive persons and what did not. Quite often, as in the case of the first three judgments cited, dominant social assumptions about AIDS influenced the view of the court, without taking into account the fact that HIV cannot be transmitted in everyday social interactions and that it is easily preventable by following a few known precautions.[19] AIDS, therefore, continued to be a contentious legal issue till Parliament passed a law protecting the rights of HIV-positive persons in 2017, prohibiting any form of discrimination, unfair treatment, stigmatisation, or incitement of hatred for them.[20] The two Hindi films that I will discuss in the following section are about the juridical framing of AIDS in India.

Phir Milenge (2004), directed by Revathy, is about an advertising company executive who is sacked by her boss when he learns that she is HIV-positive. *My Brother … Nikhil* (2005), directed by Onir, is about an HIV-positive gay man who is arrested

[19] I have discussed the legal issues in more detail in *Teaching AIDS*, 2019, chapter five, pp. 113–147 .

[20] Chapter II of the Act provides for non-discrimination in employment, education, access to healthcare, use of public amenities, residence, free movement and election to public office (Human immunodeficiency virus Act, 2017, pp. 5–6).

and detained in an abandoned sanatorium. They both show how persons with HIV have been excluded from society because of their disease, contrary to their constitutionally-guaranteed rights as citizens. Prior to the Human Immunodeficiency Virus and Acquired Immune Deficiency Syndrome (Prevention and Control) Act of 2017, there were neither laws nor legal precedents concerning the rights of persons with HIV, and decisions were most often based on norms that treated disease as an exception. To take a few examples, Epidemic Diseases Act 1897 provides for the segregation of persons with infectious disease, sections 269–270 of the Indian Penal Code criminalise transmission of lethal infections, section 16(1)(iv) of Chapter III of the Orissa Municipal Act 1950 debars persons with leprosy, mental illness and tuberculosis from contesting public office, and all the marriage acts render marriage dissoluble if a spouse has sexual disease.[21] The diseased person, therefore, is treated under an exception to law's duty to protect all citizens—he/she is 'a liminal being, a citizen who is not yet citizen' (Das, 2012, p. 114), and in the context of an incurable disease like AIDS can never achieve the rights and privileges of citizenship. Both films explore this enigma of the diseased body in law, the first pertaining to discrimination in employment and the second to custodial detention.

Phir Milenge is an adaptation of *Philadelphia* (1993), a Hollywood film about an HIV-positive gay man who is sacked from the law firm where he works. Though Andrew Beckett is a highly competent employee, he is dismissed from service on the pretext that he misplaced an important document that had to be filed urgently. He challenges the dismissal in court and wins the case, but succumbs to his illness the next day. Beckett's attorney, Joe Miller is a Black American who empathises with him because he has himself suffered racial discrimination. By clubbing homophobia and racism, *Philadelphia* is able to generalise Beckett's case in a way that was acceptable to a moral majority

[21] Earlier leprosy had also been a ground for the dissolution of marriage, but it was removed in 2019 under the Personal Laws (Amendment) Act.

that disapproved of racial discrimination but was unsympathetic to gay persons with HIV. Though the plot of *Phir Milenge* closely parallels that of *Philadelphia*, it ends on a more positive note: Tamanna Sahni not only survives but starts her own advertising firm and achieves fame when she is featured on the cover page of *Business Today*. She challenges her dismissal but loses the case in the lower court where she had filed her petition. Her lawyer Tarun is inexperienced, and is not able to argue against the more experienced counsels for the defence. The court is convinced that her boss Subramaniam has unfairly dismissed her on the pretext of professional incompetence, but holds that he has not acted outside the law. She takes it to the high court, where Tarun gives a moving summation emphasising the need for empathy. The next sequence, with which the film closes, shows Tamanna two years later as a successful entrepreneur who has gained public recognition. The film does not show the outcome of the trial, but it is presumed that she has won her case. The courtroom scenes in *Phir Milenge* are thus based on the assumption that there is nothing wrong with the rationality of law and its capacity to render justice, provided the arguments are presented convincingly—the lapse is in the lawyering, not in the decision of the judge. The lower court's decision, however, seems to be founded on a contradiction: if Subramaniam acted unjustly in dismissing Tamanna, how could this act fall *within* a law committed to guarantee justice? It can only be possible if law and justice are divergent, so that what is legally right may not necessarily be just.[22] Cases that are without precedent, which present an enigma that law has never encountered, test the capacity of law

[22] Cf. Derrida: '[F]or a decision to be just and responsible, it must … be both regulated and without regulation, it must preserve the law [*loi*] and also destroy and suspend it enough to have [*pour devoir*] to reinvent it in each case, rejustify it, reinvent it at least in the reaffirmation and the new and free confirmation of its principle. Each case is other, each decision is different and requires an absolutely new interpretation, which no existing coded rule can or ought to guarantee absolutely' (2002, p. 251). Derrida's argument is that each case opens up questions that no pre-existing rule can anticipate, which is especially applicable to those for which there is no precedent. Before the passage of the HIV/AIDS Act in 2017, that was precisely the situation in India as in other jurisdictions.

to render justice. This is the essence of the rhetorical question that the Andhra Pradesh High Court asks in *Vijaya*: can the state discriminate against persons with HIV on the sole ground that they are infected, in violation of their right to a free and dignified life as implied in Article 21 of the Constitution?[23] In resolving the matter on the concept of public good, *Vijaya* reveals the gap that exists between law as a practical instrument of the social order, and justice as the ideal on which it is premised. Though the plot of *Phir Milenge* presents an opportunity to question the court's reasoning and the fundamentally contradictory way in which it frames Tamanna's dismissal, it fails to pursue this. I argue that the reason for this failure lies not in the narrative alone, but in the presupposition of law's normativity, that law as a system is based on rational and objective rules irrespective of the social ideology within which it functions.

My Brother … Nikhil differs in this respect. Though it is based on an actual case, *Lucy D'Souza v the State of Goa* (1989), it does not have a courtroom scene and the conflict it presents is solved not by lawyering but through a public campaign for Nikhil's right to dignity. It thus shows how law cannot guarantee justice unless there is a change in social ideology, an insight that is lacking in *Phir Milenge*. The incident on which the film is based concerned the arrest and detention of Dominic D'Souza, an HIV-positive gay man, under provisions of the Goa, Daman and Diu Public Health Act, 1985. Dominic had donated blood at a local hospital, and when it tested positive for HIV the hospital alerted the local authorities. He was picked up from home on the morning of 14 February 1989 and was isolated in an abandoned sanatorium for TB patients for more than sixty days. His mother approached various health department officials, political leaders and even the chief minister of Goa, but they could do nothing for her son. Eventually she petitioned the Goa bench of the Bombay High Court, challenging the constitutional validity of the provisions

[23] This is the interpretation that *M Vijaya* gives to Article 21: 'It is well settled that the right to life guaranteed under Article 21 is not mere animal existence. It is a right to enjoy all faculties of life' (*M Vijaya*, 2001).

under which he had been arrested and detained. The court passed an interim order for his release but 'placed him under house arrest, with a police constable to stand guard' (Dube, 2015, p. 144). Subsequently, in its final order, it dismissed the petition and held that there was no infirmity in the law (*Lucy D'Souza*, 1990). After his release Dominic took an active role in creating public awareness about HIV and founded Positive People, a support group for persons with AIDS (Muller, 2017).

My Brother ... Nikhil opens with Nikhil Kapoor winning the state championship in swimming, shortly after which a routine blood test reveals that he is infected with HIV. When this becomes public, the swimming association debars him from membership and he is not allowed to use its facilities. His father, who had dreams of Nikhil winning the national championship, is devastated and throws him out of the family home. Nikhil seeks refuge in the house of his gay partner Nigel, from where the police pick him up one morning and detain him in an abandoned and dirty sanatorium. Unable to bear the stigma of a son who has AIDS, his parents leave Goa and shift to Mumbai. Only his sister Anamika, her fiancé Sam, and Nigel stand by him, and try to get him released by petitioning the court. His lawyer is sympathetic but doubtful of success since she knows how the court may rule when there is no precedent in his favour and society disapproves of his conduct. She advises them to garner public opinion in his support, while she prepares the grounds for his release. Anamika, Nigel and Sam go door-to-door, meeting people, distributing pamphlets featuring him as the champion they had once admired, and getting them to empathise with his suffering.[24] Nikhil is released after three months in custody, but finds that the firm where he worked has dismissed him. He is initially disheartened, but finds a job as music teacher in his old school. With the help of his sister and the others he sets up a support group for HIV-positive people. His parents eventually

[24] This was what actually happened in the Dominic D'Souza case, when his mother along with neighbours and activists led a massive demonstration in Panjim against his arrest (Dube, 2015, pp. 143–144).

accept him and return to their family home, where Nikhil spends his last days. After his death they take in Nigel as their son, in a gesture showing their acceptance of Nikhil's sexual orientation.

The film adheres closely to the facts of Dominic D'Souza's case, departing from it only in the way it resolves the issue when the court orders Nikhil's release. In doing so it provides an interpretation and not simply a fictionalisation of the event on which it is based. Unlike *Phir Milenge* it does not take legal normativity as granted, but shows how the norms of law intersect with social norms in the practice of law. This is especially so in cases where no statute or precedent in common law exists that fits the case and the judge has to rely on a collective sense of what constitutes a just order of society. If we read both films together, we understand why law failed to render justice to persons with HIV: on the one hand was their right to equality before law, while on the other was law's construction of transmissible lethal disease as a reasonable restriction on that right. That each disease has its own dynamics of transmission so that a restriction that is clearly reasonable for one may not be so for another is a fine distinction that the generality of any rule-system cannot include or even anticipate. Law, like social norms, prefigures disease as a negative condition, negating not only the identity of those who have it but equally their membership in society. A change in law's conception of persons with disease is possible only when there is a corresponding change in the way society perceives them. Narratives like *Phir Milenge* and *My Brother … Nikhil* both reflect social perceptions of HIV-positive persons as well as question them. Tarun's final summation before the High Court in *Phir Milenge*, for instance, distinguishes between 'us' and 'them', but is at the same time critical of stigma against those who have AIDS (Balaje & Revathy, 2004, 2:03:54–2:04:19). *My Brother … Nikhil* presents both the social ostracism that Nikhil and his family face as well as the efforts to counter it. Cultural performance, writes Victor Turner does not simply reflect the values of society but 'is often a critique, direct or indirect, of the social life it grows out of, an evaluation (with lively possibilities of rejection) of the way society handles history' (1987, p. 22).[25]

History includes both continuity and change, which are the necessary conditions for a critique of social values to emerge. My contention is that films like *My Brother ... Nikhil* and *Phir Milenge*, which present the stories of persons who have acquired HIV through sexual relationships held to be illicit and blameworthy, could be made only when social perceptions about AIDS and HIV-positive people were beginning to change. This is evident when we examine how AIDS has been constructed in *Naya Zaher*, *Nidaan*, *Ek Alag Mausam*, *Phir Milenge* and *My Brother ... Nikhil*. *Naya Zaher* was made at a time when AIDS was held to be a disease of foreigners and socially marginal 'deviant' Indians. The source of disease in the film is a group of sexually liberated women who mimic Western ways, and the protagonist is portrayed as their victim. Moreover, Avinash, who has acquired infection through premarital sex and is therefore to some extent culpable in the eyes of society, redeems himself by the end of the story. Mahesh Manjrekar's *Nidaan* which was screened in 2000,[26] tells the story

[25] Turner's work, which I have briefly discussed in chapter four, concerns continuity and change in the order of society, which happens through what he calls 'social drama.' In any society there is a structure of rules or norms that govern the conduct of its members, but all elements of this structure are not in harmony at any given moment. These instabilities of the structure—what he calls 'anti-structure' or 'communitas'—open it to change, which happens when one set of norms comes into conflict with another. These conflicts, of course, are not played out in the abstract, but are literally 'staged' by conflicts between individual social actors or groups. They begin typically in a breach of norms that leads to a crisis, followed by attempts to redress the breach through adjustments in the structure, and ending with the reintegration of the social group, but on a new level of order (Turner, 1974, pp. 33–45). Turner, thus, uses a processual approach that differs from structural anthropology in examining how social structures transform themselves over time by a dialectic that is internal to them. The relevance of this argument for what happens to the social construction of AIDS at the turn of the twenty-first century in India should be apparent.

[26] It was screened with tax exemption in several states of the country, and its title was given by the then prime minister of India Atal Behari Vajpayee (Rangarajan 2000). The government subsidised its screening because it would create awareness of the disease and sensitise people against stigmatisation of the HIV-positive.

of a teenage girl who contracts HIV through blood transfusion when she undergoes an appendicitis operation. Soumya is, thus, an 'innocent victim', in a narrative that tries to elicit sympathy for the HIV-positive even while it implicitly discriminates against those who are 'deviant'. Soumya's disease is framed against that of the high-risk groups, in the way the film constructs it. Like the haemophiliac and thalassaemic, she acquires infection due to the moral transgression of others, who are its source. Despite her being HIV-positive, therefore, she is normalised as the story progresses. She marries her childhood boyfriend with the consent and support of both their families, but they do not consummate their marriage because of the risk of transmission. Soumya had always dreamed of meeting her idol, the film actor Sanjay Dutt. This dream is fulfilled as she lies on her deathbed, providing a satisfying closure to the pathos of a life of thwarted hope. Aparna in *Ek Alag Mausam* is also an 'innocent victim', a housewife who has been infected by her errant husband; and she can culminate her relationship with George only when she learns that he, too, is an 'innocent victim'. While illness has long been treated as a major theme in Hindi film melodrama because of its capacity to evoke pathos, AIDS was not considered amenable to such treatment: it was too highly stigmatised for audiences to accept it. Avinash, Soumya and Aparna could be recruited into cinema as HIV-positive protagonists only to the extent that they did not transgress the moral code. In contrast to them, Tamanna and Nikhil contract HIV through acts that are clearly transgressive: premarital sex in the one case and gay sex in the other. What was it, then, that reversed the moral logic of Hindi film melodrama? As we have seen in the previous section, intervention projects by the government as well as non-governmental agencies prioritised sensitisation of the public to persons with AIDS, because stigma was found to actually contribute to the spread of disease. It was this conjuncture of events that made it possible to make films like *Phir Milenge* and *My Brother ... Nikhil* for release in the commercial circuit. Yet there does seem to be some hesitation in

Phir Milenge to take up the subject of AIDS openly, as if the film was 'testing the waters'. Tamanna does acquire infection through a transgressive act, but it is symbolically legitimised in the scene where she performs *saat phere* with her lover, a ritual in which the bride and groom exchange vows while going round the sacred fire (Balaje & Revathy, 2004, 49:53–50:25). Despite its bold attempt to portray her character non-judgmentally, thus, it continues to frame the epidemic as a crisis of morality, as it had been done in the early years of the outbreak. It is only in *My Brother … Nikhil* that Hindi cinema could effect a break in this framing. In 2005, when the film was made, homosexuality was still considered deviant and criminalised under Section 377 of IPC. This changed in 2009, when Delhi High Court ruled to decriminalise adult consensual same-sex acts in *Naz v NCT of Delhi*. Earlier however, on two occasions, the same court had dismissed petitions challenging the constitutional validity of Section 377, the first in 1994 filed by AIDS Bhedbhav Andolan and the second in 2001 by Naz Foundation. What happened in between was the growth of a gay rights movement in India, especially in metropolitan centres, which began with the first Gay Pride March in Kolkata on 2 July 1999. In 2006, Naz appealed against the dismissal of its petition before the Supreme Court, which directed Delhi High Court to take it up again on merits. It was at this historical conjuncture that a change in the social understanding of non-normative sexuality became possible, of which the Naz judgment is the juridical, and *My Brother … Nikhil* the narrative outcome. The way in which the HIV-postive individual is constructed in *Nidaan*, *Ek Alag Mausam*, *Phir Milenge* and *My Brother … Nikhil* corresponds to changes in the social reality of AIDS, and a growing willingness to think, however tentatively, beyond moral frames. HIV, writes K. Sujatha Rao, a former director-general of the National AIDS Control Organisation, 'is no ordinary disease. Unlike any other, it challenged the social order and value systems, and in the process helped enhance a measure of social acceptability of different sexual orientations and behaviour' (2017, p. 290).

7.6. Pedagogical Narratives

An account of AIDS narratives will not be complete without looking at those that figure in public health campaigns. In public health policy it is commonly assumed that an epidemic spreads because people lack knowledge of its modes of transmission and prevention, which can be rectified by creating awareness. This is indeed true of many disease outbreaks that are not directly linked to lifestyle or behaviour pattern, as HIV/AIDS is. Awareness creation alone has not worked in the case of AIDS, because it requires more than just knowledge of how it is transmitted and how it can be prevented. Public health efforts can work only if they combine this knowledge with strategies for lifestyle change. The public health agency tasked with mitigating the epidemic in India is the National AIDS Control Organisation, which formulates and implements the different phases of the National AIDS Control Policy. When the first awareness programmes were launched under NACP-I (1992–1998) the emphasis was on scientific information about HIV/AIDS, often presented in the format of facts-versus-myths. Under NACP-II (1999–2006), however, there was a shift of emphasis 'from raising awareness to changing behaviour through intervention, particularly for groups at high risk of contracting and spreading HIV' (NACO, 2000, p. 25). Behaviour change communication is an approach to health promotion based on the understanding that lifestyle preferences are motivated more by subjective factors than objective knowledge, so that merely imparting information is not enough. It targets individuals whose lifestyles expose them to risk, and teaches them how to live safely by utilising their emotions and aspirations. As a pedagogic technique, therefore, it induces people to refashion themselves, its objective being to produce prudential subjects in a potentially life-threatening situation (Das, 2019, pp. 162–170).[27] Stories of people having similar

[27] Behaviour change strategies, however, fail to take account of the structural factors underlying vulnerability to disease. As Arvind Singhal and Everett Rogers explain, they unproblematically assume that all people have more or less the same degree of control over their situation, that they all enjoy an 'even playing field', and that they make choices about health rationally and

lifestyles and exposed to the same risks who have successfully changed their ways to keep themselves safe provide a culturally available format for inducing behaviour change. People tend to identify personally with the characters, as a result of which such stories have a greater impact on them than an impersonal list of dos and don'ts. Let me take as example a film made by the Border Security Force in collaboration with UNAIDS.

Saavdhaan—It's a battle against HIV/AIDS was released on World AIDS Day, 1 December 2007. The main title refers to the command for attention during drill in the armed forces. It was made to be screened for BSF soldiers when a growing number of HIV cases were reported in the paramilitary forces. On the occasion of the film's release, Director–General A.K. Mitra stated that there were 122 recorded deaths and 335 cases of infection in the BSF, the most vulnerable being young soldiers posted in remote stations ('BSF produces'). This was generally true of the armed forces in the early 2000s.[28] Two of the strategies that NACP-II emphasised were targeted awareness campaigns and promotion of testing, both of which are the primary objectives of *Saavdhaan*. It is about a voluntary testing camp set up for its personnel by a BSF unit, and includes a sequence where a doctor explains to the viewer about the modes of transmission and prevention of HIV. Some of the soldiers are reluctant to test and Constable Suresh tries to persuade them. He tells the story of a brave soldier named Rajesh Kumar who never hesitated to risk his life in the service of his country. Rajesh used to visit local sex workers and contracted HIV, which he unknowingly transmitted

voluntarily (Singhal & Everett, 2003, pp. 211–212).

[28] A 2002 report published by Healthlink Worldwide in collaboration with Panos Institute stated that in many countries the incidence of HIV in the armed forces was higher than that in the general population. 'Long-term sexual relationships where both partners are mutually faithful are an integral aspect of HIV/AIDS prevention. Military life makes such relationships difficult to maintain. Younger soldiers find it difficult to establish long-term relationships, while older soldiers may be married but separated for long periods from their wives. Facilities for married couples may not be provided or may be overcrowded and unsuitable' (Healthlink Worldwide, 2002, p. 14).

to his pregnant wife and three-year-old son because he did not get tested. Meanwhile Rajesh donates blood for a soldier injured in a mission, which is tested and found to be HIV-positive. Soon after this, his son dies and the hospital tells his wife that there is a risk of her unborn child being affected with HIV. Rajesh is devastated by this personal tragedy as well as the ostracism he now faces in the unit where once he had been treated as a hero. The message is clear: risk-taking may be ideal in the battle against the nation's enemies but it is not so in the 'battle' against HIV/AIDS. The unit's medical officer Dr Ashraf Khan gives him moral support and persuades his friends not to avoid him because the virus does not spread through casual contact. He also tells Rajesh that there are medicines to prevent the virus being transmitted from his wife to the child she is carrying, and that all is not lost. Rajesh goes back home with this message of hope, and his wife soon delivers a healthy child who grows up to join the BSF and fulfil his father's dream. The film juxtaposes Rajesh's story with that of the owner of a local eatery, Chaudhury. Chaudhury contracts the virus when a quack doctor gives him an injection to boost his sexual prowess using an unsterilised syringe. Tests show that both he and his wife are infected. The double-plot structure is used to show that AIDS can affect anyone, 'guilty' or 'innocent', if they do not protect themselves from risk. [29]

At the end of his story, Constable Suresh reveals that he is Rajesh Kumar's son. If he is alive today and is able to fulfil his father's dream, it is because Rajesh learnt of his HIV status in

[29] In using the stories of Rajesh and Chaudhary, however, the film actually reinforces the moral frame. It recurrently refers to Rajesh's sexual relation with sex workers as a 'mistake', for which the death of his first child was a 'punishment', even while it presents Chaudhary's story as a counter to this logic. But the implied moralism of the film is best seen in the way it avoids any discussion of condom-use, especially since the ABC approach to AIDS prevention had promoted it as prophylactic against infection. The approach, which was introduced in 2002 by USAID and was soon adopted in India, emphasised three behaviours: *abstain* from sex, *be faithful* to your partner, and use *condoms* otherwise. While the first two are clearly moral ideas, the third is not, and the approach was a tactical way of deploying all three.

time. The soldiers must all, therefore, take the test because 'the first step towards getting cautious about the disease is to get the HIV test done' (UNAIDS & BSF, 2007, 36:25–37:09). They are convinced and report for the test next morning. The closing sequence of the film is a documentary clip from an actual voluntary testing camp set up by the BSF, where A.K. Mitra and other senior officials take the test with the soldiers. Mitra urges the soldiers to test because the sooner they know their serostatus the better they can protect themselves if negative and can get treatment if positive.

The film uses a number of techniques to induce the soldiers to test. The first is viewer-identification with Rajesh and his son, both of whom are in the BSF. Secondly, the closing sequence shows their highest officials taking the test with soldiers like them from the rank and file. Mitra does not use his authority to order them to test, but explains why it is in their interest. Finally, and most importantly, the film uses the emotions of the viewers—their concern for their families and their dream of having a son in the armed forces—to motivate them. This is the crucial part of the narrative, towards which both the story and the lesson that it imparts lead. Self-formation, argues Michel Foucault in 'The Subject and Power', is the outcome not only of the exercise of power but equally of the aspirations of those subjected to it (2000, pp. 341–342). Corresponding to the techniques by which power acts upon a subject, Foucault posits what he calls 'technologies of the self' (1988, p. 18), or the ways in which subjects act upon themselves to achieve a desired goal. It is in this reciprocity of power and subjectivity that behaviour change pedagogy works—it induces people to refashion their selves by adopting the practices that it promotes.[30] In using the soldiers' concern for themselves and their families as its instrument, the pedagogic narrative of *Saavdhaan* tries to ensure their compliance. It also mobilises another emotion ideologically associated with the soldier: patriotism and commitment to the cause of the nation.

[30] For a more detailed discussion of how this works in a neo-liberal context, see Das, 2019, pp. 180–181.

'You have a responsibility towards this country', says Mitra in his speech in the closing sequence. 'You can fulfill this responsibility only if you are perfectly fit' (UNAIDS & BSF, 2007, 39:21–40:43).

Saavdhaan is thus an apt example of a behaviour change campaign that uses narrative to produce its effect. Narrative, more than any other genre, has the power to evoke in the reader a sense of the real world and the emotional and cognitive responses to it. If the early AIDS narratives, in prefiguring those with AIDS as the 'other', produce effects of stigma and ostracism, later narratives by refiguring the HIV-positive as the 'self' produce the effects of empathy and identification that are key motivators of lifestyle change. Let me end with a final point about *Saavdhaan*. Like *My Brother ... Nikhil* and *Phir Milenge*, it creates a positive construction of the person with HIV. Unlike them, however, it is not about the middle class: the people it addresses are the ordinary soldiers of the armed forces who come from less privileged backgrounds than their officers. This shift in focus is typical of interventions that target risk-groups rather than the general population, an emphasis in NACP-II, but it also indicates a changed perception of AIDS as a social concern.

7.7. Conclusion

The AIDS epidemic is now levelling out and has become more like an endemic, thanks to a whole range of factors: blood safety; better surveillance methods that enable more accurate estimates of disease incidence; proactive governance policies; legislation to end stigmatisation and protect the rights of HIV-positive persons to access healthcare, education and employment; anti-retroviral therapies to prevent mother-to-child transmission, improve the health of ill persons and prolong life; and extensive support networks for the care and rehabilitation of persons with HIV/AIDS. It is no longer a 'death sentence' but a manageable condition like other lifestyle diseases such as cancer, coronary heart disease and diabetes. This was not so in the early years, when lack of knowledge about HIV's mode of transmission and prevention, stigma and the dominant perception that it was a disease of deviants served to fuel its spread. Narratives of AIDS provide an access to the changing contexts and constructions of the epidemic—its social history. This is what I have attempted in the present chapter by tracing through stories belonging to different genres and media the shifts from AIDS as a disease of foreigners to that of marginal groups and classes to a crisis that concerns all, requiring empathy and support to enable the HIV-positive to deal with their illness, secure a sense of dignity and well-being, and adopt practices of safety that can prevent further spread of disease. I have tried to correlate these shifts in narrative to historical conjunctures that configure and refigure the social understanding of AIDS. At the same time, I have tried to show how these narratives do not simply reproduce that social understanding, but quite often call it into question. This is where the real value of the narratives lies—the insights into the condition of crisis that they are especially positioned to offer, since they are not entirely restricted to the social contexts that engender them. There is wisdom in what Sontag says about the need to detach the meaning of AIDS from its metaphors: the stories I have discussed, not individually but collectively as a source of knowledge, bear the stamp of this wisdom. Every crisis, as Rosenberg says of epidemic, calls for its storytellers, to remind us of the mistakes we made, the lessons we learnt and the use we could make of these lessons in times of future crisis.

References

ActionAid. (2006). Claiming rights: Theme HIV&AIDS—2006. https://www.actionaidindia.org/wp-content/uploads/2018/06/Claiming-Rights.pdf

Arnold, D. (2005). *The tropics and the travelling gaze: India, landscape, and science 1800–1856*. Permanent Black.

Balaje, S. (Producer) & Revathy (Director). (2004). *Phir milenge* [Film]. Precept Picture Co.

Bariah, F. (1997, March 1–15). AIDS: striking home. *India Today*, pp. 101–108.

Beck, U. (1992). *Risk society: Towards a new modernity*. Sage.

'BSF produces film on HIV/AIDS awareness.' (2007, December 1). *The Times of India*. https://timesofindia.indiatimes.com/india/bsf-produces-film-on-hiv/aids-awareness/articleshow/2588311.cms

Common Cause v Union of India (1996) 1 SCC 753.

Crimp, D. (2002). *Melancholia and moralism: Essays on AIDS and queer politics*. Massachusetts Institute of Technology Press.

Das, D.K. (2019). *Teaching AIDS: The cultural politics of HIV disease in India*. Springer Nature.

Das, D.K. (2022). Epidemic narratives: Two paradigms. In S. Venkatesan, A. Chatterjee, A.D. Lewish & B. Callendar (Eds.), *Pandemics and epidemics in cultural representation* (pp. 12–27). Springer Nature.

Deb, S. (2008). The lost generation of Manipur. In N. Akhavi (Ed.), *AIDS sutra: Untold stories from India* (pp. 199–215). Random House India.

Demme, J. (Producer & Director). (1993). *Philadelphia* [Film]. Tristar Pictures.

Derrida, Jacques. (2002). Force of law: The 'mystical foundation of authority'. In G. Anidjar (Ed.), *Acts of Religion* (pp. 230–298).

Douglas, M. (1966). *Purity and danger: An analysis of the concept of pollution and taboo*. Routledge.

Dube, S. (2015). *No one else: A personal history of outlawed love and sex*. HarperCollins.

Faleiro, S. (2008). *Maarne ka, bhagaane ka*. In N. Akhavi (Ed.), *AIDS sutra:Untold stories from India* (pp. 79–98). Random House India.

Foucault, M. (1988). *Technologies of the self: A seminar with Michel Foucault* (L.H. Martin, H. Gutman & P.H. Hutton, Eds.). University of Massachusetts Press.

Foucault, M. (2000). The subject and power. In J.D. Faubion (Ed.), R. Hurley et al. (Trans.), *Power* (pp. 326–348). New Press.

Frank, A.W. (1993). The Rhetoric of Self-Change: Illness Experience as Narrative. *The Sociological Quarterly*, *34*(1), 39–52.

Gangopadhyay, S. (2008). Return to Sonagachhi. In N. Akhavi (Ed.), *AIDS sutra: Untold stories from India* (pp. 157–175). Random House India.

Grover, J.Z. (1988). AIDS keywords. In D. Crimp (Ed.), *AIDS: Cultural analysis, cultural activism* (pp. 17–30). Massachusetts Institute of Technology Press.

Healthlink Worldwide. (2002). *Combat AIDS: HIV and the world's armed forces*.

Helmers, M. & Mazzeo, T.J. (2005). Introduction: Travel and the body. *Journal of Narrative Theory, 35*(3), 267–276. http://www.jstor.org/stable/30225801

Human Immunodeficiency Virus and Acquired Immune Deficiency Syndrome (Prevention and Control) Act, The. (2017). https://naco.gov.in/sites/default/files/HIV%20AIDS%20Act.pdf

Jain, K. (2002). *Positive lives: The story of Ashok and others with HIV*. Penguin India.

Kesavan, M. (2008). Nowhere to call home. In N. Akhavi (Ed.), *AIDS sutra: Untold stories from India* (pp. 179–295). Random House India.

Kleinman, A. (1988). *The illness narratives: Suffering, healing, and the human condition*. Basic Books.

Kleinman, A. (1995). *Writing at the margin: Discourse between anthropology and medicine*. University of California Press.

Kramer, L. (1989). *Reports from the holocaust: The making of an AIDS activist*. St Martin's Press.

Levine, P. (1994). Venereal disease, prostitution, and the politics of empire: The case of British India. *Journal of the History of Sexuality, 4*(4), 579–602.

Lucy D'Souza v State of Goa AIR 1990 BOM 355.

McGrail, K., Lavergne R. & Lewis, S. (2016). The chronic disease explosion. *British Medical Journal, 352*.

Mishra, S. (2000, July 24). Damned to Death. *India Today*. https://www.indiatoday.in/magazine/living/story/20000724-entire-village-in-up-ostracises-an-hiv-positive-labourer-dies-inhuman-death-779109-2000-07-23

Mishra, S.S.R. (1999). Laws of pleasure: The making of the Indian Contagious Diseases Act, 1868. *Proceedings of the Indian History Congress, 60*, 550–561. https://www.jstor.org/stable/44144123.

Morrison, J. (1992). The return of the repressed: AIDS and allegory. In E.S. Nelson (Ed.), *AIDS: The literary response* (pp. 167–174). Twayne Publishers.

M. Vijaya v Chairman and Managing Director, Singareni Collieries Company Limited AIR 2001 AP 514.

Mr X v Hospital Z (1998) 8 SCC 296.

Mr X v Hospital Z (2003) 1 SCC 500.

MX v ZY AIR 1997 BOM 406.

Muller, S. (Producer & Director). (2017). *Dominic's Dream* [Film]. Henderson Productions.

NACO. (2000). *Combating HIV/AIDS in India 1999–2000*. Ministry of Health and Family Welfare, Government of India.

NACO. (2021). *Sankalak: Status of national AIDS response*. 3rd ed. Ministry of Health and Family Welfare, Government of India. https://naco.gov.in/sites/default/files/Sankalak_Status_of_National_AIDS_Response_Third_Edition_2021.pdf.

Pandit, R.V. (Producer) & Manjrekar, M. (Director). (2000). *Nidaan* [Film]. Pan Pictures.

Park, K. (2015). *Park's textbook of preventive and social medicine*. 23rd ed. Bhanot Publishers.

Patton, C. (1986). *Sex and germs: The politics of AIDS*. Black Rose Books.

Pratap, A. (1986, May 11–17). AIDS comes to India. *Sunday*, pp. 49–50.

Puri, N. (1986, December 1–27). AIDS in India. *Sunday*, pp. 24–30.

Raghunathan, K. (1986, May 17–30). A spreading AIDS scare. *Frontline*.

Rahman, M. & R. Chengappa. (1986, July 1–15). Countering the scare. *India Today*.

Ramachandran, P. (2012). ICMR's tryst with HIV epidemic in India: 1986–1991. *Indian Journal of Medical Research*, *136*, 13–21. https://pmc.ncbi.nlm.nih.gov/articles/PMC3461712/pdf/IJMR-136-13.pdf

Ramasubban, R. & Rishyasringa, B. (Eds.). (2005). *AIDS and civil society: India's learning curve*. Rawat Publications.

Ramasubban, R. & Rishyasringa, B. (2005). Introduction. In R. Ramasubban & B. Rishyasringa (Eds.), *AIDS and civil society: India's learning curve* (pp. 1–38). Rawat Publications.

Rangarajan, M. (2000, June 19). Scoring with a message. *The Hindu*. http://www.thehindu.com/thehindu/2000/06/19/stories/09190222.htm, accessed 20 December 2017.

Rao, K.S. (2017). *Do we care? India's health system*. Oxford University Press.

Reed, A.C. (1930). Medical sketches in the Orient. *The Scientific Monthly*, *31* (3), 193–216.

Rosenberg, C.E. (1989). What is an epidemic? AIDS in historical perspective. *Daedalus*, *118*(2), 1–17.

Rosenberg, C.E. (2008). Siting epidemic disease: 3 centuries of American history. *The Journal of Infectious Diseases*, *197*(Suppl. 1), S4–S6.

Said, E. (1995). *Orientalism*. Penguin India.

Sarin, R. (1990, July 22–28). The outcast. *Sunday*, pp. 22–25.

Sasi, K.P. (Producer & Director). (2005). *Ek Alag Mausam* [Film]. Penta Enterprise.

Sen, A. (2008). Foreword: Understanding the challenge of AIDS. In N. Akhavi (Ed.), *AIDS sutra: Untold stories from India* (pp. 1–15). Random House India.

Shilts, R. (1987). *And the band played on: Politics, people, and the AIDS epidemic*. St Martin's Press.

Singh, N.K. & Pillai, S. (1987, January 16–31). Campus jitters. *India Today*.

Singhal, A., & Rogers, E.M. (2003). *Combating AIDS: Communication strategies in action*. Sage Publications.

Solomon, S. (2005). Continuum of treatment and care: The YRG CARE model. In R. Ramasubban & B. Rishyasringa (Eds.), *AIDS and civil society: India's learning curve* (pp. 47–65). Rawat Publications.

Sontag, S. (1988). *AIDS and its metaphors*. Penguin.

Suri. S. (Producer) & Onir (Director). (2005). *My brother … Nikhil* [Film]. Four Front Films.

Thakar, P. (Producer) & Sarup, J. (Director). (1991). *Naya Zaher* [Film]. Durgaa Pictures.

Treichler, P. (1999). *How to have theory in an epidemic: Cultural chronicles of AIDS*. Duke University Press.

Turner, V. (1987). *The anthropology of performance*. PAJ Publications.

UNAIDS & BSF. (2007). *Saavdhaan—it's a battle against HIV/AIDS* [Film].

Venugopal, K. & Raghunathan, K. (1986, June 28–July 11). 'On the dreaded trail'. *Frontline*.

Venkatramani, S.H. (1986, May 31). News of AIDS detection in Tamil Nadu sends seismic waves through India. *India Today*. https://www.indiatoday.in/magazine/living/story/19860531-news-of-aids-detection-in-tamil-nadu-sends-seismic-waves-through-india-800925-1986-05-30.

White, H. (1978). *Tropics of discourse: Essays in cultural criticism*. Johns Hopkins University Press.

Yingling, T.E. (1997). *AIDS and the national body* (Robyn Wiegman, Ed.). Duke University Press.

8

Fictionalising History

Aashique Abu's *Virus*

In May 2018 Nipah virus disease broke out in Kozhikode district, Kerala, infecting twenty-three people and killing all but two. The government took immediate steps to curb the outbreak, and by mid-July it was officially declared to have ended. Aashique Abu's 2019 film *Virus* is the story of that outbreak. It depicts the sudden emergence of disease, identification of the causative agent and official declaration of epidemic, contact tracing, isolation and treatment of infected persons, and eventual decline of new infections leading to closure. The plot of the film closely follows the historical sequence of events. But *Virus* is not history—it weaves fiction and reality in a manner that reveals how stories of epidemic both derive from social understanding and in turn shape it.

8.1. Framing Epidemic Outbreak

I have elaborated in the first chapter Rosenberg's schema for the social understanding of epidemic. Let me briefly recapitulate here the main arguments in Rosenberg's essay. He outlines the stages through which public comprehension of an outbreak and the response to it develops, using the dramaturgical metaphor of a three-act play. Act one begins with the onset of epidemic, and its declaration by authorities when the number of deaths it has caused can no longer be ignored. Act two comprises explanations of the event in terms both scientific and lay, which frame the way it is perceived. An epidemic signifies a crisis that is at once medical, social, political and cosmological, and explanatory frames try to make sense of its sudden appearance, its randomness and the devastation it causes in terms of these aspects. The framing leads to public responses to curb the outbreak, which eventually comes to an end. This comprises the final act, which includes an 'epilogue' that expresses the lessons learnt. Responses to epidemic crisis in modern societies range from scientific measures that seek to arrest its spread—like quarantine, the wearing of masks and social distancing, vaccination and the safe disposal of dead bodies—to religious practices that involve worship and prayers. Rosenberg describes both types of response as rituals that ensure community solidarity and induce a sense of control over an indomitable reality. The social reality of an outbreak as it unfolds, therefore, 'stages' a typical sequence of events starting with the emergence of disease and ending with its decline.[1]

The object of Rosenberg's analysis is not the biological reality of epidemic but its perception in social consciousness, or its social reality. The 'social chronology' of an epidemic, he states, is *analogous* to the 'biologically determined chronology' and on that count cannot be *synonymous* with it (1989b, p. 15). What consciousness does is provide 'larger frameworks of meaning' for deciphering what seems otherwise inexplicable. The frameworks are the sedimented historical memory of the experience of past epidemics as well as the experience of current outbreaks, and are constituted in the interaction of 'incident, perception, interpretation, and response' (Rosenberg, 1989b, p. 3); the interaction, in other words, of reality and the way we become conscious of it. Culture as a system of signification is the source of the meanings we attribute to particular events. While these meanings derive from the functioning of a sign system that bears an arbitrary relation to the reality it represents, they frame that reality in relatively non-arbitrary ways. To put it more

[1] Though he uses the metaphor of the stage, Rosenberg's outline is equally applicable to narrative emplotment, as the following comment suggests: 'Like the acts in a conventionally structured play, the events of a classic epidemic succeed each other in predictable *narrative* sequence' (1989b, p. 3, italics added). The sole example of the structure of epidemic outbreak that he gives from literature is, significantly, Albert Camus's 1947 novel *The Plague*, and not a play.

precisely, the signification of an event bears a dialectical relation to it, such that the signification predisposes how the event is to be understood while our experience of the event delimits the way it can be signified. This is why Rosenberg emphasises the phenomenological role of experience in the way we come to know epidemic. While experience itself is necessarily mediated by the cultural sign system that we draw on to communicate and make sense of it,[2] it can still provide a valuable source of knowledge about the world. This is the point that Satya Mohanty makes in elaborating what he calls a 'post-positivist' approach to reality: 'All experience … is socially constructed, but the constructedness does not make it arbitrary or unstable in advance. Experiences are crucial indexes of our relationships with the world …, and to stress their cognitive nature is to argue that they can be susceptible to varying degrees of socially constructed truth or error and can serve as sources of objective knowledge or socially produced mystification' (2000, p. 38).[3]

8.2. Explaining Outbreak: Tradition, Modernity and the Notion of Risk

Explanatory frames of epidemic and the ideas they construct are both derived from the collective memory of past events and, in turn, act upon it to reinforce or transform it. Stories of epidemic are situated in this dialectical intersection of remembering and framing, and in the process they are able to restructure existing structures of meaning in response to changing historical contexts. Spanish flu, which did not have any religious association at the time it broke out, became reconfigured in memory a hundred

[2] 'Bodily experiences', writes Diana Fuss, 'may seem self-evident and immediately perceptible but they are always socially mediated.' As such, therefore, experience cannot be a basis for making any substantive claims about reality (1989, p. 25).

[3] Post-positivism holds that the world cannot be reduced to our conceptions of it, an assumption implicit in positivism; at the same time, these concepts can provide insights into the world because they are shaped and delimited by it. It refutes, on the one hand, the positivist assumption of realist theory, and, on the other, the relativism of postmodern theory.

years later, when COVID broke out. A memorial to those who died in 1918 became in 2020 a place of worship for those who sought supernatural intervention in a time of epidemic crisis. The worship of Corona Devi, which had been widely circulated in the media by then, provided a new perspective into which the earlier pandemic could be assimilated and remembered. In his *Hindustan Times* article on the memorial, Gerard de Souza reports how an 'oral tradition' developed around it, preserved in the memory of generations since: 'Anna Antonetta Fernandes, 88, recalled through her son, Marius Fernandes, the stories that she was told by her mother of the "gripe" that afflicted the land leading to a piling up of bodies in her village that were carried up the hill away from human habitation and buried without any ceremony' (2020). These stories, which de Souza reproduces and replenishes, transformed the reality of the 1918 pandemic in the way it came to be remembered. Stories reconfigure not only our memory of the past, but equally our understanding of the present. Take, for instance, the shift in the public image of people with AIDS at the turn of the twenty-first century. There were historical factors that led to this shift: development of effective anti-retroviral therapy, laws protecting the rights of HIV-positive people, campaigns to raise public awareness against stigma and discrimination, establishment of positive-people networks. Narratives like the stories in *AIDS Sutra*, *Positive Lives*, *Nidaan*, *Ek Alag Mausam*, *Phir Milenge* and *My Brother … Nikhil* translated this history into a compelling frame of HIV-positive people that the public could identify and empathise with, leading to a transformation in the social perception of AIDS. The relation between the cultural understanding of outbreak and narrative is, therefore, not a unilateral one in which this understanding determines how events come to be constructed and represented in stories, but a dialectical one in which stories play a potentially transformative role in the way an outbreak is understood.

Traditionally, epidemics have been understood in South Asia as events that have their origin in the anger of a deity or transgression of the cosmic order,[4] and the performance of rituals of propitiation and expiation can mitigate their effects as well as assure protection against them. The modern understanding of epidemics is based on the biomedical theory of microbial causation, which requires antibiotic and antiviral therapy, and vaccination and transmission-prevention to protect against them. In accounts of contemporary outbreaks, two new concepts emerge: environmental spillover and bioterrorism. The first holds that the pathogen accidentally crosses the human–animal barrier, while the second holds that it is genetically engineered and released as a weapon of mass destruction. We will see later how these two accounts have unfolded in recent times. What is common to both accounts is the notion of 'risk' which has increasingly come to be at the centre of the discourses of environmentalism, state security and disease control. 'The notion of risk', argues Bryan Turner, 'is crucial to any debate about modernity because the process of modernization involves an intensification and multiplication of social risk, both at the level of the individual and at the level of social collectivities' (1995, p. 219). Historically, public health paradigms have shifted from quarantine and vaccination in the early-nineteenth century, to sanitation and personal hygiene in the late-nineteenth century, and finally, since the second-half of the twentieth century, to risk assessment and lifestyle management. The quarantining of infected spaces and people, coupled with vaccination of the healthy, was the standard protocol for containing infectious diseases like plague and smallpox in early modern Europe. With industrialisation and the growth of towns and cities in the nineteenth century, attention shifted to the conditions of urban overcrowding that intensified contagion, and sanitation coupled with personal hygiene became standard measure for ensuring

---

[4] In Sri Lanka, for instance, they were believed to be caused by deities: 'It is generally believed that these deities, like the yakku and the prēteo, are able to spread diseases, mainly in the form of epidemics, which are included under the name '*dēviyo-dōsa*' (god-epidemics).' The goddess Patini, for instance, is associated with smallpox, like Sitala and Mariamma in India (Wirz, 1954, p. 140, italics in original).

health. Epidemic outbreaks declined considerably in the first-half of the twentieth century due to new therapeutic and prophylactic regimes, and were superseded by the increased incidence of lifestyle diseases. Risk assessment and management of lifestyles became the new paradigm of health. When HIV/AIDS broke out as the second major pandemic of the century, sixty years after Spanish flu, the notion of risk that had emerged in the context of non-epidemic disease became incorporated into epidemic discourse. Since then it has become generalised to include various aspects of contemporary life. As Ulrich Beck argues in *Risk Society*, risk was earlier understood as localised and obvious, but nowadays it seems more generalised, globalised and not always visible: 'Unlike the factory-related or occupational hazards of the nineteenth and the first half of the twentieth century, these can no longer be limited to certain localities or groups, but rather exhibit a tendency to globalization which spans production *and* reproduction as much as national borders, and in this sense brings into being *supra*-national and *non*-class-specific *global hazards* with a new type of social political dynamism' (1992, p. 13, italics in original). Linked to the concept of a generalised risk is a new perception of the vulnerability of life that both weakens and strengthens human solidarity. It weakens solidarity by casting everyone as a source of risk and potential danger, and strengthens it through the collective efforts necessary to ward off the danger. The social understanding of the Nipah outbreak in Kerala and its narration in *Virus* responded to these paradigm shifts in public health.

8.3. Nipah Outbreak in Kerala in 2018

Sometime in the second-half of April 2018 Mohammed Sabith, a twenty-seven-year-old plumber living with his parents and brother in Perambra town, Kozhikode district, contracted an infection; and on 2 May he was admitted to the Perambra taluk hospital with fever and body-ache. When his condition worsened, he was shifted on 5 May to the Government Medical College hospital at Kozhikode, where he died the same day without being diagnosed. Twelve days later, on 17 May, his brother Mohammed Salih, a twenty-eight-year-old architect living in the family home at Perambra, was admitted to Baby Memorial Hospital, Kozhikode with similar symptoms, and this time it was diagnosed as Nipah virus disease. Their father, V.K. Moosa and aunt Mariyam Kandoth also tested positive for the virus. Salih died on 18 May, followed by his aunt the next day and his father six days later. The diagnosis was first made by G. Arunkumar, a senior virologist at the Manipal Centre for Virus Research in Karnataka on 18 May, and was reconfirmed at the National Institute of Virology, Pune two days later . By then ten persons had tested positive and twelve (including two who were not tested) had died, and the Kerala government made an official announcement of the outbreak. Among the casualties was Lini Puthussery, a staff nurse at the Perambra taluk headquarters hospital who had attended Mohammed Sabith when he was admitted there. Of all those affected in the outbreak only Sabith contracted the virus directly from a bat, either while cleaning an unused well or during one of his frequent visits to the nearby forests. The rest were all human-to-human transmissions that occurred either within the family—Sabith's brother, father and aunt—or in the three hospitals that admitted the patients. In the hospital clusters, nine contracted infection in the taluk headquarters hospital at Perambra, ten in the Government Medical College at Kozhikode, and one in the community health centre at Balussery. Transmission of disease happened through close physical contact with persons in advanced stages of infection, when they were coughing severely, but not while handling the dead during funeral (Arunkumar et al., 2018; Pulla, 2018).

Nipah virus outbreaks have been reported from Malaysia, Singapore, Bangladesh and India. The first known outbreak occurred in Malaysia in 1988–1989, in the Kinta district of Perak. The virus was named after the Nipah River Valley, the place where it was first isolated and studied. Singapore reported an outbreak in 1999. In both countries, the virus was transmitted through direct contact with pigs that had acquired the infection from bats, which are its original hosts. From 2001 to 2013 a number of outbreaks occurred in Bangladesh and West Bengal, in places populated by fruit bats. Consumption of fresh date palm sap is popular in these areas, and it is believed that infection was caused by drinking sap contaminated with bat saliva and urine. The cases in Singapore and Malaysia were all animal-to-human transmissions, human-to-human transmission being first reported in Bangladesh and India. The Kerala outbreak was the third event in India. In terms of case fatality the Kerala outbreak was the worst ever reported, with death occurring about three to four days after the onset of symptoms. The symptoms of Nipah infection include fever, headache and body-ache, vomiting, a sense of confusion called 'altered sensorium', respiratory distress and convulsions (Kulkarni et al., 2013). The epidemic peaked in mid-May, between 12 and 18, the last death being on 31 May. It was officially declared closed in mid-July (Thomas et al., 2019).

Nipah is a zoonotic virus, or one that is transmitted to humans from its original animal hosts. While such transmissions have occurred throughout history, their frequency has increased exponentially in the last forty years. Examples of recent zoonotic disease outbreaks include: HIV/AIDS (from chimpanzees and sooty mangabeys), SARS, Ebola and Nipah (from bats), H5N1 flu (from birds), H1N1 flu (from pigs), Zika (from monkeys), MERS (from camels), Chikungunya (from monkeys), West Nile fever (from birds) and COVID-19 (whose animal host has not yet been established). The World Health Organisation includes these in what it terms emerging infectious disease, 'one that has appeared and affected a population for the first time, or has existed previously but is rapidly increasing, either in terms of the number of new cases within a population, or its spread to new geographical areas' (WHO, 2014, p. 1). 'Emerging zoonoses', observe Kulkarni et al., 'are the product of socioeconomic and anthropogenic environmental changes. Expansion of road networks, development of agricultural land, and intensification of wildlife trade have caused novel pathogens to emerge from wildlife' (2013, p. 398). Zoonotic viruses can also be transmitted when humans interact with wild animals in other contexts, as the case of Mohammed Sabith shows. Sabith, who was the index case in the Nipah outbreak in Kerala, acquired the disease from an infected bat that he had handled.

The outbreak was contained successfully by the timely intervention of public health authorities: the state's Department of Health and Family Welfare, the Ministry of Health and Family Welfare of the Government of India, Manipal Centre of Virus Research and the National Institute of Virology, Pune. Public health response included intensive contact tracing and surveillance (more than 2600 contacts were identified and followed up for possible symptoms), isolation of infected persons, enforcement of hospital infection control protocols and barrier nursing (Thomas et al., 2019). The World Health Organisation, which provided technical support, commended the efforts of the public health authorities in a report on 7 August 2018: 'The country demonstrated its capacity to rapidly contain the outbreak, including by the identification of cases, verifying cases with laboratory testing and caring for patients.' (2018).

8.4. Framing the Kerala Outbreak: Epidemiological Reports and News Stories

An outbreak of infectious disease is understood in two ways: one objective and concerning the population and the other subjective, about individual suffering. Both contribute to the social perception of the event and the public responses to it, because epidemics affect us in both ways. Objective accounts, usually in the third person, plot the unfolding of the epidemic as a series of morbidity and mortality figures, maps and timelines of spread, and rates of disease incidence. Subjective accounts, in contrast, plot it in terms of the stories of individuals affected, translating impersonal data into personal testimonies. As Catherine Belling explains, stories are especially suited to convey human suffering in concrete terms because of the way they reconstitute the subjective experience of the sufferer. In any other form suffering can only be either abstract or represented by a set of 'mechanical data' (Belling, 2009, p. 56). Belling's point is specifically about literary narratives, but it is pertinent in understanding the difference between epidemiological reports and personalised stories in the media, which narrate the unfolding of events in contrasting ways.

The epidemiological reports of the Nipah outbreak construct it as objective fact, with tables and charts detailing the transmission dynamics, demographic profiles of patients, patient outcomes and a map of the affected area (Kulkarni et al., 2013; Aditi & Sharif, 2019; 'Nipah virus in Kerala'; Arunkumar et al.). Individuals infected by the virus are referred to by case number (Arunkumar et al., 2018, pp. 1871–1873), not their personal names in order to maintain anonymity. The effect of this discursive construction, is to depersonalise the epidemic, muting the subjective experiences of those affected. Thus, the Arunkumar report begins with: 'On 17 May 2018, a 28-year-old man presented to a private facility in Kozhikode District, Kerala State, India, with encephalitis' (2018, p. 1867). In contrast, a news story by Priyanka Pulla in *The Hindu* opens thus: 'At around 2 am on May 17 morning, a grievously sick Mohammed Salih, a 28-year old architect from Perambra town, was rushed by his family to Kozhikode's Baby Memorial Hospital. Salih was vomiting, had a high fever, and was in a mentally agitated state' (2018). Media stories draw on epidemiological reports and public health frameworks to explain the outbreak, but add anecdotal material and testimonies of individuals to give them a 'human interest' perspective. A good instance is the following paragraph on the death of nurse Lini Puthussery, who acquired her infection while treating Mohammed Sabith.

> 'I spoke to her before she got hospitalised and she was really worried over the death of Mohamd Sadik [sic], one of the first persons to die in the Nipah virus outbreak in Kerala. She developed fever in a day or two after his death and passed away', said Sajish [Lini's husband], holding his children, aged five and two, close to him. He became lost for words when his younger child asked why their mother hadn't come back home after night duty. (Babu, 2018b)

Chief among those mentioned in the media stories are Sabith, his brother Salih, father Moosa and aunt Mariyam, nurse Lini and Kerala Health Minister K.K. Shailaja. They are recruited into the narrative for two reasons: to emphasise both the personal suffering that the outbreak caused and the government's determined efforts to curb it. Sabith's family represents the 'victims' of the outbreak, nurse Lini the dedicated healthcare worker who sacrifices her life in the line of duty, and Shailaja the 'saviour' of society. Thus, the media stories translated epidemiological data into a narrative format that the reader could comprehend and empathise with. The article on Lini cites the Kerala chief minister as saying: 'Her sacrifice is incomparable. Till her last she was dutiful' (Babu, 2018b) But the real 'hero' of the outbreak story was Shailaja, popularly known as Teacher: 'KK Shailaja', states one story, 'is the quiet face of Kerala's Nipah fightback' (Dutta, 2022) The article recounts how she had led the public health effort almost single-handedly, personally supervising arrangements in hospitals, meeting the public, consoling the bereaved and congratulating the two survivors. It notes how she was inspired by her grandmother, 'an Ezhava matriarch with a fierce belief in political life'. Thus, it constructs the outbreak as the 'victory' of the government, and especially of Shailaja, in the 'fightback' against Nipah—a mythicisation of epidemic that is conventional in media discourse. Myths may not coincide with the reality that epidemiological reports document, but they make it accessible to readers in a way that epidemiological accounts cannot. Like fiction, they add 'iconic' significance (Ricoeur, 1984, p. 80) to documented history in foregrounding subjective meanings that an objective record of events cannot express. While drawing on the social understanding of reality, media stories like those cited above rearticulate it in a conventional plot that shapes the reality they draw on and represent.

One of the functions of outbreak stories, as I have stated above, is to reconstitute suffering in subjective and empathetic ways—to accord it, in other words, affective or emotional valence. Statistical abstraction suppresses emotion, stories bring it to the fore. What role does emotion play in knowledge and action? Emotions are often understood to impede rational thinking, and thereby to restrict the capacity for effective and pragmatic action. Excessive emotion, argues Clifford Geertz, can lead on the one hand to the collapse of reason, and, given our 'tremendous emotional susceptibility' as human beings, this is best avoided. Yet, on the other, one 'cannot perform efficiently in the absence of a fairly high degree of reasonably persistent emotional activation'. The view that emotion is an obstacle to practical understanding and action assumes that it is personal and therefore unreliable. Geertz's argument is that it is at the same time collective, and culture provides mechanisms that assure 'the ready availability of the continually varying sort of sensory experience' that sustains and enables action (1973, pp. 79–80). Culture provides these mechanisms in the form of narratives that guide or regulate emotional responses to events. 'In order to make up our minds we must know how we feel about things; and to know how we feel about things we need the public images of sentiment that only ritual, myth, and art can provide' (p. 82). Faced with the crisis of outbreak, the community needs to have both cognitive sense as well as affective orientation, which together motivate action. What media stories of outbreak, like their literary or cinematic counterparts, do is configure the objective data of epidemiological reports in terms of their emotional implications. In the process they add to the objective record of outbreak what we may call, after Ricoeur, an affective augmentation. Of course, in mobilising the community to act, media stories may open up and activate latent social conflicts, as we saw in early reports on AIDS. But they may also, as in the later stories on AIDS, shape social responses to the outbreak in terms of empathy for those who suffer. It is this empathy that drives efforts to rebuild community by establishing networks of support.

8.5. *Virus* as Outbreak Narrative

Every outbreak, writes Christos Lynteris, comes as a new event, even if it has a parallel in past experience. It constitutes, as he puts it, a catastrophe that ruptures 'social, political and economic life' (2014, p. 25). Outbreaks are first apprehended as mysterious—Nipah was a 'mystery disease' when it first broke out (Babu, 2018a)—and it is only later that the factors causing their emergence come to be understood. It was only after the virus was identified and its transmission dynamics came to be known that a more comprehensive understanding of its zoonotic origin in the forests of Kozhikode district could emerge. Comparison with similar occurrences in other places that had witnessed Nipah outbreaks led to identifying patterns of recurrence, so that the Kozhikode outbreak was no longer a singular event but part of a series resulting from a complex of historical factors, in which increased human–animal encounters and environmental spillovers played a key role. Identification of transmission chains through contact tracing, a standard operating procedure in contemporary public health, further dissolved its singularity, enabling its assimilation into a format that has now become conventional. An outbreak, therefore, exists on 'two distinct and defining temporal registers' (Lynteris, 2014, p. 27)—one processual and the other evental. Epidemiological understanding focuses on the processes that cause the disease to emerge and subsequently decline, while social understanding focuses on the way people make sense of its irruption, unfolding and conclusion as event. This doubleness of epidemic temporality corresponds closely to the two forms of outbreak narrative that I have called biomedical and cultural (see chapter five). Aashique Abu's film, as we will see, alternates between the two.

Virus opens with scenes from everyday life: a doctor and his family returning from vacation, a group of interns and their friends playing a football game in the evening, hospital staff attending to patients in an emergency room. This is suddenly disrupted by the outbreak of a mysterious and highly contagious fatal disease. Once it is identified, the state makes a public announcement followed by the enforcement of sanitary measures, isolation of patients, safe disposal of the dead, contact tracing and surveillance of those likely to be infected, ending finally with confirmation of the source of outbreak. The outbreak is contained through the efforts of public officials and volunteers, and a meeting is held to mark the end of the epidemic, reflect on what it has portended and pay homage to the dead. The film returns to everyday life but with a difference, as many lives have been tragically cut short in the process. Except the ending, the film follows the format of what Priscilla Wald calls 'the outbreak narrative': 'a formulaic plot that begins with the identification of an emerging infection, includes discussion of the global networks throughout which it travels, and chronicles the epidemiological work that ends with its containment' (2008, p. 2). The typical plot represents three stages of the outbreak: identification of the microbe that causes it, the process of epidemiological detection that tracks transmission chains in cause and effect relationships, and implementation of control measures that result in its closure. While this seems to correspond broadly to Rosenberg's three-part structure of epidemic, there is an important difference. Wald's emphasis is primarily on the epidemiological theme of the narratives, while Rosenberg's is on the socio-cultural understanding of epidemic outbreak. This is because of the kind of outbreak they take as their object of study. Wald's outbreaks are of recent occurrence (she begins with SARS in the Chinese province of Guangdong in 2003), for which the outbreak narrative serves as 'a powerful story of ecological danger and epidemiological belonging' that links 'analyses of disease emergence' with 'changing social and political formations' in a global order (Wald, 2008, p. 33). Rosenberg's instances are historical outbreaks like those of plague, yellow fever and cholera, to which he assimilates AIDS. AIDS is essentially 'traditional' in its form, though 'modern' and 'postmodern' in the way it was identified through modern diagnostic techniques, its bureaucratisation in national and international public health institutions, and its mass-mediated reality (Rosenberg, 1989, pp. 9–14).[5] For Rosenberg, therefore, the framing of outbreak in cultural perception is a crucial aspect, not its decipherment through the work of epidemiological detection.

[5] It is pertinent that Wald excludes stories of AIDS from her definition of the outbreak narrative. Though they made the idea of emerging zoonoses popular and have the basic features of the genre, they 'cannot be directly incorporated into the mythic dimensions of communicable-disease outbreak narratives' (Wald, 2008, p. 27).

Virus fits into both Rosenberg's and Wald's models of the social reality of outbreak. The film has two storylines: identification of the 'index case' and the work of epidemiological detection in tracing the outbreak's origin, and cultural perceptions of the outbreak and its unfolding. While the first corresponds closely to what actually happened in the outbreak, its epidemiology, the second corresponds to how people made sense of it. How does the film mediate between the two? The first storyline builds on objective information gathered through contact tracing and testing, identifying the outbreak's transmission dynamics, timeline and areas of spread that are displayed by the virologist Rajan on charts and maps. The second builds on the 'human interest' angle: subjective accounts of suffering, loss and bereavement, and the struggle to comprehend the tragedy. The film, thus, combines the cognitive and the affective, resonating with both epidemiological reports and media stories in constructing the outbreak as an event invested with human significance.

The character who connects both storylines is Zakariya, the 'index case'. In him lies the secret of the outbreak's origin, as the first person to be infected; as the first to die, his story also opens the theme of suffering and loss. The plot frames the character of Zakariya in two contrary ways, corresponding to the two theories that it offers about the outbreak's cause. The first of these, proposed by representatives of the national government, is bioterrorism, which casts him as an Islamic terrorist who deliberately spreads the virus, based on evidence gathered by investigators. He goes on a 'dubious foreign stint', has in his possession 'four mobile phones' and 'more than six SIM cards', and is 'a highly religious person' who 'frequents forest areas' (Abu, 2019, 1:51:11–1:51:28). The second theory, which the state government's representatives pursue, is ecological accident: Zakariya frequents the forests because his hobby is nature photography, and he contracts the infection from a baby bat that he picks up on one of his trips.

Let us take a closer look at these two theories, and what they imply for the film's construction of Zakariya. We have discussed above how both theories have dominated contemporary biomedical thinking about new epidemic outbreaks, and how they share a common ground in the notion of 'risk'. The use of pathogens as weapons and their accidental spillover from animal to human hosts are perceived as the two most common threats to global health security. With regard to bioterrorism, a study conducted by the RAND Center for Global Risk and Security sums up this perception well. Infectious disease, it argues, must be a priority of global health security, for the microbes that cause it can be genetically engineered in laboratories into new drug-resistant strains that are not affected by existing vaccines. 'Such a bioweapon could overwhelm hospitals, reduce economic productivity, spark the chaotic spread of misinformation, and, worse, create unnecessary suffering and mortality, especially among vulnerable populations' (Bouskill and Smith, 2019, p. 19). In 'The Semiotics of Security', Carlo Carduff discusses the public unease over biotechnology research in the United States, particularly concerning the development of new influenza viruses using genetic engineering. In 2005 Dr Peter Palese of Icahn School of Medicine, Mount Sinai, Dr Jeffery Taubenbauger of the Armed Forces Institute of Pathology, Rockville, and Dr Terrence Tumpey of the Centers for Disease Control, Atlanta, reconstructed in the laboratory the virus that had caused the Spanish flu pandemic of 1918. Publication of the research had to be vetted by the National Science Advisory Board for Biosecurity, a federal committee, to ensure that it would not be used for harmful purposes. Fears of misuse that nuclear research had once provoked resurfaced in the context of biotechnology research, framed within the discourse of bioterrorism and security risk. 'At the center of the public scandal produced in the news media around the resurrection of the microbial creature', writes Caduff, 'was the circulation of scientific information. The circulation of such information in the public domain was generally considered a significant condition of possibility, enabling its potential misappropriation by malicious actors' (2012, p. 338). The possibility of Nipah being weaponised has been mentioned in scientific literature. Arora et al. open their essay on Nipah outbreaks with a paragraph on biowarfare, and conclude with the following statement: 'there is a probability that NiV may be used as a bio-weapon in the future; hence the probabilities of this should also be taken into consideration' (2018, p. 1182). Regarding the ecological accident theory, the last few decades have witnessed increased outbreaks of zoonotic disease due to human interference in natural habitats, especially in the Asia-Pacific region. As Morand et al. note: 'biodiversity changes through fragmentation and degradation of natural habitats (particularly forested areas) increase the proximity of wildlife to humans, and their domestic animals, and result in increased health risks through increased transmission of zoonotic diseases' (2014, p. 1). In fact, in the Nipah outbreak in Kozhikode it was presumed that Mohammed Sabith, who contracted the virus sometime in the second-half of April, had inadvertently 'handled a NiV-infected baby bat, as April is the birthing season of bats' (Arunkumar et al., 2018, p. 1876). The two theories that *Virus* offers must be seen in this larger context: they reflect the fears that emerging infections have provoked in public discourse. Outbreak narratives, as Wald points out, recirculate these fears in mythic representations of collective calamity (2008, pp. 10, 27).

In explaining the outbreak as either bioterrorism or ecological accident, the film presents the official views. One is proposed by officials of the Union Health Ministry, the other by those of the state government. What both views suppress is Zakariya's emotional connection with the nature that he photographs and the forests he frequents, which the film reveals in its closing sequence. As he rides his motorbike through the forest, he sees a baby bat lying on the road. He picks it up tenderly, and puts it back in the bole of a tree from which it may have fallen. It is at this time that he takes the photo which the virologist Suresh Rajan uses to prove his theory of ecological accident (Abu, 2019, 2:28:08–2:29:10). This flashback provides what I have called affective augmentation to the epidemiological plot, revealing a truth that the official interpretations fail to access. It is in such scenes that the film alternates between the biomedical and cultural modes of narration.

A characteristic theme of the outbreak narrative, Wald writes, is disease detection, or the tracking of an outbreak to its source. Epidemiology has essentially been detective work, especially after the creation in 1951 of the Epidemiological Investigation Service (EIS) within the Centers for Disease Control in the United States. The role of EIS is to train specialists in the methods of disease surveillance and field investigations, involving epidemiologists, microbiologists, veterinarians, statisticians, sanitary engineers, sociologists and anthropologists (Thacker, Goodman & Ricker, 1990). One of the well-known successes of the EIS was the tracking of the first outbreak of Legionnaires' disease to a hotel in Philadelphia in 1976 (Honigsbaum, 2020, pp. 99–120). Articles in popular magazines, as Wald shows, often drew parallels between epidemiological investigation and the work of the FBI, with a 1953 *Newsweek* story titled 'Disease Detectives' claiming that EIS officers would be most effective in cases of germ warfare (Wald, 2008, pp. 26–27). 'The creation of EIS', writes Wald, 'was fueled by the anxieties surrounding biological warfare that had intensified with the beginning of the Korean War in 1950' (Wald, 2008, p. 24). The 4 July 1983 issue of *Time* featured a cover article on HIV/AIDS titled 'Disease Detectives: Tracking the Killers', while *The New York Times* of 3 June 2021 carried a story titled 'The Disease Detective' on Dr Joe DiRisi, a professor of biochemistry at the University of California, San Francisco who pioneered the practice of metagenomic sequencing (Kahn, 2021). The *Time* cover story and the *NYT* story on DiRisi do not refer to germ warfare, but the phrase 'disease detective' continues in the popular imagination of outbreaks. In *Virus*, the work of disease detection is conducted by the virologist Suresh Rajan and medical student Annu, and it comprises a major part of the film. Towards the end of the film they discover how Zakariya contracted the virus, and how it was transmitted to Unnikrishnan when he used the ambulance that took Zakariya to the hospital ER. The detective work serves to solve the mystery of the outbreak's origin. The outbreak is finally contained by the combined efforts of Rajan, Annu and the public health officials, led by the health minister Prameela. But the film, as we will shortly see, ends with neither the containment of the outbreak nor the discovery of its origin.

One of the fears that emerging infectious diseases provoke is the vulnerability of human life, which must be viewed in the context of modern medicine's presumed 'victory' over microbes. With the aid of antibiotics, antimicrobials, vaccines and improved public health infrastructure, it was thought that epidemics had become a thing of the past. In May 1980 the World Health Organisation declared that 'the world and all its peoples have won freedom from smallpox' (WHO, 1980). 'The grandiose optimism rested on two false assumptions: that microbes were biologically stationary targets and that diseases could be geographically sequestered. Each contributed to the smug sense of immunity from infectious diseases that characterized health professionals in North America and Europe' (Garrett, 1996, p. 67). The very next year a mysterious new disease emerged, ironically, in the United States that caused *Pneumocystis carinii* pneumonia, cytomegalovirus infection and oral candidiasis, all associated with immune-suppression (CDC, 1981, pp. 250–252). Later named Acquired Immune Deficiency Syndrome or AIDS, it put paid to both assumptions. HIV was not a 'stationary target' but a microbe that mutated rapidly as it moved from monkeys to human populations in its spread throughout the world. Since there is still neither a cure nor even a vaccine for HIV, it disproves the myth of medicine's victory over disease. Outbreak narratives, as stories of HIV/AIDS show, do not necessarily celebrate 'the triumph ... of scientific authority' (Wald, 2008, p. 2), they often undermine it.

Virus is, in this sense, closer to Wald's characterisation of the outbreak narrative than stories of AIDS, for it shows how the crisis is contained through epidemiological investigation. It concludes by convincingly linking all cases to the index patient, Zakariya, and isolating those who acquired the infection from him. The final episode shows Zakariya picking up a baby bat and returning it to its nest. This may be interpreted in two ways.

It is a flashback that confirms what Rajan and Annu presume, which seems to be the most logical explanation. But it may also be read as a return to the beginning, in the cyclic recurrence of outbreaks that the present century has demonstrated so forcefully since it began. The ending of the film supports the logical reading as well as this counter-reading, in a tension that drives the plot towards both closure and the reopening of closure. '[T]he most powerful affective work done by outbreak narratives', writes Bill Albertini, 'exists in the tension between the desire for containment and an opposing and powerful desire for accidental exposure and infection' (2008, p. 444). He gives the example of the ABC television movie *Fatal Contact: Bird Flu in America* (2006): 'an inoculation is developed for the avian influenza that is killing millions, and the film appears to close on a note of a national family in the process of healing; however, in a denouement, Centers for Disease Control and Prevention (CDC) investigators travel to a village in Angola and discover that a more virulent strain of the flu has killed every person there: thus the plot moves from emergence to containment and back to emergence' (p. 445). Prevention of emerging infections requires constant monitoring and surveillance, as the WHO's document on Emerging Infectious Diseases (EIDs) and zoonoses states: 'While a strong public health system is a prerequisite to combat outbreaks of emerging infectious diseases, these outbreaks can also significantly disrupt such a system. Therefore, strengthening preparedness, surveillance, risk assessment, risk communication, laboratory facilities and response capacity … are all crucial' (2014, p. 2). In other words, accidents can always happen, and the 'combat' against disease outbreaks has no closure. This is the lesson on which Albert Camus's *The Plague* ends, that the plague bacillus—or for that matter, any microbe —'never dies or disappears for good'. It lies dormant for many years before appearing suddenly to wreak havoc once again 'in a happy city' (Camus, 1960, p. 297). Spanish flu disappeared as unexpectedly as it had come, two years after it broke out, but reappeared again in a related subtype of the H1N1 virus as swine flu in 2009. Underlying the trope of the 'accident' that reopens epidemic crisis, explains Albertini, is the vulnerability of human life and the porosity of the body to invasions from outside, a view that the last century's triumphal story of modern medicine had suppressed. Albertini's argument, therefore, is that the outbreak narrative *contra* Wald denies the very closure that it seeks. The trope of accident 'reveals a counter-discourse within the outbreak narrative – a discourse existing alongside the epidemiological narrative that would detect, track, and contain the epidemic' (Albertini, 2008, p. 460). In *Virus*, the possibility of another outbreak exists despite the public announcement that 'the districts of Kozhikode and Mallapuram have become free of Nipah virus' (Abu, 2019, 2:24:36), because reservoirs of the virus continue to exist in the region's bat population.[6]

Vulnerability refers to the way we are constantly exposed to risks in our lived environment, risks that social and political institutions try to minimise but cannot entirely eliminate. 'The concept of vulnerability', writes Bryan S. Turner in *The Body and Society*, 'is derived from the Latin for "wound". Although *vulnus* refers to the real wounds in the human body, it is in many respects itself a metaphor for frailty. Wounds are open and they open us to life; the wound is a metaphor for the human condition' (2008, p. 244). Industrial pollution, the global spread of infectious disease due to air travel, and the use of weapons of mass destruction have multiplied the risks that we are exposed to, which international agreements and agencies fail to control. Human vulnerability and the precariousness of institutions have, on the one hand, led to a scale of suffering that is unprecedented, but on the other they have also enabled the promotion of human rights within the framework of law. They constitute,

[6] In June 2019, a twenty-one-year old college student was reported to have contracted the virus after he visited a forest in Ernakulum district while a twelve-year old boy died of Nipah disease in Kozhikode on 5 September 2021 (Sudeep et al., 2021; Thakur et al., 2022). In August–September 2023, there were two more deaths from Nipah virus disease (Srivastava et al., 2024). While the film could not possibly have anticipated these recurrences, it does mention that there are reservoirs of the virus in forested parts of Kerala.

therefore, 'the *possibility* of a common solidarity, but this is always fragile, given the precariousness of institutions' (p. 260, italics in original). Judith Butler, too, proposes the notion of a 'common human vulnerability' that can counter the differential distribution of suffering in society, or the tendency to privilege the suffering of some over that of others, to see some human lives as more grievable than others. The vulnerability of the other might provoke us to violence, to inflict wounds, but it may also move us to attend to those wounds. 'From where might a principle emerge by which we vow to protect others from the kinds of violence we have suffered, if not from an apprehension of a common human vulnerability?' (Butler, 2004, p. 30). Though Butler writes these lines in the context of war and genocide, the ethical question she raises is relevant to human suffering in general, of which epidemic outbreak is an instance.

Vulnerability bears a direct link to community, as both Turner and Butler emphasise: it is the latter's condition of possibility. This has become increasingly evident in the context of bodily vulnerability, which enables affiliations based on the common experience of suffering, need for knowledge and political mobilisation in the case of stigmatised illnesses like HIV/AIDS. The Global Network of People Living with HIV (GNP+) was formed in 1992, to create awareness among HIV-positive people about their rights and to ensure dignity of life. This was soon followed in India by the Tamil Nadu Network of Positive People (TNP+) in 1994, Indian Network of Positive People (INP+) in 1997, Manipur Network of Positive People (MNP+) in 1997, Karnataka Network of Positive People (KNP+) in 1998 and Delhi Network of Positive People (DNP+) in 2000. Currently almost every state in India has a positive people network. Paul Rabinow coined the term 'biosociality' to refer to 'new group and individual identities and practices' (2005, p. 188) that coalesce around bodily conditions involving incurable illnesses. If vulnerability to disease leads (as it often does) to stigmatisation by those who presume themselves to be healthy, biosociality counters this through community-formation in acts of bonding and mutual support.

Community also bears a link to communication, which constitutes human interconnectedness at the micro level in face-to-face dialogue and the macro level in public media. [7] The national community, for instance, is imagined into being through books and newspapers 'which made it possible for rapidly growing numbers of people to think about themselves, and to relate themselves to others, in profoundly new ways' (Anderson, 2006, p. 36). Etymologically, the word 'community' means the social life that human beings live in common with each other, from Latin *communitas* or fellowship and *communis* or mutual sharing. *Communis* includes as an element *munia* or the duty that one owes to the community, and the compound word thus means that mutual sharing is a duty that one bears to others. It also includes *munus* or gift that links all together in continual exchange, for *munus* is not just any gift but one that must be reciprocated (Esposito, 2010, pp. 3–6). In many pre-modern societies, observes Marcel Mauss, the exchange of gift is a principal means of ensuring community solidarity, governed by three obligations—to give, to receive and to reciprocate. Of these, the first is the most important, for it is what initiates the cycles of exchange: 'by giving, one is giving *oneself*, and if one gives *oneself*, it is because one 'owes' *oneself*—one's person and one's goods to others' (Mauss, 1990, p. 59, italics in original). As Roberto Esposito sums up in *Terms of the Political*, 'The meaning [of community] that all etymological dictionaries suggest as most probable is the one that combines *cum* with *munus* (or *munia*). Such a derivation is important insofar as it designates precisely what holds the members of a community together. These

[7] The need to communicate becomes critical when both travel and social intercourse become impossible. Nothing illustrates this more forcefully than the global lockdown during the first wave of the COVID-19 pandemic in 2020, when there was a marked surge in the use of social media (Beech, 2020; Pandya & Lodha. 2021; Li et al., 2021). The internet became the new mode of sociality when the more traditional modes were restricted in the domains of work, education, leisure and personal interaction. In journalistic parlance online communication became the 'new normal' in the era of pandemic. I discuss this in more detail in the next chapter, on COVID-19.

members are not bound by just any relationship, but precisely by a *munus*—a "task", "duty", or "law"' (2013, p. 14). In the context that we are discussing, to 'communicate' is to participate in the common activity of meaning-making that, like the *munus* in Esposito's words, provides community its condition of being.

But what does *communicable* disease communicate? It is not the gift of meaning that sustains bonds of sociality but its negation, the *dis*-ease of communication. It is a reflexive irony of the 'community–communication–communicable disease' triad that the last term signifies the very inversion of the first two with which it is etymologically linked. This is what Wald brings to the fore when she writes: 'Communicable disease marks both the potential destruction of the community and the consequences of its survival. It is the figure of a necessary and even generative disequilibrium' (2008, p. 23). It marks the destruction of community by placing under risk the very relationships that constitute it, when social distance rather than solidarity becomes both norm and condition for survival. But it also imposes on individuals the need to preserve others as well as themselves, a responsibility to the vulnerability of the other that Emmanuel Levinas calls the 'inter-human order': '*my* responsibility for the other person, without concern for reciprocity, in my call to help him gratuitously, in the asymmetry of the relation of *one* to the *other*' (1988, p. 165, italics in original). If social distancing, which preserves one against the other, is one face of communicable disease outbreak, unconditional responsibility to the other's suffering is its other face.

If I have dwelt at length on the ideas of vulnerability, community, communication and communicable disease, it is because that is precisely what the penultimate scene of *Virus* presents. In section 8.4 above, we saw how media reports told the story of nurse Lini Puthussery's self-sacrifice and her empathy for the other's suffering. In *Virus*, Health Minister Prameela's speech announcing the epidemic's closure begins on this note. 'In this saga', she says, 'we have 21 martyrs including Sister Akhila, who laid down lives in this fight. All of them contracted with the malady while trying to help out somebody else. At the same time, the same kindness was instrumental in our victory over this tragedy.' She makes the announcement in a public hall filled beyond capacity, and the camera cuts between close-ups of Prameela and pan shots of the audience. In her speech Prameela talks about the horror of the outbreak and the lives sacrificed, as well as the 'lesson' that human kindness and solidarity teaches, that no 'disaster can defeat us anymore' (Abu, 2019, 2:25:23–2:26:40). The scene presents the reconstitution of community after it has been devastated by the virus. It is the archetypal scene of the *munus* or duty that binds people together, and the gift of sacrifice that ensures the perpetuation of these bonds.

Contagion, as Wald explains, is both that which threatens community and which holds it together. To appreciate this point, it is necessary to understand the connotative meaning of 'contagion'. It is not synonymous with 'infection': while infection refers to the proliferation of pathogens in the individual body, contagion refers to their transmission from body to body. In other words, the idea of contagion is rooted in that of community as its necessary context. Belief in contagion often serves to shore up social differences, such as those between the rich and the poor or the compatriot and the immigrant, contact with whom is fraught with danger. When plague broke out in Los Angeles in 1924, the Mexican quarter was cordoned off by the police. 'By the 1920s ethnic quarantines, spurred by fears of smallpox and typhus being introduced by migrants from across the border, had become a routine measure in Los Angeles and other southern California towns' (Honigsbaum, 2020, p. 53). In colonial India when contagion was a major urban concern, cities were modelled on the segregation 'between elites (initially European, increasingly Indian) within a plethora of protected zones with permeable boundaries, and subordinates (marginalized Indian groups) primarily residing outside these areas' (Beverley, 2011, p. 488). The subordinates were the poor, who were suspected of harbouring disease because they were unhygienic and their habitations were 'miasmas' of infection. In a study of colonial

Bombay, Prashant Kidambi notes how the poorer parts of the city were cordoned off during the plague outbreak of 1896 because of the 'anxiety that Bombay's poor, by virtue of being innately susceptible to the plague contagion nurtured in their insanitary "slums", would infect the city's elites' (2007, p. 51). In an essay on cultural configurations of the AIDS epidemic, Mary Douglas writes: 'Miasma is an instrument of total control. The mere physical presence of the Other is dangerous. Their use of the same space and times and their breathing the common air is a menace to the rest of the community. The miasmatic danger of AIDS is a reason for expelling foreign workers, restricting immigration, prohibiting sexually deviant practices, and, of course, drugs' (Douglas, 1992, pp. 114–115). In *Virus*, this is expressed in the stigmatisation of those who bear the disease or are even associated with it in any way. When Unnikrishnan requests people to take him to the hospital, they run away from him in fear. A shopkeeper refuses to serve the children of Babu, a mortuary worker who helps cremate the dead. 'When you investigate more', Zakariya's mother asks Suresh Rajan, 'will everyone hate my boy?' (Abu, 2019, 1:57:06). Contagion, therefore, is the negative condition for the securing of community. But it is also its positive condition, as people collectively act to ward off danger. '[T]he social experience of disease, the image of communicability, and the materialization of interdependence that characterize depictions of epidemics suggest an *epidemiology of belonging* through which people might experience their emergence as a "population"' (Wald, 2008, 18, italics added). Etymologically the word contagion comes from the Latin *tangere*, to touch, which may be either physical or emotional, as in the phrase 'heart- touching'. Disease puts at risk bodily contact, while a shared sense of vulnerability enables affective contact. In *Virus*, it is this positive and affective outcome of contagion that Prameela's speech emphasises. The 'kindness' that inspired Nurse Akhila and others to help the dying may have caused their own deaths, but it was also 'instrumental in our victory over this tragedy' (Abu 2019, 2:23:55). It counters the negative function of contagion—the fear and stigma that epidemic intensifies. The same ambivalence characterises the film's treatment of space. The forest is the source of both contagion and contact with nature, inspiring Zakariya's kindness for a baby bat that has fallen off its nest even as it infects him with the virus. The hospital is the site of care and tenderness, and equally the site where disease spreads. *Virus* links these two spaces, the hospital and the forest, through the double meaning of contagion as the 'touch' that both imperils and sustains human bonding.

8.6. Conclusion

In the summer of 2018, there was an outbreak of Nipah virus disease in Kozihkode and Mallapuram districts of Kerala. In just about a month, twenty-one persons lost their lives and only two of the infected survived. The outbreak was contained by timely action on the part of the public health authorities, but it brought to the fore crucial gaps in the state's healthcare system, especially its lack of preparedness to tackle a crisis of this order. At the same time, it showed how a dedicated and resourceful team could save the state from a much greater crisis given the rapidity with which Nipah virus spreads and its high case fatality. Aashique Abu's *Virus* is the story of that dramatic event.

The film closely follows the history of the actual epidemic, even as it fictionalises it. The plot of *Virus* seems to fit neatly into the schema that Rosenberg proposes for the social understanding of epidemic: its onset and acknowledgement; its framing in public perceptions, that derive from the cultural memory of past epidemics; the responses it evokes based on these frames, which lead to its closure; and reflection on the lessons it has taught. Epidemics are aleatory events, they break out suddenly, unforeseen, with unexpected effects. Explanatory frames, which exist in the cultural memory of past outbreaks, help to reduce their aleatoriness and manage the randomness of their spread. Rosenberg's schema, which explains outbreak as a factor of incident, perception and response, may be about the collective consciousness of epidemic, but it also explains how stories of epidemic are structured. The plot of *Virus* also matches the format of what Priscilla Wald calls 'the outbreak narrative', stories based on the work of disease detection in contemporary cinema and literature. If Rosenberg emphasises the cultural, Wald emphasises the biomedical dimensions of outbreak experience, and the plot of *Virus* spans both.

Cultural memory provides a formulaic structure that is replicated, circulated and reinforced by the individual stories that it generates. Traditionally, this formulaic structure derives from religion, one of its functions being to comprehend that which defies comprehension. Modern science has superseded the sense of enchantment with which religion had pervaded thought. In modern societies, therefore, the formulaic structure of the outbreak story derives its signification from broadly two sources: epidemiological reports and media accounts. The former recount the outbreak in terms of its objective facts—its aetiology, morbidity and mortality figures, timelines, and areas, dynamics and scale of spread. They necessarily suppress, as their discursive condition, the subjective and the personal: the suffering that epidemic outbreak causes. Media accounts derive from epidemiology the cause and scale of epidemic, adding to it personal testimonies of those who are affected by it and those who are charged with its control. Media stories, in other words, combine the objective and subjective in representing epidemic as an event imbued with human significance, augmenting scientific data with affective supplementation.

When a film takes epidemic as its theme, it draws on both these sources and weaves their meanings into a narrative sequence that viewers may easily comprehend and relate to. Thus, as we have seen, *Virus* builds its plot from epidemiological accounts of Nipah virus disease and media accounts of the outbreak in Kerala, recasting them as convincing fiction. In interpreting this fiction and the reality it alludes to, the audience draws on the same cultural cues that went into its making, in order to comprehend both the film and their world. This involves a mediation of three interlinked processes: the configuration of epidemic as culturally meaningful, its refiguration in the plot of the narrative, and its transfiguration as renewed knowledge of reality. Paul Ricoeur describes this as the 'circle of mimesis', the shift of meaning-making from reality to fiction and back to reality in our continual efforts to know our world. This is because we need to know the world not just in its objective properties but also in 'those aspects of our being-in-the-world that cannot be talked about directly' (Ricoeur, 1984, p. 80).

We can appreciate this point about stories of epidemic when we ourselves confront it in reality. What new meanings does a film about Nipah in Kerala acquire for viewers whose everyday life experiences are shaped by masks and protective gowns, social distancing, quarantine, lockdown, body bags and mass cremations, and alternating cycles of hope and grief? What new meanings does the everyday acquire in listening to the story of epidemics that happened in the past and are, in a sense, unfolding once again now? Why must an epidemic outbreak call for its stories, why are stories the only thing we have, to make life livable in times of crisis?

References

Aditi & Sharif, M. (2019). Nipah virus infection: A review. *Epidemiology and Infection*, *147*(e95), 1–6.

Albertini, B. (2008). Contagion and the necessary accident. *Discourse*, *30*(3), 443–467.

Anderson, B. (2006). *Imagined communities: Reflections on the origin and spread of nationalism*. Rev. ed. Verso.

Arora, A., Dogra, A., Dogra, A., Goyal, B. & Sharma, A.M. (2018). Nipah virus: An outbreak of deadly paramyxvirus. *Biomedical and Pharmacological Journal*, *11*(3). https://biomedpharmajournal.org/vol11no3/nipah-virus-an-outbreak-of-deadly-paramyxvirus/

Arunkumar, G., Chandni, R., Mourya, D.T., Singh, S.K., Sadanandan, R., Sudan, P. & Bhargava, B. (2018). Outbreak Investigation of Nipah Virus Diseases in Kerala, India, 2018. *The Journal of Infectious Diseases*, *219*, 1867–1878. https://pubmed.ncbi.nlm.nih.gov/30364984

Babu, R. (2018a, May 22). How the Nipah virus outbreak devastated a family in Kerala. *Hindustan Times* (Trivandrum ed.). https://www.hindustantimes.com/india-news/how-the-nipah-virus-outbreak-devastated-a-family-in-kerala/story-8t88BCV44SpiTTj0RSMFgO.html

Babu, R. (2018b, May 22). Nipah virus outbreak: 'Don't think I will be able to meet you all again' Kerala nurse tells her husband in letter before she died. *Hindustan Times* (Delhi ed.). https://www.hindustantimes.com/india-news/will-not-see-you-again-take-care-of-children-wrote-kerala-nurse-to-husband-before-succumbing-to-nipah-virus/story-w5bHpISMJNl6bn4cWr9AHM.html

BBC News Hindi. (2020, May 10). *Spanish Flu: Corona virus se bhi khatarnak who bemari jisne bharat me har taraf laashein bichha di thi* ....[Video]. YouTube. https://www.youtube.com/watch?v=WiDGE_Zut18

Beck, U. (1992). *Risk society: Towards a new modernity* (M. Ritter, Trans.). Sage.

Beech, M. (2020, March 25). COVID-19 pushes up internet use 70% and streaming more than 12%, first figures reveal. *Forbes.* http://www.forbes.com/sites/markbeech/2020/03/25/covid-19-pushes-up-internet-use-70-streaming-more-than-12-first-figures-reveal/?sh=4185fde83104

Belling, C. (2009). Overwhelming the medium: Fiction and the trauma of pandemic influenza in 1918. *Literature and Medicine*, *28*(1), 55–81.

Beverley, E.L. (2011). Colonial urbanism and South Asian cities. *Social History*, *36*(4), 482–497. http://www.jstor.org/stable/23072659

Bouskill, K.E. & Smith, E. (2019). Global health and security: Threats and opportunities. *Perspectives* (December). RAND Corporation.

Butler, J. (2004). *Precarious life: The powers of mourning and violence.* Verso.

Camus, A. (1960). *The plague* (Stuart Gilbert, Trans.). Penguin.

Caduff, C. (2012). The semiotics of security: Infectious disease research and the biopolitics of informational bodies in the United States. *Cultural Anthropology*, *27*(2), 333–357.

Centers for Disease Control (CDC). (1981). *Morbidity and mortality weekly report*, *30*(21). https://stacks.cdc.gov/view/cdc/1261

Das, D.K. (2019). *Teaching AIDS: The cultural politics of HIV disease in India*. Springer Nature.

Douglas, M. (1992). The self as risk-taker: A cultural theory of contagion in relation to AIDS. In M. Douglas, *Risk and blame: Essays in cultural theory* (pp. 102–121). Routledge.

Dutta, A. (2022, July 21). KK Shailaja on dealing with Nipah. *The Indian Express*. https://indianexpress.com/article/express-sunday-eye/extraordinary-measures-kk-shailaja-kerala-nipah-virus-5835834/

Esposito, R. (2010). *Communitas: The origin and destiny of community* (T. Campbell, Trans.). Stanford University Press.

Esposito, R. (2013). *Terms of the political: Community, immunity, biopolitics* (R.N. Welch, Trans.). Fordham University Press.

Foucault, M. (1977). *Discipline and punish: The birth of the prison* (A. Sheridan, Trans.). Penguin.

Foucault, M. (2004). *Security, territory, population: Lectures at the Collège de France 1977–1978* (G. Burchell, Trans.). Picador.

Fuss, D. (1989). *Essentially speaking: Feminism, nature and difference*. Routledge.

Garrett, L. (1996). The return of infectious disease. *Foreign Affairs*, *75*(1), 66–79.

Geertz, C. (1973). *The interpretation of cultures: Selected essays*. Basic Books.

Honigsbaum, Mark. 2020. *The pandemic century: A history of global contagion from the Spanish Flu to Covid-19*. Penguin Random House UK.

Kahn, J. (2021, June 3). The disease detective. *New York Times*. https://www.nytimes.com/2021/06/03/magazine/metagenomic-sequencing.html

Kidambi, P. (2007). *The making of an Indian metropolis: Colonial governance and public culture in Bombay 1890–1920*. Ashgate.

Kulkarni, D.D., Tosh, C., Venkatesh, G.D. & Senthil Kumar, D. (2013). Nipah virus infection: Current scenario. *Indian Journal of Virology*, *24*(3), 398–408. https://www.ncbi.nlm.nih.gov/pmc/articles/PMC3832692/

Levinas, E. (1988). Useless suffering (R. Cohen, Trans.). In R. Bernasconi & D.Wood (Eds.), *The provocation of Levinas*. Routledge, 156–167.

Li, J., Zhou, L., Van Der Heijden, B., Li, S., Tao, H. & Guo, Z. (2021). Social isolation, loneliness and well-being: The impact of WeChat use intensity during the COVID-19 pandemic in China. *Frontiers in Psychology, 12.* https://www.frontiersin.org/articles/10.3389/fpsyg.2021.707667/

Lynteris, C. (2014). Introduction: The time of epidemics. *The Cambridge Journal of Anthropology, 32*(1), 24–31. http://www.jstor.org/stable/43612893

Mauss, M. (1990). *The gift: The form and reason for exchange in archaic societies* (W.D. Halls, Trans.). Routledge.

Mohanty, S.P. (2000). The epistemic status of cultural identity: On *Beloved* and the postmodern condition. In P. Moya & M.R. Hames-García (Eds.), *Reclaiming identity: Realist theory and the predicament of postmodernism* (pp. 19–66). Orient Blackswan.

Morand, S., Jittapalapong, S., Suputtamongkol, Y., Abdullah, M.T. & Huan, T.B. (2014). Infectious diseases and their outbreaks in Asia–Pacific: Biodiversity and its regulation loss matter. *PLoS ONE, 9*(2): e90032.

Paul, L. (2018). Nipah virus in Kerala: A deadly zoonosis. *Clinical Microbiology and Infection, 24,* 1113–1114. https://www.clinicalmicrobiologyandinfection.com/article/S1198-743X(18)30480-4/pdf

Pandya, A. & Lodha, P. (2021). Social connectedness, excessive screen time during COVID-19 and mental health: A review of current evidence. *Frontiers in Human Dynamics, 3(*684137). https://www.frontiersin.org/articles/10.3389/fhumd.2021.684137/full

Pulla, P. (2018, June 2). Nipah virus: Anatomy of an outbreak. *The Hindu.* https://www.thehindu.com/news/national/kerala/anatomy-of-an-outbreak-how-kerala-handled-the-nipah-virus-outbreak/article24060538.ece

Rabinow, P. (2005). Artificiality and enlightenment: From sociobiology to biosociality. In J.X. India (Ed.), *Anthropologies of modernity: Foucault, governmentality, and life politics* (pp. 181–193). Blackwell Publishing.

Rajan, M.S. (2020, May 7). Vogue warriors: Meet Kerala's health minister who is taking the state out of the pandemic. *Vogue India.* https://www.vogue.in/culture-and-living/content/vogue-warriors-kk-shailaja-kerala-health-minister-covid-19-response

Ricoeur, P. (1984). *Time and Narrative,* vol.1 (K. McLaughlin & D. Pellauer, Trans.). University of Chicago Press.

Rosenberg, C.E. (1989a). Disease in history: frames and framers. *The Millbank Quarterly, 67*(Suppl. 1), 1–15.

Rosenberg, C.E. (1989b). What is an epidemic? AIDS in historical perspective. *Daedalus, 118*(2), 1–17.

Srivastava, S., Sharma, P.K., Gurjar, S. et al. (2024). Nipah virus strikes Kerala: Recent cases and implications. *The Egyptian Journal of Internal Medicine, 36*(11).

Sudeep, A.B., Yadav, P.D., Gokhale, M.D., et al. (2021). Detection of Nipah virus in *Pteropus medius* in 2019 outbreak from Ernakulam district, Kerala, India. *BMC Infectious Diseases, 21*(162).

Thacker, S.B., Goodman, R.A. & Dicker, R.C. (1990). Training and service in public health practice, 1951–1990: CDC's Epidemic Intelligence Service. *Public Health Reports (1974–), 106*(6), 599–604.

Thakur, V., Thakur, P. & Ratho, R.K. (2022). *Nipah* outbreak: Is it the beginning of another pandemic in the era of *COVID-19* and *Zika*. *Brain, Behavior, and Immunity, 99*, 25–26.

Thomas, B., Chandran, P., Lilabi, M.P., George, B., Sivakumar, C.P., Jayadev, V.K., Bindu, V. et al. (2019). 'Nipah Virus Infection in Kozhikode, Kerala, South India, in 2018: Epidemiology of an Outbreak of an Emerging Disease.' *Indian Journal of Community Medicine, 44*(4), 383–387. https://pmc.ncbi.nlm.nih.gov/articles/PMC6881878/

Turner, B. (1995). *Medical power and social knowledge*. 2nd ed. Sage.

Turner, B. (2008). *The body and society: Explorations in social theory*. 3rd ed. Sage.

Wald, P. (2008). *Contagious: Cultures, carriers, and the outbreak narrative*. Duke University Press.

Wirz, P. (1954). *Exorcism and the art of healing in Ceylon*. E.J. Brill.

World Health Organisation. (1980, May 8). 'Declaration of global eradication of smallpox'. Thirty-Third World Health Assembly. https://apps.who.int/iris/bitstream/handle/10665/155528/ accessed on 23 March 2021.

World Health Organisation Regional Office for South Asia. (2014). *A brief guide to emerging infectious diseases and zoonoses.*

9

COVID Narratives

Pandemic Precarity

> In March 2020, bookstores began selling out of a book from the 14th century—Giovanni Boccaccio's *The Decameron*, a collection of nested tales told by and for a group of women and men sheltering in a place outside of Florence as the plague ravages the city. In the United States, we were beginning to self-isolate, learning what it meant to quarantine, and many readers were looking for guidance from this ancient book. As the coronavirus spread across the world, the novelist Rivka Galchen approached *The New York Times Magazine* and told us that she'd like to write a story recommending Boccaccio's *Decameron* to help readers understand the present moment. We loved the idea, but wondered, instead, what if we made our own *Decameron*, filled with new fiction written during quarantine?
>
> Roper, *The Decameron Project*, 2020

This is how Caitlin Roper, senior editor of *New York Times* magazine, recounts the birth of *The Decameron Project*, a collection of twenty-nine short stories on the coronavirus pandemic. It was inspired, as she writes, by Boccaccio's famous narrative as well as the idea that we can best understand 'the present moment' through stories (Roper, 2020, p. ix). But what is it about this moment that stories alone can address? In this chapter, I try to answer that question by examining a sample of narratives about the pandemic in India: what is it about COVID-19 that exceeds the capacity of objectivist discourse to convey the truth of pandemic, and how do stories tell this truth? The COVID pandemic is different from earlier pandemics in two important aspects: the global lockdown of 2020 and the acute shortage of emergency medical resources in the midst of plenty that intensified vulnerability. I will discuss these two aspects in the sections that follow. In the next two sections I will discuss an unintended consequence of the lockdown, the plight of migrant workers who lost their livelihood in the cities to which they had migrated and were forced to return to their villages braving all odds.

9.1. Quarantine, Lockdown and the Spatio-Temporality of Pandemic Crisis

Quarantines and the evacuation of places of disease have been standard measure globally to contain epidemics for centuries, ever since the plague outbreak in Boccaccio's time, though their scientific basis came to be known only after the emergence of germ theory in the nineteenth century. Camus narrates in his novel how the town of Oran was sealed when plague broke out (1960, pp. 63–72). In *Samskara*, as we have seen, Manjayya thinks of evacuating the people of Durvasapura, where a number of people have been infected. In *Discipline and Punish*, Michel Foucault details the closure of plague-stricken towns and the meticulous surveillance that was invented as a new mode of visibility at the turn of the eighteenth century (1977, p. 195–198). During the Bombay plague epidemic in 1896–97, municipal authorities evacuated the areas where the number of cases was high, fumigated and lime-washed the buildings, demolished structures that blocked air and light, and razed to the ground the huts of the poor (Kidambi, 2007, pp. 57–58). But epidemics were then largely local phenomena, and their spread to other areas was relatively slow as communication systems were not highly developed. The Spanish flu pandemic presented a different scenario, as the virus was rapidly carried from the battlefields of Europe to other parts of the world by soldiers returning home—a rapidity that surpassed, as the Sanitary Commissioner of India F. Norman White put it, the speed of travel.

The speed with which COVID spread was unprecedented, even when compared to Spanish flu, solely because of the scale of international travel. In the two-and-a-half months from 31 December 2019 to 11 March 2020, it spread from Wuhan to the rest of the world (Global News, 2020, 07:10). Lockdowns to arrest this spread were an urgent measure. By April 2020 more than half the world was closed to all forms of traffic, people were ordered to stay at home, business establishments, offices and educational institutions were shut down, and the streets patrolled by police and paramilitary forces to ensure compliance—measures that were unprecedented in both scale and duration. Everyday routines were disrupted, writes Florian Mussgnug, social relationships endangered, and time 'no longer seemed to flow naturally into the future' (2021, p. 253).

Any epidemic outbreak distorts our sense of temporal order. The abruptness of its onset, the rapidity with which it spreads, and the premature loss of life on a large scale—all of these serve to intensify our sense of a present that seems unending and a future that seems too far off—*if, that is, we survive the present*. Mussgnug notes how, in one of the stories in *The Decameron Project*, the experience of temporality is marked by a deep anxiety that he calls 'chronophobia'—'a traumatic, debilitating experience of time *not* passing' (2021, p. 254, italics in original). The global lockdown added to this temporal disruption the arrest of space, restricting life to the indoors. For those infected, space became even more narrowed down to the confines of an isolation room. It is no wonder, then, that spatial and temporal disorientation became a theme common to many COVID narratives. This is one of the truths of our 'present moment' that the stories, with their emphasis on subjective experience, told.

Infected 2030, a short film directed by Chandan P. Singh, is about quarantine, not lockdown, but it conveys the same sense of spatio-temporal anxiety. Set in the year 2030 when a COVID-like pandemic breaks out, killing two hundred and fifty million people, it is about a young couple, Manik and Shivika. Shivika is infected and has to be isolated at home for two months because the hospitals are full, and Manik stays in to take care of her. The film has a simple plot with a single line of action: Shivika's isolation and the effect it has on her and Manik. Most of the time she spends in bed alone, except for the moments when Manik brings her food and medicines, covered fully in a PPE kit and face mask. 'I don't recall', she tells him in despair, 'when I last saw your face' (Singh, 2021, 11:01). The food is tasteless and unappetising, she frequently wets herself, and has a recurrent cough. Manik, too, is lonely, depressed and worried about their fate, but tries his best to endure what he thinks is a temporary condition. The film shows how each struggles against despair in the expectation that this will end someday.

Infected is about the acute consciousness of time and space when one is forced into confinement, a chronotope of epidemic that became distressingly familiar to us in COVID times. As Bakhtin explains, chronotope is not about the world in its physical dimensions but as it is perceived in human consciousness. Shivika perceives the room in which she is confined not as physical space, just as she does not perceive time in hours, days or months. It has been two months since her self-isolation, but for Shivika time has become static. It is, as Lisa Baraitser puts it, 'an affective experience of the too-much-ness of time, time that will not pass, will not unfold into a future of freedom, release or death' (as cited in Mussgnug, 2021, p. 254). Space is experienced as the contrast between claustrophobic interiors and wide-open exteriors. In one poignant shot, as Shivika stands by the window looking out on the vast cityscape of Mumbai, she moves her hands in the gesture of a bird flying out of the room, to express her emotional need for freedom. In a parallel shot we see Manik looking out at the same cityscape from the living-room window, his faced etched with tiredness and despair. Almost the entire footage is shot in the two rooms that they occupy, separated by a door that is always shut except when Shivika needs medicines or food. In one scene, Manik and Shivika sit on opposite sides of the door, trying to communicate across the physical and emotional barriers that the pandemic has built between them. Space and time are imbued with emotion, as they recollect scenes of past intimacy in a present that contagion has rendered devoid of contact. The film constructs the chronotope of quarantine (and implicitly of lockdown) as arrested time-space in which intimacy no longer exists because of the risk it carries in a communicable disease outbreak. We 'endow all phenomena with meaning', writes Bakhtin, and in incorporating them into our experience of time-space assign to them specific values (1981, p. 257). In their condition of claustrophobic existence within the four walls of a room, Shivika and Manik endow the space outside not only with the meaning of freedom but equally with its value; in contrast, the space of home, which in other circumstances would be valuable, loses its appeal. The present, too, becomes devalued as days blur into an endless time of suffering against the remembered happiness of past times and, implicitly, of a future that they hope for. Nostalgia and hope outline the contours of their despair. As viewers, we are able to relate to the film's chronotopic world because it connects our cultural memory of past epidemics with our present experience. As we comprehend the meaning that the film constructs, these meanings in turn make our own world more apprehensible. This, as Bakhtin points out, is how the fictional world and the real world augment each other dialectically (1981, p. 254). Paul Ricouer, too, makes the same point when he writes of 'the intersection of the world of the text and that of the listener or reader' (1984, p. 77). Narratives take their inspiration from the human experience of reality and reconfigure it according to specific plot-structures that endow them with a meaning which resonates with the readers' experiences in turn.

In the last scene of *Infected* Manik enters the bedroom and spends the night with his wife, throwing caution, literally, to the wind—for it is the *air* that carries the virus. In a film that is about confinement and loss of intimacy, this scene comes through as a yearning for freedom at whatever cost. Next morning, as Manik sorts out Shivika's medicines in the living room, he has a violent fit of coughing in what can only be described as the deepest irony: joined in disease now, Manik and Shivika need no longer maintain the barriers that separate them. What, the film seems to ask, is of more value in a time of epidemic—the protection of our health at the cost of intimacy, or an intimacy that can only be possible by risking our health? In a world where lockdowns, social distance, quarantine, masks and PPE kits have become the norm, this is a question worth asking—not to find an answer because there *are* no answers, but to understand how epidemic affects the time-spaces in which we struggle to survive and across which we strive to communicate. It provokes us to think of the emotional cost of the barriers we erect, even as it shows us why they are necessary. By locating its story in a moment in future, the film announces its fictive nature; but by relating it to the present context it deepens or enriches our understanding of our own moment. From a scientific perspective quarantine is the most practical way to break transmission, without any counter-effects, and that is also how it is perceived in everyday understanding. By complicating the idea of quarantine, *Infected 2030* does not contradict this objective commonsense, but recasts it through a plot that highlights its emotional costs. In an actual account of quarantine, for instance, Amrita Jha recalls how her family was isolated after they tested positive for coronavirus: 'Our neighbours maintained distance from us, 24x7 we were in close watch for all our actions, and sometimes it felt as if we are criminals rather than patients, trapped in our own house' (2021). For her, the anxiety and solitude of quarantine were more painful than the objective symptoms of disease. When Naresh Pathak and his family tested positive, 'we faced a lot of humiliation, ostracization from our neighbours and communities, they were all worried about getting infected from us' (2020). These are not fictitious accounts like *Infected 2030*, but describe the actual experience of their narrators.

9.2. Isolation and the Virtual Sociality of Care: 'My COVID Story'

Pathak and Jha posted their stories on a blogsite titled 'My COVID Story' that *The Times of India* ran during the epidemic, carrying accounts of the experiences of patients, caregivers or the bereaved. They covered a range of themes, such as the sudden disruption of everyday routine, effects of disease, quarantine, intensive care, post-COVID recovery, self-healing, lack of essential drugs and hospital facilities, and deaths of close relatives—issues, in other words, that formed the everyday of pandemic experience. They were personal narratives, as the blog's title indicates, expressing emotions of fear, vulnerability, suffering, anxiety and grief as well as courage and hope. The blog's description explains that those who have suffered and endured the trauma of COVID can, by sharing their stories, help others who are going through the same experience. It invokes the language of caring for others in distress, by reassuring them that they are not alone.

> The Covid pandemic has disrupted millions of lives across the globe. While some have been lucky to win the battle against the virus, several others have faced devastating consequences. 'My Covid Story' is a platform where you can share your Covid experience to help others tide over this unprecedented crisis. Your story can inspire, guide and give strength to others who are battling this pandemic in isolation. ('My COVID story', 2022)

Disease leads to isolation in two ways. The suffering of disease limits our ability to talk about it to others, to share with them our pain. Pain, writes Elaine Scarry, 'does not simply resist language but actively destroys it, bringing about an immediate reversion to a state anterior to language, to the sounds and cries a human being makes before language is learned.' Since it cannot be expressed in language and therefore cannot be objectively known, pain is fundamentally enigmatic: one's own pain is real, the other's always suspect: 'for the person in pain, so incontestably and unnegotiably present is it that "having pain" may come to be thought of as the most vibrant example of what it is to "have certainty", while for the other person it is so elusive that "hearing about pain" may exist as the primary model of what it is "to have doubt"' (Scarry, 1985, p. 4). The unshareability of pain is what, first of all, makes those suffering from disease isolate themselves emotionally from others. As a corollary, infectious disease leads others to isolate the infected socially, because of the fear of contracting it. Outbreaks of communicable disease destroy community, as we saw in the last chapter, stigmatising individuals affected by them. Describing her family's experience of quarantine, Jha tells us how their neighbours distanced themselves even as they kept a close watch on them, as if they were 'criminals' subjected to surveillance. The imposition of quarantine by public health authorities compounds the sense of emotional and social isolation by adding to it the coercive force of the state.

The objective of *The Times of India*'s blog was to reverse this process, by building a community of care to counter isolation, across time and space, in *hyperreal* time-space. Infectious disease epidemics, Priscilla Wald argues in *Contagious*, re-establish community even as they threaten it. 'The interactions that make us sick also constitute us as a community. Disease emergence dramatizes the dilemma that inspires the most basic of human narratives: the necessity and danger of human contact' (Wald 2008, p. 2). In the previous chapter we saw this in the solidarity that is expressed at the end of *Virus*, when Health Minister Prameela sums up the lessons they have learnt from the outbreak. The community that *Virus* represents, however, is one built on face-to-face relationships: in the meeting that Prameela holds we look at the characters *literally* looking at one another in hope and mutual reassurance. They all inhabit the same physical space and time—an over-packed public hall—which is also the symbolic space-time of community, expressed in the film's image of togetherness. The community that 'My COVID Story' constitutes, in contrast, is of digitised relationships in the virtual world of web platforms and social media sites.[1]

We can thus distinguish between two forms of the social network that constitutes community, one face-to-face and the other virtual. All communities, contends Benedict Anderson, are imaginary, except perhaps 'primordial villages of face-to-face contact' (2006, p. 6). Even these are also in part imagined, because they include not just contemporaries but equally ancestors and

[1] The stories in this blog were also uploaded on Facebook and Twitter, and could be followed there.

those yet to be born. What matters is the style of imagining. The concept of community in many traditional societies comprises of relationships that range from the real to the symbolic. As Clifford Geertz explains in the context of Bali, it is an imagined network linking consociates, contemporaries, predecessors and successors. Consociates are those who inhabit the same time and space and are likely to meet in face-to-face interaction, while contemporaries are those who belong to different spaces but the same time, and may possibly meet each other. In contrast, predecessors (ancestors long dead) and successors (those yet to be born) belong to time-space relationships that exist only in the mind. '"Consociates", "contemporaries", "predecessors", and "successors" are best seen not as pigeonholes into which individuals distribute one another for classificatory purposes, but as indicating certain general and not altogether distinct, matter-of-fact relationships which individuals conceive to obtain between themselves and others' (Geertz, 1973, p. 367). In contrast to traditional communities, the nation as a modern community is imagined into being through the media, literature and cultural icons like the national flag and anthem that homogenise regional differences into a singular national framework (Anderson, 2006, pp. 9–46). National communities are imagined in two senses of the word: they are imagined as real for those who belong to them, and they are represented predominantly through images.

I have taken this detour through Anderson and Geertz to explain how *The Times of India* blog constructs its community of care. It is imagined into being in the circulation of stories that provide concrete images of suffering, and which can, as the blog puts it 'inspire, guide and give strength to others who are battling this pandemic in isolation'. In other words, it seeks to establish what we may call a *virtual* sociality, in contrast to the *actual* sociality of face-to-face encounters which the pandemic has placed at risk. The community it imagines into being, however, is not that of the nation or kin-group but of fellowship founded on disease, in a virtualised and mass-mediated form of what Rabinow (2005) calls 'biosociality'. Since well before the COVID pandemic, devices like telephones, mobiles, messaging services and emails had been enabling relationships to continue over geographical divides, which would otherwise tend to be weakened in the absence of regular interaction. In such case, however, they served merely to extend face-to-face relationships that had become inaccessible, by providing opportunity for contact that sustains them across space (Licoppe, 2004, pp. 136–139). In a pandemic they act as lifelines for family members and friends, who are either in quarantine or unable to meet due to lockdowns and travel restrictions. 'As the ongoing health crisis constrains people's movements and social interactions because of distancing requirements, travel bans and lockdowns', write Earvin Cabalquinto and Tanja Ahlin, 'ICTs [Information and Communications Technology] have been key to sustaining relationships in already networked societies' (2021, p. 344).

Social interactions are conducted over a range of interdependent channels, from face-to-face to technologically mediated, constituting a total system that Christian Licoppe describes as a 'relational economy' of interactions (2004, p. 140). However, they do not *as such* constitute sociality because (i) they may not be enduring and (ii) they belong to the micro-level of person-to-person exchange. Virtual sociality, in contrast, refers to macro level exchanges in which a large number of people engage in conversations over issues with passionate concern, and over time some of them may go on to develop enduring relationships. Virtual sociality was possible when, at the turn of the present century, web hosting sites made it possible for users to create and upload content and establish online social networks. But it was anticipated as far back as 1993, when Howard Rheingold wrote about the 'virtual community' of relationships mediated by the internet: 'In the traditional community, we search through our pool of neighbors and professional colleagues, of acquaintances and acquaintances of acquaintances, in order to find people who share our values and interests. … In a virtual community we can go directly to the place where our favorite subjects are being discussed, then get acquainted with people who share our passions or who use words in a way we find attractive' (1993, pp. 24–25). Rheingold's 'virtual community' is, however, restricted to micro level interactions, since the web conference as he conceives it serves only to facilitate person-to-person relationships. In virtual sociality, people across geographical locations come together in some form of *collective* action that bears consequences for society and/or for their lives. One of its most common contexts has been in fostering activist movements, such as Arab Spring.[2] The COVID pandemic has provided yet another context, in which virtual sociality becomes a means of extending support to those in distress by sharing stories of endurance and hope. *The Times of India* blog is an apt example, in the way it constitutes a community of suffering grounded in an ethics of care.

We note a number of points about the blog. The first pertains to the newspaper, which has reconfigured its services from providing news to brokering relationships of care. As Cabalquinto and Ahlin observe, online platforms like Facebook and Instagram have often used the rhetoric of care to increase subscription and profits, framing 'connectedness through digital media as inevitable in maintaining personal relationships' and sharing personal experiences as 'a form of caring for valued individuals' (2021, p. 347). The format for 'My COVID Story', therefore, was already an established practice in social media. Rhetoric of care in social media sites carries an emotional appeal that disguises the economics underlying it, which operates in the form of social network advertising. In the context of pandemic, caring for readers who are encouraged to care for others in distress serves to legitimise sources of profit that are reconfigured as ethical initiatives on the part of both the newspaper and its readership. Most readers are too engrossed in reading the stories to notice the ads that pop up frequently but unobtrusively as they read. Caring for others may be a ground for ethical community, but mediatised care is obviously a lot more complex than that.

[2] The phrase refers to a series of public protests in North Africa and the Middle East from 2010 to 2012, most of which were facilitated by social media. Such movements, however, are often compromised because the private corporations that own social media permit surveillance by the state (Gray-Hawkins, 2018; Tierney, 2013).

The second point about 'My COVID Story' is the kind of stories it includes. In the chapter on AIDS, I made a distinction between outbreak narratives and illness narratives: the former are typically about collective calamity, the latter about personal suffering. An exception to this is the AIDS narrative, which personalises the epidemic because of the way it has come to be associated with lifestyle. In the early years of the pandemic it was predominantly understood as either a disease of deviance, affecting prostitutes and their clients, sexually promiscuous individuals and drug addicts, or as the undeserved suffering of 'innocent victims' like haemophiliacs, thalassaemics, children or middle-class housewives with errant husbands. This changed during the turn of the century when middle-class people with no ostensible deviance turned up positive, and narratives of their illness shifted from stigma to sympathy. AIDS stories, therefore, adopted the already-existing format of narratives about chronic illnesses like cancer and kidney disease, in which one suffers an inscrutable and unjust fate. The stories in *The Times of India* blog follow this format and all stories are of personal suffering—the pain of disease, loss and grief, and the desperation of not being able to get help. Vinay Kumar recalls his stay in 'an ICU room filled with 8 patients, many suffocating, screaming, trying to survive with monitors blinking all around' (2021). Sashi's post in 'My COVID Story' is about his father's death and the emotional trauma he suffers at a time when he himself is infected:

> I was still strong, despite having a high-grade fever; somehow, my oxygen level was normal. I managed to pull it off through home quarantine after 15 days of struggle, but the hospital informed me that my father's vital organs stopped functioning on an early morning. After some time, my dearest father left us for his heaven abode, leaving a scar in our life. My mother has already left us in 2015. I am still struggling to cope up with this and I miss dad very dearly every single day! (2021)

Sri Tatsat recalls how he lost his father: 'In the hindsight, it seems nothing was meant to work because the doctors lacked faith in themselves. They stayed in their chambers playing mobile games while the ventilators beeped like crazy. Those beeps are the scariest sounds that I will ever hear, I think' (2021). Shatarupa Sen Gupta's father dies, ironically, on her birthday: 'I sent away to death, the man who brought me into this world, held my hand, taught me to walk, taught me life lessons, always gave me courage, boosted my confidence and was my pillar of strength' (2021). A number of stories are about the lack of emergency services. 'The day I realised that my father was serious, I tried my best to get a hospital bed. I called innumerable hospitals, but there was not even a single bed and due to financial problems and being COVID+ too, I and my mother were not able to bring an oxygen cylinder at home which we have to refill every 4 hours. I tried my best to find a hospital but I was helpless' (Panesar, 2022). Pawar recounts the desperation when oxygen supplies ran acutely short: 'That time I also saw violence, people were fighting for cylinders, they were stealing them, they were mistreating and harming the doctors. … There was also black marketing and misleading information around the city for oxygen cylinders' (2021). In these examples, what especially enables the personalisation of collective suffering is the blog as a communicative genre. In an interview with Anna Poletti and Julie Rak, Lauren Berlant (who herself maintained a blog titled *Supervalent Thought*) states that 'the blog form has an amplifying function with respect to intention and voice' (Poletti & Rak, 2014, p. 263). Blog-writing, in other words, is a mode of performing selfhood in relational terms, or of presenting oneself to another in the form of intimate, yet anonymous, address.[3] The names of contributors in 'My COVID Story' are not their real names, but anonyms to protect their identities.

The third point about the blog posts is the sense of precariousness they express. Precariousness refers to the existential condition of hopelessness, vulnerability and uncertainty when social and institutional arrangements fail to provide a secure life. Aseem Prakash and Hem Borker note two moments of precariousness in the first wave of the epidemic

[3] For an account of how ICT technologies have led to a proliferation of online autobiographies, see the essays by Aimée Morrison and Philippe Lejeune in Poletti and Rak, 2014 and Sorapure, 2015 respectively.

in India: the first concerning migrant workers who lost their livelihood in the lockdown and the second 'the experience of the non-availability of medical aid, death of kith and kin followed by the struggle to cremate/bury and perform the last rituals of their family members' (2022, p. 40). We will discuss the problem of the migrants in a later section. As regards the second moment, while all outbreaks put medical resources under strain, in the COVID pandemic this became so severe that it intensified the sense of vulnerability, as we see in *The Times of India* blog posts. Because of the large number of fatalities, there was also a pressure on crematoria and funeral grounds. Though the health ministry's advisory 'COVID-19: Guidelines on Dead Body Management', issued on 15 March 2020, permitted families to perform cremation following COVID-safety norms, it was not always followed in practice. In her post on 'My COVID Story', Meenu recalls the agony of not being able to see her father before he was cremated (2021).

The fourth point about *The Times of India* blog is the sphere of sociality it constitutes. Evidently, these are people who can interact with each other in terms of knowledge of English, computer skills and access to infrastructure—in other words, a social class that possesses both economic and cultural capital. With low-cost smartphones and internet connectivity, skills and infrastructure may not necessarily be a barrier for socio-economically underprivileged groups, but access to English certainly is. This in itself does not disqualify the blog from being an ethical initiative, for newspapers in other languages can provide the same services for those who do not know English. But it points to the kind of pandemic subject it both represents and constitutes, and the ideology underlying this constitution. In addressing individuals, representations hail or interpellate them into positions of ideologically defined subjectivity with which they, in turn, identify. As Louis Althusser explains in 'Ideology and Ideological State Apparatuses', hailing elicits as its necessary condition the response of the one who is hailed: 'he has recognized that the hail was "really" addressed to him, that "it was *really him* who was hailed" (and not someone else)' (2001, p. 118, italics in original). The recognition of oneself as a caring person and the blog as a platform on which '*you* can share *your* COVID experience' (italics added), are complementary parts of the same process, and they happen, like hailing and the response of the hailed, 'without any succession'. In recruiting writers and readers into narratives of suffering, the blog constitutes them as subjects of a mass-mediated sociality based on relations of care. Since the stories are by and about middle-class people, they mirror one another's experience in what Althusser terms the '*speculary*' structure of ideological self-recognition (2001, p. 122, italics in original). 'My COVID Story', thus, constructs pandemic identity in two polar ways, as fractured by the breakdown of community and as ideologically reconstituted in mediatised relations of care.

9.3. Lockdown 2020 and the Enigma of Biopolitics

On the night of 24 March 2020 the Government of India announced a country-wide lockdown, which came into effect four hours later and was subsequently extended in three phases till 31 May. This was an urgent measure to control the pandemic, which by 22 March had recorded 360 confirmed cases and seven deaths (WHO India, 2020, p. 1). The Ministry of Home Affairs, invoking the Disaster Management Act, 2005, issued an order prohibiting movement of people without valid permission, closing down government offices, commercial and private establishments, industries, transport and hospitality services, educational institutions and places of worship, and banning gatherings of any kind.[4] Law and order agencies were tasked with ensuring compliance, and violation of lockdown rules was punishable with imprisonment of up to two years. The lockdown gave otherwise unwarranted power to the state authorities to intervene in the everyday lives of people, as seen in numerous instances of the police beating or shaming lockdown violators in the name of controlling the pandemic (Global News, 2020; *Hindustan Times*, 2020). Responding to the imposition of a

[4] See Ministry of Home Affairs order No. 40-3/2020-DM-I (A) dated 24 March 2020 and Annexure dated 24 March 2020. https://www.mha.gov.in/sites/default/files/MHAorder, accessed on 25 April 2022.

similar lockdown in Italy in February 2020, the philosopher Giorgio Agamben posted a blog on the website *Quodlibet* titled 'The Invention of an Epidemic', accusing the state of using COVID as a pretext for creating a 'state of exception' in which the rights of citizens could be suspended (Agamben, 2020). The modern state, as Foucault points out, is biopolitical, that is, the preservation of human life becomes a political obligation and a right of the state. The governance of public health, which in India is specified under Article 47 of Directive Principles of State Policy in the Constitution, is a part of that right, others being to ensure welfare of the people, their right to education, employment and a living wage, and conditions that ensure a decent standard of life. But the 'enigma' of biopolitics appears when the state's right to 'make live' is penetrated by the sovereign's right to take life, and the state subjects its citizens to death, literal or metaphorical, in the name of preserving life (Foucault, 2003, pp. 253–254). The concept of a state of exception is how Agamben explains this enigma: in exceptional situations, like that of a pandemic or a security threat, the state exercises its negative right to take life as the condition for exercising its positive right to preserve it. In short, the state must kill some in order to make others live. It is in this paradox, when the right to 'make live' becomes indistinguishable from the right to 'take life' (Foucault, 2003, p. 241), that the sovereign power of the state becomes manifest. In conditions of emergency the state suspends ordinary law, the duty of which is to guarantee the life and personal liberty of the citizen.[5] The lockdown in India created a situation contrary to a basic principle of law enforcement, when the police could themselves inflict punishment on violators instead of handing them to a court, which alone has the power judge and to punish. As Agamben explains in *Homo Sacer*, 'One of the paradoxes of the state of exception lies in the fact that in the state of exception, it is impossible to distinguish transgression of the law from execution

[5] The Emergency provision in the Indian Constitution (Articles 352–359) is a specific instance of this exceptional situation. When a state of emergency is proclaimed, fundamental rights are placed under suspension—that is, they continue to exist but they cannot be enforced in a court of law. In other

of the law, such that what violates a rule and what conforms to it coincide without any remainder' (1998, p. 57).

In his blog post, Agamben explains why people accept the suspension of their freedoms instead of opposing it, as one would expect in a liberal democracy. A pandemic of the scale of COVID-19 leads to a state of fear that calls for extraordinary measures. Governments and the media scale up this fear, even while assuring people of their safety. 'Therefore, in a perverse vicious circle, the limitations of freedom imposed by governments are accepted in the name of a desire for safety that was created by the same governments that are now intervening to satisfy it' (Agamben, 2020). One may not agree completely with Agamben's view—one respondent called it 'paranoiac' (Benvenuto, 2020)—but it is worth considering in the context of the biopolitical enigma. Roberto Esposito, while disagreeing with the way Agamben states his case, agrees that the pandemic made visible the hidden link between medicine and power. We witness on the one hand a 'medicalization of politics' that seeks to protect its subjects from risks that it has itself accentuated, and on the other, 'a politicization of medicine, invested with tasks of social control that do not belong to it—which explains the extremely heterogeneous assessments virologists are making on the nature and gravity of the coronavirus' (Esposito, 2000). Esposito's answer to the biopolitical enigma is the paradigm of immunity, which connects the positive and negative poles of biopolitics. Immunisation introduces into the biological body the very same pathogen that it seeks to exclude, as a 'negative [form] of the protection of life' (Esposito, 2008, p. 46). Likewise, in the political body, it introduces the violence that law must prohibit, in order to protect it from one that would, if not countered, destroy it. 'The negative—that which contradicts order, norms, values—

words, it is a provision within law for the law to suspend itself in a paradox under which law and lawlessness coincide. Another instance is the Armed Forces (Special Powers) Act, 1958, under which an army officer may kill any person on suspicion or hold them in custody for an unspecified period, acts that are formally illegal but for which the Act makes him immune from prosecution.

is taken on not only as an indispensable element of human history in all its singular or social configurations that it assumes periodically, but indeed as history's productive impulse' (p. 47). But under certain circumstances the immunitary apparatus rebounds against itself, as in auto-immune disorders: 'The idea of immunity, which is needed for protecting life, if carried past a certain threshold, winds up negating life. That is, immunity encages life such that not only is our freedom but also the very meaning of our individual and collective existence is lost' (Esposito, 2013, p. 61). Seen from this perspective, the lockdown in India caused more harm than good, depriving many people of their source of livelihood and thus exposing them to the very death that it was meant to avert, apart from everyday violations of the right to dignified existence. Analysing the economic impact of the lockdown, Ramakumar and Kanitkar conclude that it caused severe economic distress to the people least equipped to cope with it: 'In agriculture, farmers were faced with broken supply chains, lack of market outlets, poor demand and falling output prices.... In industry, micro and small enterprises were the most acutely affected....The crisis also led to a major loss of employment; at least 13 million people disappeared from the labour force between February and October 2020' (2021, p. 30). The people most distressed were migrant workers, who suddenly found themselves without a livelihood, driven to starvation, unable to stay in the cities to which they had migrated and unable even to return home because of lack of transport.

9.4. Pandemic Precarity and the Migrant's Story

On 27 April 2020, a little more than a month after the nationwide lockdown was announced, a group of thirty migrant workers left Ghaziabad in Uttar Pradesh for their villages in Bihar. Vinod Kapri's documentary film, *1232 KMS* and the book based on the documentary, *1232 kms: The Long Journey Home*, recount how seven of them cycled all the way home, braving hunger, mishaps, exhaustion and policemen beating them for being on the road in a curfew. Kapri first learnt of the plight of these migrants from a Twitter post. On contacting one of them, he learnt of their resolve to undertake the journey against all odds because, as one of them said, 'It's better to die on our way while trying to reach home than dying here' (Kapri, 2021b, p. 9). Kapri, who is a filmmaker, documented their journey all the way from Brijghat to Saharsa, to let the world know 'about their struggle, their pain and the threats they faced' (p. xxx). The book, which was written from notes that he made during the journey, was intended to bring out nuances of meaning that the camera could not capture: 'Things like the lingering fear that by the time they reach home, one or two might not make it; that at night, when they stopped to sleep, they would call up their family members and cry for hours' (p. xxix). I will discuss the film and the book as a single story in multimedia narration. While the film records this story mainly styled as *cinema verité* or unobtrusive documentary, the book retells it from Kapri's perspective and that of the migrants. It is in this mixed modality that the film and book bear (as Kapri aptly puts it) 'witness' to the precarity of the migrants' lives (p. xxv).

In a socio-economic analysis of migrant precarity in the pandemic, Prakash and Borker show how it was the outcome of a structural convergence of three factors that had existed well before the lockdown. One was the liminal status of migrants in the market, who, lacking both organisation and formal terms of employment, could easily be short-changed by managements and labour intermediaries. Second was the difficulty in accessing welfare entitlements from the state due to gaps in documentation, bureaucratic inefficiency and lack of political will. The third factor was the ambivalent attitude of civil society towards returning migrants, with some people trying to profit from their desperation or turning them away for fear of disease while others rallied round them with food, transportation or financial aid. A sentiment that some of their respondents expressed was, 'if I have to die, it's better to die in my village' (Prakash & Borker, 2022, p. 40). Precariousness has been understood as both personal and social, the first in terms of the frailty of the human body and its susceptibility to harm, and the second in terms of structural inequalities that magnify the sense of personal vulnerability (Turner, 2008, pp. 242–262). The posts in 'My COVID Story', *The Times of India* blog that we discussed above, are about personal precariousness, while the stories of migrants, which were narrated in innumerable media reports and Kapri's film and book, are about the social. The distinction between personal and social precariousness is, however, only theoretical, for the two actually constitute a spectrum of how one experiences and becomes conscious of vulnerability. Stories of precarious life connect the two, those of personal suffering emphasising the former while those of collective suffering emphasise the latter.

In a roundtable with Jasbir Puar, Judith Butler distinguishes between *precariousness* and *precarity*, the latter being political rather than existential and the outcome of unequal power relations. To these she adds the concept of *precaritisation* as an ongoing process not reducible to a specific time or place. 'Precaritization allows us to think about the slow death that happens to targeted or neglected populations over time and space. And it is surely a form of power without a subject, which is to say that there is no one center that propels its direction and destruction' (Butler, in Puar, 2012, p. 169). Thinking about it as a process enables us to see how precarity is not limited to specific global events like terrorism, natural calamities or pandemics, though it may be exacerbated by them. Since there is no subject directing it but a historical conjuncture of forces, it is pointless to trace it to the intentions of particular social actors. In the context of migrant workers in the lockdown in India, as Naregal argues, their vulnerability is the outcome of structural arrangements between labour and capital that have been emerging since economic liberalisation in the 1990s, irrespective of the government in power and its officials. Migrant workers are typically recruited by payment of an advance on the condition that they will complete their period of work, and a meagre living allowance till the work ends. On the one hand, they have only a 'tenuous' relation with the villages they were forced to leave due to poverty. On the other, they merely manage to subsist in their place of work, where they suffer marginalisation by being deprived of their rights and entitlements as citizen-subjects of the state. 'All of this contributed to how migrants found themselves stranded without money, food or support, during the lockdown' (Naregal, 2021, p. 38). Echoing Butler, Nancy Ettlinger writes: 'Precarity is located in the microspaces of everyday life and is an enduring feature of the human condition. It is not limited to a specific context in which precarity is imposed by global events or macrostructures' (2007, p. 320). Precaritisation takes place wherever and whenever access to entitlements is unequally distributed, on the intersecting axes of class, gender, race, caste and disability. Kapri's story of the seven migrants who cycled their way from Ghaziabad to home can be best understood from this perspective.

1232 KMS, the documentary that Kapri made, opens with shots of migrants lining up for government dole, scrambling for food that even dogs do not eat, a kitchen with empty bins and oil-bottles, hordes of them walking back home, and, on reaching their destination, being locked up in a dirty hall without food or water. The opening sequence highlights their hopeless condition as the lockdown deprives them of livelihood, their wages withheld by contractors and their meagre savings spent, when survival becomes impossible in the city. It serves to place in perspective the journey of seven migrants from Ghaziabad to Saharsa district in Bihar, a distance of 1232 kilometres that they cover in seven days on bicycle and by hitching the occasional ride on trucks. Ritesh, Ashish, Ram Babu, Sandeep, Mukesh, Sonu and Krishna are part of a larger group of returning migrants that is stopped by the police at a checkpost in Brijghat, abused, beaten, and ordered to go back. They decide to break up into smaller groups, and this group of seven led by Ritesh crosses the Ganga and takes village roads and forest paths to avoid police barricades set up on main thoroughfares.

In documenting their journey, the film uses visual techniques associated with the plot of travel narratives—maps showing their progress each day; the towns, villages and natural landscapes they traverse; and the roadside dhabas where they stop for food and rest. But the context of their journey, a *reverse* migration not freely chosen but forced, and the many setbacks they suffer reframes the travel plot in underlining their precarity. Rhetorically, it recasts the travel as 'exodus', at one point comparing it with the exodus of refugees during the historic Partition of India and Pakistan. It is in this tension between the generic form of the travel documentary and the context of this particular travel that Kapri constructs the meaning of their return. This is complemented on the soundtrack by the two theme songs that play at key moments in the film, *Marenge to wahin jaa kar jahan par zindagi hai* ('If we are to die we will die there, where there is life') and *O re bidesia jaane pardesia ib ghar aija re* ('O migrant who has left for another land, come back home now'). While the first is composed specifically in the context of the lockdown, the second belongs to a traditional genre in Bhojpuri song and theatre culture, the *bidesiya*. During colonial rule the Bhojpuri people had been drafted, often forcibly, to work as indentured labour in sugar plantations in Caribbean colonies, and the origin of the *bidesiya* genre lies in this migration to other lands. Contemporary versions like the song in *1232 KMS* re-contextualise it to internal migration, thus linking the two. The genre, which is popular in Uttar Pradesh and Bihar, expresses the anguish of separation from the homeland, serving to resolve the emotional conflicts of the migrant and his family as well as restoring their sense of symbolic community. The term '*bidesiya*' refers to both the migrant (also called '*pardesiya*') and the genre in which his life is imagined. '*Bidesiyā* emerged as a cultural expression in which aesthetic experience from *viraha* or longing in separation transformed the essential negativity from a dire socio-economic condition to a new hope of rebuilding the community' (Prakash, 2016, p. 63). The two songs augment the film's theme of return migration with affect, imaginatively reconstructing it as subjective experience. This also points to another creative tension between the film's form and its technique of narration. It belongs to the genre of what Bill Nichols calls the 'observational mode', a non-intrusive representation of characters' lives. Except for the intertitles at the beginning and end of the documentary that are necessary to establish the theme, Kapri offers no interpretations of the migrants' experiences nor comments on them. Nor does he appear on screen except in one brief sequence. The film's representational mode is objective, the camera recording events as they unfold in reality with little intervention by the filmmaker. Nichols's account of the observational mode can be an apt description of Kapri's cinematography: 'We look on life as it is lived. Social actors engage with one another, ignoring the filmmakers. Often the characters are caught up in pressing demands or a crisis of their own. This requires their attention and draws it away from the presence of the filmmakers' (Nichols, 2001, p. 111). At the same time, Kapri weaves into this objective rendering a subjective story, captured in scenes of intimacy and the emotional tenor of the theme songs. We will see in a while the significance of this interweaving.

When large numbers of migrants started returning to their homes during the initial days of the lockdown, the media gave it wide publicity. As Naregal points out, 'there was frequent mention of how the COVID-19 pandemic had exposed the "invisibility" of migrant labour to Indian planners and policymakers' (2021, p. 38). This invisibility seems deeply ironical, since migrants constitute a substantial part of the workforce in the informal sector. The fact that the decision to impose lockdown was taken without anticipating its impact on them, points to their invisibility with regard to the political decision-makers. For the government the lockdown was primarily a public health decision, without considering the way the health of a population is linked to its conditions of existence as a whole. Moreover, as Faizi and Royal argue, the incidence of cases was not uniform across the country, with some states reporting zero or low prevalence, and a nationwide lockdown was not in order. The presumed public health benefits could have been achieved by imposing lockdown in high-prevalence states, providing welfare to the most vulnerable populations in these states, and sealing interstate borders. Faizi and Royal conclude that the lockdown, which forced large groups of migrant workers to move from highly affected cities to villages not yet affected, contradicted not only its own logic but equally the ethics of public health governance (2021, p. 41). Instances of police abusing and beating the migrants for violating lockdown orders were commonplace, as too was the stigma against returning migrants. In *The Long Journey Home*, Kapri recounts how the police treated the migrants: 'The policemen turned their attention to another batch of labourers. Ashish could hear their heart-rending screams as they were mercilessly beaten' (2021b, p. 17). They punished even those who tried to help the returning migrants. When Ritesh requests a fisherman to ferry them across the Ganga, he refuses because of the fear of police reprisal (p. 29). When Ram Babu requests a truck-driver to give them a lift, he initially refuses because the police would beat him, seize the truck and impose a penalty of twelve thousand rupees on him (p. 88). A dhaba-owner they approach refuses to help for the same reason. 'With the police threatening punitive action against dhabas that provided them food or shelter, the owners were understandably scared' (p. 62). Even cycle-repair shops are unwilling to come to their aid (p. 102). To add to their suffering at the hands of the police, they are also subjected to stigma by people they encounter. In a village that the group passes through they are not allowed to drink water from a hand pump because, as one of the villagers says, 'We don't know what kind of ailments you may be carrying with you. … It's a pandemic. There are places where people who have returned from Mumbai and Delhi are not being allowed to enter the village boundary' (p. 49).

Kapri's documentary and book confirm what social commentators have written about the migrant's precarity. Subjected to harassment by the police and administration, the migrants take it for granted as their fate, to (as Ritesh puts it) suffer 'hardships throughout life and then just die' (Kapri, 2021b, p. 182). They are often reduced to a subhuman condition, a dehumanisation expressed through animal imagery. When they are locked up in a filthy hall in Saharsa, Ram Babu protests:

'You will let us sleep here? During a pandemic? Are we stray animals? Cats or dogs? If something happens to us, who will be responsible?' (p. 166). Narrating their experience at Brijghat, Ashish says: 'there is no place for the poor. They are treated like caged animals' (Kapri, 2021a, 0:21:39). When an NGO at Shahabad distributes food, they 'pounced on the dinner like a pack of hungry wolves' (Kapri, 2021b, p. 83). At the Gopalganj camp 'the labourers were packed like cattle inside the bus' (Kapri, 2021b, p. 151). In the first twenty-one days of the lockdown, Kapri writes, the migrants realised 'that they were valued as a stinking pest in a city drain, and it didn't matter if they and their families were alive or dead' (p. xxvii). 'When you are not seen by others as a human being you probably start agreeing with them' (p. 83). In Sitapur when they are given food by the police and district officials, it seems like a 'stroke of luck' and not what they are entitled to as legitimate subjects of a biopolitical state. Kapri comments: 'This was the first time in more than 100 hours, since they had begun their journey from Ghaziabad, that I saw the seven men being treated as fellow human beings by those in authority' (p. 91). To paraphrase Judith Butler, what makes a human life grievable, and in this context who counts as 'human'? As she clarifies in the roundtable with Puar, the point is not about the distinction between human and animal, with animal life being subhuman, but to rethink the ways in which dominant norms of sociality exclude certain human lives as subhuman and therefore ungrievable (Butler, in Puar, 2012, pp. 173–174). Kapri's documentary ends with the words: 'Approximately 30 million migrants returned to their villages between 25th March and 15th June, mostly those from UP and Bihar. As per media reports, more than 350 died in different incidents during the lockdown. Government claimed in Parliament that there were no official statistics to confirm deaths.' Against this monumental apathy is the image of a woman grieving for her husband who died while they were returning home (Kapri, 2021a, 1:22:16). Ritesh and his friends learn that a migrant was killed in an accident near Panipat: 'Everyone was shaken by the story, but what could they have done?' (Kapri, 2021b, p. 90). The precariat is the one whose life is either unrepresentable as a human life, effaced and rendered invisible, or represented as less than human (Butler, 2004, pp. 146–147)—and, we may add, whose death cannot be mourned except by the precariat themselves.

Kapri's narrative seeks to counter the effacement and dehumanisation of the migrant in two ways. One involves his own growing awareness and acknowledgement of their humanity. This is a major theme of his book, a self-narrative that the documentary, because of its observational mode, precludes. The other is the off-screen conversations that Kapri has with the migrants in the film, drawing out their personal stories without intruding on their privacy. I have mentioned above the interweaving of the objective and subjective: it is in these conversations that the film constructs and represents their subjectivity. We learn that Ritesh lives with his father, mother, brother and wife Santul Devi and dreams of someday having his own house (Kapri, 2021a, 0:47:58); that Ashish is married with a daughter named Anjali Kumari and a son named Neelkamal, that they want him to bring chocolates, a bicycle and a small chair, and that he is a graduate but works as a migrant labourer due to poverty (0:53:40); that Ram Babu, who has studied till class two, left for Kolkata at the age of ten or twelve to work in a tea-stall to support his family, and that the lockdown has wiped out all his savings (1:07:20). We learn also how deeply Ashish loves his mother, who had supported his desire to study (1:06:06). There are emotional scenes of Ashish weeping as he reassures his mother (1:37:02) and Ram Babu breaking down as he talks to his family (1:11:46). *The Long Journey Home* opens with the effacement of the daily-wage workers who 'are our lifelines, but we know them only for the service they provide' (Kapri, 2021b, p. xxii). It ends with Kapri's recognition of the humanity of the migrants to whose ordeal he bears testimony: 'Not only these seven labourers, but all the labourers in the world were no more nameless, faceless humans for me' (p. 180). 'The face', writes Emmanuel Levinas in *Totality and Infinity*, 'opens the primordial discourse whose first word is obligation, which no "interiority" permits avoiding' (1979, p. 201). To *ef*-face the other is to avoid the responsibility that one bears to humanity; to see the face of the other is to be obliged to respond. *The Long Journey Home* ends with that Levinasian obligation to the other's humanity which, as Kapri states, 'brought about a sea change in my life and attitudes' (2021b, p. 180).

Let me now turn to the self-narrative that Kapri weaves into his account of the migrants' story. Making the documentary on their lives was not an easy choice: 'many times I wondered if I was trying to turn their tragedy into an opportunity' (Kapri, 2021b, p. xxx). This doubt lingers, and he often realises that 'it was my self-interest driving my enthusiasm' while 'Ritesh and his fellow labourers may have found it difficult even to secure food' (p. 38). He even doubts whether the documentary would change the migrants' condition: 'I didn't have the answer then, and neither do I have one now' (p. 72). Before the epidemic, like most middle-class people, he was barely aware of the lives of the working class: 'They really belonged to a different world' (p. 45). In documenting their stories his perspective changed, and the book is a record of that change. 'This book', he tells the reader, 'will not only take you on their journey but will also help you understand their lives from close quarters; *people invisible to the better off*, but who have played an important role in society, generation after generation, for centuries' (pp. xxviii–xix, italics added). It is one thing to observe as an outsider the suffering of people or to read about it in the news; it is entirely another thing when one participates directly in this suffering, as Kapri does in making the documentary. On each occasion when Ritesh and his companions suffer a setback, he suffers with them too. And every time their luck turns and they get unexpected help, he joins them in their elation. At no point in the narrative does this appear as a deliberate effort to empathise with them: on the contrary, he tries to keep himself outside the frame both physically and emotionally. In a sentence in the middle of the book, shortly after they have had a series of good turns, he reveals this, almost inadvertently, in his choice of pronouns: 'Whenever disappointment and dejection cast a dark shadow on *us*, *we* received help from angels from unexpected quarters' (p. 115, italics added). During the course of the journey he not only develops a tacit empathy with the migrants but also discovers the depths of their personal lives, the hardships they suffer and their strength to endure, their dreams of a better time: they are no longer a faceless and invisible populace but individuals with unique selves. It is in responding to and acknowledging each of them as a valuable human life that he grows ethically, so that the journey of the migrants becomes in a sense his own journey. Levinas's meaning in the line from *Totality and Infinity* I cited above is that, in responding to the face of the other we transcend our self-absorption ('interiority') and realise our own humanity simultaneously as we recognise the humanity of the other. Elsewhere, Levinas calls this the 'inter-human order': '*my* responsibility for the other person, without concern for reciprocity, in my call to help him gratuitously, in the asymmetry of the relation of *one* to the *other*' (1988, p. 165, italics in original). Narrating the story of the migrants becomes for him a lesson in Levinasian ethics, and an intuition of social justice that may remain an ideal but provokes us to ask what we have made of our society. The documentary may not change the conditions under which migrants live, but it will certainly make those conditions ethically unacceptable. As Kapri returns to his home in Noida, the people he had once taken for granted as 'different' are no longer '*faceless, nameless humans for me*' (2021b, p. 180, italics added).

When Ritesh and his companions enter the state of Bihar, they are jubilant. Ashish tells Kapri: 'I am now with my senior mother [Bihar] and tomorrow I will meet my junior mother [Saharsa]' (Kapri, 2021b, p. 137). But they are disillusioned by the treatment they receive at Gopalgunj and Saharsa: 'They had suffered unimaginable risks, pain and privations to reach this far. Sadly, the indifference and callous behaviour they had encountered in big cities ... was now being meted out to them in Bihar—their home state' (p. 152). Unable to bear their condition any longer, they collectively revolt against the authorities at Saharsa stadium. The passage is worth quoting in full:

> The government officers lost their nerve when they saw hundreds of labourers walking towards the stadium gates. There was pandemonium all around. The police was told to immediately shut the gates. But they knew closed gates were a poor bulwark against a determined tsunami of people. Some labourers started climbing the gates. Some were on the stadium wall. Ritesh and Ram Babu were leading the pack. For us, their new avatar was a revelation. They were leading the entire agitation. (p. 174)

How could people who had accepted their precarity as fate become so transformed? What they demand of the officials is humane treatment, the most basic entitlements of food and water that a state should provide to all its subjects. 'You people were being told since yesterday that we were hungry. We were hungry!' shouted Ram Babu. 'But you think we are idiots. We are animals. Let them die of hunger. Isn't it?' (p. 174). As Butler explains, it is at such moments that the precariats' agency, which conditions of precarity tend to suppress, becomes manifest: 'What, then, is the political significance of assembling as bodies, stopping traffic or claiming attention, or moving not as stray and separated individuals, but as a social movement of some kind?' These are people who can no longer been ignored or rendered passive, people who literally *perform* their agentiality in disrupting the social order that excludes them. It is ethically necessary, therefore, 'always to link precarity with forms of social and political agency where that is possible' (Butler, in Puar, 2012, p. 168).

Precariousness, even as it disrupts 'the bonds that support life,' (Butler, in Puar, 2012, p. 169), calls for the re-establishment of those bonds in sustaining interdependencies. What we see of Ritesh and Ram Babu is not a 'new avatar'—it had all along been there on the many occasions they stuck to each other and refused to abandon a straggler. The avatar seems 'new' because it had not been noticed earlier, just as migrants' lives had not. 'I had heard and read accounts', writes Kapri, 'of people sticking it out together through thick and thin, and the bond they developed; but here I was witnessing it first-hand in these seven men' (Kapri, 2021b, pp. 109–110). Perhaps the most illuminating instance of such bonding is an incident that is not there in the documentary but is recounted in the book. As they pass through a forest, Sonu's cycle breaks down and three strangers offer to help. They lead the migrants to a deserted area and set upon them, to steal their bicycles and cell phones. Eventually the migrants manage to overpower them, and they confess that they are not really burglars but poor workers out of a job who thought this could be a way of surviving till the lockdown was lifted (pp. 121–128). When Kapri asks them why they did not seek his assistance to call the police, Ram Babu replies: 'What would we achieve by lodging a complaint with the police? ... The police would have harassed an already harassed lot. What would we have gained out of it?' (p. 130). Instead, they give the would-be burglars some food out of their meagre stock. It is in such banal gestures of bonding that the precariat's agency is constituted, not just in the political struggle that Butler highlights. More precisely, the two—the precariat's bonding and struggle—are continuous in the continuity that links the everyday to the exceptional. On their way a number of people help the migrants in unexpected ways, without seeking return—a cycle mechanic, a dhaba owner, truck drivers, a police constable—in other words, all belonging to the migrants' own social class. Kapri comments: 'During the journey, Manav [the cinematographer] and I noticed something unique. The labourers—abandoned by the leaders, the administration, the police and the people living in the big cities where they had worked—were being embraced by those who were in many ways one with them' (p. 115). Precariousness is ultimately about forms of sociality: if social conditions fail to secure their lives, the precariat find security in mutual interdependencies. When it is the outcome of political structures, more volatile forms of protest stage not just an anger that is justified but 'the assertion in their very social organisation, of principles of equality in the midst of precarity' (Butler, in Puar, 2012, p. 168).

The migrants' jubilation on reaching their villages is, however, short-lived. Unable to find employment in the village, they go back to the city, some of them 'to live in the same rented house … where they had lived when the lockdown had been announced' (Kapri, 2021b, p. 187). They have emotional ties to the village, as the theme songs emphasise, but limited means of livelihood. The city provides no emotional support but there are opportunities for employment. The migrants' sense of precariousness is the outcome, therefore, of differences that are geographical as well as economic. Labour migration to urban areas is not a new phenomenon: what is new is its scale under economic liberalisation. From construction work to manufacturing, transportation, security services and waste disposal, cities require people willing to work for lower wages and under the informal terms decided by employers and their intermediaries. With farming becoming increasingly unviable due to high input costs and unpredictable climate, villages provide the bulk of migrant labour in the cities. Ram Babu was the first of the seven migrants to return to Delhi, because his crops had been washed away in floods and he had no money left to look after his large joint family (p. 186). Conditions of life in the city are difficult: they are forced to live in cheap tenements or overcrowded slums without basic amenities, and have no access to welfare or security. The plight of construction workers is the worst, as they have to live in makeshift tents at work sites that move from one location to another. The migrant worker in the urban landscape of neoliberal economy is the 'anomalous figure … who cannot be dispensed with and who cannot be settled' (Sammadar, 2016, p. 52). Precariousness becomes deeply entrenched, as Solange Muñoz writes, 'in the everyday life worlds of urban dwellers struggling to live in the city' (2018, p. 412). In her ethnographic study of female migrant workers in Buenos Aires, Argentina, she argues how their precarity is the outcome of spatial processes that limit opportunities for a more settled existence.

Kapri's film is essentially about spaces—its plot is about a journey, the camera tracks the space traversed by the migrants, and there is the recurrent image of the map. It charts the journey from Ghaziabad to Saharsa in two ways, graphically on the route map and experientially as they inch closer home, counting at every stop the distance covered and left to cover, the kilometers they lose by taking a wrong detour and the kilometers they gain on a truck ride. We have, in other words, two relations to space, one abstract and the other concrete.[6] In the cartographic representation, space is homogeneous and all places are the same; in the way the migrants experience them, places bear differential value. Brijghat, where they first experienced the violence of the police, signifies a trauma that haunts them every time they are stopped at a barricade, even the one at Sitapur where they are given food. As they cross the border into Bihar, they are jubilant (Kapri, 2021a, 1:00:32) because they have returned to their 'mother'—a metaphor that expresses an affective relation to space that maps cannot express. They are detained by the police at Gopalgunj, but Ram Babu is confident that they will slip through because it is home turf: 'If we could dodge the Uttar Pradesh police in Brijghat, then this is *our* state, *our* village; who has the power to stop *us*?' (Kapri, 2021b, p. 142, italics added). There are spaces of precarity and spaces of hope, places where they fear a setback but find support unexpectedly and places where they expect support but suffer setbacks. It is in this lived relation to space, as Lefebvre argues, that we become conscious of its meaning and value. Habitations are not mere physical enclosures within which we exist, they are formed in the practices by which we inhabit

[6] Lefebvre, as I have mentioned in chapter six, calls these 'representations of space' and 'representational spaces', the former referring to the knowledge of space as conceptualised in architectural and geographic discourse, and the latter to the symbolic meanings of particular spaces in lived experience (1991, p. 38–39). Lefebvre's cultural Marxist analysis of space as socially produced critiques objectivist assumptions about space that are ideologically grounded: 'instead of uncovering the social relationships … that are latent in spaces, instead of concentrating our attention on the production of space and the social relationships inherent to it', such assumptions treat 'space as space "in itself", as space as such. We come to think in terms of spatiality, and so to fetishize space in a way reminiscent of the old fetishism of commodities, where the trap lay in exchange, and the error was to consider "things" in isolation, as "things in themselves"' (p. 90).

them. Space is always produced as social space, through relations of economic production (the neoliberal city), social relations (the neighbourhood), relations of affect (the village), and the practices associated with them. To the extent that affective, social and economic relationships are embedded in space, we may say that precariousness is the outcome of the precariats' relation to the space they inhabit. In this sense the migrant worker and the refugee are one—*they live in a space they cannot belong to, they belong to a space they can no longer live in.*[7] The precarious life of the migrant and the refugee cannot be grasped without an understanding of the cultural geography of precarity, and its links with the political and affective economy of spaces.

In what way does Kapri's story add to our understanding of the COVID pandemic? Social commentators have written extensively on the precarity of the migrant worker that the lockdown made visible. Prakash and Borker examine it as 'pre-existing structural inequities' that can be studied empirically (2022, p. 40). Precarity, as they rightly point out, is a structure that can be objectively known. But *precariousness*, as the consciousness of one's existence, can only be known subjectively, by bearing witness to the precariat's suffering. This is what Kapri highlights in his multimedia testimony of the migrants' journey home. It is a meaning that the social scientist's data cannot capture, but the camera can show and the book illuminate in all its nuances.

9.5. Conclusion

Let me return to the question with which I began: what is it about our present moment that only stories can tell? For most if not all of us living now, more than a hundred years after Spanish flu, this is our first direct experience of an outbreak of such global magnitude. More than the disease itself, it is the fear of suffering, the sense of vulnerability and uncertainty of the future that most mark this moment, as the virus mutates and breaks out in wave

[7] I have discussed the refugee's enigmatic relation to space in Deep Haldar's *Blood Island* and Amitav Ghosh's *The Hungry Tide* in an essay on interdisciplinary humanities and refugee studies (Das, 2022, pp. 14–15).

after wave. Except for its scale, however, the COVID pandemic is in no way unique in this: all epidemics, to the people affected by them, are fearsome events. What makes COVID unique is the governmental response to it in terms of control measures: the restrictions it has imposed on the lives and livelihoods of people, on the everyday interactions and obligations that constitute social life, and on the freedom from state interference that forms the basis of a democratic polity. When this crisis is hopefully over, that is the lesson we will take from it: enforcement of quarantine on a massive scale and a global lockdown are not only ineffectual, but they also raise ethical questions that our common humanity impels us to ask. Life seems to be hemmed in by a state committed to the life and well-being of its subjects. The paradox is that this hemming in of life seems necessary for life to thrive—in Esposito's eloquent metaphor, the paradox of immunity. It is the negative protection of life, when a new pathogen with no known cure or vaccine makes positive protection impossible. What constitutes the meaning of our present moment, more than the effect of the virus on the body, is the subjective impact it has had on us: the pain of suffering in isolation, the disruption of everyday social interactions, the disorientation of time and space, the loss of livelihoods, the insecurity caused by lack of institutional support—in a word, the precariousness of our lives. The stories of COVID that we have discussed bring out this subjective dimension of pandemic experience in its various nuances. Broadly, this involves two forms of narration that are not distinct except as conceptual schemas—personal tragedy and collective calamity. I read *Infected 2030* and *The Times of India* blog posts as emphasising the former, and Kapri's story of the migrants from Saharsa as emphasising the latter.

Precariousness refers to the subjective sense of vulnerability and uncertainty that people experience in conditions of extreme distress. In the COVID pandemic, this manifested in two contexts. One was the acute shortage of beds in government hospitals, the high cost of private healthcare, and hoarding and black-marketing of oxygen and essential drugs, all caused by the failure of public health infrastructure combined with profiteering by the private sector. When these incidents were given wide publicity in the media, it created a panic that intensified uncertainty and vulnerability of pandemic times. The other context of precariousness was the sudden imposition of a national lockdown on grounds of epidemic control, without giving due consideration to its impact on the livelihoods of people engaged in small businesses or employed in the informal sector. Millions of migrants working in cities were forced to return to their villages due to loss of wages, inability to access the government's welfare schemes, and the depletion of whatever money they had saved. Since public transport was closed they had to travel long distances by foot or on bicycles, many of them dying on their way home due to accidents, hunger or exhaustion.

The precariousness of life in the COVID pandemic can be traced to a number of different factors, the most critical of which was the failure of institutional mechanisms to ensure safety and security. In the first context, which involved a crisis of healthcare, the government failed to anticipate the pandemic's impact on medical resources despite ample warning. The first confirmed case of COVID in India was reported from Kerala on 27 January 2020, by which date it had spread to fifteen countries with total infections amounting to 4593, most of which had been reported from China, and 80 deaths (Andrews et al., 2020, p. 490; WHO, 2020). In the second, an economic crisis, district and state authorities had made no arrangements for the safe return of migrants: on the contrary, as Kapri's film and book show, they were subjected to harassment by the police and administrative officials. It was not just the failure of the Indian state in particular, for the situation was more or less the same in most countries where the pandemic raged. It was not due, also, to the irresponsibility of particular individuals and their lack of sensitivity to the plight of sufferers. 'The notion of social and political precariousness', writes Turner, 'includes the inability of political institutions to protect and serve the interests of individuals' (2008, p. 247). As the responsibility of managing risks to life shifts from the social security net to individuals, their vulnerability to unforeseen crises increases: 'it is precisely individualized private existence which becomes more and more obviously and more emphatically dependent on situations and conditions that completely escape its reach' (Beck, 1992, p. 131).

The plight of the contributors to 'My COVID Story' and of the migrants whose journey Kapri documents is a clear instance of the institutional conditions of precarity. These narratives illuminate their suffering in the only way suffering can be expressed—as the sense of bewilderment and helplessness that people feel when distress exceeds their capacity to bear it. Narratives, as Paul Ricoeur says, enhance our understanding of reality by bringing out meanings that cannot be expressed directly. Some of these meanings augment that reality iconically, some affectively.

References

Agamben, G. (1998). *Homo Sacer: Sovereign power and bare life.* (D. Heller-Roazen, Trans.). Stanford University Press.

Agamben, G. (2020). The invention of an epidemic. *The European Journal of Psychoanalysis.* https://www.journal-psychoanalysis.eu/articles/coronavirus-and-philosophers

Althusser, L. (2001). Ideology and ideological state apparatuses: Notes towards an investigation. In B. Brewster (Trans.), *Lenin and philosophy and other essays* (pp. 85–126). Monthly Review Press.

Anderson, B. (2006). *Imagined communities: Reflections on the origin and spread of nationalism.* Rev. ed. Verso.

Andrews, M.A., Areekal B., Rajesh K.R., Krishnan J., Suryakala R., Krishnan B., Muraly C.P. & Santhosh, P.V. (2020). First confirmed case of COVID-19 infection in India: A case report. *Indian Journal of Medical Research, 151*, 490–492. https://www.ncbi.nlm.nih.gov/pmc/articles/PMC7530459/pdf/IJMR-151-490.pdf

Bakhtin, M. (1981). Forms of time and of the chronotope in the novel. In M. Holquist (Ed.), C. Emerson & M. Holquist (Trans.), *The dialogic imagination* (pp. 84–258). University of Texas Press.

Baraitser, L. (2017). *Enduring time.* Bloomsbury.

Beck, U. (1992). *Risk society: Towards a new modernity* (M. Ritter, Trans.). Sage.

Benvenuto, S. (2020). Welcome to seclusion. *The European Journal of Psychoanalysis.* https://www.journal-psychoanalysis.eu/articles/coronavirus-and-philosophers

Cabalquinto, E.C. & Ahlin, T. (2021). Care within or out of reach: Fantasies of care and connectivity in the time of the COVID-19 pandemic. In L. Manderson, N.J. Burke & A. Wahlberg (Eds.), *Viral loads: Anthropologies of urgency in the time of COVID-19* (pp. 344–361). University College London Press.

Camus, A. (1960). *The plague* (S. Gilbert, Trans.). Penguin.

Das, D.K. (2022). Disciplinarity or dissent? A paradigm for critical interdisciplinary studies in the humanities. *Guineis journal: An Interdisciplinary Journal of North East India Studies, 9*, 1–22.

Esposito, R. (2008). *Bios: Biopolitics and philosophy* (T. Campbell, Trans.). University of Minnesota Press.

Esposito, R. (2013). *Terms of the political: Community, immunity, biopolitics* (R.N. Welch, Trans.). Fordham University Press.

Esposito, R. (2020). Cured to the bitter end. *The European Journal of Psychoanalysis.* https://www.journal-psychoanalysis.eu/articles/coronavirus-and-philosophers

Ettlinger, N. (2007). Precarity unbound. *Alternatives: Global, local, political, 32*(3), 319–340.

Faizi, N. & Royal, A. (2021). Adherence to pandemic ethics during India's COVID-19 lockdown. *Economic and Political Weekly, 56*(29), 37–42.

Foucault, M. (1977). *Discipline and punish: The birth of the prison* (A. Sheridan, Trans.). Penguin.

Foucault, M. (2003). *'Society must be defended': Lectures at the College de France, 1975–76* (D. Macey, Trans.). Picador.

Geertz, C. (1973). *The interpretation of cultures: Selected essays.* Basic Books.

GlobalNews.(2020,March25).*Coronavirusoutbreak:Indianpolicepunish lockdown offenders with violence, push-ups* [Video]. YouTube. https://www.youtube.com/watch?v=VdDGUvLoJvI

Gray-Hawkins, M. (2018). Collective movements, digital activism, and protest movements: The effectiveness of social media concerning the organisation of large-scale political participation. *Geopolitics, History, and International relations,10*(2), 64–69.

Gupta, S. (2020, November 28). My COVID story: With all the precautions we were taking, I never imagined

I would catch COVID. *The Times of India*. https://timesofindia.indiatimes.com/life-style/health-fitness/health-news/my-covid-story-with-all-the-precautions-we-were-taking-i-never-imagined-i-would-catch-covid/articleshow/79443856.cms

Hindustan Times. (2020, March 24). *Covid-19 | Watch how Police is dealing with people stepping out amid lockdown* [Video]. YouTube. https://www.youtube.com/watch?v=5wNQ_V-Ol78

Jha, A. (2021, June 9). My COVID story: Anxiety and solitude were worse than getting COVID-19 symptoms. *The Times of India*. https://timesofindia.indiatimes.com/life-style/health-fitness/health-news/my-covid-story-i-was-in-denial-that-i-wasnt-affected-by-covid-virus/articleshow/83370544.cms

Kapri, V. (2021a). *1232 km: The long journey home*. HarperCollins.

Kapri, V. (2021b). *1232 KMS* [Film]. Bhagirathi Films.

Kidambi, P. (2007). *The making of an Indian metropolis: Colonial governance and public culture in Bombay, 1890–1920*. Ashgate.

Kumar, V. (2021, May 28). My COVID story: I was in an ICU with patients suffocating, screaming, trying to survive. *The Times of India*. https://timesofindia.indiatimes.com/life-style/health-fitness/health-news/my-covid-story-i-was-in-an-icu-with-patients-suffocating-screaming-trying-to-survive/articleshow/83034942.cms

Lefebvre, H. (1991). *The production of space* (D. Nicholson-Smith, Trans.). Blackwell.

Levinas, E. (1979). *Totality and infinity: An essay on exteriority* (A. Lingis, Trans.). Martinus Nijhoff Publishers.

Levinas, E. (1988). Useless Suffering (R. Cohen, Trans.). In R. Bernasconi & D. Wood (Eds.), *The Provocation of Levinas: Rethinking the Other* (pp. 156–167). Routledge.

Lejeune, P. (2014). Autobiography and new communication tools. In A. Poletti & J. Rak (Eds.), *Identity technologies: Constructing the self online* (pp. 247–258). University of Wisconsin Press.

Licoppe, C. (2004). 'Connected presence': the emergence of a new repertoire for managing social relationships in a changing communication technoscape. *Environment and planning D: Society and Space*, *22*, 135–156.

Meenu. (2021, June 17). My COVID story: I couldn't even see my father's body due to COVID protocols. *The Times of India*. https://

timesofindia.indiatimes.com/life-style/health-fitness/health-news/my-covid-story-i-couldnt-even-see-my-fathers-body-due-to-covid-protocols/articleshow/83604902.cms

Morrison, A. (2014). Facebook and coaxed affordances. In A. Poletti & J. Raks (Eds.), *Identity technologies: Constructing the self online* (pp. 112–131). University of Wisconsin Press.

Muñoz, S. (2018). Precarious city. *Cultural Geographies, 25*(3), 411–424.

Mussgnug, F. (2021). Afterword: Covid-19 or the vulnerability of the future. In A. Masschelein, F. Mussgnug & J. Rushworth (Eds.), *Mediating vulnerability: comparative approaches and questions of genre*. University College of London Press.

My COVID story. (2022, April 25). *The Times of India.* https://timesofindia.indiatimes.com/blogs/my-covid-story

Naregal, V. (2021). Labour 'invisibility' during COVID-19 times. *Economic and Political Weekly, 56*(34), 37–43.

Nichols, B. (2001). *Introduction to documentary.* Indiana University Press.

Panesar, S. (2022, January 11). My COVID story: We heard that nebulizer could be used when the oxygen dropped; it cannot be! *The Times of India.* https://timesofindia.indiatimes.com/life-style/health-fitness/health-news/my-covid-story-we-heard-that-nebuliser-could-be-used-when-the-oxygen-dropped-it-cannot-be/articleshow/88833986.cms

Pathak, N.M. (2020, December 21). My COVID story: Me and my family faced social stigma from the community. *The Times of India.* https://timesofindia.indiatimes.com/life-style/health-fitness/health-news/my-covid-story-me-and-my-family-faced-social-stigma-from-the-community/articleshow/79839023.cms

Pawar, P. (2021, June 22). My COVID story: I wish I could have arranged oxygen for my father. *The Times of India.* https://timesofindia.indiatimes.com/life-style/health-fitness/health-news/my-covid-story-i-wish-i-could-have-arranged-oxygen-for-my-father/articleshow/83746751.cms

Poletti, A. & Rak, J. (2014). The blog as experimental setting: an interview with Lauren Berlant. In A. Poletti & J. Rak (Eds.), *Identity technologies: Constructing the self online* (pp. 259–272). University of Wisconsin Press.

Prakash, A. & Borker, H. 2022. Pandemic precarity: Life, livelihood, and death in the time of the pandemic. *Economic and Political Weekly*, 57(5), 40–45.

Prakash, B. (2016). Performing 'Bidesiyā' in Bihar: Strategy for survival, strategies for performance. *Asian Theatre Journal*, *33*(1), 57–81.

Puar, J. (2012). Precarity talk: A virtual roundtable with Lauren Berlant, Judith Butler, Bojana Cvejić, Isabell Lorey, Jasbir Puar, & Ana Vujanović . *TDR*, *56*(4), 163–177.

Rabinow, P. (2005). Artificiality and enlightenment: From sociobiology to biosociality. In J.X. Inda (Ed.), *Anthropologies of modernity: Foucault, governmentality, and life politics* (pp. 181–193). Blackwell Publishing.

Raikar, V. (2021, September 4). My COVID story: I was responsible for infecting my wife and my in-laws. *The Times of India*. https://timesofindia.indiatimes.com/life-style/health-fitness/health-news/my-covid-story-i-was-responsible-for-infecting-my-wife-and-in-laws/articleshow/85833329.cms

Ramakumar, R. and Kanitkar, T. (2021). Impact of COVID-19 pandemic on the Indian economy, *Investigación Económica*, *80*(315), 3–32.

Ricoeur, P. (1984). *Time and narrative,* vol. 1 (K. McLaughlin & D. Pellauer, Trans.). University of Chicago Press.

Roper, C. (2020). Preface. *The Decameron project: 29 new stories from the pandemic. New York Times Magazine* (pp. ix–xi). Scribner.

Sammadar, R. (2016). Migrants and the neo-liberal city: An introduction. *Economic and Political Weekly*, *51*(26/27), 52–54.

Sashi. (2021, September 19). My COVID story: My dearest dad left us for his heaven abode, leaving a scar on our life. *The Times of India*. https://timesofindia.indiatimes.com/life-style/health-fitness/health-news/my-covid-story-my-dearest-dad-left-us-for-his-heaven-abode-leaving-a-scar-on-our-life-/articleshow/86342422.cms

Scarry, E. (1985). *The body in pain: The making and unmaking of the world*. Oxford University Press.

Sen Gupta, S. (2021, July 27) My COVID story: COVID took my dad and my ability to carry on. *The Times of India*. https://timesofindia.indiatimes.com/life-style/health-fitness/health-news/my-covid-story-covid-took-my-dad-and-my-ability-to-carry-on/articleshow/84785386.cms

Singh, C.P. (Director). (2021). *Infected 2030*. [Film].Eros Now.

Sorapure, M. (2015). Autobiography scholarship 2.0? Understanding new forms of online life writing. *Biography*, *38*(2), 267–272.

Sri Tatsat. (2021, September 2021). My COVID story: My father passed away just when we thought he was recovering. *The Times of India*. https://timesofindia.indiatimes.com/life-style/health-fitness/health-news/my-covid-story-my-father-passed-away-just-when-we-thought-he-was-recovering/articleshow/86396562.cms

The Decameron project: 29 new stories from the pandemic. (2020). *New York Times Magazine*. Scribner.

Tierney, T.F. (2013). Disentangling public space: Social media and internet activism. *Thresholds, 41*, 82–89.

Turner, B.S. (2008). *The body & society: Explorations in social theory*. 3rd ed. Sage.

Wald, P. (2008). *Contagious: Cultures, carriers, and the outbreak narrative*. Duke University Press.

World Health Organisation. (2020, January 28). Novel coronavirus (2019-nCOV): Situation report–8. https://www.who.int/docs/default-source/coronaviruse/situation-reports/20200128-sitrep-8-ncov-cleared.pdf

World Health Organisation India. (2020, March 22). Novel coronavirus disease (COVID-19): Situation update report–8. https://www.who.int/docs/default-source/wrindia/situation-report/india-situation-report-8.pdf?sfvrsn=cd671813_2

10

Why Narratives?

Whether we take fiction, autobiography, epidemiology or myth, epidemics have always been recounted as events, rarely described, though nothing actually precludes their description. Take, for instance a liturgical tale or *katha* of Sitala, the smallpox goddess, which begins: 'Once upon a time, pox (*chechak*) appeared on the oldest son of a king …' (Wadley, 1980, p. 38). Or take E. Selby Phipson's report on the outbreak of Spanish flu in Bombay in 1918: 'As early as June 10th, a group of 7 A Ward police sepoys, one of which was employed at the docks, were admitted to hospital suffering from a non-malarial fever …' (p. 442). The Spanish flu episode in Suryakant Tripathi's memoir *A Life Misspent* begins thus: 'There was a violent outbreak of influenza about this time' (2016, p. 53); while that in Ahmed Ali's novel *Twilight in Delhi* opens with: 'The summer of 1918 was more terrible than the summers of the previous years' (1940, p. 229). As these opening lines suggest, epidemic as an event that occurs in space and time calls to be recounted. What ties the social understanding of outbreak so closely to the form and content of narrative, so that its story must be told in a particular way, and not merely described? What are the essential elements of narrative that make this correlation a generic compulsion in representing an outbreak? In this concluding chapter I pose two questions that I have touched upon in many of the preceding chapters. Why is narrative the most appropriate genre for representing outbreak? Why does outbreak call for narration? To answer these questions, I draw on concepts in literary and social theory supported by illustrations from different narratives, some of which I have discussed in the previous chapters. I begin with the argument that emplotment in narratives is composed of three essential elements: event, time and space. In the next three sections I discuss each element to bring out its aptness for representing epidemic. In the final section, I try to explain why outbreaks need to be represented as narrative.

10.1. Emplotment and the Representation of Outbreak as Event

Narrative plots construct a sequence of events arranged in their causal and chronological order, with event being that which transcribes a change of state—as Aristotle said of dramatic plots, from good fortune to bad or its reverse, from bad fortune to good. This correlates with how we experience an epidemic outbreak: it emerges abruptly, disrupting the normalcy of everyday life, and over time it declines and normalcy is restored. In Charles Rosenberg's 'What is an Epidemic' this corresponds to act one and act three of his dramaturgical schema for epidemic outbreak. In its narrated form the outbreak unfolds as change from good fortune to bad, and is resolved in the change from bad fortune to good. In Aashique Abu's *Virus*, for instance, Nipah breaks out in Kozhikode, disrupting its normalcy as people fall ill and die, and fear prevails. The outbreak eventually subsides, and life returns to normal, though on a different level, as people come to terms with the loss of their loved ones. The Netflix web series *Kaala Paani* (2023) opens with a tourist festival in the Andamans in 2027, when a mysterious disease suddenly breaks out and the holiday mood is shattered. It is traced to a bacterium named LHF-27, which spreads when a construction company digs up a graveyard where it had remained confined for long. It is highly destructive, and those who are infected die horrible deaths. In the final episode the doctors manage to find a cure, while arrangements are made to evacuate the islands. *Kaala Paani* weaves a number of plots—outbreak, disease detection, environmental crisis, the destruction of the aboriginal peoples' habitat, and the tragic fate of a tourist who loses his wife and son to the disease, and kills, in an act of desperation, the very same woman who had saved his daughter's life. It ends by bringing about a resolution of sorts to each of these plot lines. At its minimal level, a narrative event comprises an initial state of equilibrium, a complication that disrupts it, and an unraveling that restores equilibrium though not the original state. Linguistically it comprises a stasis statement describing a condition, a process statement transcribing change, and a final stasis statement that describes a new condition. Plot is the sequential organisation of stasis and process statements, in which the former serves its spatio-temporal setting and the latter its causal order (Chatman, 1978, p. 32). 'The minimal complete plot', writes Tzvetan Todorov (1969), 'can be seen as the shift from one equilibrium to another.... The two moments of equilibrium, similar and different, are separated by a moment of imbalance, which is composed of a process of degeneration and a process of improvement' (p. 75).

Event, then, is the fundamental unit of narrative plot, serving to represent both states and their transformation. Seymour Chatman distinguishes between two types of events: those in which human agents act to transform their state, and those in which they are subjected to a new state. Events 'are either *acts* or *actions*, in which an existent is the agent of the event, or *happenings*, where the existent is the patient' (Chatman, 1978, p. 32, italics in original). A narrative in which actions predominate may imply an ideal agency that can act on the world and transform it, whereas that in which happenings predominate may imply passivity. Viewed on the basis of this distinction, the schema for epidemic plot is a two-part structure that opens with a series of happenings that express human vulnerability to disease, and ends with a series of agential acts to remedy the situation and restore health, with actual narratives either representing both parts or only the first. *Virus* and *Bombay Fever* are examples of the first kind, while the Spanish flu episode in *Twilight in Delhi* is an example of the second. This is because the episode does not stand on its own, but is framed by a main narrative line that is about the gradual disintegration of a community unable to cope with change. Disease outbreaks are contingent events that we neither directly bring about nor anticipate, we suffer them as they rage, till eventually our efforts at containment as well as herd immunity lead to their decline. Quite often, an outbreak subsides as mysteriously and abruptly as it came. Pranay Lal narrates how a strange new illness popularly called 'sweating sickness' suddenly appeared in England in 1483, continued to recur across Europe for almost a century before it went away as suddenly with a final outbreak in 1551. After a long dormancy it broke out again in 1718, and once again in 1906, claiming a large number of lives over the span of three centuries (2021, p. 123–127). *Virus* closes on the ambiguous note that the epidemic has ended but may break out again. The story that best illustrates this recurrent pattern of rise and fall is Albert Camus's *The Plague*, in which the disease that begins innocuously with the deaths of a few rats spreads rapidly to claim human lives and eventually declines, but only to reappear later in another time or place. '[R] eviewing the last hundred years of epidemic outbreaks', writes medical historian Mark Honigsbaum, 'the only thing that *is* certain is that there will be new plagues and new pandemics. It is not a question of if, but when. Camus was right. Pestilences may be unpredictable, but they *will* recur' (2020, p. 283, italics in original). The COVID-19 pandemic is the latest in this cycle of historical recurrence and return.

Narratologists and Russian formalists distinguish between two levels of narrative: an abstract level of discrete events that constitutes the *story*, and a concrete level of the events organised into a whole that constitutes the *plot*. 'Plot is distinct from story. Both include the same events, but in the plot the events *are arranged* and connected according to the orderly sequence in which they were presented in the work' (Tomashevsky, 1965, p. 67, italics in original). Gerard Genette distinguishes between the signified content (which corresponds to story) and the signifying discourse (which corresponds to plot): 'I propose … to use the word *story* for the signified or narrative content [and] to use the word *narrative* for the signifier, statement, discourse or narrative text itself' (Genette, 1980, p. 27, italics in original). In other words, story comprises of the events in their singularity while narrative is their organisation into a coherent and unified plot.

This distinction is important in understanding how separate events are configured into a unified whole, investing it with significances that are not inherent in the events themselves. In narratives of epidemic the factors that underlie this configuration are temporality and spatiality, since epidemics are by definition a series of connected events that unfold in time and space. To explain how the temporal organisation of events happens in a narrative, let me draw on arguments from Paul Ricoeur's *Time and Narrative*, volume one, some of which I have already discussed.

10.2. Emplotment and the Representation of Time

It has often been observed that structuralist and formalist theories of narrative pay less attention to the temporal dimension of plot than to patterns and techniques. This observation may at first seem inaccurate, for the ratio of story-time to plot-time figures as an important element of analysis in these theories. For instance, Viktor Shklovsky, a Russian Formalist, points out how in *Tristram Shandy* the 'action is continually interrupted; the author repeatedly goes backward or leaps forward .... Such digressions are unrelated to the basic narrative' (1965b, p. 27). That is, they are part of plot-time and not the time of the story, which is what he refers to as 'basic narrative'. Genette devotes three of the five main chapters of *Narrative Discourse* to the relation between story-time and the time needed to read the narrative in '*crossing* or *traversing* it, like a road or a field' (Genette, 1980, p. 34, italics in original). He identifies three classes on which this relation is determined: order, duration and frequency. The first refers to the 'connections between the temporal *order* of succession of the events in the story and the pseudo-temporal order of their arrangement in the narrative' (p. 35, italics in original). It includes dissonances like flashbacks and flashforwards, retrospective and prospective narration. The second refers to the contrast between the duration of an event in the story 'measured in seconds, minutes, hours, days, months and years' and the space devoted to it in the narrative text 'measured in lines and in pages' (pp. 87–88). Plot-time here is measured in units of space and not time, which is why Genette calls it 'pseudo-temporal'. The third refers to the ratio of the number of times an event occurs in the story and the number of times it is represented in the text: 'Schematically, we can say that a narrative, whatever it is, may tell once what happened once, *n* times what happened *n* times, *n* times what happened once, once what happened *n* times' (p. 114). Accounts of the temporal structure of narratives in Chatman (1978, pp. 63–84) and in Shlomith Rimmon-Kenan (2002, pp. 43–58) derive from and elaborate Genette's classification.

What Shklovsky, Genette, Chatman and Rimmon-Kenan underemphasise, therefore, is not time itself but *the human perception of time*, which includes but is more than just the measurement of time. It is this perception which Paul Ricoeur considers central to narrative emplotment. This is important in understanding how epidemic narratives construct temporality, in representing epidemics as human phenomena. Narratology 'in its ambition to dechronologize narrative' reduces the representation of time to 'achronic systemic relations' like those between story and plot, neglecting the way we experience temporality as significant human time (Ricoeur 1984, p. 85).[1]

In chapter five we saw how Ricoeur argues that the human experience of time is not that of a linear series of moments divided into past, present and future, as in calendar or clock, but as a 'three-fold present' comprising a structure of memory, attention and expectation. It is in terms of this structure that we become conscious of the phenomena around us. In a narrative

[1] The narratological approach to the representation of space is marked also by what we may call a *despatialisation*. Ruth Ronen, for instance, begins 'Space in Fiction' with the assumption that 'space is a *semantic construct* built with linguistic structures employed by the literary text' (1986, p. 421, italics in original). It is produced in structured relationships between textual devices that indicate space, like frames and settings, and elements of the plot like characters, objects and events. Its realism lies not in the way it draws on our understanding of real places, but on that of stereotypical situations that she calls 'Frame' (p. 432). The Frame itself is a textual construct that bears no relation to the real world and 'does not emerge from an extra-textual information-structure' (p. 433). Literary space is ruled by generic conventions of what constitutes an appropriate place for an action or event, and is relatively independent of our consciousness of the world we inhabit.

plot, actions and happenings draw on this consciousness and reinforce it: 'What counts here is the way in which everyday praxis orders the present of the future, the present of the past, and the present of the present in terms of one another. *For it is this practical articulation that constitutes the most elementary inductor of narrative*' (Ricoeur, 1984, p. 60, italics added). Our consciousness of time comes from our embodied existence of being-in-the-world, in relation to which the mathematical representation of time is an abstraction. In representing moments as they pass, narrative rearticulates this abstract conception into a lived reality that is marked not by hours, days, months or years, the units of horological time, but by memory and anticipation of the time of life and death, of generations that have passed and those yet to come, the acceleration of active time and retardation of idle time, the circadian coordination between the body's time and the time of diurnal and seasonal cycles. In *Outline of a Theory of Practice* Pierre Bourdieu notes how the ethnographer's account of time differs from that of the native informant. In constructing an abstract calendar of the time and duration of ritual festivities, the ethnographer 'substitutes a linear, homogeneous, continuous time for practical time, which is made up of incommensurable islands of duration, each with its own rhythm, the time that flies by or drags, depending on what one is *doing*' (Bourdieu, 1977, p. 105, italics in original). It is this 'practical' articulation of time that narrative seeks to represent in organising its events into a meaningful whole. Ricoeur describes this process of articulation as an interaction of the 'episodic' and 'configurational' dimensions of plot. The first relates to the episodes presented as discrete moments of past, present and future, which serve a purely referential function with regard to chronology. The second relates to the causal connections that make of these moments an integrated complex of actions and happenings directed towards a logical end. The configurational dimension of narrative, thus, reconstitutes its episodes into a teleological whole that approximates how we perceive time in phenomenological experience through memory, attention and expectation (Ricoeur, 1984, pp. 67–68).

In chapter five I discussed, as examples of the narrative representation of time, Phipson's report on the outbreak of Spanish flu in Bombay and the Spanish flu episode in *A Life Misspent*. Phipson's report configures the temporality of the outbreak in terms of a mathematical division of time typical of the epidemiological narrative, as it tracks the spread of disease from one day to the next. It is the equivalent of Bourdieu's ethnographer drawing up a festive calendar from the account given by informants. Nirala's memoir configures time in terms of his memory of loss and bereavement, in which the exact times and dates of death recede out of focus and what stands out is the way his family disappears 'in the blink of an eye', as one death is followed by another seemingly without break. It also configures the present in continuity with past and future, looking forward to an eternity as he sits ruminating on the mound of sadhus. Another example of how time is configured in the process of emplotment is the autobiography of Damodar Hari Chapekar. The opening of the narrative anticipates its end, the assassination of Rand, as an act of patriotism that deserves to be told and acclaimed. This is why he writes a long and apparently superfluous preface that explains why one should write an autobiography, what kind of life deserves to be recorded in writing, and what must be its objective. On the one hand he is deeply conscious that, as an uneducated man lacking in any distinction, it may seem presumptuous to write about his life. His conscience, on the other hand, directs him to the task so that others may know why he sacrificed his life for his country and faith, and then judge whether it was right or wrong (Chapekar, n.d., pp. 956–958). The rest of the autobiography is a chronology of selected incidents in his life from his birth to just before his arrest and trial, attributing to each a significance that is linked to his assassination of Rand. Chapekar tells us how he had been inspired by heroic deeds of Nana Saheb Dhondu Pant, the second peshwa of the Maratha empire who fought the British in the Revolt of 1857, and Vasudev Balwant Phadke, a revolutionary who fought for India's independence. He had also been inspired by the *kirtans* that his father, an itinerant singer performed. These were the two major influences that led him to fight for land and faith. Nothing is left out, not even the most trivial of incidents, in his account of why he killed Rand, as he imbues in each a significance he was not conscious of when it occurred, and which he retrospectively adds. The configuring of the past in terms of a meaning and value that he attaches to his present 'sacrifice' and the anticipation of future glory, transforms what appears to be a chronology of discrete events and happenings into a temporal whole that makes the killing of Rand intelligible as well as his act of writing the autobiography legitimate: 'It is probable, therefore, that like the victim of sacrificial rites, I shall be consumed in the furnace of fire into which I am going to plunge. Perhaps God in His mercy may extricate me from all difficulties and vouchsafe fame to me, as that Supreme Soul rescued Pralhad[2] from burning fire by cooling its flames and made him renowned' (p. 958). The plot of the autobiography, thus, reveals how narratives organise time in subordinating chronology to causality so as to give what would otherwise be only discrete events of a chronicle. It is in this organisation of time as an articulation of past, present and future that it is perceived in human consciousness: '*time becomes human to the extent that it is articulated through a narrative mode, and narrative attains its full meaning when it becomes a condition of temporal existence*' (Ricoeur, 1984, p. 54, italics in original).

10.3. Emplotment, Chronotope and the Representation of Space

Space is as crucial to narrative emplotment as time, for it is in space, too, that events (as we say) take *place*. This is especially so in the case of epidemics, which are measured in terms of

[2] Prahlad's father Hiranyakashyapa was a *daitya* king who vanquished the gods and ruled the world. He demanded that his subjects worship him instead of the gods. Prahlad, however, was a firm devotee of Vishnu, and refused to worship Hiranyakashyapa. Enraged, his father tried various means to kill him. In one story Hiranyakashyapa's sister Holika, who could not be burned by fire, took Prahlad in her lap and sat on a pyre so that he would burn to death. But Vishnu saved his devotee, took away Holika's magic power and she, herself, was destroyed.

timelines of spread. In chapter five we saw how narratives of Spanish flu organise temporal and spatial elements in different ways. A concept that is useful in understanding this organisation is 'chronotope', by which Bakhtin explains the way the two are fused in human consciousness and how narratives configure it as both a formal device and a generic type. Epidemic narratives as a genre represent the time and space of outbreak in the figure of what I have called the chronotope of contagion. Within the genre different narratives construct primarily two forms of this chronotope, one representing it objectively, from the point of view of the neutral observer, in terms of chronological time and cartographic space, while the other represents it as the subjective perceptions of those who experience the outbreak. We saw how these two forms differentially structure the unfolding of epidemic events in Phipson's epidemiological report on the outbreak of Spanish flu in Bombay and in Nirala's memoir. As a further example, let us look at two texts that are about the outbreak of COVID and the global lockdown in 2020.

On 20 March 2020 Global News, the current affairs division of the Canadian Global Television Network telecast a documentary titled *Coronavirus outbreak: A timeline of how COVID-19 spread around the world*. It covers the period from 31 December 2019 to 20 March 2020, and represents the spatiotemporal unfolding of events in a montage of shots indicating locations and dates of spread, complemented by a metronomic score on the soundtrack. It tracks the journey of the virus from its source in Wuhan (31 December) to Thailand (13 January), Japan (16 January), South Korea (20 January), the US (21 January), France (24 January), Canada, Australia and Malaysia (25 January), Germany (27 January), Phillipines (2 February), Egypt and Iran (14 February), Lebanon, Morocco, the Democratic Republic of Congo, Panama, Mongolia (10 March), to Turkey, Ivory Coast, Honduras and Bolivia (11 March). There are shots of empty city streets, hospital wards and intensive care units, the WHO headquarters at Geneva, national borders closed to traffic, airports with planes standing idle, a ship quarantined in the dock—in brief, spaces associated in different ways with the pandemic and the lockdown that followed (Global News, 2020).The video constructs its chronotope in terms of objective timeline and geography of spread, a formal characteristic of biomedical narratives of outbreak.

In clear contrast to this is the representation of time-space in a YouTube video *Corona Pandemic Lockdown Effect on Wild Animals*, uploaded on 20 April by the Indian vlogger Verily Vagabonding. It opens with an aerial shot of a rainforest, followed by shots of a cityscape with a wooded hill in the foreground, flowing water, the earth seen from space, dolphins swimming in the sea and a herd of deer walking down an urban street. These are captioned: 'One of the positives within all this negativity of the pandemic is … its giving our mother nature a break … air is getting cleaner …water sources are getting cleaner … ozone is healing … earth is healing … wild animals are enjoying their freedom too' (Verily Vagabonding, 2020, 0:00–0:15). This is followed by still shots of wild animals venturing into human spaces across the globe—a puma in Santiago, a peacock in Mumbai, elephants in Thailand, lions sleeping on a road in South Africa, a neelgai in Delhi, a rhino in Nepal, deer in Japan, mountain goats in Wales, geese strutting across an empty airport tarmac. The shots are put together from various media sent by contributors from different locations, and they show how during the lockdown the distinction between human spaces and spaces of animals became blurred, in a symbolic renewal of nature within urban habitations. In bringing out the 'positive' side of the outbreak, the video juxtaposes the idea of a lockdown with that of 'freedom', and 'pandemic' with that of 'healing'. It presents this 'positivity' not in the quantitative terms of lower pollution levels and enhancement of air and water quality, as many scientific studies at the time did, but as *healing*, a word that carries symbolic overtones in the context of a devastating outbreak. Healing, as I have explained in chapter one, restores well-being as a whole—physical, emotional and spiritual—and these are the significances that the video attributes to the lockdown in its positive aspect. The space it represents is not an 'environment' but a symbol of 'mother nature', suggesting a primordial relation to it that we broke when we made it an object of exploitation—for which the lockdown becomes, as it were, a sign of expiation. The events it depicts refer to the present, but they also allude to a primordial time in which the order of nature and not human beings ruled. It evokes, in other words, a symbolic spatio-temporality that reverses the actual history of human interventions in nature. *Corona Pandemic Lockdown Effect on Wild Animals*, thus, constructs a mythic chronotope that contrasts with that of the Global News video. It represents time-space, not realistically as in biomedical narratives, but figuratively as in cultural narratives of outbreak.

Our consciousness of space, as Ricouer says of time, is not that of a Euclidean cartography in which all spaces are equivalent and homogeneous, differentiated only by gridlines. In lived reality space is a heterogeneity of places that bear various meanings and affective valences in the way we inhabit and relate to them. We owe this insight to Lefebvre's account of how space is not a given, but a product of our relation to it. In extending the Marxist theory of production from economy to culture, and in extending it further from relations of production to the space of production, Lefebvre may very well be said to have inaugurated what Foucault called the 'epoch' of space (Foucault, 1986, p. 23). Space is produced materially by clearing sites for a factory or a city, building roads, rails and air lanes that traverse different spaces. But it is also produced discursively when we represent it in maps and blueprints, in geometry, in landscape painting, and in constructing the scapes of contagion. Lefebvre, as we have seen, called this the 'representation of space', to distinguish it from the way we experience, comprehend and value different spaces as lived reality, or 'representational space'. Space becomes representational when it is no longer an object of reflection but 'directly *lived* through its associated images and symbols' (Lefebvre, 1991, p. 39, italics in original). When Phipson tracks the passage of a microbe from the dockyards of Bombay to the Hong Kong and Shanghai Bank, the Government Telegraph

Department and the Mint, he produces a representation of space; but when Nirala tracks the 'passage' of an emotional experience from his village to Dalmau and thence to the mound of sadhus on the bank of Ganga, he produces representational spaces imbued with symbolism and affect. 'Representational space is alive: it speaks. It has an affective kernel or centre: Ego, bed, bedroom, dwelling, house; or: square, church, graveyard. It embraces the loci of passion, of action and of lived situations, and thus immediately implies time' (p. 42). Epidemic outbreaks, to repeat a point that has already been made, are objective processes that have subjective effects on those they affect. In configuring spaces as locations of pathogenicity as well as of human suffering, narratives of outbreak emplot space as both representation and representational. Thus, emplotment takes on the function of what Lefebvre calls 'spatial practice', or the activity through which we produce space to make it signify meanings both material and figurative. Spatial practice demarcates spaces as homogenised in objective representation or as heterogenised in subjective experience, and narrative emplotment takes this as its model. Epidemiological accounts imagine all spaces as the same, differentiating—as done by Snow in his map of Soho, by Phipson in mapping the Spanish flu outbreak, and by the Global News video in tracking the path of coronavirus—only between those places where people died and those where they were spared. Cultural accounts code every space as different: a place of death and suffering, a place of contemplation or of worship, places like the forest and hospital in *Virus* that both renew life and transmits death, or a space of confinement when one looks out of the window, as Shivika does in *Infected 2030*, onto wide open spaces of freedom. Such spaces are sites of singularity in the way we inhabit and imbue them with meaning, what Foucault, in a figure that corresponds closely to Lefebvre's representational space, calls 'heterotopias': 'we do not live in a kind of void, inside of which we could place individuals and things. We do not live inside a void that could be colored with different shades of light, we live inside a set of relations that delineates sites which are irreducible to one another and absolutely not superimposable on one another' (1986, p. 23).

10.4. Why *Narratives*?

The narrative mode, as we have seen, is the most suited for representing outbreaks, because of the correspondence between narrative emplotment and epidemic unfolding, in the way epidemics are understood to happen. At the centre of this is the moment of outbreak as turning point in the plot, and as rupture of everyday life in phenomenological experience. It is perceived as rupture primarily for three reasons: the scale on which it happens, the devastation that it causes, and, most importantly, its sheer unpredictability and randomness. Epidemic outbreaks may not objectively be either unpredictable or random: considered as a single event with a singular cause, a microbe, they appear to be so. Medicine has characteristically assumed that diseases are discrete and definable events that can be identified once the cause is known. This assumption has led to the development of nosologies or classificatory systems that help in identifying specific disease conditions, their causes, symptoms, diagnosis and treatment. Recent thinking in public health medicine, however, questions this approach: disease is not a single event but a process involving the interaction of several events in a given period of time and in a specific location. It is the outcome of synergic relations between biological factors and social conditions. Diseases, write Merill Singer and Scott Clair, 'do not exist in a social vacuum nor solely within the bodies of those they inflict', and are therefore not reducible to biology. 'Ultimately, social factors, like poverty, stigmatization, racism, sexism, ostracism, and structural violence may be of far greater importance than the nature of the pathogens or the bodily systems they infect' (2003, p. 428). On this view, the scale of an epidemic outbreak, its unpredictability and randomness are the outcome of long-term processes that seem random because they are not readily apparent, but are actually predictable. To take an example, the extreme virulence of Spanish flu in British

India in 1918 was in part caused by the widespread poverty, famine and the panic that resulted from death and food scarcity, as well as colonialism and the war. Instead of the irruption of a singular epidemic, its origin lay in a 'syndemic' process that could well have been anticipated and mitigated. While the newspaper reports mentioned these factors, they did not make the necessary connections that would recast discrete events as a continuous process. Syndemic theory, however, overlooks an important aspect of outbreaks: the fact that they are 'more often than not, *experienced* by their victims as ruptures in social, political and economic life; that they are experienced not as long-term processes but as short-term catastrophic events, which are often attributed not to a multiplicity of causes, but to a single or unilateral cause' (Lynteris, 2014, p. 25, italics added).

It is in such experience that the event-character of epidemic outbreak lies, and social understanding frames it as such. The course of an outbreak, likewise, is understood as a series of events unified in consciousness as a whole: a rapid succession of deaths leading to a peak, followed by a slow decline. As Rosenberg explains, this sequence corresponds closely to the plot of a novel—rising action, climax and falling action or denouement. If narrative is the mode of representation most suited for outbreaks, it is because of this correspondence; and Rosenberg implies this by taking the example of *The Plague* to explain what an epidemic is. At the same time, a question arises: *why* is the unfolding of an outbreak like the unfolding of a narrative plot? Is it something intrinsic to the nature of an outbreak? The answer lies in culture as a signifying system. Culture provides the paradigmatic plot-forms—what Hayden White calls 'archetypal story-forms' (1978, p. 58)—that guide our understanding of the events we experience as well as those that we imagine and represent, it is what makes these events sensible to us. It also provides the spatial and temporal cues or the chronotopic forms that link events to their unfolding, both in real epidemic outbreaks and in the way they come to be imagined. Narrative is, therefore, the most appropriate genre for representing outbreaks, not because there is some intrinsic link between the two, but because of the way cultural understanding prefigures the event-ness of an event.

Let me turn to the other question now: why do epidemics seem to *call forth* narrative? What is it in our experience of epidemic that makes it imperative to narrate them? In an essay on the social psychology of narration, Jerome Bruner explains its function in knowledge. He begins with the question, how do we come to know reality? We know it, first, empirically, through observation; next, we know it rationally, by reflecting on what we observe; and third, we know it narratively, by *telling* stories in a double sense—the act of telling in story-form as well as stories that are 'telling', evidential and unquestionable. These, according to Bruner, constitute the three predominant ways in which we process knowledge of reality, both individually and collectively. Of these three, the last consists of a conventional way of knowing that is based neither on observation nor reason, and yet is a compelling account of reality. The first two—empiricism and rationalism—are effective ways of explaining the causes of natural phenomena, but less so in explicating 'the rich and messy domain of human interaction'. We 'organise our experience and our memory of *human happenings* mainly in the form of narrative—stories, excuses, myths, reasons for doing and not doing, and so on' (Bruner, 1991, p. 4, italics added). Unlike observation and reflection that aim to know the truth through provable facts or laws, stories do not aspire for verifiability but verisimilitude—the truth they express is ruled by convention rather than demonstration, and narrative necessity rather than the necessity of a law. Now, the important point is that these three modes of cognition—observing, reasoning and narrating—are not mutually exclusive, but are interlinked and simultaneous. In knowing and representing worldly phenomena, we use all three at the same time, though any specific form of knowledge and representation may privilege or accord priority to some over the others. Thus, in narratives, reason and observation do not become redundant but are shaped by the privileged function of telling a plausible story. As a corollary, in scientific reports narration does not disappear altogether, but continues to function with priority given to reason and observation. Anyone who has written a lab report will agree: a good lab report records not only what one sees and how one connects the things seen, but also the sequence of acts by which seeing and connecting happen in the first place. We may not be aware of its narrativity, but this has more to do with the way scientific discourse suppresses the 'I' that observes and reasons. Take, for example, Phipson's report on the outbreak of Spanish flu in Bombay: 'The earliest cases among the civil population appear to have occurred in the Indian ranks of the City Police…' To whom does it 'appear' to be so? By using the detached third-person point of view, Phipson, like a good scientific reporter, erases his presence on the scene, or that of someone else who reported it to him.

If we accept this argument, then epidemiological reports on outbreak are narratives, just as novels, memoirs and films are. Let me now move to the next point. What distinguishes an epidemiological account from a literary (or cinematic) one lies in the perspective from which it is narrated, which is objective in the former and subjective in the latter This is another way of saying that the narrator of an epidemiological report assumes a detached third-person position in relation to the outbreak, while that in a literary/cinematic account assumes an engaged first-person position. This is, however, merely a schema: actual narratives may alternate between the two modes. Thus, Phipson and White while reporting on the Spanish flu as medical officers also feel compelled to express their subjective response to the distressing scenes they witness, in the 'messy domain of human interaction'. As a corollary, in *Virus* the camera-eye (which stands for the 'I' of the narrator) continually shifts between objective and subjective framing, the latter underlined in the sound track. In Kapri's *1232 KMS*, which uses the objective technique of *camera verité*, there are close-ups of the migrants in their moments of hope and despair, sorrow and jubilation.

So, the question is: what is it about outbreak that calls for an explanation, either objective or subjective, or alternating between the two? An outbreak is experienced as a calamitous event that strikes abruptly and randomly, an 'intractable reality' in Rosenberg's phrase (1989, p. 7). As such, it demands explanation: why does disease break out suddenly in one place while sparing those next to it, why does it strike one person and not another just as equally vulnerable? It is at such times that we seek explanations that have conventionally existed in culture, explanations that may be realistic or mythic, cognitive or affective. Narrative constitutes a mode of thinking about reality that concerns particular events and actions, the beliefs and theories that motivate people to act, and the particular interpretations they put on what happens to them. These interpretations are conventional in the sense that they tend to reiterate earlier interpretations stored in cultural memory, which is why anthropologists increasingly turn, not to other anthropologists who can hypothesise about a particular situation, but to 'indigenous participants immersed in the culture's own processes for negotiating meaning' (Bruner, 1991, p. 19). Like all human calamity, epidemics call for explanations of why they happen and how they can be mitigated which draw on the cultural knowledge of what had worked best in the past, whether it is based on a scientific, cosmological or affective orientation of the world. Stories that mobilise these orientations—what Bruner calls 'narrative accruals'—both draw on the lived reality of epidemics and in turn construct or frame it. It is by way of these accruals that '"life" comes to imitate "art" and vice versa' (p. 21).

10.5. Coda: 'Rebati' and *Kocharethi*

Let me end with two examples of cultural narratives of smallpox and cholera, diseases that broke out in much higher frequency and accounted for many more deaths totally than the ones I have discussed. The outbreaks were severe enough to have deities assigned to them, who provided the cosmological frames for outbreaks of new diseases like plague, HIV/AIDS and COVID-19. Sitala and Mariamma were worshipped in different parts of India, the former in the east, north and west and the latter in the south, as goddesses of smallpox. The worship of a cholera goddess, known to Hindus as Ola Chandi and to Muslims as Ola Bibi, was prominent in the east, primarily Bengal. Vaccination, improved sanitation and the use of antibacterial therapy in the twentieth century led to a decrease in incidence of the two diseases, though sporadic outbreaks have occurred since. Smallpox was eradicated in the late 1970s, after the outbreak in Bihar, Uttar Pradesh and West Bengal. The last recorded case occurred in 1975. Cholera epidemics are few, though the endemic form of the disease is not infrequent. Insofar as narratives are concerned, I was not able to find enough material available in English or English translation to constitute a chapter, and it is this limitation that I seek to redress here, if briefly, in a discussion of an Odia short story by Fakir Mohan Senapati and a chapter in the Malayalam novel *Kocharethi* by Narayan.

Senapati's 'Rebati', published in 1898, is a criticism of a patriarchal norm prevalent in nineteenth-century Odisha that denied women access to education. Rebati, the eponymous character, has a great desire to study, which her father Shyambandhu encourages but her grandmother disapproves of. Shyambandhu Mohanty works as the accountant of a local zamindar, and is reasonably well off. The zamindar has given him a rent-free plot of land to cultivate, and the harvest is enough for his small family comprising his wife, daughter and aged mother. Once, the deputy inspector of schools had visited their village, Patapur, and Shyambandhu had petitioned him on behalf of the village to establish a school there. The school soon opens with a single teacher, Basudev, who is of the same caste as Shyambandhu and a man of high personal integrity. He becomes a frequent guest in the Mohanty household, and during one of his visits he informs Shyambandhu of a girls' school in Cuttack. Hearing this, Rebati is filled with a desire to study, and Basudev begins her education at home. This was a practice quite common at the time for those girls who wished to study but could not, for various reasons, attend school. Shyambandhu's plan is to send Rebati to Cuttack after she has learnt the basics. His wife agrees to the plan, but his more conservative mother is opposed to it. When Rebati shows her the primer that Basudev had given her, she gets annoyed and shouts, 'Take that silly thing away from me' (Senapati, 2019, p. 207). Gradually, as Basudev's intimacy with the family grows, Shyambandhu thinks of getting his daughter married to him. At this point, complication emerges in the form of an outbreak of cholera. Shyambandhu and his wife are taken ill and die; the zamindar takes back the rent-free land he had given and the farmhands leave; the buffaloes are sold; and finally the zamindar confiscates the cows, on the pretext that Shyambandhu had not deposited the revenue he collected from tenants. Rebati and her grandmother are suddenly reduced to poverty, and are forced to pawn household goods to buy food. Others in the village are indifferent to their plight, and only Basudev visits them every day to provide support. The grandmother takes her frustrations out on Rebati, cursing her every now and then for calling misfortune on the family because of her ill-advised decision to study:

> … the wretched girl was at the root of all her misery and misfortune; her education had caused it all—first her son had died, then her daughter-in-law; the bullocks had been sold off; the farmhands had left; the cows had been taken by the zamindar; and now her eyes had gone bad. Rebati was the evil eye, the she-devil, the ill-omened. (Senapati, 2019, p. 210)

The question of women's education was a major issue for social reformers in nineteenth-century Bengal, especially those belonging to the Brahmo Samaj. Orthodoxy disapproved of any form of public presence for women, and the fear was that modern education might encourage it. Kadambini, the wife of Brahmo reformer Dwarkanath Ganguly, was one of the first women graduates of Calcutta University, the first woman doctor to be appointed to government service in 1888, and one of the first women to be accorded membership of the Indian National Congress in its session the following year. The *Bangabasi*, a weekly newspaper representing orthodox opinion, accused her of sexual immorality, virtually calling her a 'whore', reflecting the conservative fear that 'a career and life outside the home threatened traditional notions of chastity and femininity' (Karlekar, 1986, p. WS27). Reformists strongly opposed the orthodox standpoint, arguing that the education of women was essential if India was to be a modern society. British authors had blamed India's civilisational backwardness on the low status which it accorded to its women, and nationalist reformers responded by emphasising women's education as a crucial need (Chakraborty, 2009, p. 88). This led to the establishment of an increasing number of schools and colleges for women in Bengal Presidency, for which Bethune College, from which Kadambini had graduated, provided the model. For most reformers, however, women's education meant learning subjects that would help them become better wives and mothers, like the humanities, hygiene, domestic science, and useful crafts like needlework. 'Converting women into grihalakshmis (Lakshmi of the household) through the novel means of formal education, was the self-appointed task of a civilizing nationalism' (Chakrabarty, 1994, p. 60). The need for women's education was felt in Odisha, too, and a primary school for girls was established at Cuttack in 1869. It was upgraded to a middle school subsequently, and, in 1873, renamed Ravenshaw Hindu Girls' School (presently Ravenshaw Girls' School situated at Gourishankar Park, Cuttack). It is perhaps this school that Basudev refers to in 'Rebati'.

To return to the story, after the death of Shyambandhu and his wife it is Basudev who provides support. Though the grandmother refuses to accept money from him, she depends on him for help in clarifying Shyambandhu's rent records to the zamindar. A few months later, Basudev falls ill and dies of cholera. On hearing of his death, the old woman blames it on her granddaughter's education: 'he had perished in his prime because he had been foolish enough to want to teach Rebati' (Senapati, 2019, p. 212). When Rebati falls ill, she blames it on her desire to learn: 'Rebati had brought the fever on herself by daring to study'. Within a week both Rebati and her grandmother die, and Shyambandhu's family is wiped out. 'The last words which had emanated from his house were: 'Rebati! Rebi! You fire that turns all to ashes' (p. 214).

In 'Rebati', the outbreak serves to focus the crisis that the question of women's education precipitated in a society bound to patriarchal norms. Senapati's critique of this society is also expressed in a passage about the outbreak, which people associate with the malevolence of the cholera goddess. When news of Shyambandhu's death spreads, 'the immediate response was to bolt the doors and windows, and keep out of the path of the demonic deity, as though the old evil hag was out with her basket and broom sweeping up heads' (Senapati, 2019, p. 208). It is easy to misread the view expressed in these lines and the old woman's curses as that of the author, as Sachidananda Mohanty does: 'In the hands of Fakir Mohan, this dreaded epidemic that used to be a real scourge in the early part of this century, becomes a formidable symbol of retribution' (Mohanty, 1994, p. 48). Senapati's style of narration was marked by an irony that served to distance himself from the characters as well as the narrator, and 'Rebati' provides many instances of such style. When Shyambandhu dies there is no one to help cremate him, out of fear of catching disease. Only Bana Sethi, the washerman, agrees to help: 'Bana was rather philosophical about it: cholera or not, if your time's up you've got to go, whether today or tomorrow, but why miss out on a set of new clothes?' (Senapati, 2019, p. 209) When the grandmother goes to Hari to pawn a utensil for a measure of rice, the shopkeeper turns her away saying that he has none in stock. 'Of course, he had both rice and the inclination to sell it, but getting the brass bowl for a song was what interested him' (p. 213). The belief in a disease goddess, like the grandmother's belief that Rebati's education brought on misfortune, is due to ignorance, which modern education alone can expel. Senapati, himself, was a schoolteacher, besides holding administrative positions as diwan of the princely state of Nilgiri and assistant manager of Dhenkanal state. It is erroneous, therefore to consider the outbreak a 'retribution', for if that were the case Rebati's decision to go to school would not be, as Mohanty puts it, 'an act of defiance against the dominant patriarchy and the feudal ethos of the village community of Patapur' (1994, p. 45), The outbreak episode would, instead, be an unambiguous condemnation of women's education, which it evidently is not. The outbreak is both a realistic detail of life in nineteenth-century rural India when cholera broke out frequently, as well as a device to direct the story's criticism of orthodoxy. In that sense it functions somewhat like plague in *Samskara*, a realistic texture that concretises the narrative's allegorical structure.

Narayan's *Kocharethi: The Araya Woman* is an ethnographic novel about an adivasi community living in the Western Ghats of Kerala. Set in the early-twentieth century, it narrates the story of Kochuraman and Kunjipennu who, through hard labour, manage to eke out a living on the hilly tracts that the Arayars inhabited. When a forest fire destroys their village and their son dies, things take an unfortunate turn. They are reduced to poverty and forced into a cycle of debt, their land is taken away from them, and Kochuraman takes to drinking to drown his sorrows. Their daughter Parvati, who manages to get an education and finds employment in the city, sends home money; but this stops when she falls in love and marries against her parents' wishes. Separated from Parvati, unable to adapt to the changes that were sweeping out the old values that Kochuraman and Kunjipennu still clung to, they feel completely lost. In narrating the story of the Arayar couple, the novel depicts the fate of these simple hill people who were exploited by traders, missionaries, and government officials, and were alienated from their cultural traditions and ways of being in the name of development.[3]

One summer the rains are delayed and the hillside lies scorched. The Arayars till the soil and plant paddy seeds in the hope that it may rain, but the few that sprout dry up when the expected rain fails to come. One night, they hear the cry of the 'chaviliyan', a bird of ill-omen, and they fear for their lives: 'No one knew how, but suddenly fear spread across the hillside. Stillness all around. People did not venture out of their homes' (Narayan, 2011, p. 47). Smallpox suddenly breaks out in a nearby

[3] Narayan himself belongs to the community. In an interview with the translator of the novel, Catherine Thankamma, he recounts how he and other educated Arayars decided to write about their community, to counter the stereotypes reproduced in mainstream literature: 'We wanted to tell the world that we have our own distinctive way of life, our own value system. We are not demons lacking in humanity but a strong, hardworking and self reliant community' (Thankamma, 2011, p. 209).

village, and news reaches them every day of people dying and their huts being burnt down. There are rumours that some people living near a temple of Bhagavathi had offended her, and the goddess had sent the disease to punish the whole community: 'She threw a handful of small pox seeds all around, that too the very virulent variety called *karinjapatta*. The boils swelled up and burst open; the flesh split and pus oozed. People just fell down and died in hordes … it was terrible'. One morning, Kochuraman and Kunjikela go down to the village where the disease had broken out, and find it deserted. Most people had left the village out of fear, and the market, which had once been bustling, looked desolate and empty. The lone toddy-shop owner tells them that at night Parayars came to bury the dead, and looted the houses of those who had left. 'I haven't seen anything so dreadful in all my life', says the shopkeeper, 'haven't even heard of anything like this' (p. 48). They come across an acquaintance, who informs them of people who have died, and warns them: 'Don't wander about here. This evil spirit is blind. But they say it has ears and a nose' (p. 49). Kochuraman goes to the house of Kopallan Pilla, whom he knows, and finds him lying still on a mat.

> Was there a slight movement? Kochuraman moved forward. He tried to draw back the cloth that covered the face. Oh! He let out a cry, shuddering. The cloth stuck to the body wherever the pustules had burst open to release the pus. The face looked torn and covered with pus. It was Kopallan Pilla. Suddenly Kochuraman thought he heard the sound of anklets ... the Goddess of small pox was somewhere around … Kochuraman ran out …

Running away in fear, Kochuran thinks: 'Smallpox had no eyes. But suppose it had ears and a nose …' (Narayan, 2011, p. 50)

In *Kocharethi* and 'Rebati', thus, popular understanding constructs the outbreak of disease in cosmological terms, as punishment for transgression of norms or the work of a malevolent deity. However, they treat this differently: in 'Rebati' it is a superstitious belief that the author is critical of, while in *Kocharethi* it reflects the simplicity of the Arayars who believe that a divine order rules their fate. Narayan's objective, unlike that of Senapati, is to depict the life of the Arayars without passing judgment on it. The novel ends on a contrast between their belief in a cholera goddess and the scientific ethos of the city. Kochuraman falls seriously ill, and is admitted to a hospital in Kochi. The hospital seems foreboding, and when Kunjipennu learns that he is to undergo a surgery, she is terrified. 'They tie up your arms and legs and cut you up live, just like that', she tells her husband (Narayan, 2011, p. 207). They leave the hospital at once, without anyone seeing them, and walk back to the village, though Kunjipennu fears that her husband may not live long enough to reach it.

The belief in supernatural causes, as we saw in chapter one, is one way in which outbreak comes to be framed in social understanding. Unlike biomedical explanations, what it serves is not to explain epidemic objectively but to allay the fear it causes, through the performance of rituals of propitiation. Driven to the limits of their capacity to make sense of chaos, as Geertz says, people turn to a deity or to a cosmological realm that may help restore order, or at least make suffering bearable. Outbreaks call for such explanations in narratives that serve emotional functions, just as they also call out for other explanations that serve cognitive functions. As long as there are epidemics—and epidemics are to come again and again—there will be the need to recount them in stories that constitute their objective reality as events and their subjective reality as calamities that befall us and cause untold death and suffering. 'We tell stories', says Ricoeur, 'because in the last analysis *human lives need and merit being told*' (1984, p. 75, italics added).

References

Abu, A. & Kallingal, R. (Producers). Abu, A. (Director). 2019. *Virus* [Film]. OPM Cinemas.

Bakhtin, M.M. (1981). Forms of time and of the chronotope in the novel: Notes towards a historical poetics. In M. Holquist (Ed.), M. Holquist & C. Emerson (Trans.), *The dialogic imagination* (pp. 84–258). University of Texas Press.

Bourdieu, P. (1977). *Outline of a theory of practice* (R. Nice, Trans.). Cambridge University Press.

Bruner, J. (1991). The narrative construction of reality. *Critical Inquiry, 18*,(1), 1–21. https://www.jstor.org/stable/1343711

Camus, A. (1960). *The plague* (S. Gilbert, Trans.). Penguin.

Chakrabarty, D. (1994). The difference-deferral of a colonial modernity: Public debates on domesticity in British India. In D. Arnold & D. Hardiman (Eds.), *Subaltern studies VII: Essays in honour of Ranajit Guha* (pp. 50–88). Oxford University Press.

Chakraborty, R. (2009). Women's education and empowerment in colonial Bengal. In H. Hägerdal (Ed.), *Responding to the west: Essays on colonial domination and Asian agency* (pp. 87–102). Amsterdam University Press. http://www.jstor.org/stable/j.ctt46mt0s.9

Chapekar, D. H. (n.d.). *Autobiography of Damodar Hari Chapekar.* Bombay Police Abstracts of 1910, (pp. 50–107). https://cultural.maharashtra.gov.in/ english/gazetteer/VOL-II/ autobiography.pdf,

Chatman, S. (1978). *Story and Discourse: Narrative Structure in Fiction and Film*. Cornell University Press.

Genette, G. (1980). *Narrative discourse: An essay in method* (J. E. Lewin, Trans.). Cornell University Press.

Foucault, M. (1986). Of other spaces (J. Miskowiec, Trans.). *Diacritics, 16*(1), 22–27.

Global News. (2020, March 20). *Coronavirus Outbreak: A timeline of how COVID-19 spread around the world* [Video]. YouTube. https://www.youtube.com/watch?v=ST-cn2JQ31M

Honigsbaum, M. (2020). *The pandemic century: A history of global contagion from the Spanish Flu to Covid-19*. Penguin.

Karlekar, M. (1986). Kadambini and the bhadralok: Early debates over women's education in Bengal. *Economic and Political Weekly, 21*(17), WS25–WS31. http://www.jstor.org/stable/4375594

Lal, P. (2021). *Invisible empire: The natural history of viruses*. Penguin Random House.

Lefebvre, H. (1991). *The production of space* (D. Nicholson-Smith, Trans.). Blackwell Publishing.

Mohanty, S. (1994). Rebati's sisters: Search for identity through education. *India International Centre Quarterly, 21*(4), 41–52. http://www.jstor.org/stable/23003845

Narayan. (2011). *Kocharethi: The Araya woman* (C. Thankamma, Trans.). Oxford University Press.

Orban, C. and Rosenblum, L. (2017). Powerlines: The discourse of power in the medical chart. *Journal of Contemporary Thought*, *46*, 35–53.

Ricoeur, P. (1984). *Time and narrative*, vol. 1, (K. McLaughlin & D. Pellauer, Trans.). University of Chicago Press.

Rimmon-Kenan, S. (2002). *Narrative fiction: Contemporary poetics*. 2nd ed. Routledge.

Ronen, R. (1986). Space in fiction. *Poetics today*, *7*(3), 421–438. https://www.jstor.org/stable/1772504

Rosenberg, C. E. (1989). What is an epidemic? AIDS in historical perspective. *Daedalus*, *118*(2), 1–17. http://www.jstor.com/stable/20025233

Senapati, F.M. (2019). Rebati. In L. Mohapatra, P. St-Pierre & K.K. Mohapatra (Trans.). *The greatest Odia stories ever told* (pp. 204–214). Aleph.

Singer, M. & Clair, S. (2003). Syndemics and public health: Reconceptualizing diseases in bio-social context. *Medical Anthropological Quarterly*, *17*(4), 423–441. http://www.jstor.org/stable/3655345

Shah, K. (Executive Producer). Saxena, S. & Golani, A (Directors). (2023). *Kaala Paani* [TV series]. Posham Pa Pictures; Netflix. https://www.netflix.com/watch/81314383?trackId=255824129

Shklovsky, V. (1965). Sterne's *Tristam Shandy*: Stylistic commentary. In L.T. Lemon & M.J. Reis (Trans.), *Russian formalist criticism: Four essays* (pp. 25–27). University of Nebraska Press.

Thankamma, C. (2011). '*We want to be understood ... and allowed to live with dignity*': An interview with Narayan. In Narayan, C. Thankamma (Trans.), *Kocharethi: The Araya woman* (pp. 208–216). Oxford University Press.

Todorov, T. (1969). Structural analysis of narrative (A. Weinstein, Trans.). *Novel: A Forum on Fiction*, *3*(1), 70–76.

Tomashevsky, B. (1965). Thematics. In L.T. Lemon & M.J. Reis (Trans.), *Russian formalist criticism: Four essays* (pp. 61–95). University of Nebraska Press.

Verily Vagabonding. (2020, April 22). *Corona Pandemic Lockdown Effect on Wild Animals* [Video]. YouTube. https://www.youtube.com/watch?v=WYB8febAorM

White, H. (1978). *Tropics of discourse: Essays in cultural criticism*. Johns Hopkins University Press.

Epilogue

'*Agni* Plague, Buffalo Plague and Mad Plague'

The Cultural Representation of an Epidemic in *Plague Sindhu*

S. MUKUNDAN

The profoundly impactful experiences of the COVID-19 pandemic have sparked renewed interest in the popular understanding and expression of epidemics in history. People have turned to cultural works produced in the context of major epidemics for myriad reasons, not in the least to understand how societies and communities from different times and spaces have negotiated similar experiences. The third bubonic plague pandemic, which lasted roughly from 1894 to 1950, is estimated to have taken at least fifteen million lives, spanning five continents (Echenberg, 2007, p. xi). The majority of these deaths occurred in India. The history of this pandemic in India, which significantly reconfigured the nature of the colonial empire and its relationship with its subjects, has been reconstructed and extensively analysed (Arnold, 1993; Lynteris, 2022; Echenberg, 2007; Kidambi, 2004). Echenberg has insightfully observed that the global spread of plague coincided with the era of Western cultural imperialism, and in India, the confrontation of Western biomedicine with older medical traditions such as Ayurveda and Buddhist and Islamic medicine (Echenberg, 2007, p. xii).

In a groundbreaking study, David Arnold examines the history of Indian medicine, public health, and the responses to Western biomedicine and colonial medical intervention during the period of unparalleled crisis prompted by the spread of bubonic plague, beginning in 1896 (1993). According to him, 'Plague posed important questions about the place of medical science and the authority of medical practitioners in the colonial order and about the political constraints on medical and sanitary intervention' (p. 202). Another significant aspect of the plague outbreak in colonial India was that it dramatised the importance of the bodies of the colonised 'as a site of conflict between colonial power and indigenous politics' (p. 392). It is precisely these tensions that animate the text that is examined in this chapter.

Artistic expressions relating to epidemics are not only rich sources of historical knowledge but also crucial sites that enable us to glean insights into the popular understanding of disease and contagion. The encounters with plague in Tamil Nadu in the late-nineteenth century and early-twentieth century found expression in various oral and literary traditions. The societal experience of these outbreaks forms a part of the cultural memory of the region, leading to the creation of folklore surrounding it as well as new customs of worship. This is demonstrated by the prevalence of disease goddesses in South Asia and the existence of temples such as the 'Plague Mariamma' temple where people offered prayers, seeking divine intervention to recover from the deadly disease. Mariamma had been worshipped for centuries as the goddess of smallpox, which occurred almost every year in epidemic form during the hot summer months and abated with the monsoon, and her name was derived from the Tamil word for rain, 'mari' (Bhattacharya, 1999; Das, 2019). In the typical manner in which new deities are incorporated into already existing traditions of worship in South Asia, plague came to have a goddess etymologically linked to the goddess of smallpox though the two diseases had nothing in common.

In literature, the ordeals of plague outbreak were documented and chronicled through a form of musical composition known as *Sindhu Paadalgal* and were recorded in the printed folklore of the time (Muralidharan, 2020). The word *sindhu* refers to a particular poetic metre in the Tamil tradition, which was popular in the early-twentieth century. There is a variety of *sindhus*, labelled according to their subject matter: *Cholera Sindhu*, *Kavadi Sindhu*[1], *Jodhida Sindhu* (Astrology Sindhu) etc. (Perumal, 2021). *Sindhus* are a versatile form and can be set to various rhythms and tempos to reflect the content being expressed. This chapter explores a marginal text known as *Plague Sindhu*, written by Anthony Muthu Pillai and published in 1924, which records the experience of plague in Uttamapalayam, as well as several other towns in southern India (in the region known today as Tamil Nadu) in the early-twentieth century. An analysis of this text is undertaken in order to explicate the popular social understanding of an epidemic, and glean insights into the cultural memory of the region. A detailed translation of excerpts from this text is presented at the end of this chapter.

Born in 1863 in Hanumanthanpatti, a village in the Uttamapalayam taluk, Theni district, Anthony Pillai composed songs for and about the events he witnessed in his lifetime: plague outbreak, flood, *jallikattu*, the governor's visit to his district etc. (Perumal, 2021, p. 29). Based on the composition of *Plague Sindhu*, the historian A.K. Perumal observes that Anthony Pillai was trained in *yappu*, the grammar prescribed for writing verses (Muralidharan, 2020). He was also well versed in the classical music tradition; elements of *raagam* (raga) and melody are evident in some of his compositions. Most of his compositions have the rhythms of *nattarmarabu* (folk tradition). Anthony Muthu was rooted in the Catholic literary tradition and won accolades for his contribution in disseminating the Tamil epic *Thembavani*. He also wrote several plays, songs and *sindhus* for important occasions; some of them were published but these books are no longer available (Perumal, 2021, p. 30).

Plague in Colonial Madras

The arrival of the plague in the port city of Bombay in 1986 and its subsequent ravages as epidemic outbreak contributed significantly to an already alarming mortality rate in the

[1] These were sung by devotees while carrying the 'kavadi' (a semi-circular decorated canopy) for Lord Muruga, typically during an uphill journey.

subcontinent during the second-half of the nineteenth century (Klein, 1973, p. 639). It is estimated that by 1930, plague claimed over twelve million lives in India (Arnold, 1987, p. 391). In Madras Presidency, starting from 1897, the colonial government implemented stringent preventive measures and public health policies to contain the spread of plague. This was preceded by the introduction of what David Arnold called 'one of the most draconian pieces of sanitary legislation ever adopted in colonial India'—the Epidemic Diseases Act of 1897 (2000, p. 143). This unique act imparted special powers to the colonial government, which wielded it to specifically target the poor and migrant workers (Chakrabarti, 2020). The suffering and distress of poor people during this period finds expression in the various plague *sindhus* that were composed around that time.

The activities of the colonial government in south India have been compared to a 'great military campaign', albeit one with glaring weaknesses such as ineffective travel restrictions and impractical quarantine measures (Klein, 1988, p. 746). Stemming from the misconception that plague was spread by infected travellers, passports were issued in a measure aimed at surveillance, but the passport stations were easily evaded (p. 746). The effects of colonial surveillance and control in this regard, and the counter-measures undertaken by the people to evade it, figure in several other plague *sindhus*, including *Salem Sindhu* composed by Annusamy Pillai (1910).

Popular Literature in Early-Twentieth-Century Tamil Nadu

A brief note on the literary landscape of early-twentieth-century Tamil Nadu is in order before moving to the analysis of the text. The historian A.R. Venkatachalapathy, in his book *The Province of the Book: Scholars, Scribes, and Scribblers in Colonial Tamilnadu*, writes that the world of popular publishing 'was a more or less distinct and autonomous domain which the middle class could not hegemonize' (2015, p. 19). Various terms have been used to designate this stream of publishing: 'quarter anna songbooks', *Sindhu Paadalgal*, *Thannane Paatukkal* and *Gujili* literature (p. 131). These were a heterogeneous media of mass communication with an unparalleled reach especially among lower socio-economic classes, dealing with a wide range of themes and subjects, such as religion, medicine, astrology, fables, parables, local scandals and nationalism (p. 139). Naturally, these works were viewed with scorn and contempt by the elite, who derided them as lewd, vulgar and repulsive (p. 131). Today, they would be called 'subaltern literature'.

The logistics of disseminating these chap-books had a bearing on their subject matter. Considering that they were sold at crossroads and marketplaces—often by hawkers or other people (and sometimes the poets themselves) who sang the compositions to attract sales—they tended to speak of 'topical and sensational news' (Venkatachalapathy, 2015, p. 141). Venkatachalapathy notes that 'local scandals, murders ... and epidemics interested the common folk greatly in an age when mass media had not come into being'. L.D. Barnett, who prepared the catalogue of Tamil books in the library of the British Museum, remarked that:

> An interesting feature is the wealth of popular ballads [...] which deal with a great variety of themes: the attack of the German cruiser Emden during the War, local riots and murders, the ravage of the guinea-worm, the wonders of the aeroplane, social absurdities, and many other matters of topical interest are described in rhymes which, though usually of slight literary merit, are nevertheless of real value for the light which they throw upon the thought and feeling of the masses. (as cited in Venkatachalapathy, 2015, p. 142).

The aspersions on the literary value of those popular ballads aside, Barnett partly captures the driving argument of the present chapter: that artistic expressions are indispensable sources in examining the social understanding of epidemics. While it does not provide a window into the 'thoughts and feelings' of the homogenously aggregated 'masses', *Plague Sindhu* is a text that is extremely illuminating in terms of providing a glimpse at a mode of understanding and talking about the epidemic that was popular during the period. As will be outlined later, this mode involved a selective merging of the colonial scientific understanding of the epidemic with local legends, beliefs and practices.

Plague Sindhu

It was in this context that Anthony Muthu Pillai composed *Plague Sindhu*, which narrates the experience of plague in the Theni region. Though there is not much information regarding the total number of editions that were printed, the text accessed for this analysis is the revised second edition (priced at two annas), of which there were six hundred copies printed. By employing different registers, adopting the musical metres of popular songs during their time, and incorporating diverse forms of performance, *sindhu*s were widely disseminated and consumed beyond just their existence in print. *Plague Sindhu* is an endlessly fascinating text that paints a vivid picture of the ravages of the plague and the crises it sparked. Starting off with customary salutations to the local deity and the respected elders of the village, the poet goes on to speak about the 'terrible, evil plague'. Anticipating the opening scene of Albert Camus's *The Plague* and the memorable sequences in U.R. Ananthamurthy's *Samskara* involving the death of rats in huge numbers, the poet says that rats, as though they were 'messengers' forewarning the spread of the plague, fell dead all over the village:

> Like messengers forewarning the coming
> of the fast-spreading plague,
> rats fell dead all over.
> Opening their houses and seeing this,
> the people who went to the forest survived.
> The ones who proclaimed that they
> would not leave, can their passing be shared?[2]
>
> (Pillai, 1921, p. 1)

The text posits several possible causes for the coming of the plague and recounts the devastation that followed in its wake. Different types of plague, their symptoms and the nature and trajectory of their spread are also forcefully described in these lines:

[2] All translations of *Plague Sindhu* quoted here are by the author of this chapter.

'*Agni* plague', causing fever as hot as fire
'Buffalo plague', when people lie unmoving[3]
'Sleep plague', when people die while unconscious
'Blood plague', where people vomit blood
and 'Mad plague', when people suffer from wearied madness
—these are the five kinds. (p. 2)

Plague Sindhu throws light on the suffering of poor people in particular and observes how wild animals roamed the villages in broad daylight. The narrator reports that thieves capitalised on this unique opportunity to steal as much as they could, unafraid of the plague:

Wild dogs and foxes enter houses.
Hyenas roam the streets.
People were afraid to set foot in houses.
The whole village reeked.
The forest became home and—*Aiyyo*[4]!
The home became a forest.
This is a great joy for a few thieves,
as empty houses become theirs.
No one to question them if
they steal through the night.
As though the plague itself
fears the thief … (Pillai, 1921, p. 6)

There is also a description of the crisis of burial that was prompted by a large number of deaths, highlighting the changing social relations during this period:

Countless corpses of the poor
are rolled by Thotti–Madhari[5] people
reaching out with rods
and pushed into holes.

[3] The Tamil word used in the original text is *erumai*, which translates to buffalo, an animal which can often be seen as inactive and idle. In colloquial use, people considered lazy are often referred to disparagingly as *erumai*.

[4] A common exclamation of distress in Tamil.

[5] Thotti and Madhari are Scheduled Caste communities in Tamil Nadu. Also referred to as 'Untouchables' and Dalits, these communities are outcastes in the Hindu ritual order and are historically oppressed due to their 'low status' in the caste system.

All because there are no people
to dig holes … (Pillai, 1921, p. 7)

The undercurrent of the text seems to be the urge to document the pain and suffering of the people, to record the progression of the disease, the places that were affected and the people that died. As Perumal notes, the district gazettes and manuals of the time failed to record the details of outbreaks accurately, and in some cases, colonial officials did not even visit certain affected areas (2020). Most of the enquiries and investigations on plague in India primarily focused on Bombay, Calcutta and a few other regions, overlooking the Madras Presidency (Mahammadh, 2020). It is against this backdrop that *Plague Sindhu* must be analysed: as documenting the experiences of people (largely rural), spreading the news and raising awareness regarding plague outbreaks. As mentioned earlier, *sindhu*s were tools of mass communication and often conveyed sensational news; as such, it would have been standard practice to embellish and exaggerate the occurrences to augment their profitability.

Considering that these were essentially poetic compositions, Anthony Pillai employed rhetorical devices such as hyperbole, metaphors and rhetorical questions to convey the scale of destruction and to evoke the appropriate dramatic atmosphere. This is how the text performs this function in these lines:

The ones who proclaimed that they
would not leave, can their passing be shared? [...]
We haven't seen or heard of a thing like this—
or even dreamt of a disease like this
From Europe, it flies
and comes to Bombay in India,
it walks in Coimbatore and Dindugal
leaps and arrives at Theni,
it flies with desire—
This bird without wings called plague …
(Pillai, 1921, p. 1–3)

To convey its rapid spread, the disease is narrated as flying 'with desire', walking and leaping from Europe to the affected regions. However, Perumal argues that because they were usually brought out in the year that the outbreak occurred (or soon after), the *sindhus* dealing with epidemics would not be fabricated or exaggerated (2020). Therefore, the application of poetic and rhetorical devices (which are easily discernable) does not detract from its value as a source to explore the social understanding of the plague. In fact, the choice of rhetorical devices provides us with further insight into how the epidemic was popularly constructed.

The death of rats is repeated multiple times in the text, no doubt to stress the importance of recognising it as a sign of plague, reminding the reader that 'the people who went/to the forest survived' and that 'towns where people leave as soon as rats fall dead/will not be affected by the plague' (Pillai, 1921, p. 1, 9). Anthony Pillai was evidently motivated to utilise this form of mass communication to educate and guide the masses, to warn them of the effects of the epidemic and caution them to recognise its signs. There are strong visual metaphors that are deployed here to communicate the seriousness and catastrophic effects of a plague epidemic. For instance, to emphasise the rapidity of its spread, the plague is couched in the metaphorical vocabulary of a 'bird without wings'. While it would not be entirely accurate to consider *Plague Sindhu* a 'health communication'[6] text, it nevertheless stakes a claim to be considered what Das calls an 'incipient pedagogy' (2019).

Writing in the context of AIDS narratives and related discursive formations, Das observes that incipient pedagogies are those texts that 'do not take up teaching about AIDS as their objective' but which nonetheless 'shape opinion about the disease and how it can be comprehended' (2019, p. 6). They are not strictly 'pedagogical' because their intended objective is not to teach people but to provide news; but by considering them as incipient sources this formulation takes a far-reaching view of how people are taught about the disease in modes that are not 'restricted to institutionalized pedagogies and their formal

[6] Health communication refers to the use of visual, textual and oral strategies to inform and influence individual as well as community decisions, to make healthier choices and prevent the spread of disease.

contexts of implementation' (p. 70). *Plague Sindhu* serves the crucial social function of carrying knowledge regarding the cause, symptoms and prevention of the epidemic, and its narrative form ensures wider purchase among the populace than a formal pedagogical text would.

Kinds of Plague in *Plague Sindhu*

In a remarkable verse in *Plague Sindhu* (quoted above), the poet talks about different 'kinds' of plague: '*agni* Plague', 'buffalo Plague', 'sleep Plague', 'blood plague' and 'mad plague'. While this is decidedly not a scientific classification of the types of plague, they reflect the popular understanding of the illness. As Eisenberg observes, 'illness' (as distinct from disease) is a model that constructs a certain reality, 'imposing meaning on the chaos of the phenomenological world' (as cited in Helman, 1981, p. 548). Drawing on Helman's discussion of the disease/illness model developed in the Western medical tradition, the classification of different types of plague in *Plague Sindhu* is one that falls under the model of illness, which 'refers to the subjective response of the patient to being unwell; how he, and those around him, perceive the origin and significance of this event'.

Subjective experience provides the foundation for Anthony Muthu's classification of plague, as distinct from its scientific classification as bubonic, septicemic and pneumonic. In India, it was bubonic plague that was the most prevalent form of the disease (Mahammadh, 2020). The descriptions of various kinds of plague in *Plague Sindhu* are largely symptoms of the bubonic plague, which causes high fever ('*agni* plague'), buboes, chills and fatigue ('buffalo plague'). Bleeding from the mouth, anus and nose ('blood plague') occurs in cases of septicemic plague, which may develop from untreated bubonic plague.

However, the construction of plague in *Plague Sindhu* does not entirely fall under the illness model. A larger 'folk model of illness' would be more appropriate, within which 'illness is only a specialised form of misfortune or bad luck' (Helman, 1981, p. 549). This is evidenced in the possible causes for the plague advanced by Anthony Pillai in these lines:

Perhaps owing to the accumulated sins of unjust people,
or the consequent curse of divine wrath,
or the earth's unbearable burden of humans,
or the birth of the year *rowthri*[7].
The disease spread—its name?
Aiyyo! Plague! (Pillai, 1921, p. 1)

The 'sins of unjust people', 'divine wrath', overpopulation, astrological causes, unfair practices like 'adding water to rice' or charging high interest, 'abandoning our dharma' and 'not performing the proper rituals for the dead' are all posited as potential causes of the plague. In his essay 'What Is an Epidemic?', Rosenberg writes that the outbreak of an epidemic involves the collective agreement on an explanatory framework within which its 'dismaying arbitrariness' can be managed (1989, p. 5). He states that, historically, there have been two explanatory frameworks: one that understands it in terms of 'spiritual assumptions' and the other that understands it in terms of 'secular and mechanistic styles of explanation'. Building on Rosenberg's observation, Das argues that there are 'biomedical' and 'cosmological' explanatory frames: a biomedical frame attributes the epidemic to a natural cause (such as a pathogen) which acts according to natural laws and can be contained by applying those laws whereas a cosmological frame attributes it to magical causes and supernatural forces, such as the actions of a spirit or deity, and redressal is sought through rituals to appease them (2022, p. 18).

The biomedical frame generally adopts a realist mode of narration and the cosmological frame adopts a mythic mode, which leads Das to formulate two 'paradigmatic forms of epidemic narrative': the biomedical–realist and cosmological–mythic. It is evident that in *Plague Sindhu* the cosmological–mythic form predominates, but it is interesting to note that scientific explanations rephrased for popular use regarding transmission and spread are present in the text as well. This is most apparent in the following lines:

[7] *Rowthri* is the name of the particular year in which the plague occurred in the Tamil calendar.

Rats falling dead all over the house,
and as they fall
poisonous insects inside them fly
and stick to people—Oh! (Pillai, 1921, p. 2)

This notion is reflective of contemporary medical understanding. As Mahammadh states, 'The Indian Plague Commission believed that plague was an air-borne contagion transmitted from travellers to other humans. Rat fleas get attached to humans after abandoning rat carcasses for a new live host' (2020, p. 327). *Plague Sindhu* also describes how rats would 'drill' and 'gnaw' their way into houses and 'gorge on foodstuff in the house', which corresponds with the scientific knowledge at the time, that 'initial transmission was thus through contaminated food grains, due to black rats' activities in grain stores' (ibid). As touched upon earlier, the text also recounts the transmission pattern of the plague in these lines, 'From Europe, it flies / and comes to Bombay in India, / it walks in Coimbatore and Dindigul / and leaps and arrives at Theni' (Pillai, 1921, p. 3). While it may or may not reflect contemporary efforts at mapping the spread of the disease, recent scholarship has suggested that the outbreak originated in China, and travelled to Hong Kong from where it spread to colonial India and other parts of the world (Mahammadh, 2020).

Plague Sindhu, however, does a lot more than merely corroborate colonial understanding of the plague. It is very likely that Europe was identified as the source because it was largely ships engaged in colonial trade that brought the disease to India. The places in India that are identified by name in the text—Bombay, Coimbatore, Dindigul and Theni (which was then part of Madurai district)—were all major plague hotspots, connected by commercial relations (Mahammadh, 2020). Knowledge of the dynamics of its spread and the role of travellers therein was, thus, prevalent at the time. The claim that this disease had European origins is a significant aspect of *Plague Sindhu*, as it offers an indictment of Europe by reversing the popular stereotype that viewed 'the East' as the source and a hotbed of disease (Arnold, 2020, p. 570). Further, an indication that the knowledge regarding plague came from an assimilation of Western medical science into existing ideas about contagion in India is the fact that the word 'plague' (in Tamil transliteration) is used in the original text.

A common thread running through the arguments outlined above is that biomedical knowledge was filtered through indigenous frames of understanding illness to form a complex and contradictory explanatory framework about epidemics, which circulated in narratives such as *Plague Sindhu*. There is a cohabitation of the two distinct paradigms referred to earlier: biomedical–realist and cosmological–mythic. Despite the presence of biomedical elements, the epidemic still retains its religious associations and is framed in terms of ill luck, misfortune and divine wrath. The response of indigenous beliefs to Western medicine is evident in the verse that describes doctors visiting villages to inoculate people:

> Doctors gather as if to inoculate against smallpox.
> '*Aiyyo*! We can't do this', the people say
> 'Our life will leave us'.
> 'Our left hand will decay'.
> They say, 'You cannot touch
> even cold water'... (Pillai, 1921, p. 3)[8]

Though the opposition to being vaccinated has surface-level parallels with modern-day anti-vaccination sentiments in the context of COVID-19, it is more likely that the resistance expressed in *Plague Sindhu* stems from a cosmological basis, as opposed to the individualistic resistance to vaccinations in Western societies. This is revealed in the villagers' belief that 'our life will leave us' and that the 'left hand will decay' if they were to be inoculated by government officials. As David Arnold observes, rumours regarding the plague and the containment measures enacted by the colonial government flourished in the atmosphere of uncertainty and panic during this period (1993, p. 218). Arguing that rumours provide us with a closer window

[8] The indigenous responses to plague vaccination described here evoke similarities with the popular resistance to smallpox vaccination when it was introduced in the nineteenth century. See Ferrari, 2015, pp 135–141.

to popular perceptions and responses than other sources, he goes on to state, 'One striking feature of the plague rumours, in seeming contrast to many other examples of this form of popular discourse in India, was their preoccupation with the body' (p. 219). The fear expressed by the villagers and the popular resistance to Haffkine's antiplague serum derived from earlier fears about Jenner's vaccine for smallpox, with the rumours associated with the smallpox vaccine being transferred to plague by a logic that belongs to cultural semiosis. These rumours are, in part, expressions of a deep-seated suspicion and hostility towards the methods of Western medicine, particularly in the context of the intense and unprecedented scale of medical intervention by the colonial administration in the late-nineteenth century and the coercive nature of the measures adopted (p. 223).

Plague Sindhu also offers a potent illustration of the way 'medical pluralism' operates in a society, shaping popular understanding of diseases in complex and seemingly conflicting modes. Medical pluralism refers to the 'availability of different approaches, treatments, and institutions that people use to maintain health or treat illness' (Khalikova, 2021). Despite the putatively hegemonic position of Western biomedicine, traditional and alternative medical practices did not disappear (ibid). Extending this observation to the broader conception and interpretation of epidemics by the general public, *Plague Sindhu* demonstrates how the outbreak of plague can be understood both as spreading through the bite of infected fleas in rodents (biomedical) *as well as* resulting from astrological causes or the displeasure of deities.

Epidemic as Social Crisis

The social disorder prompted by plague outbreaks was unprecedented in scale, with millions losing their lives and millions of others forced to evacuate their homes, camping in fields or detained in observation camps (Klein, 1988, p. 724). *Plague Sindhu* consistently constructs the epidemic as a crisis of disastrous consequence, leading to loss of life and a breakdown of social order. A mythical explanatory framework is developed, which as Priscilla Wald observes of outbreak narratives as a genre, 'is not specifically authored but emerges from a group as an expression of the origins and terms of its collective identity' and whose 'strong emotional appeal derives from and affirms the fundamental values, hierarchies, and taxonomies that are the preconditions of that identity' (2008, p. 9). The epidemic is constructed as a cosmological punishment for the wrongdoings of people, specifically the acts that society deems unfavourable and grievous. Plague here also becomes a metaphor for a larger social crisis: in positing certain social acts as potential causes of the epidemic, a strong moral position is assumed by the author, who then censures practices that are deemed immoral by the 'community'. These include charging unfairly high rates of interest, abandoning one's dharma and not performing ritual acts in the prescribed manner.

The suffering caused by the epidemic is capitalised on by social authorities to reinforce norms and discourage practices that the dominant sections of the community consider deviant. There are 'inevitable deaths' and 'countless corpses'; people die 'with convulsions and shudders' and sometimes 'all of a sudden'. If the 'evil disease' emerges in a village, the people are forced to leave it by colonial officials and the police, and go to the surrounding forests where temporary segregation camps are set up. When plague breaks out in a locality, the plague officers—the 'sub-magistrate' in Anthony Muthu's song—with the help of soldiers or police shift the affected to hospitals and the healthy to those temporary segregation camps, and their houses sanitised and lime-washed. This is the practice that Anthony Muthu alludes to when he writes that 'Doctors gather as if to inoculate against smallpox' (Pillai, 1921, p. 3). Other plague *sindhus* also speak of government officials isolating the infected people in huts and doctors inoculating the healthy with Haffkine's antiplague serum, while the towns and villages were sanitised (Mudaliar, 1906).

Fleeing from sites of contagion was very common in the case of smallpox and cholera, as it was in the case of famines.

Tiruvannamalai Plague Sindhu by Munisamy Mudaliar, which narrates the experience of plague in the Tiruvannamalai region and was published in 1906, contains a section in which the collector attempts to reassure the scared populace but they take flight to other regions anyway (p. 5). In the case of plague outbreaks, people were quick to leave town not just because of the epidemic itself, but also out of fear about the state measures deployed against it. In *Plague Sindhu*, Anthony Muthu highlights the deterioration of social order in the sections where he writes that poor people suffered and 'wept tears' as they were compelled to take apart their houses and build a makeshift *tompar* (a crude wooden housing structure), placing their children and paltry belongings in it, and leave the village (1921, p. 4). The poet describes how wild dogs and foxes entered houses and hyenas roamed the street, expressing distress at the fact that 'the home became a forest' (p. 6). Villages emptied of their occupants provided a unique opportunity for thieves because there was 'no one to question them'.

The local administration and police coerced people to leave the settlement but did not make any effort to safeguard their property, and the thieves were free to 'steal through the night'. In a memorable verse (quoted above), Anthony Muthu details the way in which 'countless corpses' of the poor and dispossessed people were rolled into a mass grave because there were too many bodies and not enough people to dig holes for all of them. He draws our attention to the fact that the Thotti–Madhari people pushed the corpses with makeshift rods and sticks. Anthony Muthu highlights the peculiarity of the so-called 'untouchables' not wanting to touch the corpses; it is the infected people that have become 'untouchable'.

Plague Sindhu thus constructs the epidemic as a multiplicity of crises: a public health crisis, an existential crisis, an administrative (law and order) crisis and a social crisis. This resonates with Arnold's argument that the epidemic years in India constituted a crisis of state medicine, and more generally, a crisis of confidence in Western medicine and public health (1993,

p. 237). In the text, the degradation of values, people abandoning their 'dharma' and not performing the proper rituals for the dead are proclaimed as the causes of the epidemic. By inculcating this fear of transgressing, the norms and hierarchies of society are reinforced. Through its deployment of metaphors, the text also provides crucial insights into the popular perception of plague, demonstrating how biomedical and cosmological explanatory paradigms coexisted in a state of tension.

Translation of *Plague Sindhu*[9]

Kaapu[10]

Praying to god, I will speak of
some atrocities of the cruel plague, listen! Verse 1

Sandha Virutham[11]

Like messengers forewarning the coming
of the fast-spreading plague,
rats fell dead all over.
Opening their houses and seeing this,
the people who went to the forest survived.
The ones who proclaimed they would not leave
can their passing be shared? Verse 2

Kovam Seyyathir[12] *Mettu*

Look at the injustice—listen
to the spread of the plague Verse 3

Injustice! The world has not seen
trouble like this disease. Verse 4

[9] This text contains forty-six verses in the first section, of which nineteen have been selected and translated here. These verses were selected for their instructiveness in analysis and their ability to illustrate key aspects discussed in this chapter.

[10] A call to the singer's deity to protect their literature or song.

[11] A kind of verse, with seven words (University of Madras, n.d.).

[12] A popular song of that time, which provides the metre for this section.

Day by day, this disease grew and
left some towns, expanding
all over Paalayam[13].
With the blessings of the elders,
  I will dolefully sing
  of its cruel spread. Verse 5

Perhaps owing to the accumulated sins of unjust people,
or the consequent curse of divine wrath,
or the earth's unbearable burden of humans,
or the birth of the year *rowthri*,
  the disease spread—its name?
  Aiyyo! Plague! Verse 6

Like cattle and goats affected
by *thullunoi*[14],
dying with convulsions and shudders,
the accounts of inevitable deaths
  caused by this evil disease
  I will share. Verse 7

Drilling through the base of houses
and gnawing through the roofs,
causing suffering to its residents,
gorging on foodstuff in the house,
  they become stronger—
  rats and bandicoots. Verse 8

This disease moves fast, to destroy.
Rats falling dead all over the house,
and as they fall
poisonous insects inside them fly
  and stick to people—Oh!
  The mind becomes weary. Verse 9

[13] A village in Dindugal district, Tamil Nadu.

[14] Possibly referring to the *thullumari* disease, known as 'enterotoxemia' in English; it could also refer to anthrax, which results in bleeding from the orifices, fever and death.

'*Agni* plague', causing fever as hot as fire
'Buffalo plague', when people lie unmoving
'Sleep plague', when people die while unconscious
'Blood plague', where people vomit blood
 and 'Mad plague', when people suffer from wearied madness
 —these are five kinds. Verse 10

Fever beyond normal measure,
buboes form on the body
which then rupture in a few days,
and people die all of a sudden.
 We haven't seen or heard of a thing like this—
 or even dreamt of a disease like this. Verse 11

From Europe, it flies
and comes to Bombay in India,
it walks in Coimbatore and Dindugal,
leaps and arrives at Theni,
 it flies with desire—
 This bird without wings called plague … Verse 12

This the government officials realising,
police came with the sub-magistrate.
'You need to leave your homes quick
and go to the forest', they say.
 'We shall go', some people say, scared—
 'Let whatever happen, according to fate', say others. Verse 16

Doctors gather as if to inoculate against smallpox.
'*Aiyyo*! We can't do this', the people say.
'Our life will leave us'.
'Our left hand will decay'.
 They say, 'You cannot touch
 even cold water' … Verse 17

Some poor people take apart their houses,
then collect the wood,

and construct *tompars*[15] with it
place their children and belongings in it and leave.
  They suffered—the poor people
  wept tears … Verse 21

Wild dogs and foxes enter the town.
Hyenas roam the streets.
People were afraid to set foot in houses.
The whole village reeked.
  The forest became home and—*Aiyyo*!
  the home became a forest. Verse 28

This is a great joy for a few thieves,
as empty houses become theirs.
No one to question them if
they steal through the night.
  As though the plague itself
  fears the thief … Verse 29

Countless corpses of the poor
are rolled by Thotti–Madhari people
reaching out with rods
and pushed into holes.
  All because there are no people
  to dig holes … Verse 34

Perhaps the transgression of adding water to rice,[16]
or the dishonesty of charging extremely unjust interest
or because we abandoned our dharma
or not performing the proper rituals for the dead
  did these provoke?[17]
  Could this be false?[18] … Verse 38
Towns where people leave as soon as rats fall dead,

[15] A crude, temporary wooden housing structure.

[16] A 'dishonest' practice by vendors to increase the weight of rice while measuring for customers.

[17] Referring here to the plague and its effects.

[18] A rhetorical tone, implying that the mentioned reasons are true.

will not be affected by the plague.
This is Anthony Muthu's word Verse 46

Professor A.K. Perumal, who has long studied Tamil folklore and the *sindhus*, provided invaluable assistance in locating a copy of *Plague Sindhu* and in its translation. My grandmother Kamala Ramaswamy also helped with the translation. I take this opportunity to thank them.

References

Arnold, D. (1993). *Colonizing the body: State medicine and epidemic disease in nineteenth century India*. University of California Press.

Arnold, D. (2020). Pandemic India: Coronavirus and the uses of history. *Journal of Asian Studies*, *79*(3): 569–577.

Arnold, D. (2000). *Science, technology and medicine in colonial India*. Cambridge University Press.

Arnold, D. (1987).Touching the body: Perspectives on the Indian plague, 1896–1900. In R. Guha (Ed.), *Subaltern studies V: Writings on South Asian history and society*. Oxford University Press.

Bhattacharya, N.N. (1999). *The Indian Mother Goddesses*. 3rd ed. Manohar.

Chakrabarti, P. (2020, July 14). Covid-19 and the spectres of colonialism. *The India Forum*. www.theindiaforum.in/article/covid-19-and-spectres-colonialism

Das, D.K. (2022). Epidemic narrative: Two paradigms. In S. Venkatesan, A. Chatterjee, A.D. Lewis & B. Callendar (Eds.), *Pandemics and Epidemics in Cultural Representation*. Springer Nature Singapore.

Das, D.K. (2019).*Teaching AIDS: The cultural politics of HIV disease in India*. Springer Nature Singapore.

Echenberg, M. (2007). *Plague ports: The global urban impact of bubonic plague, 1894–1901*. New York University Press.

Ferrari, F.M. (2015). *Religion, devotion and medicine in North India: The healing power of Śītalā*. Bloomsbury.

Helman, C.G. (1981). Disease versus illness in general practice. *The Journal of the Royal College of General Practitioners*, *31*, 548–52.

Khalikova, V. (2021). Medical pluralism. In F. Stein (Ed.), *Cambridge encyclopedia of anthropology*. https://www.anthroencyclopedia.com/entry/medical-pluralism

Kidambi, P. (2004). 'An Infection of locality': Plague, pythogenesis and the poor in Bombay, c. 1896–1905. *Urban History, 31*(2), 249–67.

Klein, I. (1973). Death in India, 1871–1921. *The Journal of Asian Studies, 32*(4), 639–659.

Klein, I. (1988). Plague, policy and popular unrest in British India. *Modern Asian Studies, 22*(4), 723–755.

Lynteris, C. (2022). Mahamari plague: Rats, colonial medicine and indigenous knowledge in Kumaon and Garhwal, India. *Medical Anthropology, 41*(4), 373–386.

Mahammadh, V.R. (2020). Plague mortality and control policies in colonial South India, 1900–47. *South Asia Research, 40*(3), 323–343.

Mudaliar, M. (1906) *Tiruvannamalai plague sindhu* [Tiruvannamalai plague sindhu]. Tam C 1730. British Council Library, Chennai.

Muralidharan, K. (2020, April 21). Memories of another epidemic occupy Tamil culture even as coronavirus fears rage. *The Wire*. https://thewire.in/society/tamil-nadu-plague-literature-mariyamman

Pillai, A. (1910). *Selathil nadandha thothhuvyadhi yennum plague kalakkola sindhu* [Sindhu on the havoc caused by the contagious disease known as Plague in Salem]. Tam. C 1486. British Council Library, Chennai.

Pillai, A. M. (1921). *Plague sindhu*. Tam. C 1773. British Council Library, Chennai.

Perumal, A.K. (2021). *Plague, kula udaipu pattri sindhu paadiya kambam kavignan* [Cumbum poet who sang about plague and pond breakage]. In *Thaarukan peruram kizhitha pennum allal* (pp. 29–35). New Century Book House.

Perumal, A.K. (2020, June 7). Plague sindhu. *Hindu Tamil Disai*. https://www.hindutamil.in/news/literature/558256-plague-sindhu-5.html

Rosenberg, C. E. (1989). What is an epidemic? AIDS in historical perspective. *Daedalus, 118*(2), 1–17. http://www.jstor.org/stable/20025233

University of Madras. (n.d.). Virutham. *Tamil Lexicon*.

Venkatachalapathy, A.R. (2015). *The province of the book: Scholars, scribes, and scribblers in colonial Tamilnadu*. Permanent Black.

Wald, P. (2008). *Contagious: Cultures, carriers, and the outbreak narrative*. Duke University Press.